The Medieval Translator 4

MEDIEVAL & RENAISSANCE
TEXTS & STUDIES

VOLUME 123

The Medieval Translator 4

Edited by

Roger Ellis and Ruth Evans

MEDIEVAL & RENAISSANCE TEXTS & STUDIES
Binghamton, New York
1994

Published in the United States by

Medieval & Renaissance Texts & Studies
State University of New York
Binghamton, New York 13902–6000

ISBN: 0–86698–128–4

Published in Great Britain by

University of Exeter Press
Reed Hall, Streatham Drive
Exeter, Devon EX4 4QR UK

ISBN: 0 85989 412 6

This book is made to last.
It is set in Times Roman, smythe-sewn,
and printed on acid-free paper
to library specifications

Printed in the United States of America

CONTENTS

CONTENTS

ACKNOWLEDGEMENTS

The editors wish to thank the British Academy and the School of English Studies, University of Wales College of Cardiff, whose generous financial assistance has made this publication possible. Thanks are also due to the Master and Fellows of University College, Oxford, for permission to reproduce a page from a manuscript owned by the Library; to the Bibliothèque Nationale for permission to use the manuscript illumination which appears on the cover of the volume; and to Anthony Dale of Oxford University Press for generously providing access to a photograph of this illumination. We also wish to thank Jane Erskine for invaluable help with the preparation of the camera-ready copy.

NOTES ON CONTRIBUTORS

Mary-Jo Arn teaches in the English Department at Bloomsburg University. She has produced a critical edition of the English poetry of Charles of Orleans and is currently finishing a book on *Piers Plowman*.

Rina Drory is a lecturer in the Department of Arabic at Tel Aviv University, Israel. Her paper in this volume forms part of a project concerning Jewish-Arabic cultural contacts in twelfth- and thirteenth-century Christian Spain and Provence. A larger version of this study, entitled 'Literary Contacts and Where to Find Them: on Arabic Literary Models in Medieval Jewish Literature', will be published in *Poetics Today* 14:2 (1993). She is the author of *The Emergence of Jewish-Arabic Literary Contacts at the Beginning of the Tenth Century* (Tel Aviv: Ha-kibutz Ha-meuḥad, 1988); 'The Hidden Context: on Literary Products of Tri-Cultural Contacts in the Middle Ages' *Pe'amin* (*Studies in Oriental Jewry*) 46–7 (1991); ' "Words Beautifully Put": Hebrew versus Arabic in Tenth-Century Jewish Literature' in J. Blau and S.C. Reif (eds) *Geniza Research after Ninety Years: The Case of Judaeo-Arabic* (Cambridge: Cambridge University Press, 1992). Her study, 'Introducing Fictionality into Classical Arabic Literature: the *Maqāma*' is forthcoming in *Studies in Arabic and Comparative Poetics*.

Roger Ellis is Senior Lecturer in the School of English, Communication and Philosophy at the University of Wales, College of Cardiff. His publications include *Patterns of Religious Narrative in the* Canterbury Tales (Croom Helm, 1986) and an edition of *The 'Liber Celestis' of St Bridget of Sweden* for the Early English Text Society (1987). He has published widely on the medieval English mystics, and on aspects of medieval translation, and has edited the previous three volumes of *The Medieval Translator*.

Ruth Evans is a lecturer in the School of English, Communication and Philosophy at the University of Wales, College of Cardiff. With Lesley Johnson she has edited *The Wife of Bath and All Her Sect* (Routledge, forthcoming, 1994), a collection of feminist re-readings of medieval texts. She has published essays on courtly literature, medieval drama and medieval translation. She is one of the joint editors, with Ian Johnson, Nicholas Watson and Jocelyn Wogan-Browne, of *The Idea of the Vernacular: Medieval Prologues* (University of Exeter Press/MRTS, Binghamton, forthcoming).

Ian Johnson is a lecturer in the Department of English at St Andrews University, Fife, Scotland. His publications include 'The Latin Source of Nicholas Love's *Mirrour of the Blessed Lyf of Jesu Christ*: A Reconsideration' *N&Q* (1986); 'Walton's Sapient Orpheus' in A.J. Minnis (ed.) *The Medieval Boethius: Studies in the Vernacular Translations of 'De Consolatione Philosophiae'* (1987); 'Prologue and Practice: Middle English Translations of the Life of Christ' in R. Ellis *et al.* (eds) *The Medieval Translator* Vol. 1 (1989); a section on literary theory and translation in Middle English in A.J. Minnis (ed.) *The Cambridge History of Literary Criticism* Vol. 2: *The Middle Ages* (forthcoming); 'Vernacular Valorizing: Functions and Fashions of Literary Theory in Middle English' in Jeanette Beer (ed.) *Proceedings of the International Conference on Translation in the Middle Ages, Kalamazoo* (forthcoming). He is one of the joint editors, with Ruth Evans, Nicholas Watson and Jocelyn Wogan-Browne, of *The Idea of the Vernacular: Medieval Prologues* (University of Exeter Press/MRTS, Binghamton, forthcoming).

Veronica Lawrence was an Assistant Librarian at New College, Oxford, England, and has published in Exeter Symposium V on the Middle English Mystics (1992).

Helen Phillips is a lecturer in the Department of English Studies, Nottingham University. She is the editor of *Langland, the Mystics and the Medieval English Religious Tradition* (1990), to which she contributed '*The Quatrefoil of Love*'. The following articles are forthcoming: 'The Complaint of Mars' and 'The Complaint of Venus' in P. Ruggiers (ed.) *Chaucer Enclyclopedia*; 'Chaucer's French Translations' *NMS* (1993); 'Chaucer and Deguileville: The ABC in Context' *MAE*. She has also written on later literature.

Denis Renevey is currently finishing his DPhil on Richard Rolle at Lincoln College, Oxford, England.

Anne Savage is an associate professor in the Department of English at McMaster University, Canada. With Nicholas Watson she has translated, with notes and commentary, various anchoritic texts in *Anchoritic Spirituality: Ancrene Wisse and Associated Works* (1991). The following articles are forthcoming in 1993: '*Piers Plowman*: the Translation of Scripture and Food for the Soul' *English Studies*; 'Shifts and Transformations of the Narrative in *Beowulf*' in the festschrift for Elspeth Kennedy, edited by Karen Pratt; 'The Solitary Heroine: Meditation and Mysticism in the *Ancrene Wisse*, the Katherine Group and the Wooing Group' in W. Pollard (ed.) *The English Mystical Tradition* (University of Florida Press).

René Tixier is Professor of English Literature at the University of Social Sciences in Toulouse, France. His main research and teaching areas are medieval devotional literature, with a special interest in the 14th century English mystics. He has published a number of articles on *The Cloud of Unknowing*. Future publications include that of his thesis, *Mystique et pédagogie dans* The Cloud of Unknowing.

Scott Westrem teaches at Lehman College, City University, New York. His book-length study on *Johannes Witte de Hese's* Itinerarius is scheduled for publication by the Medieval Academy of America.

Jocelyn Wogan-Browne is a Senior Lecturer in the Department of English at Liverpool University, England. She is one of the joint editors, with Ruth Evans, Ian Johnson and Nicholas Watson, of *The Idea of the Vernacular: Medieval Prologues* (University of Exeter Press/MRTS, Binghamton, forthcoming).

Introduction

Introduction

ROGER ELLIS

This volume of papers heard at the 1991 Cardiff Conference on the theory and practice of translation in the Middle Ages complements the three volumes of papers generated by the two previous Conferences on the subject.[1] As with the previous volumes, the papers offer a blend of theoretical and practical approaches, either inferring the former through their study of the latter, or (in the papers of Jocelyn Wogan-Browne, Rina Drory, Ian Johnson and Veronica Lawrence) making direct reference to it by studying the explanatory material translators often produced to accompany their work. Several literary genres are represented: different kinds of religious writing (hagiography produced in the twelfth and thirteenth centuries by female religious and in the fifteenth century by an Austin friar; religious apologetic produced in the thirteenth century by the anonymous author of the *Ancrene Wisse*, in the fourteenth century by two English mystics, and in the sixteenth century by an English Brigittine monk); courtly poetry (Chaucer in the late fourteenth, Charles of Orleans in the early fifteenth, centuries); medieval travel books (an anonymous fifteenth-century translation of a Dutch travel writer); narrative collections (a twelfth-century Arabic *Maqāmāt*, used in the thirteenth century for a Hebrew translation, then as model for a Hebrew *maqāmāt*). The volume is distinguished from its predecessors in that most of the papers consider translations produced by named narrators, all but one working in England in the high Middle Ages—Marie of Chatteris and Clemence of Barking (Wogan-Browne), Rolle (Denis Renevey), Chaucer (Helen Phillips), Charles of Orleans (Mary-Jo Arn), Bokenham (Johnson) and Whitford (Lawrence):[2] the one exception, the late twelfth/early thirteenth-century Hebrew translator al-Ḥarīzī, takes us to medieval Spain, whose obvious and considerable importance for students of medieval translation has been barely acknowledged in previous volumes.[3] A further departure from previous practice is signalled by the appearance of two papers, by Anne Savage and René Tixier, considering modern translations of medieval texts. Modern translation as such has never been the

1

central focus of the Conference, but the questions its study raises so clearly complement those addressed by the study of translation in and into medieval vernaculars that it was felt appropriate to include the two papers in the present volume. Finally, the volume breaks new ground in that one of the editors is providing a general introduction on the state of—what this and the previous volumes will show to be—a very flourishing art.[4]

★   ★   ★

It is appropriate for several reasons, and not just for the sake of chronology, to begin the volume with Wogan-Browne's paper on female translators of Anglo-Norman hagiography. One concerns the possibility of identifying 'schools' of translators grouped in a single place, whether at Toledo, or Paris, or Vadstena, and even evolving what might be called a 'house style' of translation. Wogan-Browne is cautious about the possibility of discovering in the work of these female religious a distinctively 'female school of hagiographic translation' associated with the nunneries of Barking and Chatteris.[5] She prefers to speak of 'temporarily constituted groups' of female writers, which suggests the serendipitous nature of the contacts which may have produced many translations in the Middle Ages. All the same, such groupings may have made it possible for one translator to base her work on that of a predecessor: ready parallels exist later in the Middle Ages to show that women writers 'read each other intensely'; at the end of the period, the Brigittine monk Richard Whitford, as Lawrence's paper demonstrates, reveals himself to be operating, if not in a tradition, certainly in just such a 'temporarily constituted group' of male religious translators.

Wogan-Browne's paper brings into focus two further points of considerable interest for the study of translation, both developed elsewhere in this volume: (i) the status and significance of the target language; (ii) the gender of the translator.

On the first point, her paper reminds us of the complex trilingual situation which obtained in England, in varying degrees, from the Norman Conquest almost to the end of the Middle Ages. If the decision to translate into Anglo-Norman, as into English, was, in David Burnley's words, 'a tacit admission that a linguistic barrier had to be crossed' (*Medieval Translator* (1989) p. 41), it does not follow that those who translated these texts out of Latin into Anglo-Norman saw the target language as inferior to the source language: for these aristocratic women in the post-Conquest church insular French was not 'a ghetto language confined to the less Latinate nunneries, but the language of instruction in monastic schools and . . . used by . . . the secular aristocracy and gentry'. They may, of course, have seen their own Anglo-Norman as superior to English, just as they themselves were socially superior to most native speakers of English. Perceived differences in status between the two vernaculars seem to have obtained into the mid-fourteenth century: in his *Polychronicon*, completed some time after 1352, the Chester monk Ranulph Higden, as translated by John of Trevisa, notes the difference between the 'gentil men' who teach their children to speak French in the cradle and the 'oplondysch men' who, wishing to be thought 'gentil', and so 'more ytold of', take great pains to speak French: this picture Trevisa is at pains to modify in respect of the education which grammar-school children are receiving later in the century, where English has taken over from French as the medium of instruction.[6] As for Latin, if it enjoyed an authority greater than any vernacular throughout the Middle Ages—its ultimate authority clearly indicated, for example, by the decision to translate vernacular works into Latin—the power relations are by no means always or only one-way when a text is being translated from Latin into the vernacular. As Copeland's work has shown, vernacular translation of Latin texts was often part of an ambitious project of linguistic rehabilitation:[7] the act of translation then demonstrates the adequacy of the target language for the presentation of material hitherto confined to the source language, and, by implication, for the production of original material which might previously have been written only in the source language. It is not by accident that linguistic and national self-consciousness regularly go hand-in-hand, and that Chaucer, for example, defends his translation of scientific Latin in his *Treatise on the Astrolabe* by appealing to King Richard II who is 'lord of this langage'.[8]

This understanding that translation involves fundamental questions about the status and significance of the target language receives powerful confirmation from the next paper, whose subject is the complex cultural and linguistic relations that obtained between Arabic and Hebrew in north Spain and in the near East in the twelfth and thirteenth centuries. When the Hebrew translator al-Ḥarīzī, having translated the Arabic *Maqāmāt* of al-Ḥarīrī into Hebrew in Spain, travelled to the near East and there composed his own Hebrew *Maqāmāt, Sefer taḥkemoni*, on the model of the Arabic one, we may be tempted to draw the conclusion, as scholars have done, that both acts of translation witness to an ongoing dependence of Hebrew on Arab literary culture. The situation, argues Drory, is more complex. Prior to this time Arabic had been used by Jews, for all but 'literary-aesthetic and ceremonial functions', throughout the lands where Jews and Arabs existed side-by-side; Hebrew itself was understood to be 'short and sparse' by comparison with the 'ample' resources of Arabic. Possibly in reaction to the prevailing cultural climate in Spain at the time, where Arabic texts were being translated into Latin, and local vernaculars were being increasingly used for writing purposes, translation from Arabic into Hebrew seems to have been envisaged as a way of 'marking a particular collective or ethnic identity, that could be called "national"'. Admittedly, as Drory describes it, the battle was not immediately won, even in Spain: and it was a much harder fight in the East. Some Jewish translators doubted the adequacy of the target language to contain the riches of the source language: in the prefaces to two separate works Judah Ibn Tibbon declared that 'all we have of the Hebrew language is that which is found in the books of the Bible, and this does not suffice for all of a speaker's needs'. (This situation has suggestive parallels in late medieval England when the Wycliffites began producing their English translations of the Bible, and had to defend themselves against the view that, since 'English was impoverished by comparison with Latin', such translations ought not to be attempted.)[9] So al-Ḥarīzī's Hebrew *Maqāmāt* needs to be seen as his response to that situation of Arab cultural dominance which he and other Hebrew translators in Spain had been working to displace, and which had received most pointed exemplification in his translation into Hebrew of works written before his time by Jews in Arabic. Hence, by contrast with the earlier-noted view of Judah Ibn Tibbon, al-Ḥarīzī declared that 'even the little Hebrew that has survived is adequately equipped to ensure the composition of some splendid literary works', and planned *Sefer taḥkemoni*, in part, to develop his readers' facility in Hebrew (by including 'many words that are obscure and difficult to understand so that . . . a reader . . . will have acquired a good deal of knowledge about the Hebrew language'). Hebrew is to become as 'ample' as Arabic, in particular—and the quoted material demonstrates the claim very neatly—by appropriating Biblical language and figures for purposes of ordinary communication.

These latter feature as an important element in the defence of the whole enterprise: according to al-Ḥarīzī the situation whereby Jews can hardly read their own language has Biblical precedent both literal and metaphoric.[10] The literal precedent is provided by Nehemiah 13:24, twice cited, which tells how half the Jews at the time of Nehemiah 'could not speak the language of Judah'; the metaphoric, for example, by a repeated allegorisation of Genesis 16, which tells how Abraham's lawful wife Sara (the Hebrew language) was barren, whereas her handmaid Hagar (Arabic) was fertile. Though the sexual context of this metaphor is overlaid by questions of legitimacy and illegitimacy—questions, as Drory notes, of considerable interest to those in the vanguard of any revolution—it figures prominently elsewhere in al-Ḥarīzī's writing. Thus, as a result of his marriage to a maiden called 'the Holy Tongue', 'a [new] literary composition', the *Sefer taḥkemoni*, was born. Such translation is the freeing of a king from prison, an echo, perhaps, of Jeremiah 52:31–33. This metaphor could obviously accommodate or acquire erotic meaning—

think of the great prince lying in prison in Donne's 'The Ecstasy'—but its real significance is to be found in occasional partnering references to swords elsewhere in his writing: that is, a subject people must be freed from slavery by force of arms. This metaphor may, in turn, remind us of the way in which Roman writers often theorized their relation to their Greek forebears in terms of warfare, or of the way in which St Augustine and St Jerome used Biblical metaphors to justify their expropriation of material from pagan writers.[11] In each case, 'translation' involves a determined assertion of the superiority of the target over the source language.

But Wogan-Browne's paper, to return briefly to that, provides a further point of departure for other papers in the volume, in respect of its awareness of the importance of the gender of translator or of reader: an item as important as often neglected.[12] As Wogan-Browne is able to demonstrate, not all aspects of a translation are necessarily, in themselves, 'gender-specific'—an understanding which some of those who have fuelled the debate about the gender of the narrator of Chaucer's *Second Nun's Tale* might have done well to take on board. At the same time, clear differences exist between the hagiographic translations of male clerics and those of female religious. Where the former create for themselves 'a place in both the spiritual and material economy, claiming an instructive relation with the whole community', the latter conceive their work, almost literally, as an act of generating analogous to the Incarnation. The literary offspring thus produced is, in the Senecan phrase, which it distantly echoes, like and unlike its parent (the Saint whose story is being translated).[13] Consequently, we should not read the women translators' use of their sources simply 'in terms of stereotypes of women—and translation—as derivative and timid, creating no significant difference from the source material'.

This finely-nuanced understanding is extended in a number of ways in the present volume, notably in '*The Complaint of Venus*: Chaucer and de Graunson' by Phillips. This paper demonstrates once again Chaucer's importance for the development of translation in the late Middle English period, by now a commonplace of medieval English literary studies, as indicated by contributions to earlier volumes (see above n. 2). In it Phillips offers a detailed study of Chaucer's translation of three balades by the 'floure of hem that make in France', Oton de Graunson. Chaucer's translation is also a transformation. Most significantly, it turns the male voice of the originals into a female voice; then, it adds an *envoi* in the translator's own, male, voice at the end of the work. The male voice in de Graunson's fiction has a much wider range of possibilities open to it than either the female voice in Chaucer's fiction or Chaucer's own voice as he dedicates the work to his princely readers. The 'humble faithfulness' which characterises the female speaker—Phillips insists that this characterisation 'is not unequivocally an antifeminist position'—links with the translator's self-presentation in the *envoi* and elsewhere in the canon, and reinforces a standard modern distinction between original writing ('masculine') and translation ('feminine'). Yet the offered characterisation proves no more adequate as an expression of the translator's role(s) than was the stereotyping of women ('derivative and timid') noted by Wogan-Browne. The ironies of Chaucer's claiming 'humble faithfulness' to the original even as he rewrites it to realise in it yet another of his, usually female, emblems of patient suffering are well caught in this paper, and bring sharply into focus the instability of the metaphors used to describe the translator's role.[14] In the light of what later papers will have to say about the ways in which a male, clerical, translator worked to meet the expectations of a female readership, we may also find it significant that one scribe of the text read Chaucer's text as directed to a 'princesse', 'my lady of York'.

The translation of female saints' lives by the Austin friar Osbern Bokenham, the subject of the next paper by Johnson, overlaps with those produced by the women religious studied by Wogan-Browne. Thus for Bokenham, as for Clemence of Barking and her religious contemporaries male and female, translation of a saint's life is an act of Christian witness, 'not just to his sources but also to the reality of the power of the saint'. All the same, the differences may be almost as great as the similarities: first, and obviously, because Bokenham is a cleric, like the male Anglo-Norman translators briefly noted by Wogan-Browne; then, because he is writing, as they could not, in the light of late medieval developments in scholasticism.

The difference is clearly focussed in Bokenham's realisation in his work of what, following Genette, Johnson calls the 'para-text' of his work, in particular the traditional translator's prologue, regularly influenced by 'the traditional scholastic categories of *accessus*-tradition'.[15] Bokenham's prologue 'translates' the terms of the academic prologues both literally and metaphorically. Literally, in that it provides a general account of the *Legendys* initially based on the standard pattern of Aristotelian causality and, moreover, translating its very terms. Bokenham's invoking of the Aristotelian category of efficient cause allows him to claim for himself the status not just of translator but, more importantly, of *auctor*. Inevitably this role pulls in a different direction to that earlier noted, of one who witnesses to, or, in Wogan-Browne's phrase, engenders the divine (a term also used by Johnson). Nevertheless, Bokenham's assumption of the two roles reminds us yet again of the commonplace that the translator must always be, on some level, an author as well.

As his own *auctor*, Bokenham is able, in the prologues to the individual *legendys* as well as in what we might call his General Prologue, to provide an extraordinary amount of authoritative circumstantial information about the production of his own work: information which his models, the academic prologues, had to glean from the pages of the *auctores* whom they were prefacing, or from the pages of other commentators on them. Hence, in Johnson's telling phrase—though its relevance is perhaps more immediately apparent for students of critical than of translation theory—'autobiography is bisected and presented through/by theory': and the reverse, obviously, too. Hence, too, whatever we might wish to say about Bokenham's specific translational strategies,[16] his real value for the student of medieval translation, as Johnson presents him, lies in the way he lets himself be seen, if not acting as a translator, in the different social contexts which generated his translations: (i) in his need to secure the spiritual assistance of female saints; (ii) in his need to meet the expectations of the gentlewomen who commissioned several of the translations;[17] (iii) in his dependence on the literary models he is 'translating', specifically Chaucer, whose *Second Nun's Tale* he may have used (so p. 119 below) when preparing his own translation of the life of St Cecilia, and other works by whom—*The Legend of Good Women*; even possibly *The Canterbury Tales*—cast long shadows over his pages.

★   ★   ★

The other named translators studied in this volume are all male, and several of the works to be discussed were produced primarily for a female readership, but questions of gender do not directly inform the next group of papers. Instead, the reader will find detailed discussion of matters of practice like those addressed in Phillips' paper. These papers are also linked in their awareness that what passes for mistranslation may have originated with a copyist of the translation, and, in any case, may as well indicate conscious intention as incompetence on the part of the translator; and in their implied criticism of the view that translators necessarily aimed at a consistency of performance, so that translations can be ascribed to them, or withdrawn from them, on the basis of perceived inconsistencies between those translations and the rest of their works.

Arn's paper neatly complements that of Phillips, since it too considers the question of translation of aristocratic love poetry from French to English by a named translator, Charles of Orleans. Charles has a special interest for students of translation because he is both author and translator of the same works.[18] Like Phillips, Arn assembles evidence to suggest that translators could be as responsive to sound as to sense, sometimes at the expense of the sense, when carrying over details of the original into a translation: thus *effacé du livre* becomes, in translation, *with face delyverid.* Some critics have wished to use the evidence of such (mis)translations to disprove Charles's authorship of the translation, on the assumption that only a translator, and an inept one at that, could possibly mangle an original text so badly (as, to take a strikingly parallel case, Pistol does with the words of the captured Frenchman in *Henry V* IV. iv). But parallels for the practice occur elsewhere in the period,[19] and cannot be put down simply to a translator's incompetence: consequently, argues Arn, evidence of (mis)translation cannot be used to deny authorship of a translation.[20] The evidence suggests that throughout his career as a translator of his own work Charles was ready to take such liberties with his originals, and leads Arn to conclude, with several of the contributors to earlier volumes, that medieval writers make no meaningful distinction between translation and literary composition. In presenting a translator who appears to have responded line-by-line to his original, she describes a practice subtly different to that noted by Burnley and Mills, of translation not line-by-line but by larger units of sense, and tangibly demonstrates that no one model covers all translation situations.[21]

Questions of practice also inform the subject of Lawrence's paper, the sixteenth century Brigittine monk, and prolific writer and translator, Richard Whitford. Brigittine contributions to the development of medieval spirituality, by way especially of the publication of original and translated works of religious edification, have been considered elsewhere.[22] A contemplative order like the Brigittines naturally understood its religious vocation to include the production by the monks of spiritual classics for the sisters and for seculars. Lawrence's paper shows clear y that, in the sixteenth century, translation was a flourishing industry at the Brigittine monastery of Syon. Thus Whitford refers to translations begun by other monks and completed or revised by him, and on one occasion sends his monastic readers to a translation previously produced by himself. It would be difficult to claim that any of his practices are distinctive to Syon: in his regular provision for his readers of prologues explaining his aims and methods, and providing information about the authorship and composition of the originals, and in his use of the abbreviation 'a.l.' in the margins of his works to indicate where he had emended what he took to be a faulty original, Whitford was treading what were, by then, very well-worn paths.[23] For the most part, his translation practices are equally familiar to students of medieval translation:[24] which might make one cautious of using their evidence, even when paralleled in original works by Whitford, to claim for him the authorship of other, anonymous translations which share these particular features, a subsidiary interest of the paper and a perennial interest for students of the many medieval translations to which we are at present unable to assign a translator's name.[25]

The obverse of this desire to credit a named translator with anonymous translations is neatly demonstrated in the next paper, by Scott Westrem, on the translation into Dutch of the Latin *Itinerarius* of Johannes Witte de Hese. The *Itinerarius* is a work in the, by then, flourishing tradition, of books, usually of clerical authorship, describing travels to the Far East. The three Dutch texts of the *Itinerarius* 'seem so discrepant as to represent three separate translations': yet, 'despite differences in spelling, syntax, and even vocabulary', Westrem concludes that they derive from a single ancestor. Scribal alterations to a translated text, that is, can sometimes be sufficiently great to make us think a new translation has been produced. Consequently, as noted above (n. 14), the study of translation cannot be undertaken without a full account of its transmission: in which connection a number of points very relevant to the study of translation emerge. (i) Westrem describes several phases in the development of the Latin original, and identifies a number of scribal strategies, some of which can be readily paralleled in the work of translators (transformation of first- into third-person narrative; increasing rhetorical sophistication; turning 'one of two independent clauses into a participial phrase or a gerundive'; replacement of active voice by passive; reduction of the earlier version's 'numerical extravagance').[26] (ii) Translations of these travel books often circulated simultaneously with the originals. Consequently, the possibility exists, though the evidence leads Westrem decisively to reject the hypothesis, that the translation was from Dutch into Latin and not the other way around. As earlier noted, the decision to translate a Latin work into the vernacular signifies something subtly different to the decision to translate a vernacular work into Latin; and the simultaneous appearance of Latin and vernacular versions may well suggest, as David Burnley implied, that the translator would see himself as producing not a translation so much as a version of the original (*Medieval Translator* (1989) p. 41). (iii) Fascinatingly, the translation has survived only in two post-medieval copies and a detailed account of a medieval copy now lost: which should remind us once more of the need to cast our net beyond the narrow confines of the Middle Ages in our trawl for information about medieval translation.[27]

This account raises further interesting questions. When, as Whitford does, translators tell us that, instead of producing a new translation intended to displace an existing version or versions of the original, they are revising an existing translation, is it necessary to distinguish the two 'voices' of the newly-revised translation, or even possible, if we do not have access to the earlier of the two versions? More critically, if the functions of scribe and translator overlap, what evidence points most clearly to the hand of a scribe-redactor of an existing translation, and what indicates a new and separate translation? Though Westrem does not address this latter question directly, perhaps because a simple answer is almost unachievable, it is obviously of cardinal importance.[28] And the paper has other noteworthy features, too. In particular, the place where it starts— with Defoe's account of a Somerset boy reading aloud from the Authorised Version of the Bible and translating what he read, as he read it, into the words of his own dialect—provides a vivid image of one kind of translator at work, which we might use to supplement the much fuller picture Bokenham offers of himself in his paratext.

★   ★   ★

The remaining papers differ from their predecessors in taking a much wider cast at the question of translation. Though, in all of them, we observe male clerics translating religious texts—in two instances, for a female religious readership—the act of interlingual translation is, for Savage, Renevey and Tixier, merely one element of a much larger hermeneutic question. And there is a further, not entirely fortuitous, link between the three. They are all concerned with religious texts, and religious texts can be notorious for the ways in which they 'translate' the inconvenient immediacy of sense experience into a spiritual sense. In all of the texts being studied, consequently, suppressions or displacements of sexual material can be observed. This feature is not restricted to the trans- lation of religious texts, and may have been undertaken for other than religious motives,[29] but it is a fair guess that sexual material will stand out more dramatically in religious than in other texts, and its suppression or adaptation may seem more urgently necessary.

Savage's paper takes the widest cast at the question of translation. To change the metaphor, her cast list includes translators and readers male and female, medieval and modern, religious and secular, academic and non-academic; all of them, confronting the anchoritic option which three nobly-born sisters embraced early in the thirteenth century, have to find some way of making sense, within their own different cultural sets, of this difficult way of life.

'Translation' as a term thus covers a number of human experiences, not all of them literary. The first, and the formal cause of the literary transla- tions which resulted, is the literal removal ('translation', as of bones from one shrine to another) of the anchoress from the world into the anchorhold. This provides the occasion for a further, metaphorical, trans- lation, the anchoress's spiritualising of her human (specifically, her sexual) nature. The latter activity has to be seen both negatively and positively: negatively, in that the life of the anchorhold systematically negates normal human expectations and appetites in the anchoress herself, and in that medieval attitudes hold woman responsible not only for her own sexual

appetites but also for the desire she arouses inadvertently in men; positively, in that the anchorhold represents a liberation—or, at least, a
protection—from the all-too-real pressures of those expectations, as
expressed particularly by parents and would-be lovers. In addition, the
negatives provide the occasion for the anchoress to identify her own
suffering with, and hence translate it into, the redemptive suffering of
Christ.

To encourage the three sisters in this staggeringly challenging way of
life, an anonymous cleric produced a number of translations of religious
works, including three lives of women saints who heroically resisted
marriage to heathens and suffered frightful martyrdom as a result. His
treatment of these works can provide the basis for telling comparison with
the saints' lives discussed earlier in the volume by Wogan-Browne and
Johnson: inevitably a male cleric like Bokenham will produce a different
version of the same text if he is translating it for a secular gentlewoman,
and a nun like Clemence of Barking if she is translating it for her sisters.[30]
Savage stresses the ambiguities of the enterprise. On the one hand, the
writer must satirise the male suitors of the female saints so as to
encourage the anchoresses to read their own anchorhold as a spiritual
martyrdom and the occasion for a literal withdrawal from men; on the
other, he cannot, even if he wishes to do so, undermine the authority of
the patriarchal establishment from which he derives his own authority, an
establishment deeply implicated with the 'discourse of male sexual authority'. Nevertheless, his great regard for the sisters—Savage insists that his
position is not the archetypal one of 'hatred in disguise'—and his sense of
the heroic spiritual struggle in which they are engaged, lead him, in some
respects, into unavoidable conflict with 'inherited literary tradition'.

The problems are differently focussed by the decision to produce a
modern translation of this medieval material, but ambiguity is once again
the linchpin of the exercise. On the one hand, feminists may feel the
underlying attitudes revealed in the medieval texts are all too familiar.
Now as then woman is often presented as an imperfect 'translation', even
biologically, of man: Savage quotes tellingly from a medical text-book
reissued in 1984 which describes 'the female urogenital triangle' only in
relation to male 'formations and functions'. Yet more pointedly, she notes
(her n. 23) how 'some male academics' in the field of mystical studies
continue to operate in a tradition whereby the male religious institution
intellectualises religious experience, and mystics like St Bernard entirely
reject the body 'while insisting on . . . the heavily physical, erotic literary
vehicle of the Song of Songs as the ideal expression of mystical experience' (a medieval precedent for this attitude is discussed below, in
Renevey's paper). At the same time, a decisive change has occurred in
basic cultural assumptions, as a result of which the same word, 'freedom',

for example, means drastically different things to most modern readers from what it meant to most medieval readers. The writer of the original texts could take it for granted that the sisters shared his understanding of their own fallen natures and absolute dependence on God, so that freedom was the end of the ascetic process, and could be paradoxically symbolised by their ongoing renunciation of other human choices. The modern translator knows that freedom is now understood differently, as the condition of every human choice, and as a right rather than as something needing to be earned. How then to produce a translation which makes readers aware of such simultaneous similarity and difference?

A last point is worth making, about the reader's role as shaping and completing the act of translation. Thus Savage contrasts the response of one modern reader whom we might expect to be sympathetic to the anchoritic option (a nun) with that of another whom we might expect to be completely turned off by it (a mother of three): yet it is the first who read the texts 'with a lot of anger', and the second who 'read them with a lot of love'. The student of such translations must somehow find a way to negotiate both these responses so as to shortchange neither.

Richard Rolle, the subject of Renevey's paper, has been studied both as an actual translator of Biblical and other religious texts for enclosed nuns, and as a tireless self-propagandizer whose work, repeatedly devoted to an exposition of what he took to be normative spiritual experiences, represents, at least metaphorically, an attempted translation into prose of those experiences.[31] Renevey refers only in passing to Rolle the Biblical translator; his particular quarry is the way in which Rolle's acts of self-translation depend fascinatingly upon his reworking of material from the commentary tradition, in particular the Song of Songs, so as to authorise his spiritual experiences and, like Bokenham, appropriate for himself the role of *auctor*, a role at odds with the received image of the translator as the copyist of another writer's work. The ironies of this appropriation are profound. Where the commentary tradition typically read the erotic imagery of the Song of Songs through a spiritual filter, and thus produced the kind of translation-with-commentary widespread in the Middle Ages, Rolle needs to recoup as much of the erotic charge of the original as he can, to read the erotic metaphors as metaphors of *themselves*, so as to produce a version of them which, in the measure that it is slewed towards the immediacy of actual sense experience, though not carnally erotic experience, goes some way to restoring the literal sense of the original text. This picture is further, and fascinatingly, complicated by Rolle's susceptibility to women—what Renevey calls his 'propensity for feminine beauty and his desire for concupiscence'—so that Rolle's reinstatement of the literal level of the spiritual metaphor may give us the sense that Rolle is, at the same time, covering his tracks and producing a spiritual reading of his own erotic instincts. For Rolle, then, the problematics of translation are foregrounded precisely at the point where the two loves, divine and carnal, meet, and where the carnal metaphors necessary to translate the experience of divine love must simultaneously be affirmed and denied.

Tixier's paper comes appropriately at the very end of the volume. He writes in passing about several English, and considers in detail two twentieth-century French, translations of the anonymous Middle English mystical text *The Cloud of Unknowing*. One, the work of the learned Benedictine monk Noetinger, is accompanied by an extensive scholarly apparatus; Noetinger's translation, more an act of interpretation than a translation (so Tixier), makes a regular practice of glossing the text. By contrast, the translation of Armel Guerne minimises the commentary in an attempt to let the text speak nakedly for itself. Tixier identifies in the two strategies, which he calls the roles of the theologian and the poet, something like the two poles between which a translator must situate himself, and both have ready parallels in the works of medieval translators. Tixier's paper, however, does much more than merely develop this variant of a translational commonplace. It positions the translator of a mystical text in a precisely analogous position to that of the reader—and, one might add, the writer—of the work, compelled like them to seek the God hidden *between* the words of the text.[32] His paper also foregrounds the difficulties of producing a translation of a text which itself, directly and indirectly, is operating within well-established traditions of spiritual writing: put crudely, how far ought one to go in embedding these traditions in the language of the translation, and how?[33] The paper further shows how modern translators are, in a whole variety of ways, operating like their medieval predecessors. In particular, they frequently depend on earlier commentaries on, and versions of, the work, reproducing their details to the frequent detriment of the original. Tixier notes how, for example, Noetinger's translation was based not on the original text, which had not appeared in a critical edition when he produced his translation, but on the English translation of Dom Justin McCann: precisely the situation that obtains in many medieval translations, based not on an original text but on a dependent, translated, version of it.[34] Now, as then, translation of so difficult a text implies an active interpretation which is in constant danger of distorting its meanings.

One such distortion, unsurprisingly, concerns the presence of sexual material in the original. The author writes twice about the 'preue membres' of the body, once in the context of a warning against extremes of ascetic practice, and once as a way of stigmatising heretical licence, the one use of the phrase a negative of the other, and the two phrases linked perhaps by the understanding that heresy is often orthodox belief or practice carried to extremes. Noetinger's source McCann was himself at this point dependent on a translation of Evelyn Underhill which suppressed the adjective 'preue', and thus transformed the specifically sexual reference of the original into a more neutral bodily one in the translation. Tixier rightly complains at this suppression for future readers of 'une donnée ascétique d'un intérêt non négligeable'. At the opposite end of the scale he also finds disheartening the translators' unwillingness to let the text speak for itself when the central question of God's relation to the soul is being discussed. A text which insists on the soul's equality with God through love is regularly presented in translation so as to insist on the inequality of the relationship: in several of the translations God *condescends* or *comes down* to the level of the soul. Small wonder that an entry in the *Dictionnaire de Spiritualité* complains that the translations have paradoxically rendered the medieval mystics inaccessible to monoglot French readers. The most careful translation, that is, modern no less than medieval, inevitably represents, on whatever level, in however concealed a way, a rewriting, a new version, of its original.

Similarity-and-difference, then, as between original and translation, the binary oppositions linked in Trinitarian fashion through, with, and in each other, seems to be a constant defining feature of medieval translation. Several of the translations here studied describe themselves in such a way as to emphasise their affiliations with, rather than their difference from, their originals. This is figured typically in sexual terms. On the one hand, translation is a process of bringing to birth, the translator or the translation presented as female to the original text's, or the reader's, male. Hence the generative metaphors noted by Wogan-Browne, Drory and Johnson, where translation is understood, almost literally, as a labour of love; hence, too, with suppression of the specifically sexual dimension of the image, Chaucer's description of the translator, in the paper of Phillips, as the subservient female to the original text's, and the readers', maleness, where the emphasis is placed rather on the labour than on the love. Alternatively, the translator or the translation can be figured as the male principle to the original text's, or the reader's, female: this time, one might guess, it is not labour but pleasure or power which is foregrounded in the act of translation. Hence, in Drory's paper, al-Ḥarīzī marries himself to 'the Holy Tongue' and begets on her a new literary composition; hence, in a most striking version of the metaphor, Rolle presents himself in his English epistle *Ego Dormio*, noted at the start of Renevey's paper, as a paranymph who wishes to bring his (literally female) reader to the (barely metaphoric) bed of her (literally male) master.

These variations on a metaphoric theme partner another term which reappears several times in the course of the volume: that of the betweenness of translation. Thus Arn urges us to 'read one of [Charles's] French poems, then its English counterpart, and finally to explore the space between the two'; thus, to adapt Johnson, translation is a 'zone of transaction' anologous to the place where the text constitutes itself a text; or, to adapt the author of *The Cloud of Unknowing*, translation is the place where the word of God lies hidden and where the disciple's fractured language must engage with it, like Jacob wrestling with the angel, so as to secure a blessing for those who come after. This metaphor, of course, reminds us that the obverse of love is struggle and warfare, a metaphor of considerable relevance to the study of translation, if not one much in evidence in these pages.

NOTES

1. R. Ellis (ed.) assisted by Jocelyn Price, Stephen Medcalf and Peter Meredith *The Medieval Translator: The Theory and Practice of Translation in the Middle Ages: Papers Read at a Conference Held 20–23 August 1987 at the University of Wales Conference Centre, Gregynog Hall* (Woodbridge, Suffolk: D.S. Brewer, 1989); R. Ellis (ed.) *The Medieval Translator II* Westfield Publications in Medieval Studies 5 (London: Centre for Medieval Studies, Queen Mary and Westfield College, 1991); R. Ellis (ed.) *New Comparison* 12: *Translation in the Middle Ages* (1991).

2. Some of these figures have received attention in previous volumes of *The Medieval Translator*: for Clemence of Barking, see C. Batt, 'Clemence of Barking's Transformations of *Courtoisie* in *La Vie de Sainte Catherine d'Alexandrie*', *New Comparison* 12 (1991) pp. 102–23; for Rolle, N. Watson, 'Translation and Self-Canonization in Richard Rolle's *Melos Amoris*' in *Medieval Translator* (1989) pp. 167–80; for Chaucer, T.W. Machan, 'Chaucer as Translator' in *Medieval Translator* (1989) pp. 55–67, and N. Thompson, 'Translation and Response: *Troilus* and the *Filostrato*' in *Medieval Translator II* (1991) pp. 123–150.

3. For an exception to this generalisation, see C. Foz, 'Pratique de la traduction en Espagne au Moyen Age: les travaux tolédans' in *Medieval Translator II* (1991) pp. 29–43.

4. In the early stages editorial work was undertaken by both editors; in the later stages, Ruth Evans had the time-consuming task of preparing the camera-ready copy for the publishers.

5. Such caution reminds us how careful we may need to be when pronouncing on 'schools' of translation. Thus on Toledo, the subject of a paper by Foz (above n. 3), an unpublished paper communicated to me by Dr Anthony Pym claims that 'the school of Toledo is mostly the invention of two nineteenth-century historians'. For Paris (at the court of Charles V), see L.A. Shore, 'A Case Study in Medieval Nonliterary Translation: Scientific Texts from Latin to French' in J. Beer (ed.) *Medieval Translators and their Craft* Studies in Medieval Culture XXV (Kalamazoo, Michigan: Western Michigan University, 1989) p. 310, and my comments in reviewing this book, *Allegorica* 12 (1991) p. 55; and for Vadstena, Wollin (full reference n. 22 below).

6. See K. Sisam (ed.) *Fourteenth Century Verse and Prose* (Oxford: Clarendon Press, 1921) pp. 148–9.

7. R. Copeland, *Rhetoric, Hermeneutics, and Translation in the Middle Ages: Academic Traditions and Vernacular Texts* (Cambridge: Cambridge University Press, 1991).

8. L.D. Benson (ed.) *The Riverside Chaucer* 3rd edn. (Oxford: Oxford University Press, 1988) p. 662.

9. For further comment see R. Ellis, 'The Choices of the Translator in the Late Middle English Period' in M. Glasscoe (ed.) *The Medieval Mystical Tradition in England* (Exeter: University of Exeter Press, 1982) p. 29 and n. 38 and references.

10. The example of the Bible was similarly invoked in the late fourteenth century to authorise the translation into Latin of the Swedish revelations of St Bridget: see my 'The Divine Message and its Human Faces: St Bridget and her Editors' in J. Hogg (ed.) *Studies in St Brigitta and the Brigittine Order* (forthcoming).

11. For an example of the former, in the *Ars Poetica* of Horace, see Copeland, *Rhetoric, Hermeneutics, and Translation* p. 28; for quotations from Sts Augustine and Jerome, D.W. Robertson Jr., *A Preface to Chaucer: Studies in Medieval Perspectives* (Princeton, New Jersey: Princeton University Press, 1963) pp. 340–1.

12. Granted, it has been treated by A. Barratt, 'Dame Eleanor Hull: a Fifteenth-Century Translator' in *Medieval Translator* (1989) pp. 87–101, and R. Evans, 'Women Inside and Outside the Text: Translation and Position', *New Comparison* 12 (1991) pp. 89–101.

13. For the Senecan phrase, see Copeland, *Rhetoric, Hermeneutics, and Translation* p. 27.

14. The paper's opening remarks about the difficulties of determining the precise status of de Graunson's original, and Chaucer's translated, texts also provide a timely reminder that the study of translations requires a knowledge of the total manuscript context of original and translated works before we can pronounce, even tentatively, on the relation of one to the other. On this point see further C.W. Marx, 'Problems of Editing a Translation: Anglo-Norman to Middle English' in *Medieval Translator II* (1991) pp. 253–67.

15. On translation prologues, see I. Johnson, 'Prologue and Practice: Middle English Lives of Christ' in *Medieval Translator* (1989) pp. 69–85, and the forthcoming edition of such prologues by R. Evans, I. Johnson, J. Wogan-Browne and N. Watson; on the ultimate origin of these prologues, the so-called academic prologues, A. Minnis, *Medieval Theory of Authorship: Scholastic Literary Attitudes in the Later Middle Ages* (London: Scolar Press 1984: rev. ed. Aldershot: Wildwood House, 1988) chs. 1–2.

16. Johnson has little to say about Bokenham's translational theories or practices. For comment about Bokenham as translator, see M.S. Serjeantson (ed.) *Legendys of Hooly Wummen by Osbern Bokenham*, Early English Text Society OS 206 (London: Oxford University Press, 1938) pp. xv–xxiv; R. Ellis, 'Choices of the Translator' pp. 35–6, 40–1, 45; and D. Burnley, 'Late Medieval English Translation: Types and Reflections', *Medieval Translator* (1989) pp. 39–40. For a modern translation of Bokenham's text, with critical comment, see Sheila Delany, *A Legend of Holy Women: a Translation of Osbern Bokenham's Legends of Holy Women* (Notre Dame, Indiana: University of Notre Dame Press, 1993).

17. On women as readers of certain kinds of translations, and on the influence their expectations might have exerted on the production of the translation, see Ellis, *Allegorica* 12 (1991) p. 65; J.R. Goodman, 'William Caxton and

Anthony Woodville, Translators: the Case of the *Dictes and Sayengis of the Philosophres*', *New Comparison* 12 (1991) pp. 16–19; and, in the present volume, comments *passim* by Wogan-Browne, Phillips and Savage.

18. For other instances of interlingual self-translation (Latin into French) see K. Lloyd-Jones, 'Humanist Debate and the "Translative Dilemma" in Renaissance France'; for an instance of the parallel practice of intralingual self-translation, J. Beer, '*Le Bestiaire d'amours en vers*', both in J. Beer (ed.) *Medieval Translators and their Craft* pp. 356–64 and 285–96 respectively.

19. Parallels for the practice occur as well in prose as in poetry: for example, 'la feste estoit par tel maniere establie' becomes Malory's 'stable their horsis' (see E. Vinaver (ed.) *The Complete Works of Sir Thomas Malory* 3 vols., 2nd edn. (Oxford: Clarendon Press, 1967) vol. I, p. lxii n. 3); or, in the translation of the *Liber Celestis* of St Bridget of Sweden, 'expresse nominauerim' becomes 'excusede . . . be nam' (see R. Ellis (ed.) *The Liber Celestis of St Bridget of Sweden*, Early English Text Society 291 (Oxford: Oxford University Press, 1987) p. 131 l. 6). In some cases, of course, translators may have been faithfully following errors introduced in their copy of the original.

20. It should also be used with caution to argue that a translator was or was not a native speaker of English: the case does seem proved, though, for example, by W.O. Ross (ed.) *Middle English Sermons Edited from the BM MS Royal 18 B xxiii*, Early English Text Society 0S 209 (London: Oxford University Press, 1940) pp. xxvi (addressing the question of authorship of sermons 44–46 in the collection).

21. See Burnley, *Medieval Translator* (1989) pp. 44–5, and M. Mills, 'Techniques of Translation in the Middle English Versions of *Guy of Warwick*' in *Medieval Translator II* (1991) pp. 209–29 *passim*.

22. On translation activity at the Swedish mother house, Vadstena, see L. Wollin, 'The Monastery at Vadstena. Investigating the Great Translation Workshop in Medieval Scandinavia', *Medieval Translator II* (1991) pp. 65–88; and at Syon Abbey, R. Ellis, 'Further Thoughts on the Spirituality of Syon Abbey' in W. Pollard (ed.) *The English Mystical Tradition* (forthcoming); J. Hogg, 'The Contribution of the Brigittine Order to Late Medieval English Spirituality' *Spiritualität Heute und Gestern. Internationaler Kongress vom 4 bis 7 August 1982*, Analecta Cartusiana 35 (1983) pp. 153–74; A. M. Hutchison, 'Devotional Reading in the Monastery and in the Late Medieval Household', and M.W. Driver, 'Pictures in Print: Late Fifteenth- and Early Sixteenth-Century English Religious Books for Lay Readers' in M.G. Sargent (ed.) *De Cella in Seculum: Religious and Secular Life and Devotion in Late Medieval England* (Cambridge: D.S. Brewer, 1989) pp. 215–27 and 229–44 respectively; M. Denley, 'Elementary Teaching Techniques and Middle English Religious Didactic Writings' in H. Phillips (ed.) *Langland, the Mystics and the Medieval English Religious Tradition* (Cambridge: D. S. Brewer, 1990) pp. 223–41; and J. Rhodes, 'Syon Abbey and its Religious Publications in the Sixteenth Century' *Journal of Ecclesiastical History* 44 (1993) pp. 11–24.

23. On the translation prologues, see above n. 15; for abbreviations comparable to Whitford's 'a.l.', see examples noted by Ellis, 'Choices of the Translator' pp. 24–5, 27. Whitford's practices can be paralleled in other translations emanating from Syon, for example *The Myroure of Oure Ladye*, also discussed art. cit.

24. So, for example, his use of proverbs to enliven his material, a practice earlier followed by Chaucer in his *Melibee* (cf. R. Ellis, *Patterns of Religious*

Narrative in the Canterbury Tales (London: Croom Helm, 1986) p. 108). Whitford's claim, however, to have translated a text 'after the same metre/ in maner and measure' as the original would, if the claim received scholarly substantiation, constitute a notable instance of distinctive translational practice not much in evidence in the Middle Ages.

25. Lawrence's account of Whitford's practice when translating Bible verses, though the evidence itself is of variable quality, may give pause to those who would use comparable evidence to remove from the canon of the *Cloud* author's works the anonymous translation of Richard of St Victor's *Benjamin Minor*: see R. Ellis, 'Author(s), Compilers, Scribes and Bible Texts: Did the *Cloud*-Author Translate *The Twelve Patriarchs*?' in M. Glasscoe (ed.) *The Medieval Mystical Tradition in England* Exeter Symposium V (Cambridge: D.S. Brewer, 1992) pp. 200–5.

26. Some of these changes (first- to third-person narrative; active and passive interchange; interchange of main clause and participial phrase/gerund) are briefly noted as features of translation practice by Ellis, 'Choices of the Translator' pp. 30–4.

27. For further comment on this point see M. Kalinke, 'Translator or Redactor? the Problem of Old Norse-Icelandic "Translations" of Old French Literature', *New Comparison* 12 (1991) pp. 34–53.

28. A rule of thumb, though, might be advanced as follows: major syntactic divergences between two translated versions of the same text, which cannot be directly explained by reference to the different linguistic situations (for example, the different dialects) in which the scribes might have been producing their different versions, probably indicate two independent translations of the same text rather than two copies of the same translation. For fuller discussion, using as test-case the Middle English versions of the *Revelations* of St Bridget of Sweden, see R. Ellis, 'An Edition, with Commentary, of Certain Sections of BM MS Claudius BI of the Fourteenth Century Brigittine *Revelations*' (University of Oxford: DPhil thesis, 1974) pp. l–lxxii.

29. For comment on the practice, though not in translations of religious texts, see R. Field, '*Ipomedon* to *Ipomadon A*: Two Views of Courtliness' in *Medieval Translator* (1989) pp. 135–41, and J. Beer, 'Julius Caesar, Philip Augustus and the Anonymous Translator of *Li Fet des Romains*' in *Medieval Translator II* (1991) pp. 89–97.

30. With this observation, one might compare the different uses made of the image of Christ as mother by male and female religious: see C.W. Bynum, *Jesus as Mother: Studies in the Spirituality of the High Middle Ages* (Berkeley and Los Angeles: University of California Press, 1982).

31. See in particular N. Watson, *Richard Rolle and the Invention of Authority* (Cambridge: Cambridge University Press, 1991); V. Gillespie, 'Mystic's Foot: Rolle and Affectivity,' in M. Glasscoe (ed.) *The Medieval Mystical Tradition in England* (Exeter: University of Exeter Press, 1982) pp. 199–230; R. Allen, '"Singular Lufe": Richard Rolle and the Grammar of Spiritual Ascent', and R. Copeland, 'Richard Rolle and the Rhetorical Theory of the Levels of Style', both in M. Glasscoe (ed.) *The Medieval Mystical Tradition in England* (Cambridge: D.S. Brewer, 1984) pp. 28–54, 55–80.

32. The metaphor of the mystic as translator has been made much of by Nicholas Watson: see, in particular, 'Misrepresenting the Untranslateable: Marguerite Porete and the *Mirouer des simples âmes*', *New Comparison* 12 (1991) pp. 124–37.

33. See comment on this feature in *Allegorica* 12 (1991) pp. 55–6. For comparable developments in eighteenth-century Germany, where translations from English were produced initially through the medium of French translations, see W. Graeber, 'German Translators of English Fiction and their French Mediators' in H. Kittel and A.P. Frank (eds) *Interculturality and the Historical Study of Literary Translations* (Berne: Erich Schmidt Verlag, 1991) pp. 5–16, kindly communicated to me by Professor Kittel.

Translating Past Cultures?

RUTH EVANS

> Fundamental difference . . . always contains an element of violation
> . . . we could accept each other's irreducible otherness . . . we could
> declare each other products of different cultures . . . But that would
> leave us separate and impermeable.
>
> Eva Hoffman[1]

In her compelling book, *Lost in Translation: Life in a New Language*, Eva
Hoffman narrates her memories of being 'translated' from Poland to
Canada in 1959 when a young girl, and her subsequent, often awkward,
sometimes painful, accommodation to an alien culture.[2] The problem, as
she sees it, is how to articulate a sense of her own identity and cultural
difference while assimilating herself to another culture: not quite Polish
nor quite North American, Hoffman forges a hybrid subjectivity in the
borderland between the two. Complete cultural translation is impossible,
but neither, according to Hoffman, is it desirable, for if it were then an
important 'untranslated' residue would be lost, the residue that helps to
construct a subjective sense of self: 'if I don't want to remain in arid
internal exile for the rest of my life, I have to find a way to lose my alienation without losing my self. But how does one bend toward another
culture without falling over, how does one strike an elastic balance
between rigidity and self-effacement?'[3] Her title, then, alludes to the
traditional notion of translation as a site of loss, but does so ironically,
making 'loss' problematic because it is also a (precarious) site of self-
making.

Hoffman is Polish, Jewish and a woman; these are her most obvious
(though not her only) markers of difference, aspects of herself that have
to be articulated and negotiated in that space between cultural boundaries.[4] And in her account translation is also a figure for what happens to
whole peoples and cultures as they try to construct forms of solidarity in
the modern fragmented world: 'I share with my American generation an

acute sense of dislocation and the equally acute challenge of having to invent a place and an identity for myself without the traditional supports. It could be said that the generation I belong to has been characterized by its prolonged refusal to assimilate—and it is in my very uprootedness that I'm its member. It could indeed be said that exile is the archetypal condition of contemporary lives.'[5]

In our current historical period, marked by unprecedented levels of exile, emigration, immigration, diaspora, deportation, decolonising, civil war and new peace initiatives, 'translation' has come to be a powerful critical trope naming various activities of displacement and transformation within and across cultures that produce what Homi Bhabha calls 'the third space':[6] a process in which there can never be a full translation of the subject-matter of ourselves or of forms of culture, but which is hybrid and which bears, like a translation, traces of former meanings that can give rise to new identities and positions.[7] In *Siting Translation: History, Post-Structuralism and the Colonial Context* Tejaswini Niranjana describes hybridity as 'living in translation'.[8] Hoffman's book not only explores this powerful metaphor of 'living in translation', but also forces the reader's acknowledgement of the human subjects whose identities are formed in and through translation(s). I understand 'translation' here as both a metaphor *and* a practice, since it is in and through actual translated texts that human subjects are contained and constructed, and enact their resistance to various forms of power. Translation, still thought of as marginal to academic literary culture and criticism, is, when viewed from a wider cultural perspective, absolutely central to the experiences of men and women in our modern, post- and neo-colonial world.[9]

Yet previous historical periods, including the Middle Ages, have been just as deeply marked by the processes of cultural hegemony, by the concomitant need for translations, and by the shaping and containment of human subjects through and by translations. The contest between Latin and the vernaculars, played out across so many cultural and social scenes, is only one major site of the complex, varied and shifting relations of power in Europe in the Middle Ages, though few critics have so far explored that contest in those terms. Rita Copeland's work is a notable exception: she argues, for example, that the classical, rhetorical model of translation-as-displacement is seen at work in the later Middle Ages in 'continuing efforts of translators to define the range of vernacular literary languages and to generate a vernacular canon which will substitute itself for Latin models in the very process of replicating them'.[10] Her account of the relationship between rhetoric and hermeneutics, 'a nexus within which the character of medieval vernacular translation was largely defined',[11] views translation as a site for a disciplinary contest that has, or could have, considerable ramifications in terms of wider institutional power structures in the Middle Ages. Her book thus raises some large questions about how medievalists use 'translation' as a site for representing past culture(s).

I will return later and in more detail to the kinds of questions that I think Copeland's work *fails* to ask. What is important is that her model offers a significantly different representation of medieval 'translation', one that shifts attention away from the traditional formalistic emphasis on linguistic and stylistic source-comparison, with its attendant moralizing idiom of fidelity and error, word-for-word or sense-for-sense, and its normative aesthetic assumptions, and puts the *cultural* issue of vernacularity firmly on the agenda. It is also obvious that there is a radical disjuncture between the notion of 'living in translation' which I started with and Copeland's particular historical model: both have very different objects at their centres. And this raises important questions. Which model provides appropriate critical tools for reading *medieval* texts? What is the relative heuristic value of different translation theories when used in relation to the texts and cultures of the Middle Ages? Underlying this is a much more fundamental question that I cannot possibly answer because it is dependent upon the kind of reading agendas that we individually set for ourselves: what do we want to know about the past?

My intention here is not to offer a historical survey of 'translation' in general or 'medieval translation' in particular, or to frame the papers presented in this volume in terms of either medieval or modern 'theories' of translation.[12] Nor, since this is a point of contention, do I so much want to defend the right of medievalists to frame their work within current translation theories, since some of them, as the essays in this volume by Jocelyn Wogan-Browne, Helen Phillips and Anne Savage demonstrate, are anyway already successfully doing this, and in ways that suggest they are not simply appropriating the models uncritically.[13] However, I do want, at least partly, to look at this question of historical portability and to suggest some problematic areas raised by medievalists' appropriation of modern understandings of translation. And, since Rita Copeland has proposed a clearly-articulated *historicist* model, one that aims to sweep aside previous 'understandings', explicit or implicit, of translation in the Middle Ages, I also want to engage with her work.

It will be clear throughout this essay that I privilege a particular understanding of 'translation', namely the greatly expanded notion of 'translation' found in the poststructuralist critique of classical notions of representation and reality, especially the appropriation and development of this critique by feminist and colonial discourse theory critics. This understanding of translation has, I believe, the potential to go deeper into questions of politics and power relations in medieval translation than, say, Copeland's model. The discussion of hybridity and hybrid identities in border zones with which I opened is *potentially* enormously valuable for rethinking some of the questions about vernacularity, *translatio studii* and *translatio imperii* as zones of *cultural* transaction in the Middle Ages. The kind of hybridity displayed in early fifteenth-century sets of proto-Lollard sermons such as the collection in MSS Lambeth Palace Library 392 and Cambridge University Library Additional 5338, which draws verbatim on the English Bible translations from the Wycliffite cycle but on orthodox Latin material for the scriptural exegesis, might be susceptible to just this kind of analysis, leading, perhaps, to a new understanding of the kinds of political initiatives established by Lollards in the wake of the *De heretico comburendo* of 1401.[14] However, colonial discourse theories cannot be appropriated unproblematically for an earlier period. It will also be clear from this essay that some aspects of what comes under the rubric 'translation' are in fact also part of 'critical theory', despite Roger Ellis's distinction between 'translation theory' and 'critical theory' (see above, p. 7), although my argument recognises that for some medievalists these areas are incommensurable and their juxtaposition produces anxiety: that anxiety and incommensurability need to be addressed.

I see my arguing for the importance of medieval translation scholarship as part of a much wider project of making visible a period whose differences are often unacknowledged by scholars working in post-medieval disciplines. Although Translation Studies is now a growing field, the medieval period is often ignored or downplayed when the genealogy of Translation Studies is established.[15] Conversely, medievalists often show a lack of interest in situating their work within the wider disciplinary, and interdisciplinary, field of translation, with the result that it goes largely unnoticed by non-medievalists. This is a familiar scene: there is no need to rehearse here the well-known arguments about the status of medieval studies in relation to other academic disciplines and to the marking out, and privileging, of specific periodisations within the academic institution.[16] Implicit in my argument is the need for work on medieval translation to be sited in a wider field if it is to achieve greater academic visibility and contribute to the redrawing of the historical maps of 'translation'.

The new visibility and importance of medieval translation as a distinct subject of academic enquiry (for English speakers, at any rate) is attested by a number of recent ground-breaking volumes. These include four collections of papers (of which this volume forms one collection) chosen from those delivered at the series of Cardiff conferences on the Theory and Practice of Translation in the Middle Ages, inaugurated by Roger Ellis;[17] the volume edited by Jeanette Beer, *Medieval Translators and Their Craft* (1989), a collection of contributions from the sessions on The Medieval Translator's Craft convened annually by Jeanette Beer at the

International Congress for Medieval Studies, Kalamazoo, Michigan;[18] and Rita Copeland's rigorously-argued study, *Rhetoric, Hermeneutics, and Translation in the Middle Ages* (1991).[19] This important work is not, however, an isolated phenomenon, comfortably cordoned off in a place called 'the Middle Ages'. It is related, though in asymptotic and sometimes equivocal ways, to the much larger and now critically significant field of 'translation'.

This field of 'translation', as it has developed within the academy over the past decade or so, is extremely heterogeneous. It would be difficult to do justice here to its range and history. It comprises the largely subjective, New Critical approaches of the American literary translation workshop of the 1960s; the more systematic, linguistically-based approaches evolved by the 'science of translation' school associated chiefly with the American theorist Eugene Nida, whose highly influential work on Bible translation drew on Chomsky's transformative-generative grammar and its underlying notions of universal mental structures, and who contributed to the vocabulary of translation *inter alia* the notions of formal and dynamic equivalence; the wide-ranging, humanist, interdisciplinary and largely empirical knowledges about translation, known collectively under the rubric of 'Translation Studies' (and this is far from being a homogeneous category), of which probably the best-known and most controversial is Hamar Even-Zohar's 'polysystem theory', partly developed by Gideon Toury; and the critique of those knowledges made possible by radical revisions of the Western philosophical notions of representation, textuality, authorship and knowledge upon which 'translation' has conventionally depended. I draw here on Edwin Gentzler's very useful recent taxonomy of the 'field',[20] to which I would add the important area of colonial discourse theory, in which 'translation' is understood both as a metaphor and as a set of practices crucial to the 'strategies of containment', as Niranjana puts it, of human subjects.[21]

Interest in translation generally, both from an academic and a 'professional' standpoint, is attested by the many conferences on translation, such as the annual one sponsored by The Center for Research in Translation (CRIT) at SUNY-Binghamton, New York, and by the establishment of a number of journals concerned specifically with 'translation', such as *Target, TRANSST, Translation and Literature, TTR* and *Testo a Fronte*.[22] The enormous hold which 'Translation Studies' has within the academic field of translation is evidenced by the inauguration of a new series, Translation Studies, from Routledge.[23] The importance of the topic of literary translation in poststructuralist and colonial discourse theory is witnessed by volumes such as Joseph Graham's *Difference in Translation*, Tejaswini Niranjana's *Siting Translation*, and Lawrence Venuti's *Rethinking Translation: Discourse, Subjectivity, Ideology*.[24] I will return to this last area in more detail since it radically challenges the premises of even the 'new' Translation Studies approach.

The most recent work in Translation Studies seeks, in the words of Susan Bassnett-McGuire, 'to avoid the old hackneyed evaluative approach that simply set translations alongside one another and discussed differences in a formalist vacuum'.[25] Current work on medieval translation has largely (though not completely) abandoned this arid formalist and evaluative approach, and is recognisably, though not always explicitly, situated in the field of 'Translation Studies'. Thus it broadly conforms with the statements made by Gideon Toury and José Lambert in their editorial manifesto to the first issue of *Target: International Journal of Translation Studies*: it recognises the 'pluralism inherent in the various possible approaches to translation'; it is 'goal-oriented', concerned with the fortunes of the translated text as it enters the 'target' culture; it recognises that acceptance of the translation in the target culture is 'determined largely by the constellation of that culture and the functions the target text is to fulfil in it' (further glossed by Toury and Lambert as the 'target-oriented constraints of a cultural-semiotic nature' which shape 'the cognitive processes involved in individual acts of translation'); and it is empirical: 'translated texts . . . are observational facts . . . which lend themselves to actual study'. And its perspective, like that of Translation Studies, is interdisciplinary, characterized, in the words of Susan Bassnett-McGuire, by 'the combining of work in linguistics, literary studies, cultural history, philosophy and anthropology'.[26] However, I am cautious about arguing that all current work on translation by medievalists can be categorized under the heading of TS. There is still a tendency to accumulate formalistic evidence at the expense of understanding the role(s) of the translated text in the target culture, and there is still relatively little attention paid to some of the categories felt important by TS scholars, such as 'the role of ideology in the shaping of a translation'.[27] Before I discuss Rita Copeland's ground-breaking work, I want to clarify a little more the project of current work on medieval translation. It would be difficult to do justice here to what is a very wide orbit of activity, so I will look briefly at some statements by scholars in the field. Just as the proclamations of intention in medieval translators' prologues and introductions embody particular cultural and political values, so Beer and Ellis's prefaces to their medieval translation volumes set out their project in translating past culture into the present.[28]

Beer is well-versed in the 'Translation Studies' approach, and tries to locate the various projects of medieval translators in relation to this, but not because she is sympathetic towards it. The major thrust of her introduction is to crusade on behalf of the *historical* specificity of the Middle Ages, to defend the lack of theoretical self-consciousness exhibited by medieval translators, and to assert that 'modern theorists' have got it wrong. She discusses, for example, the inappropriateness of 'audience response equivalence' (= dynamic equivalence) for the Middle Ages, because translators were much more focussed on the response of a particular target audience, and she notes with some acerbity the value judgments inherent in the terminology of 'modern theorists' ('adaptation'; 'paraphrase'; 'imitation'), and its inadequacy for describing 'the complexity of the translative process in the Middle Ages'. She castigates 'those modern theorists who, for the sake of anachronistic criteria, categorize a milennium of translative vitality as one thousand years of non-translation'.[29]

Beer's points about the historical portability and inadequacy of certain terms and concepts current in translation theory deserve greater elaboration. Savage's essay in this volume interestingly acknowledges the failure of a teleologically-oriented 'dynamic equivalence' approach ('what has often been seen as the ultimate goal of translators, to reproduce in the target audience the same responses as the original language did for its contemporary one . . .') to her own, modern, translation of medieval texts. Yet Nida's notions of formal and dynamic equivalence[30] can, in a sense, be mapped only too easily onto the Middle Ages, especially onto religious texts, since Nida's theory arose out of his practice as a Bible translator, and was very much governed by his sense of a transcendental signified: an inviolable, divine core message. His primary concern was 'the communication across cultures of the spirit of the original message . . . The particular form in which that message appears is superficial as long as the meaning of that message is clear.'[31] Put this way, the notion of formal and dynamic equivalence is a recognisably Robertsonian mode of understanding translation. But it is also a reductive mode which would, ironically, exclude Wyclif's understanding of the materiality of the signifier: 'in the whole of scripture no single syllable has been set down without a meaning'.[32] It would of course be impossible wholly to recover the relationship between the original receptors and message in the Middle Ages. Constraints of partial and fragmentary historical evidence would dog the project, but the overriding critique here must be directed towards the search for origins, essential meaning and (authorial) intentions. This is admittedly a different critique of the terminology from that of Beer.

One obvious, and non-medievalist, objection to Nida's formulation is that it is dependent on problematic communication models of coding and encoding which assume a pre-linguistic (divine) 'message'. While it is true that all scriptural authority in the Middle Ages was defined as absolute,[33] it is not true that as a result all textual signifiers were defined as having minimal significance, and certainly not true of the complex situation in relation to Wyclif, as is most stimulatingly demonstrated by Nick Davis.[34]

A Robertsonian understanding of medieval translation (not that this is by any means the case amongst medievalists) would preclude other, non-Robertsonian and re-routing approaches, like Davis's. Beer's suspicion of the adequacy of some modern translational terms for the situation in the Middle Ages is right, but this is not the fault as such of 'modern theorists': Translation Studies, like colonial discourse theory, *is* concerned (albeit in very different ways) with historical specificity.[35] The question is, *which* terms are adequate to describe the historical situation in the Middle Ages? This is a question that Copeland tries to answer more rigorously.

Ellis is less concerned than Beer to justify his project to 'modern theorists' or to knock the pronouncements of the latter, but like Beer he is cautious about modern blanket theorising of what is a complex historical situation. Implicit in vol. 1, and explicit in vol. 2,[36] is a view of medieval translational activity as heterogeneous (a point also made by Beer), but the problem that is not fully addressed here is how to focus or understand this heterogeneity. Ellis reiterates in vol. 2 his earlier point that 'every instance of practice that we may be tempted to erect into a principle has its answering opposite, sometimes in the same work'.[37] This is an entirely reasonable caveat, yet it is possible to advance *other* kinds of generalisations about medieval translation apart from what constitutes 'medieval translation theory', and it is possible to work with *both* generalisations *and* meticulous attention to textual detail. The establishing of frames (a form of theorising) is what makes it possible to consider 'translation in the Middle Ages' as more than a set of disparate stylistic practices. The question is, what kind of frames?

In vol. 1 Ellis loosely structures his discussion around Copeland's finely-nuanced historical understanding of the Ciceronian and Hieronymic models of translation as, respectively, displacement and replication, although Ellis applies this with an eye more to how authorial activity might be classified[38] than to the 'discursive systems and practices' that Copeland arguably wished to emphasise, including such matters as the lack of patristic concern for 'generating a distinct literary culture'.[39] In his prefaces to all four volumes Ellis gives more weight than does Beer to the medieval construction of the translator, represented as a composite continuity of the roles of scribe, compiler and author/interpreter.[40] Yet this focus on the multiple functions of *auctoritas*, important as it is, does not sufficiently acknowledge that translating is an act that transforms (largely) Latin clerical culture as it passes into the European vernaculars (or even very occasionally vice versa), or that transforms the cultural products of high-status vernaculars as they are rewritten into lower-status vernaculars (and vice versa), or that transforms the cultural products carried over between languages of equal prestige, and that this has enormous cultural importance for all the various constituencies (in terms of nationality, race, ethnicity, class, gender, sexuality) who are constructed in, by and through those translated texts.

Beer identifies medieval translators' address to a public as the feature which distinguishes the later Middle Ages from the much earlier period, when the dialogue was between Augustine and Jerome and not between translator and public. Yet, despite this awareness of the 'public', Beer's discussion is still focussed on the translator (as 'servicer' of authority)[41] and on aspects of the style and structure of the translated text itself. However, in vol. 2 Ellis draws attention to how 'translation into the vernacular can be part of a programme of creating national identity . . . or it can assist powerfully in the creation of a standardised written vernacular',[42] and in his introduction to this volume, vol. 4, he also raises the question of the relationship between 'linguistic and national self-consciousness' (p. 3). It is these sort of points that need to be developed, especially as for many the question of *national* self-consciousness in the Middle Ages is non-existent. Ellis's prefaces, then, increasingly gesture towards some rather different and important ways of understanding translation: as a set of activities with specific and detailed *cultural* significance, rather than as simply a range of heterogeneous practices. What is at stake in Beer and Ellis's paratexts is that *how* one understands the meaning of 'translation', whether as a metaphor, as a set of interlingual processes, as a tool of cultural transformation, or as revelatory of the functions of medieval *auctoritas*, is crucial in determining *what* can be said about the medieval translated text or the cultural situation in which the act of translating takes place.

For Beer, though not for Ellis, the translator in the Middle Ages is invariably male, whereas this is disproved by Catherine Batt's discussion of Clemence of Barking's Anglo-Norman version of the Catherine legend,[43] and actively challenged by both Alexandra Barratt's discussion of three named female translators, Juliana Berners, Eleanor Hull and Margaret Beaufort,[44] and Jocelyn Wogan-Browne's paper on Marie of Chatteris and Clemence of Barking in this volume. One important area in which 'translation' is imbricated with cultural and ideological meanings is in the growing recognition, shown by several of the papers in this volume, of the gendered metaphorics of translation. This dimension deserves more than the cursory treatment I will be able to give it here.

In an important essay by Lori Chamberlain which is drawn on, not uncritically, by Helen Phillips in her essay in this volume, it is argued that translation is to original as woman is to man: in this sealed analogical system writing is coded primary and masculine, and translating, derivative and feminine. This metaphorics, according to Chamberlain, has a lineage stretching from the seventeenth century to Derrida, who may critique the metaphorics but, *pace* Chamberlain, not in an entirely unproblematic way.[45] But the lineage goes back much further than the seventeenth century: Carolyn Dinshaw offers an excellent brief account of the medieval ancestors, as part of her wider argument about the figurative identification of the text with woman or the principle of the feminine in the Middle Ages.[46] It is time that the historical force of this metaphorics, and of translation as a *libidinal* activity, even as an activity in which various kinds of identifications suggest psychoanalytic models of transference at work,[47] informed the work of writers on medieval translation and was developed further. There may, perhaps, have been a parallel understanding of vernacularity itself as 'feminine', with interesting consequences for Copeland's argument, and for the study of the negotiation of Latin sources and models.

Rita Copeland's magisterial book *Rhetoric, Hermeneutics and Translation in the Middle Ages* (1991) represents a major scholarly attempt to redraw completely the boundaries of the map of medieval translation theory and practice, and to establish the Middle Ages as a significant period in the genealogy of translation. It does this by redirecting the heuristic project of medieval translation study towards an understanding of larger discursive and institutional frames:

> A theoretical history of translation in the Western Middle Ages cannot be written as if translation represents a semi-autonomous development of stylistics. Considered in this way, medieval vernacular translation is little more than a collection of disparate practices, united by a few inherited commonplaces which center on the distinction between word for word and sense for sense, and useful for diachronic source study, stylistic analysis, or the study of particular literary or historical relationships. But the earliest theories of translation which the Latin West received from Cicero, Horace, and Quintilian did not emerge as critically transparent and historically portable reflections on practice. These theories of translation were formulated at Rome within a certain academic environment and in response to a certain disciplinary agenda.[48]

This is a call to move the discussion on to a higher level: the choices governing acts of translation in the Middle Ages are not purely individual and voluntaristic, nor are they determined by a few translational commonplaces (the precise historical function and nature of which have often been poorly understood by modern readers), but emerge instead as the result of the discursive force of a disciplinary frame. In place of interpretatively narrow analyses of the work of single authors, Copeland proposes that translation be understood in terms of Foucauldian discourse theory: 'In studying vernacular translation I am also asking how the discourse of criticism [rhetoric, hermeneutics and the commentary tradition] defines the status of both Latin and vernacular textuality in the

Middle Ages'.[49] Her aim is to decentre the received history of Western translation theory, which views the contribution of the Romans to be the inauguration of the 'literal v. loose' polarised debate, and to shift the parameters of the debate altogether, so that it is not the polarity which is the issue but the whole cultural question of the intersection of grammar and rhetoric, and the disciplinary nature of the academic commentary tradition. The details of Copeland's argument, 'that [medieval] translation . . . was . . . a primary vehicle for vernacular participation in, and ultimately appropriation of, the cultural privilege of academic discourse', are by now too well-known to repeat here.[50] Instead, I want to go straight to some of the problems raised by her account.

Despite its debt to a non-traditional critical theoretical framework, the book is conservative. Copeland's representative 'translators' are Notker III of St Gall, Chaucer and Gower, and the translated texts she draws on include the French and English translations of Boethius' *Consolatio*, and the *Ovide moralisé*. These are high-culture writers and high-culture literary products. Her notion of the processes of appropriation of 'cultural privilege' is a very circumscribed one: a Bloomian version of the Middle Ages in which 'great authors' vie with their forefathers in order to generate a productive new canon of texts that will subvert paternal authority only to reinstall anew, but by ever more subtle literary means, the (masculine) line of authority. Her model of the emergence of vernacularity as a force to be reckoned with in the Middle Ages is thus implicitly masculinist, and perhaps also one in which a vernacularity coded feminine must struggle to assert its masculinity—or hide its femininity—in relation to a Latin culture coded masculine. Nor can her argument accommodate those vernacular writers, female and male, that because of various combinations of gender, class or religious orientation negotiate 'cultural privilege' in very different ways but who nevertheless stand in important relations to authoritative Latin sources: writers such as Rolle, Margery Kempe, Bridget of Sweden, Wyclif, Christine de Pisan, to name only some of the more problematic examples. The contest for the vernacular was played out in some rather more downmarket forms, and with some very different strategies and effects. This is openly acknowledged by Copeland,[51] but the initial choice of focus nevertheless reinforces a dominant, and dominantly conservative, view of the Middle Ages. Nor does it seem entirely adequate to represent a writer like Chaucer as a triumphant appropriator and maker of an élite literary tradition, since many readers today have so radically extended the range of options for reading Chaucer's texts that it no longer seems appropriate to see in them the invariable inscription of cultural privilege.

Yet in refining Copeland's thesis I still tacitly accept the terms of her model; it is the model itself that should be under scrutiny. This is really a question of how Copeland understands 'discourse'. I take it that her use of this Foucauldian vocabulary carries the force of its meaning in Foucault's work, although it is possible that Copeland does not intend this:[52] the production of knowledge-power in specific institutional arenas, embodied in particular forms of language and specific practices—in this case, the medieval commentary tradition. The specific historical knowledges about textuality produced by that tradition operate both as forms of power and as indications of the power-relations at work in culture. It is thus slightly disappointing to discover that the main consequences of this are that writers like Chaucer and Gower can successfully, and apparently unreflexively, manoeuvre themselves into positions of unassailable cultural privilege. Despite the gestures towards Foucault, 'discourse' in Copeland's book is shorn of the potential for political radicalness it has in Foucault's work and becomes another way of talking about 'context', rather than a way of understanding how subjects are constructed through and within various nexuses of power-relations, whether it is through the discourses of the confessional, the penal system, or the face-off between grammar and rhetoric.[53] But in order to encompass all the different groups who might be constructed by, through and in these powerful discourses Copeland would have had to write a different book: this is an impressive, meticulously-researched, historical, scholarly study of the cultural significance of certain medieval modes of translation for a small élite group of literary writers. We learn a great deal about the shaping of a modern idea of medieval vernacular 'literary' culture, and very little about the subjects that were marginalized or problematically represented by that culture's confident appropriation, through vernacular translation, of *auctoritas*.

The writings of colonial discourse critics, such as Tejaswini Niranjana, Samia Mehrez, Richard Jacquemond and Sherry Simon,[54] represent a significant body of work in which questions of history, power, institutions, subjectivity and *actual translation processes and practices* are intertwined, and in which the notion of 'translation' circulates with a highly-charged metaphoricity. 'Translation' is understood by these critics in a greatly expanded sense:

> I use the word *translation* not just to indicate an interlingual process but to name an entire problematic. It is a set of questions, perhaps a 'field', charged with the force of all the terms used, even by the traditional discourse on translation . . . In my writing, *translation* refers to (a) the problematic of translation that authorizes and is authorized by certain classical notions of representation and reality; and (b) the problematic opened up by the poststructuralist critique of the earlier one . . .[55]

31

'Translation' here identifies not a distinct genre (and I'm reminded here of Beer's remark that translation 'was not . . . and is not now a literary genre at all, and medieval translators never classified it as such, despite their strong generic awareness')[56] but rather a zone for engaging with the possibility and impossibility of 'an absolutely pure, transparent, and unequivocal translatability'[57] where what is at stake is the question of the historical constituencies that are represented in translation(s).

In colonial discourse theory the metaphorical sense of translation, indicating a 'displacement or liminality' which 'opens up the possibility of articulating *different*, even incommensurable cultural practices and priorities'[58] (the one with which I opened this essay), relies to a great extent on Derrida's notion of translation as a specific instantiation, or even as *the* instantiation of the principle of difference, or more precisely *différance*, at work in language as a whole.[59] This has implications for many of the hallowed hierarchies upon which translation has traditionally depended and which are thus called in question: original/copy, author/translator, equivalence/difference, text/preface, presence/supplement. Much of this ground is already generously covered in Gentzler's recent survey of translation theories.[60] However, deconstruction is not a 'theory of translation' *per se*. Its lack of a clear heuristic model and its fundamentally post-Romantic, and therefore possibly anachronistic, challenge to the dualism of Augustinian/Aristotelian sign-theory make it not only alien but genuinely problematic for many medievalists.

While Derrida recognises that translation 'practices the difference between signified and signifier', and that this opposition or difference is at times indispensable '*within certain limits*' (italics mine) for 'no translation would be possible without it', nevertheless 'we will never have, and in fact have never had, to do with some "transport" of pure signifieds from one language to another, or within one and the same language, that the signifying instrument would leave virgin and untouched'.[61] Derrida proposes that for the (classically understood) notion of translation we substitute a notion of '*transformation*: a regulated transformation of one language by another, of one text by another'. Not equivalence, then, as in the traditional model, but transformation. This position is however very different from the idea that 'pure translatability' is an impossible ideal, but nevertheless an ideal; it is precisely this desire for presence that Derrida critiques.

We cannot overestimate the force and significance of the deconstructive critique of the classical representational subject for subaltern and subcultural studies, which is where I see it used with the greatest political impact. Yet neither can medievalists easily appropriate this critique in relation to translation. Colonial discourse theory is focussed on a specific historical period and a specific configuration of power relations. As

Niranjana says in the introduction to her volume on translation:

> The postcolonial desire for 'history' is a desire to understand the traces of the 'past' in a situation where at least one fact is singularly irreducible: colonialism and what came after.[62]

A rapprochement on some level between medieval studies and subaltern studies would have to recognise very different desires behind the desire of each for 'history'. The project of medievalists cannot be to rewrite the specific history of *colonialism*: but it could be to rewrite other sociopolitical histories, such as those of women or heresy, using translation as the focus for a study of the dialogue between cultures in the Middle Ages. In the Prologue to the Middle English translation, known as the *Knowing of Women's Kind in Childing*, of part of a Latin medical treatise *Cum auctor*, a text sometimes known as the *Trotula major* because supposedly written by Trotula, an eleventh- or twelfth-century woman doctor of Salerno, the translator begins by saying that

> whomen ben more febull and cold be nature than men been and have grete travell in chyldynge

and then justifies his (or her?) Englishing of the Latin work:

> And because whomen of oure tonge cunne bettyre rede and undyrstande thys langage than eny other, and every whoman lettyrde [may] rede hit to other unlettyrd and help hem and conceyle hem in here maladyes, withowtyn scheuynge here dysese to man, I have thys drauyn and wryttyn in Englysch.[63]

Here, in the 'outwork' to the translation, a specific constituency of medieval women are constituted as subjects, although in highly equivocal terms.[64] The translation is offered as a bridge between several cultures: a learned, clerical élite, with access to medical knowledge, and both literate and illiterate English-speaking (married?) women. While the translation offers itself as extending and sharing knowledge, and is evidence that we shouldn't be too reductive about medieval spheres of knowledge, about assuming that the male élite kept medical knowledge to themselves, nevertheless we cannot necessarily read this as a gesture of humanist understanding. The translator's sympathy for his (or her?) female readers is born out of traditional and misogynist understandings of female physiology which of course serve to naturalize and contain women's difference. However, we can also recognize that this translation participates in a major cultural shift: the necessity for the vernacular here arises in a very specific context, and precisely because of women's unequal access to Latin culture. Presumably even 'lettyrde' women did not have access to the *Latin* texts. On one level we are looking here at new value structures, including the granting of access to technical and scientific material to those groups normally excluded from its domain. On the other hand, this is done to effect a speaking *amongst women* rather than a dialogue between the dominant patriarchal group and its subordinates, who might perhaps thereby have challenged the 'knowledges' about themselves contained within the text.[65]

Walter Benjamin's essay 'The task of the translator', written in 1923, has become an obligatory dancing partner for many theorists of translation, especially for deconstructive and colonial discourse theory critics.[66] This is because it anticipates questions of language and difference which are at the centre of current thinking in continental philosophy, and because it articulates a view of the signifying power of language(s) and a notion of 'untranslatability' which have proved extremely suggestive and productive as *metaphors*, producing/naming a 'space' between cultures, nations, peoples, races, which is not about humanist 'cultural diversity' but is rather a simultaneous recognition of the incommensurability of cultures and cultural practices and the possibility of their being articulated together. The events surrounding the publication of Salman Rushdie's *Satanic Verses* provide one such example, where traditional humanist and democratic beliefs in pluralism have proved inadequate for understanding the situation. Bhabha aims to produce 'a theory of culture which is close to a theory of language, as part of a process of translations'. From Benjamin's essay Bhabha derives the notion of 'cultural translation'. Benjamin's statement that 'Translation . . . serves the purpose of expressing the central reciprocal relationship between languages'[67] suggests to Bhabha that all forms of culture are in some way related to each other because culture is a signifying or symbolic activity. The articulation of cultures is possible not because of the similarity of *contents* (cultures do not share an equivalence of subject-matter), but because all cultures are 'symbol-forming and subject-constituting, interpellative practices'.[68]

For Benjamin, translation 'is only a somewhat provisional way of coming to terms with the foreignness of languages';[69] the element of transfer can never be total: what Benjamin refers to as 'the element that does not lend itself to translation', since, 'even when all the surface content has been extracted and transmitted, the primary concern of the genuine translator remains elusive. Unlike the words of the original, it is not translatable, because the relationship between content and language is quite different in the original and the translation.' It is this notion of that which does not lend itself to translation that is picked up by Bhabha to argue about cultural transfer as a site where 'newness enters the world'.[70]

At first sight, Benjamin's essay—and the dominant contexts in which it has recently been re-read[71]—looks incommensurable with the projects of those who write about medieval translation. It is undoubtedly very difficult to understand and to come to terms with. According to Kelly's history, Benjamin can be sited at the pole of the 'hermeneutic' understanding of language: language as having creative and productive power, as Logos, as divine presence. 'Language transcends man [sic], and to some extent creates him' but this is 'not adequate as a full theory of translation'.[72] It is largely the product of German Romantic thinking and an essentially German preoccupation: Benjamin belongs to a lineage that includes figures such as Heidegger, a lineage characterized by a 'mixture of mysticism, aesthetics and philosophy'.[73] Put that way, there are few indications that this might be a productive way of thinking about translation. Kelly quotes George Steiner on the Heidegger strand: 'Ordinarily translation, even literary translation, moves on no such wilful lofty plane. It aims to import and naturalise the content of the source-text and to stimulate, so far as it is able, the original executive form of that content'.[74] At stake here is the value of work like Benjamin's as a heuristic model, but the development of Benjamin's work in the politicized readings of critics like Bhabha and Niranjana shows how important it can be not for its explanatory power but because it shifts the way in which we might conceptualize the dialogue between cultures, not in humanist, pluralist terms that *contain* cultural difference but in terms that revision it as hybrid. The implications of this rethinking of 'culture' in relation to medieval translations and their functions are as yet unexplored but potentially exciting.

However, some signs that traditional understandings of 'translation', based on a purely linguistic epistemology (to borrow Kelly's terms), are inadequate for particular texts and cultural situations, and that those texts and the cultural configurations in which they are produced might be better served by reference to other epistemologies of language, is indicated by, for example, Copeland's brief references to Benjamin's 'suprahistorical kinship of languages'[75] and Nicholas Watson's invocation of Benjamin's 'pure language' [*reine Sprach*] in an essay on Marguerite Porete's *Mirouer des Simples Ames*, in which he attempts to yoke together the '"horizontal" problem of untranslatability and the "vertical" one of ineffability'.[76] Much more work needs to be done on the problems of the historical specificity of these apparently incommensurable models, but perhaps we should not assume that the conventional dualist Augustinian/Aristotelian model of the sign, that which is bequeathed to Saussure,[77] is the only epistemological base for understanding language in the Middle Ages. Nor does Benjamin have to be appropriated uncritically: when in this volume Anne Savage discusses the 'untranslatability' of the feminine in medieval anchoritic texts she is both invoking Benjamin's central trope and extending it to encompass gender difference. Arguably, an awareness of Benjamin's essay, its opening up of teasing questions about the nature and function of language, and its importance for deconstructive critics, would give greater visibility to work on translation by medievalists that negotiates various kinds of border zones (between medieval and modern, orthodox/non-orthodox sensibilities, and masculine and feminine) and that urges a complex view of that interstitial space as *not necessarily* producing containment of the (medieval and modern) subjects located there.

What I've been arguing is that medievalists be aware of the much larger field of translation. I've privileged the greatly expanded notion of 'translation' found in the work of colonial discourse theorists because it is in this work that I find the most convincing tools for beginning to construct maps of the problematic dialogue between cultures. Such dialogues are also part of the history of the Middle Ages, although their specificities are of course significantly different. Colonial discourse theory, it seems to me, can negotiate between a particular cultural awareness and the acts and products of translation that construct that knowledge. Its critique of the classical notions of representation and reality has been invaluable in shaping new histories of subjectivities, and its foregrounding of translation as a metaphor for some kind of cultural in-betweenness has been extremely powerful in rewriting the politics of cultural studies. 'Translation' is a powerful site of cultural transformation in which there are equal ratios of loss and gain, and in which new modes of thinking through the notion of 'difference', which is at the heart of the problematic of translation, are born.

Translation is itself a metaphor for the kind of negotiation between past and present cultures which medievalists constantly perform. Two such important negotiations which will continue to prove problematic are the question, felt keenly by medievalists, of how to negotiate the boundaries between empirically-driven scholarship and more recent, theoretically-informed approaches (the two are not necessarily mutually incompatible), and the related question of how to set about changing the way 'in which the study of the Middle Ages in the academy today is often consigned to the unexamined margins of contemporary thought'.[78] And this is where medievalists need to be aware that they also have to address their modernist colleagues, have to persuade them, perhaps in the way that New Historicists have opened up the Renaissance, or Foucault the eighteenth century, that the medieval period can speak to the present in complex ways. In the words of the American cultural historian James Clifford:

In the kind of translation that interests me most, you learn a lot about peoples, cultures, and histories different from your own, enough to begin to know what you're missing.[79]

NOTES

1. Eva Hoffman, *Lost in Translation: Life in a New Language* (London: Heinemann, 1989; repr. London: Minerva, 1991) pp. 209–10.
2. I would like to thank Alan Grossman for drawing this book to my attention, and for discussing with me issues to do with translation.
3. Hoffman, *Lost in Translation* p. 209.
4. It would be difficult to argue from Hoffman's account that any one of these differences was primordial. However, it is worth pointing out that in certain discussions of the articulation of subjective identity in interstitial spaces there is a downplaying of the specific difference of gender.
5. Hoffman, *Lost in Translation* p. 197.
6. Homi Bhabha, 'The Third Space' (interview with Jonathan Rutherford) in Jonathan Rutherford (ed.) *Identity: Community, Culture, Difference* (London: Lawrence and Wishart, 1990) pp. 207–21. Bhabha links this displacement and transformation with similar activities within the linguistic sign, in a trajectory which goes from Walter Benjamin through Derrida to colonial discourse theory. Hoffman makes a similar analogy between the linguistic and the cultural: 'You can't transport human meanings whole from one culture to another any more than you can transliterate a text' (p. 175).
7. Such an understanding of translation is of course radically at odds with traditional, post-Romantic views of translation, which have emphasised it as a site of lack, betrayal and melancholia, the inevitable outcome of the failure of linguistic equivalence in a fallen world: implicit in this kind of thinking is the notion that the 'copy', the translated text, is inferior to the 'original'. Bhabha draws on the work of Derrida to rewrite this notion, arguing rather that in the translated, or hybrid, text the traces of other meanings give 'rise to something different, something new and unrecognisable, a new area of negotiation of meaning and representation': Bhabha, 'The Third Space', p. 211.
8. Tejaswini Niranjana, *Siting Translation: History, Post-Structuralism, and the Colonial Context* (Berkeley, Los Angeles and Oxford: University of California Press, 1992) p. 46. Niranjana's approach, while just as anti-humanist as Bhabha's, gives greater recognition to questions of subjectivity and, while just as theoretical as Bhabha's, moves in a much less abstract mode.
9. It is of course a commonplace that translation is seen as a secondary or low-status activity in the hierarchy of cultural practices: cf. Theo Hermans' introduction to his collection, *The Manipulation of Literature: Studies in Literary Translation* (London and Sydney: Croom Helm, 1985) p. 7: 'works of literary theory almost universally ignore the phenomenon of literary translation . . . Educational institutions . . . treat translations with barely veiled condescension'; and also his review of Paul Chavy's *Traducteurs d'autrefois. Moyen âge et Renaissance: Dictionnaire des traducteurs et de la littérature traduite en ancien et moyen français (842–1600)* (Paris-Genève: Champion/Slatkine, 1988), 2 vols.: 'It may well be symptomatic of the present state of translation studies—a discipline busy pulling itself up by its own bootstraps—that the

preface to a reference work of this size and scope should still open on a defensive note, with an assertion of the importance of literary translation for literary history and a reminder that although translated literature is necessarily "du second degré" it is not therefore "de second ordre"' (*Target* 1:1 (1989) p. 123). However, Venuti, who also recognises that translation is 'an invisible practice' in our culture, nevertheless challenges the kind of complicity in constructing translation as a low-status activity evinced by Chavy's analysis (and, incidentally, Hermans' reproduction of it), pointing out that translation's marginalisation is due to 'an essentially romantic conception of authorship': Lawrence Venuti, 'Introduction' in Lawrence Venuti (ed.), *Rethinking Translation: Discourse, Subjectivity, Ideology* (London and New York: Routledge, 1992) p. 3.

10. Rita Copeland, *Rhetoric, Hermeneutics, and Translation in the Middle Ages* (Cambridge, New York and Melbourne: Cambridge University Press, 1991) p. 93.

11. Copeland, *Rhetoric, Hermeneutics, and Translation* p. 3.

12. To do this last would, anyway, be to impose a misleading and problematic homogeneity upon the papers, all of which are attempting very different things. Examples of the consideration of specific translations and practices in the light of medieval theories of translation are exemplified by Karen Pratt, 'Medieval Attitudes to Translation and Adaptation: the Rhetorical Theory and the Poetic Practice' and N.S. Thompson, 'Translation and Response: *Troilus* and the *Filostrato*', in Ellis (ed.) *The Medieval Translator II* (1991) pp. 1–27, 123–50; Copeland, *Rhetoric, Hermeneutics, and Translation passim*, but esp. chs. 4–7; Nancy Vine Durling, 'Translation and Innovation in the *Roman de Brut*' in Beer (ed.) *Medieval Translators and Their Craft* pp. 9–39.

13. There are several medievalists who explicitly frame their work in terms of theories of translation; at the Fourth Cardiff Conference on the Theory and Practice of Translation in the Middle Ages, Conques en Aveyron, France, 26–29 July 1993, this deliberate framing was seen, for example, in Brenda Hosington's paper, 'Proverb Translation as Linguistic and Cultural Transfer in Some Middle English Versions of Old French Romances' and in Bernd Weitemeier's paper, '*Visiones Georgii*: Their Latin Transmission and Late Medieval German Translations'.

14. See Ruth Evans, 'An Edition of a Fifteenth-Century Middle English *Temporale* Cycle in MSS Lambeth Palace 392 and Cambridge University Library Additional 5338' (University of Leeds: PhD thesis, 1986), and also Ruth Evans, 'Women Inside and Outside the Text: Translation and Position', *New Comparison* 12 (1991) pp. 89–101. Another such hybrid sermon collection is edited by Gloria Cigman, *Lollard Sermons* Early English Text Society OS 294 (Oxford: Oxford University Press, 1989).

15. Two Translations Studies scholars in particular, André Lefevere and Susan Bassnett, are in fact quite open to the project of writing the 'Middle Ages' into translation history. The volume edited by André Lefevere, *Translation/ History/ Culture: a Sourcebook* (London and New York: Routledge, 1992), which has an ambitious programme (it aims to cover 'the most important, or at least most seminal texts produced over centuries of thinking about translation in Western Europe in Latin, French, German, and English'), includes four medieval statements about translation: Augustine's *De Doctrina Christiana*, Trevisa's 'Dialogue between a Knight and a Clerk', Roger Bacon's *De Linguarum Cognitione*, and Jerome's 'Letter to Pammachius'. However,

Lefevere's introduction is rather more interested in categorising these statements according to 'lines of approach', such as 'Patronage' and 'The Role of Ideology', than in situating them historically. In Susan Bassnett-McGuire's chapter on 'History of Translation Theory' the Middle Ages is represented in both the 'Bible translation' and 'Education and the vernacular' sections. However, despite her caveats about periodization and the usefulness of a 'lines of approach' division, these sections are still sandwiched between 'The Romans' and 'The Renaissance': see Susan Bassnett-McGuire, *Translation Studies* rev. ed., New Accents (London and New York: Routledge, 1991). The important collections edited by Venuti (*Rethinking Translation*) and Theo Hermans (*The Manipulation of Literature*) do not include any essays on medieval translation(s). Disappointingly, André Lefevere's very recent book, which aims to place 'the production and reception of literature within the wider framework of a culture and its history', does not deal with any texts or theories from the Middle Ages: see André Lefevere, *Translation, Rewriting, and the Manipulation of Literary Fame* (London and New York: Routledge, 1992). The work of Jeanette Beer and Roger Ellis has done a great deal to promote medieval translation as a significant area.

16. See, for example, David Aers, 'Rewriting the Middle Ages: some suggestions', *Journal of Medieval and Renaissance Studies* 18:2 (1988) pp. 221–40; David Aers, 'A Whisper in the Ear of Early Modernists', in David Aers (ed.) *Culture and History 1350–1600: Essays on English Communities, Identities and Writing* (Hemel Hempstead: Harvester Wheatsheaf, 1992) pp. 177–202 (for an earlier version of this essay, see 'Reflections on the Current History of the Subject', *Exemplaria* 2:2 (1991) pp. 20–34); Lee Patterson, 'On the Margin: Postmodernism, Ironic History, and Medieval Studies' *Speculum* 65 (1990) pp. 87–108; Thomas Hahn, 'The Premodern Text and the Postmodern Reader' *Exemplaria* 2:1 (1990) pp. 1–21. Recognition of the elision of the Middle Ages in current critical genealogies is the starting point for a telling series of questions posed by Sarah Kay, who asks why critics pass over the Middle Ages in silence: 'Do the conventions of literary history succumb to the seduction of the Renaissance, as it points to the writers of Antiquity and says "these are our fathers"? Do they turn their back on the medieval period as though it were faintly indecent, like the body of an ageing mother?' See Sarah Kay, 'Sexual Knowledge: The Once and Future Texts of the *Romance of the Rose*' in Judith Still and Michael Wortin (eds) *Textuality and Sexuality* (Manchester: Manchester University Press, 1993) p. 69.

17. For details of these volumes consult the bibliography to the present volume.

18. Full reference, n. 12 above (see also the review of this volume by Roger Ellis, *Allegorica* 12 (1991) pp. 55–58); a second volume of papers is forthcoming.

19. Copeland, *Rhetoric, Hermeneutics, and Translation.*

20. These categories are clearly mapped out and evaluated in Edwin Gentzler, *Contemporary Translation Theories* Translation Studies (London and New York: Routledge, 1993). Gentzler implicitly advances deconstructionist theories of language as of value for those interested in translation theory; in his last chapter he also points to the value of considering questions of gender, noting Bassnett's useful work in this area. For a critique of 'Translation Studies' and valuable deployment of a critical theory approach towards translation, see Niranjana, *Siting Translation* p. 48.

21. Niranjana describes how the representation of Others in colonial discourse produces 'strategies of containment': *Siting Translation* p. 3.

22. *Target: International Journal of Translation Studies* is edited by the prominent translation scholars Gideon Toury of Tel Aviv University and José Lambert of the Katholieke Universiteit, Leuven, Belgium. *TRANSST: An International Newsletter of Translation Studies* is published by the M. Bernstein Chair of Translation Theory and the Porter Institute for Poetics and Semiotics, Tel Aviv University (Israel). It is edited by Gideon Toury, with the help of José Lambert. It serves as an information clearing-house for the Committee for Translation Studies of the International Comparative Literature Association (ICLA/AILC) and for the Scientific Commission on Translation and Interpreting of the International Association of Applied Linguistics (IAAL/ AILA), and thus has a practical orientation. *Translation and Literature* is a new annual series launched by Edinburgh University Press in 1992, and devoted to literary translation from an historical and academic perspective. *TTR* (*traduction terminologie rédaction*) is the periodical journal of the Canadian Association for Translation Studies (CAT). *Testo a Fronte* is a newly-established Italian review fully devoted to the theory and practice of literary translation, and edited by Franco Buffoni of the Università degli Studi di Torino. The titles and sponsoring institutions of these journals make clear their particular theoretical affiliations.
23. Gentzler, *Contemporary Translation Theories*; André Lefevere (ed.) *Translation/History/Culture: a Sourcebook* Translation Studies (London and New York: Routledge, 1992); André Lefevere, *Translation, Rewriting, and the Manipulation of Literary Fame* Translation Studies (London and New York: Routledge, 1992); Palma Zlateva (ed.) (with chapter introductions by André Lefevere) *Translation as Social Action: Russian and Bulgarian Perspectives* Translation Studies (London and New York: Routledge, 1993); Romy Heylen, *Translation, Poetics, and the Stage: Six French* Hamlets (London and New York: Routledge, 1993).
24. Joseph Graham (ed.) *Difference in Translation* (Ithaca: Cornell University Press, 1985). For Niranjana and Venuti, see above, n. 8 and n. 9.
25. Bassnett-McGuire, *Translation Studies* p. xii.
26. Bassnett-McGuire, *Translation Studies* p. xi.
27. This is one of the categories from André Lefevere's Translation Studies Series anthology, *Translation/History/Culture* (London and New York: Routledge, 1992) pp. 14–18.
28. See above, n. 17 and n. 18.
29. Beer, *Medieval Translators* p. 2.
30. I borrow Nida's definitions: 'formal equivalence' focuses on 'attention on the message itself, in both form and content', whereas dynamic equivalence aims to ensure that 'the relationship between reception and message should be substantially the same as that which existed between the original receptors and the message': Eugene Nida, *Toward a Science of Translating* (Leiden: Brill, 1964) p. 159. On these terms, and for a brief critique, see further Susan Bassnett-McGuire, *Translation Studies* p. 26. For further information on Nida's work on the 'science' of translating, and especially on its debt to the work of Chomsky, see Gentzler, *Contemporary Translation Theories* pp. 44–60.
31. Gentzler, *Contemporary Translation Theories* p. 46.
32. *De ecclesia* p. 9, as translated in Anne Hudson, *The Premature Reformation: Wycliffite Texts and Lollard History* (Oxford: Oxford University Press, 1988) p. 244.

33. 'God, who had guaranteed the superlative *auctoritas* of Scripture, was the *auctor* of all created things as well as an *auctor* of words': Minnis, *Medieval Theory of Authorship* p. 36.

34. Nick Davis, in his draft of a very brief paper provisionally titled 'Wyclif and scriptural translation', discusses the mutually inconsistent approaches towards Biblical translation adopted by Wyclif's followers, namely the moving from a literal to a free rendering as the work progressed, and finds a rationale for this inconsistency in Wyclif's own thought: 'the highly Latinate approach seems to have had as its rationale the willed non-replacement of a Vulgate text saturated with meaning down to the last syllable; while the freer, "sense-for-sense" approach seems to align itself with that part of Wyclif's thought which seeks to deny the relation between scriptural truth and the empirical properties of any given text' (this latter disdain for the empirical properties of the text is perhaps the more familiar aspect of Wyclif's thought). Davis argues that the letter of the scriptures in Wyclif thus has the status of a Derridean 'supplement', as 'necessary manifestation of and denaturing replacement for scriptural truth'. The discerning of supplementarity in Wyclif's thought is fundamental to Davis's point: Wyclif's statement about the meaning-saturated nature of single syllables is not a *complement* to his thought (i.e. in the sense of being a self-sufficient statement) but has all the force of the Derridean supplement. The supplement is a manifestation of presence. And Davis shows how this has practical consequences for the actual Bible translation which derives its rationale from Wyclif's apparently contradictory statements. I am grateful to Nick Davis for allowing me to see his draft paper.

35. One example of just such an historical appropriation of the concepts of Translation Studies is an article by Maria Tymoczko which uses the 'polysystem' hypothesis: 'Translation as a Force for Literary Revolution in the 12th Century Shift from Epic to Romance', *New Comparison* 1 (1986) pp. 7–27.

36. *The Medieval Translator II* (1991) p. xiv.

37. *The Medieval Translator II* (1991) p. xiv, quoting himself in *Allegorica* 12 (1991) pp. 65–6.

38. E.g. 'We might almost say that he [Malory] is replacing the Hieronymic-type model of his source with a Ciceronian-type one': *The Medieval Translator* (1989) p. 11.

39. Rita Copeland, 'The Fortunes of "Non Verbum Pro Verbo": Or, Why Jerome is Not a Ciceronian', *The Medieval Translator* (1989) pp. 15–35; for the quotation, see p. 20.

40. *The Medieval Translator* (1989) pp. 4–5.

41. Copeland's work has considerably complicated such observations: see Copeland, *Rhetoric, Hermeneutics, and Translation* p. 3: 'Medieval arts commentary does not simply "serve" its "master" texts: it also rewrites and supplants them.'

42. *The Medieval Translator II* (1991) pp. xv–xvi.

43. Catherine Batt, 'Clemence of Barking's Transformations of *Courtoisie* in *La Vie de Sainte Catherine d'Alexandrie*', *New Comparison* 12 (1991), pp. 102–23.

44. See Alexandra Barratt (ed.) *Women's Writing in Middle English* (London and New York: Longman, 1992) pp. 12–17. She also proposes that some anonymously-translated texts, especially those translated from French, may have been

done by women. On Eleanor Hull, see further Alexandra Barratt, 'Dame Eleanor Hull: A Fifteenth Century Translator', *The Medieval Translator* (1989) pp. 87–101.

45. Lori Chamberlain, 'Gender and the metaphorics of translation' in Venuti *Rethinking Translation* pp. 57–72. Chamberlain is rather uncritical of Derrida. While she points out that he is at least partly able to contest the 'classical' view of translation by exposing gender as 'a conceptual framework for definitions of mimesis and fidelity' (p. 69), she states that he draws his terms 'invagination' and 'hymen' from 'the lexicon of sexual difference'. Yet with these terms the concept of *anatomical* difference makes an appearance. Thus Derrida's anti-essentialist argument risks having a whiff of essentialism about it.

46. Carolyn Dinshaw, *Chaucer's Sexual Poetics* (Madison, Wisconsin and London: University of Wisconsin Press, 1989) pp. 42–7, and ch. 5, 'Griselda Translated', pp. 132–55.

47. Dinshaw, *Chaucer's Sexual Poetics* p. 137 and p. 248 n. 12.

48. Copeland, *Rhetoric, Hermeneutics, and Translation* p. 1.

49. Copeland, *Rhetoric, Hermeneutics, and Translation* p. 1.

50. Copeland, *Rhetoric, Hermeneutics, and Translation* p. 3 (for elaboration, see, for example, Ellis's discussion in his Introduction to *The Medieval Translator* (1989)). Cicero's famous, and famously misunderstood, dictum, 'non verbum pro verbo', functions not as prescription, description or proscription, but rather articulates translation as a site of contest in which rhetorical *inventio* establishes itself as distinct from, and superior to, grammatical and hermeneutical *narratio*. Translation in the Roman period, then, is the site for a disciplinary contest: Cicero constructs himself, through translation, as orator not interpreter, in a culture in which the function of an orator is seen as superior. The Middle Ages inherits the Ciceronian dictum but Jerome is not a Ciceronian; he borrows the terminological apparatus, but in order to generate a theory of translation directed almost entirely at meaning and signification 'outside the claims of either the source or target-language' (p. 43). The Middle Ages conceptualises language in a radically different way from the classical period: textual meaning has a core, an inviolable divine essence, whereas Roman theories of translation were about and between *human* languages. And the Middle Ages lacks the Roman political agenda of 'cultural disjunction and aggressive contestation' (p. 36). But Jerome's early patristic model, which necessarily cannot be about *displacement* of the Biblical source, is inadequate as an explanation of the nature of vernacular translation. The later vernacular model, however, draws on the Roman theory of translation as displacement: in fact, it is a process of simultaneous replication and substitution, developed out of the commentary tradition, which itself depends on the relative status of the disciplines of hermeneutics and rhetoric. Writers like Chaucer and Gower seek both to replicate the authority of their *auctoritates* and to substitute in their place their own authoritative texts.

51. 'This book does not propose itself as a "key" to vernacular translation. My arguments do not necessarily extend to the emergence of "popular" translation in genres such as the *lai* or the metrical romance from one vernacular language into another, nor to hagiographical or devotional writings, nor to translation of scientific or technical works.' (Copeland, *Rhetoric, Hermeneutics, and Translation* p. 5)

52. The Foucauldian frame is rather submerged in Copeland's narrative: I infer it from references such as that on p. 239 n. 38 to Foucault's *Archaeology of Knowledge* where Copeland talks about 'the need to locate individual critical practices in larger discursive systems'.

53. Soon after writing this sentence I came across the following: 'Writing as a social function—as differentiated from the ideal of art for art's sake—is the aim that Third World writers, in defining their roles, highly esteem and claim. *Literacy* and *literature* intertwine so tightly, indeed, that the latter has never ceased to imply both the ability to read and the condition of being well read— and thereby to convey the sense of *polite learning* through the arts of *grammar* and *rhetoric*': Trinh T. Minh-ha, 'Commitment from the Mirror-Writing Box' in Gloria Anzaldúa (ed.) *Making Face, Making Soul: Haciendo Caras: Creative and Critical Perspectives by Feminists of Color* (San Francisco: Aunt Lute Books, 1990) p. 249. Bearing in mind that Copeland and Minh-ha are writing about completely different histories and cultures, the above comment does point to a certain lack in Copeland's work of the socio-political dimensions of literacy and literature.

54. Niranjana, *Siting Translation*; Samia Mehrez, 'Translation and the Postcolonial Experience: The Francophone North African Text'; Richard Jacquemond, 'Translation and Cultural Hegemony: The Case of French-Arabic Translation'; and Sherry Simon, 'The Language of Cultural Difference: Figures of Alterity in Canadian Translation', these last three collected in Venuti, *Rethinking Translation* pp. 120–38, 139–58, 159–76.

55. Niranjana, *Siting Translation* p. 8.

56. Jeanette Beer 'Introduction' in Beer (ed.) *Medieval Translators* p. 1.

57. Jacques Derrida, *Positions* trans. and annotated by Alan Bass (London and Chicago: Athlone Press, 1987) p. 20.

58. Bhabha, 'The Third Space' (full reference n. 6 above) pp. 210–11.

59. For an excellent brief summary of Derrida's *différance*, see Toril Moi, *Sexual/ Textual Politics* (London and New York: Methuen, 1985) pp. 105–7. See also the lucid discussion by Gentzler, *op. cit.* pp. 146–7: 'The process of translation offers . . . a mode of differing/deferring that subverts modes of traditional metaphysical thinking that have historically dominated assumptions about translation specifically as well as philosophy in general . . . The subject of translation theory has traditionally involved some concept of determinable meaning that can be transferred to another system of signification. Deconstruction questions such a definition of translation and uses the practice of translation to demonstrate the instability of its own theoretical framework . . . In translation, what is visible is language referring not to things, but to language itself.'

60. Gentzler, *Contemporary Translation Theories* ch. 6 'Deconstruction' pp. 144–80. Gentzler suggests that one value of deconstructive thinking about language is that while it does not offer another, 'better', theory of translation, it 'deepens and broadens the conceptual framework by which we define the very field itself', thus breaking 'a logjam of stagnated terms and notions' (p. 145). Gentzler notes that translation recovers a property of language itself, coming to terms with that which *language* denies and 'which no theory in this book remotely approaches' (p. 157). In *The True Interpreter: a History of Translation Theory and Practice in the West* (Oxford: Basil Blackwell, 1979) Louis G. Kelly outlines two theories of language, the 'linguistic' and the 'hermeneutic', which offer complementary epistemological frames and entail

different consequences for theories of translation. Perhaps unsurprisingly in 1979 Kelly does not discuss Derridean *différance* in his discussion of the 'hermeneutic', although it is a development of it. However, deconstructive critiques of language are integral to the recent volumes by Niranjana and Venuti.

61. Derrida, *Positions* p. 20.
62. Niranjana, *Siting Translation* p. 41.
63. See Barratt, *Women's Writing in Middle English* p. 30. The text is edited from a fifteenth-century manuscript, Oxford Bodleian Library MS Douce 37, ff.1–5v. According to Barratt, the Middle English compilation had a wide circulation in the fourteenth and fifteenth centuries.
64. I borrow the term 'outwork' from Niranjana, *Siting Translation* p. 13, just as I borrow, with an awareness of its very different context, her description of the way that translations construct subjects.
65. In fact, Barratt suggests that this text offers some interestingly different knowledges about the female body; see Barratt, *Women's Writing* p. 28.
66. Walter Benjamin, 'The task of the translator: an introduction to the translation of Baudelaire's *Tableaux Parisiens*', in Walter Benjamin, *Illuminations*, ed. Hannah Arendt, trans. Harry Zohn (New York: Schocken Books, 1968) pp. 69–82. On its focal importance in deconstructive criticism, see Paul de Man, 'Conclusions: Walter Benjamin's "The Task of the Translator"', in *The Resistance to Theory*, Theory and History of Literature, vol. 33 (Minneapolis: University of Minnesota Press, 1986); Jacques Derrida, 'Living on/Borderlines', trans. James Hulbert, in Harold Bloom, Paul de Man, Jacques Derrida, Geoffrey H. Hartman, J. Hillis Miller, *Deconstruction and Criticism* (London and Henley: Routledge and Kegan Paul, 1979) pp. 75–176; John Johnston, 'Translation as Simulacrum' in Venuti *Rethinking Translation* pp. 42–56; Niranjana *Siting Translation* chs. 3, 4 and 5.
67. Benjamin, 'Task of the Translator' p. 72.
68. Bhabha, 'The Third Space' (full reference n. 6 above) pp. 209–10.
69. Benjamin, 'Task of the Translator' p. 75.
70. The phrase was used by Homi Bhabha in a paper, 'Spatialism, Time and Postmodern Theory', delivered on 12 February 1993 in the Cardiff Centre for Critical and Cultural Theory, in which he drew extensively on Benjamin's essay 'The Task of the Translator' to argue for a new position on the ethics of representation, one which does not resolve the issue either by a moral pietism or by recourse to autobiography.
71. See above, n. 64.
72. Kelly, *The True Interpreter* pp. 30–1.
73. Kelly, *The True Interpreter* p. 30.
74. George Steiner, *After Babel* (London and Oxford: Oxford University Press, 1975) p. 333, quoted in Kelly, *The True Interpreter* p. 241.
75. See Rita Copeland, 'The Fortunes of "Non Verbum Pro Verbo": Or, Why Jerome is Not a Ciceronian' in *The Medieval Translator* (1989) p. 23 and the slightly revised version of this in Copeland, *Rhetoric, Hermeneutics, and Translation* pp. 44 and 238 n. 27. Interestingly, in the later version the direct reference to Benjamin is relegated to the footnote.
76. 'To win back pure language, formed in the flux of language, is the violent and single power of translation': Nicholas Watson, 'Misrepresenting the Untranslatable: Marguerite Porete and the *Mirouer des Simples Ames*' in *New Comparison* 12 (1991) p. 124.

77. See Kelly *The True Interpreter* pp. 8 and 12.
78. Linda Lomperis and Sarah Stanbury (eds) *Feminist Approaches to the Body in Medieval Literature* (Philadelphia: University of Pennsylvania Press, 1993) p. xii.
79. James Clifford, 'Traveling Cultures' in Lawrence Grossberg, Cary Nelson and Paula Treichler (eds) *Cultural Studies* (New York and London: Routledge, 1992) p. 110.

Chapter 1

Wreaths of Thyme: the Female Translator in Anglo-Norman Hagiography

JOCELYN WOGAN-BROWNE

Give thyme or parsley wreath, I ask no bays.
(Anne Bradstreet, *The Prologue*)

The authorial prologues of medieval romance translators and adaptors have been much discussed in modern scholarship, whether with reference to individual authorial practice or collectively in order to examine generic developments and relations with socio-economic contexts.[1] Hagiographic prologues have been less frequently considered in studies of vernacular translation and its poetics than those of romance writers.[2]

In various kinds of relation to both Middle English and Anglo-Norman romance texts, and the continental traditions generally held to have influenced them, is a large corpus of texts (given, so far, much less attention)—that of the Anglo-Norman saints' lives. There are some 70 texts concerning some 37 saints.[3] This is a considerable corpus but one which has tended to fall between the concerns of Middle English and Old French scholars. Nevertheless these texts and their strategies of translation deserve attention especially given insular culture's early tradition of vernacular translations and its heightened experiences of linguistic and cultural disruptions and continuities in the Norman conquest.

I want here to consider the translating strategies of Anglo-Norman women hagiographers by foregrounding the particular problems of female *translatio* against the (culturally and numerically) more dominant male hagiographers. The women writers concerned worked in the late twelfth

46

and thirteenth centuries: they are an anonymous nun of Barking; Clemence of Barking; and Marie [of Chatteris?]: the first, the writer of a Life of Edward the Confessor; the second, of a Life of St Catherine of Alexandria; the third, of a Life of St Audrey [Etheldreda] of Ely.[4] (Though it has been suggested that the two Barking Lives are by the same woman, the evidence for common authorship is not conclusive and may testify to imitation or influence. I am therefore, in the current state of the evidence, neither excluding nor assuming the possibility of single authorship.)[5] Socially and economically the context for these translators is the aristocratic and privileged nunnery of Barking and (probably) the less wealthy but still aristocratic house of Chatteris.[6] The women living in these nunneries, though part of an enclosed female sub-culture, were largely from noble and gentry Anglo-Norman families and in many cases remained closely connected with Anglo-Norman courtly society.[7] The linguistic context of these Lives—insular French—is not a ghetto language confined to the less Latinate nunneries, but is the language of instruction in monastic schools and in some monastic texts and the language used by and to the secular aristocracy and gentry. Like the monastic and clerical authors of vernacular Lives, the women translators seem to have produced Anglo-Norman *vitae* for the use, in the first instance, of their communities and colleagues (male and female), though the reception evidence suggests that secular audiences also used these Lives.[8]

In generic and literary terms, the context for the translating stances of the three women writers is the other prologues and translations of Anglo-French hagiography. Among the few studies of these prologues, Karl Uitti's is notable for its articulation of the paradigm, very frequent in insular as in continental hagiographic texts, of 'the clerkly narrator' as translator.[9] This explicitly clerical narrative persona is a communicator and officiant mediating between saint, text and audience: 'to those who have not learnt Latin . . . clerks must show the faith.'[10] As the audience is to the cleric, so the clerical translator is to the saint: this tripartite model of *translatio* is at once hierarchized and as inclusive as possible. The translator and the audience are inscribed as a particular Christian textual community, in which all can serve God with their various talents and estates. In Wace's *Vie de St Nicolas*,

> some are lay, some are learned, some are foolish, some are sensible, some small and some great, some poor, some rich. Thus God diversely gives various goods to different people. Each one must make manifest the benefit of what God has given him. The knight and the citizen, the peasant and the aristocrat must have faith in God and honour him with their goods. They must willingly listen when they hear discourse about God. Whoever knows what is best must teach

the best and whoever has greater capabilities must give more help. The stronger must bear more, and whoever has more must give more. Each must demonstrate his knowledge, his gifts and his ability, and serve God, his creator, and, in his honour, the noble saints.[11]

In this account of hagiographic *translatio studii*, the clerk transmits the saint and the audience co-operates by listening attentively, so continuing hagiography's special historical transmission of the saint's power and efficacy. This power reaches out through the saint's posthumous miracles and through the responses of hagiographers and their readers and hearers in an unbroken chain of contact with the saint's life. The hagiographic text is thus not a mimesis but a continuation of the saint's historical life, and has its own virtual power. 'A genuine *translatio* takes place' and a strong set of credentials for vernacular translation is established.[12]

Viewing the hagiographic text as an extended form of ritual, or, at least, as hospitable to ritual elements and uses, illuminates hagiographic *translatio*'s simultaneous disestablishment and empowerment of narrator figures, its apparent indifference to originality in *matière* if not *sens*, and its claim of mere service in relation to its inscribed textual communities. The idea of the translated text as having virtual historical power, of being in effect a form of contact relic, is however not exclusive of political and socio-economic dimensions in the manoeuvres of the hagiographic prologue, and these too need attention. In invoking estates theory, Wace's clerkly narrator is creating for himself a place in both the spiritual and material economy, claiming an instructive relation with the whole community. The obverse of humble universal availability is indispensability, and although shared ritual assumptions can be appealed to in the prologue, this does not exclude a bid for social control and the valorization of the clerkly profession. Once visible through his own restatement of estates and functions, the translating cleric privileges and justifies his social utility. Recent work on continental hagiography and lineage by Vauchez and others extends perspectives on the development of literacy first opened by Clanchy and Stock to reveal just how pervasively the strategies of hagiographic texts are constituted by clerical claims to power and resources.[13] St Alexis for instance, like other virgin saints, frustrates his parents' hopes of lineage: the resources and expectations channelled through him are 'diverted' to the church, while his family comes to a biological and genealogical dead end.[14] The transfer of power and resources over time and space can be claimed for communities of celibate men as well as for the secular nobility's propagation of lineage. The written word—the text iconically present as contact relic in the tripartite saint's life-clerk-audience model—and its control and transmission empower the clerk as the cultural, if not the biological, hero of *translatio*.

The hagiographic prologue topics of transience, *ubi sunt*, the world's decline and the use of time and resources (whether or not mapped onto estates theory as in the example from Wace quoted above) function partly as topics of social and behavioural control, but they also privilege clerical access to the past as a dimension open to textual control and fixed form on the one hand, but requiring informed decoding and renewal—*translatio*—on the other.

Several kinds of intertextuality operate in these prologues: each text needs to make its bid for attention and legitimacy and does so partly with reference to established convention and precedent and partly through carving out its own position in the genre's legitimating clerical discourse. The prologue from the Life of St Clement is a good example:

> Clerks of the schools who have learnt so much that they understand something exert themselves making books and discussing opinions at length, in order to show their knowledge and have the world's praise. They make new books and adorn them beautifully and compose them beautifully, but lay-people and clerks who are not well-instructed derive little profit from this. The clerks themselves who make these books are not specially apt or ready to teach the unlettered and to make whatever it may be they have said in the books they have written understood in the common language. For it is enough for them that they should be praised by other clerks and that this can be said: 'It's a good clerk who wrote that.' Because it is a silly idea to waste intelligence for nothing in this way, and because there are enough books to suffice for the learned, it would be much better and would turn out to greater profit if the books of antiquity . . . were turned into a language in which more people could have the benefit of them. I am not one of the learned who are thoroughly grounded in clerisy; nevertheless the little that I know I intend to write to such effect that clerks and laypeople who hear it will be well able to understand it.[15]

Here the 'cleric-without-[stuffy]-clerisy' at once rejects and renews predecessors' strategies of modesty and humble utility; the narrative *persona* locates and legitimates its translating activity in its own evocation of a market in clerical *translatio*.

Given the pervasively clerical assumptions and claims of the hagiographic translator's stance, and given the essentially clerical nature of the whole project of vernacular hagiographic translation to lay people, the opportunities for women writers to position themselves in this genre's discourses seem limited. Women are not clerics and officiants, and cannot deploy an estates structure or claims to a social function in the manner of Wace's clerkly narrator. Bishop Étienne de Fougère's *Livre des Manières*, contemporary with Wace's *Nicolas* Life and written for Cicely, countess of Hereford, pays unusual attention to the position of women in estates structures, but, even here, they come last, only noblewomen are dealt with, and these are divided only into the bad (lecherous and/or lesbian) and the good (givers of alms, exemplified by the countess herself).[16] Nevertheless, at least three Anglo-Norman saints' lives by women exist. What are the women writers' strategies for entering into hagiographic translation and what if anything distinguishes their texts?

Areas with which I am particularly concerned here are the Lives' 'narratorial signatures', their prologues, and some aspects of the handling of their material. By 'narratorial signature' I mean the presentation, included in most Anglo-Norman hagiographic texts, of a narrator figure which may be named or anonymous, but which in any case personifies a translating stance. In the case of the three texts by women these 'signatures' are all at the end of the Lives rather than in the Prologues: and in the case of the nun of Barking pointedly anonymous: 'sun num n'i vult dire a ore,/Kar bien set n'est pas digne unkore' ('she does not wish to tell her name at present/For well she knows she is not yet worthy' ll. 5308–9). Since this is followed by an appeal that her narrative 'should not be scorned/Because a woman has translated it' ('Qu'il ne seit pur ço avilé,/Se femme l'ad si translaté' ll. 5314–5), this seems at first sight evidence of timidity and reticence.[17] Yet these aspects of the nun's strategies here are not in themselves gender-specific, since a good proportion of the male hagiographers who give their names place them at the end of their texts rather than the beginning (7 cases against 6), while there are 19 cases of anonymous (and probably mostly male) authorship, and a few cases of male authors who give their names at both end and beginning or who name themselves in some texts but not in others known to be by them.[18] The *Edouard* writer in any case says that her name 'n'est pas digne *unkore*' (italics mine) of mention in the same text as the saint, which may be translated as 'indeed, unworthy' or as '*not yet*'. (Similarly the *Audrée* writer, while giving her name in the very last couplet of her text, does so in order 'that I may be remembered', see below p. 57). The *Edouard* writer also seems confident of audiences beyond her immediate one ('toz les oianz/Ki mais orrunt cest soen rumanz': 'all the hearers who will ever hear this, her [vernacular] narrative' ll. 5312–3), envisaging transmission of her text to future audiences in her own community or to outside groups of listeners (as the manuscript evidence shows did indeed happen).[19] It is by no means clear that narratorial modesty is to be taken more literally here than in the case of other hagiographic texts. Although gender is made the particular occasion of the *Edouard* writer's modesty topoi, this can equally well be seen as an effective deployment of hagiographic humility, extending the saint's transmissible and recuperative powers beyond the usual boundaries of the envisaged textual community to include women, and extending the narrative stance of the 'cleric without clerisy' (as deployed in the example from the *Vie de Clement* above, p. 49) to the gender without clerisy. The underlying model of text production here moreover is quietly, but radically, different from that of clerical service and indispensability. The translator asks her audience to seek the Son of Mary's blessing ('le fiz Marie', l. 5324) on her convent and on herself as the handmaid of God ('cele Deu ancele' l. 5326) who has made this new Life ('ceste vie nuvele' l. 5327). As a virgin handmaiden of God, the translator fits her own Marian model for the production of the Word: she too produces a new Life under God's aegis. For the nun of Barking, it seems, the metaphorics of *translatio* require neither strong assertions of authenticity nor assault and dismemberment of the source text, but a process of generation. Here the translation's target language acquires resonances which do not seem to have been used by male Anglo-Norman hagiographers: given the narratorial presence of a woman, the creation of a new Life ('vie nuvele' l. 5327) puns on biological and literary creation.

In the narratorial signature to the Life of St Catherine, Clemence of Barking gives her name, and says that she has undertaken to translate Catherine's Life for love of the community at Barking:

> I who have translated her life am called Clemence by name. I am a nun of Barking, for love of which I took this work in hand.[20]

This concluding 'signature' is brief, but noteworthy for its affirmation of female community: this life of the female patron saint of learning has been undertaken for love of one of the longest enduring female institutions of learning in England.[21] The narrative stance of the text is more extensively created in the prologue to the Life of Saint Catherine. In addition to invoking a Latin source, Clemence of Barking specifies a vernacular precedent:

> It [the *vita*] was translated before, and well set out, according to the standards of the time. But people were not then so hard to please nor so critical as they are at present (and will be even more so after our day). Because times have changed and people's nature has altered, the verse, having become somewhat corrupted, is considered poor. It must therefore be corrected and the times made to conform to the people.[22]

The necessity of translation through time is here extended beyond the conventional Latin-based claim in one of the earliest literary reworkings to use a vernacular source declared as such.

This awareness of linguistic and behavioural change is counterpointed by the topos of Christ's plenitude and permanence, since, like the Barking

Edouard, the *Catherine* prologue uses a model of (spiritual) birth, generation and nurture as a pattern for text production. Clemence of Barking turns for legitimation and support directly to Christ. She emphasizes not the social structure of conventional estates inventories such as Wace's (where women are not mentioned), but Christ's distribution of grace throughout them.[23] No groups are excluded and Christ is perceived as a source of nourishment and universal distribution:

> he who alone is good by his very nature gave us both precept and example. He did not wish to conceal his goodness from us, but to reveal it publicly. His goodness suffices for everyone, for it alone is common to all. From his great bounty he feeds us, and all our goodness has its source in [lit. is born from] his goodness.[24]

In her narratorial strategy here, Clemence of Barking is reminiscent of the later medieval women studied by Bynum who, when denied institutional access to priestly offices and the eucharist, by-pass these structures via direct emotional appropriation of Christ.[25] Having secured personal if not official writing space (anyone who knows what is good should distribute it according to their power to do so, ll. 1, 6), the writer now weaves a courtly poetics of grace through the estates framework. *All* have access and sufficiency ('*cumunement* demustrer', l. 10, 'a *tuz commun*' l. 12, '*nostre* bien', l. 14) and *all* have work ('labur', l. 24) through grace, through Christ's great 'largesce' (l. 13) and 'bunté' (l. 9) of sweetness ('dolçur', l. 23). This is open to all who desire it and cannot fail ('Unkes a nul ne volt failir/Ki de lui oust desir' ll. 19–20). As a clerk without (official) clerisy Clemence uses an economy of salvation and desire, rather than that of the academic marketplace.

The prologues from Barking show women writers adapting and extending generic conventions of the hagiographic translator's stance: though they testify to women writers' need to develop particular strategies for entering into composition, they should no more be read as literal confessions of inability and modest timidity than those of male hagiographers. They also provide important suggestions for the thematic programmes of their texts. Though the women translators' handling of source material has sometimes been perceived in terms of stereotypes of women—and translation—as derivative and timid, creating no significant difference from the source material, such arguments cannot survive detailed attention either to text or context and particular thematic emphases and interest are readily apparent in these lives. I have explored elsewhere the significance of writing in French for a female community in the case of the Catherine Life and in the reception differences between Marie's Life of Audrey and its source material in the *Liber Eliensis*.[26] The latter text apparently follows its source very closely, but large scale changes of *dispositio* are not needed in order for the Anglo-Norman Life to have a very different effect. The translator's hundreds of small changes create a subject status for this Life's virgin heroine whereas the Latin source material uses her virginity as a symbol of intact monastic property rights. In the case of the Lives from Barking, the source material is also completely refocussed in the light of particular thematic interests and relations with inscribed and future audiences. These are signalled in the prologues, as part of the creation of narratorial stances.

The *Edouard* prologue, for example, announces thematic concern with spiritual *plenté* and earthly riches and poverty. No source is known for this prologue's thematic play on power, desire, riches and poverty: it can perhaps be accounted for as an experiment in *amplificatio* on the Life's themes, with possible use of reminiscences of other material. As in the accounts of the joys of heaven often present in treatises for religious women at this period, the prologue envisages angels desiring and being fulfilled with the 'plenté suvraine,/La plenté de la grant duçur' (ll. 24–5) of the creator's presence, a 'plenté' (l. 39) in which King Edward now shares, having desired it amidst his earthly 'plenté' (l. 45).[27] In the case of this *Edouard* Life, there is the opportunity of comparison with Matthew Paris' later Anglo-Norman reworking of the same Latin *vita* by Anselm: the nun of Barking's play on spiritual and material desires is very different from the monk of St Alban's invocations of epic nationalism ('In all the world, there is not, I dare well say to you, a country, realm, or empire where there have been so many good kings and saints as in the island of the English . . .').[28] A major strategy of Anselm's in presenting this passive, childless king is to make him a figure of the new ideals of charity and personal compassion for the poor given so much late twelfth-century theological discussion, and Matthew Paris has hard work to create epic nuances around Edward's unheroic figure.[29] The nun of Barking's reading of Anselm's concern with alms-giving involves not only the prologue's stress on Edward's dual crown of earthly and heavenly plenty in his service of a God who 'les povres n'ad en despit/Ne sul de riches n'est suffit' (ll. 63–4), but retention and development of all the Confessor's acts of charity and miracles for the poor. For example, an apparently trivial incident—the king observes a thief in his own treasury and, at the approach of his treasurer, warns the thief to escape—focuses concern with the issue (much discussed by twelfth-century theologians and canonists) of whether the needy have a right to go beyond their spiritually-useful position as an occasion of charity in others and actually steal what they need to live.[30] In the nun of Barking's version this is celebrated as the greatest of all Edward's miracles, and the king, in discussion with the treasurer, is made to point out that they have plenty left and the thief has only (as in orthodox poverty theory) taken the rich man's surplus.[31] The basis for this is present in the Latin source, but the nun of Barking amplifies the praise of Edward's saintly charity and benevolence: he not only feels no covetousness but has saved the life of the 'maveis garcun' (l. 1063). In this Life's version of Edward's many encounters with beggars, there is, moreover, a strong and compassionate sense of the smell, filth and physical infirmity of the very poor.[32]

In addition to this concern with spiritual and material 'patient poverty', the *Edouard* writer also develops the poetics of chastity and desire signalled in her prologue's account of the angels' infinitely consummatable desirous gaze at the creator. I have elsewhere argued that hers is the only version among the Lives of the Confessor to pay adequate attention to the virgin marriage which is a major point of his sanctity.[33] Her sympathy for the virgin subject extends from her distinctive portrayal of the Confessor's queen to the reluctant Edward's own efforts to cope with the politics of dynastic propagation. Her development of the poetics and politics of chastity is one of the first literary treatments of 'fin' amur' (*Edouard*, l. 1360).[34] Comparable and arresting treatment of affective themes can be seen in the Barking Life of St Catherine, where the prologue's emphasis on Christ as a personal and desirable source of grace is developed, as Catherine Batt has noted, via the appropriation of courtly terms ('largesce', 'bonté', 'dolçur', see above, p. 52) and through a complex integration and displacement of courtly discourse in relation to spiritual throughout the Life.[35]

These women translators thus bring some different kinds of subjectivity and historical experience to bear on the writing of hagiography of which better account needs to be taken than hitherto. I would nevertheless be wary of claiming their work as a separate and distinctively female school of hagiographic translation. Their works constitute not a disruption of the genre's assumptions and conventions, but rather a series of unconsolidatable extensions of them. Even if one could irrefutably isolate gender-specific aspects of their texts, these would need to be seen as one strand in texts which also and necessarily use the dominant discourses of their genre and of their socio-economic milieu. Stephen Nichols has recently argued that the margins are a potentially enabling place to write from: that writers like Heloise, Constance of Le Ronceray from the convent of Angers, and Marie de France can use the poetics of the body and a legitimation of emotion and sensuality to command a range of expressiveness unavailable to male clerics.[36] The margins, however, by definition are marginal, and the dominant discourses re-contain these extensions without strain. (Thus, for instance, the nun of Barking's attention to the politics of the chaste body is an inward, but not fundamentally disruptive account of life on the inside of dynastic structures of kinship and exchange, see p. 54 above.) One should, of course, not expect or seek as a sign of feminist engagement evidence that these writers radically dissent from their class outlook and habits of thought, any more than one should condemn Christine de Pisan (as some recent commentators have done) for 'failing' to extend the politics of gender to those of class.[37] In any case what is at issue here is not just the particular stances of individual women translators but the conditions of literary production for post-Conquest women.

Their literary language—'rumanz'—was an empowered language for the use of and for clerical address to the upper classes of insular culture. It had its own function and resources and was by no means only *faute de mieux* for the Latinless. The aristocratic religious houses and courts in which Anglo-Norman women writers lived had literary resources available to women who chose to interest themselves in writing and some upper-class Anglo-Norman women did have means and leisure for such a choice. There is a relatively large amount of Anglo-Norman female literary patronage by women of high socio-economic standing, large property resources and some degree of personal autonomy. The Anglo-Norman women translators are themselves privileged in socio-economic terms. Why, in these circumstances, is there not more writing by Anglo-Norman women?

In fact there is a relatively large amount of literary activity by women if we count patronage, book ownership and use; there may be women writers among anonymous works; and many texts that have been presented in literary histories as gender-neutral become part of women's writing and reading when their manuscript context is attended to.[38] The relative infrequency with which women *authors* can nonetheless be identified is part of the wider problem of the absence of institutional underpinning of female achievement in anything other than sexo-biological terms. Post-Conquest literary production by women occurs within particular networks and circles, it is not an institutional practice to which women have a right of entry but one which happens as the practice of temporarily constituted groups. There are few institutional structures which host or nurture women's engagement in the production of texts, and those there are (such as all but the very richest nunneries) tend to exist on conceded, often grossly underfunded (and sometimes begrudged, sometimes withdrawn), territory. In court circles, in insular gentry kin and family networks and in nunneries, Anglo-Norman women did create or exploit some social contexts for female literary interests: examples, apart from Barking itself, include the Conqueror's Latinate daughters and their correspondents, the Angevin courts and their female patronage, some insular gentry circles, some groups of female readers associated with Matthew Paris and St Albans, some indications of 'vertical' networks (from one generation to another) such as Eleanor of Provence and her granddaughter, princess Mary, at Amesbury.[39] But a female literary written tradition independent of or extending beyond temporary social groups and literary practices established only for one or two generations is harder to find in post-Conquest Britain.[40]

None of the women translators has open, unreflected-upon access to the traditional marketplace of discourse into which the *Vie de Clement* so confidently and professionally inserts itself: each woman has to negotiate and validate a route into composition without female 'auctores' (though the presence of two Lives from Barking suggests either that the one writer found her strategy fruitful or that it was seen as imitable by a second writer in the same community). Work on later women writers has shown that they read each other intensely: since all need to seek particular legitimation for writing to counter their gender's invisibility, precedents (when discoverable amidst the recurring phenomenon of the 'transience of female writers' fame') are specially valued.[41] How far could or did Anglo-Norman women read each other?

It is possible, though (given the imprecise dating of both oeuvres and the absence of much secure biographical information) not provable, that Clemence of Barking saw a precedent in Marie de France or that Marie de France found a precedent in Clemence of Barking. The *Lais* of the 'dame Marie' whom we know as Marie de France seem to have been circulating in British courts in the 1170s and 80s, contemporaneously with the production of the Lives at Barking.[42] The manoeuvres of the *Catherine* Prologue are very similar to those of the much-better known Prologue to Marie de France's *Lais*:

> Ki Deus ad duné escience
> E de parler bon' eloquence
> Ne s'en deit taisir ne celer,
> Ainz se deit voluntiers mustrer
> Quant uns granz biens est mult oïz,
> Dunc a primes est i fluriz,
> E quant loëz est de plusurs,
> Dunc ad espandue ses flurs.

[Anyone who has received from God the gift of knowledge and true eloquence has a duty not to remain silent: rather one should be happy to reveal such talents. When a truly beneficial thing is heard by many people, it then enjoys its first blossom, but if it is widely praised its flowers are in full bloom.][43]

Clemence of Barking's opening makes use of the same topoi but with lexis geared to the spiritual *cortoisie* earlier discussed: she sees the translator's utility in terms of spiritual fruit rather than the flowers of rhetoric:

> Cil ki le bien seit e entent
> Demustrer le deit sagement
> Que par le fruit de sa bunté
> Seient li altre amonesté
> De bien faire e de bien voleir
> Sulunc ço qu'en unt le poeir
> (ll. 1–6).

[All who know and understand what is good have a duty to make it known wisely, so that by the fruit of its goodness others may be encouraged to do good deeds and to want what is good as far as they are able (see also ll. 7–14, quoted above n. 24).]

Here then we have at least two distinguished female writers, both using courtly and religious discourses, and both extending and redirecting topoi from within the clerical hagiographic translator's prologue repertoire to create their own narrative authorization.

To this admittedly (and unsurprisingly) tenuous possibility of a female tradition, we can add, again tentatively, the author of the Life of St Audrey, who writes (perhaps 10, perhaps as much as 70 or 80, years later), 'Ici escris mon non Marie/Pur ce ke soie remembree' ('Here I write my name, Marie, so that I may be remembered', ll. 4619–20). Perhaps she had seen the late twelfth-century collection of *Fables* whose epilogue reads 'al finement de cest escrit,/Que en romanz ai treité e dit,/Me numerai pur remembrance:/Marie ai nun, si sui de France' ('At the end of this book, which I have composed and related in French, I will name myself so I may be remembered: My name is Marie and I am from France').[44] Or perhaps she knew the late twelfth/early thirteenth-century prologue to the *Espurgatoire seint Patriz*:

> Jo Marie ai mis en memoire
> Le livre del'Espurgatoire,
> En romanz k'il seit entendables
> A laie genz e covenables;
> Or preiom Deu ke pur sa grace
> De nos pechiez mundes nus face.[45]

This Marie, author of *La vie sainte Audrée*'s biography of a 'blessed queen' (l. 18) and her struggles to remain God's rather than anyone else's spouse, may have been a nun or perhaps a widowed vowess at Chatteris: her text certainly presents a heroine who is both widowed and then separated with her second husband's agreement, and who is materially, personally, and spiritually better off as a result.[46] Given the dating of Marie de France's oeuvre in the late twelfth century, the language of the extant thirteenth-century manuscript of *Audrée* is too late for the two writers to have been the same person. But the extant manuscript is clearly

57

not the original and Marie de France's canon is not only not fixed beyond
doubt to any one of the several candidates proposed in the late twelfth
century, but the order of the works in that canon is a matter of inference
based on literary historians' images of the differing genres within it.[47]
Even if the author of *Audrée* is not a strong candidate for the authorship
of the *Espurgatoire* (and/or the *Fables*, and/or the *Lais*) she may serve as
a reminder that we still do not know enough about these women writers
to have a proper estimate of what they did.

This is not the place to develop these questions of identity, authorship
and tradition at the length they need. Nevertheless, taking even provisional account of the work of post-Conquest women translators raises
some interesting questions. With what sense of their own history, personal
and social, did these women work? The old, royal, female communities
continued, in the 1080s, to commission updated biographies of their foun-
dresses and patronesses from Goscelin (a writer cited by the *Vie sainte
Audrée* author and a major writer of the Latin hagiography of Barking's
own saints) and perhaps did not feel themselves to be living in so very
different a world from that of pre-Conquest England.[48] Christina of
Markyate may have had *Alexis* copied for her by the monks of St Albans,
but perhaps had heard her (probably late Old English) *Cecilia* from an
Ælfric manuscript.[49] Linguistic conservatism is the hallmark of the English
version of the Wintney Regula for nuns as it is of the Katherine Group
and *Ancrene Wisse*, and as it must have been of those nunneries which,
on the evidence of the commissioners' reports, were still using French at
the Dissolution.[50] The relation of post-Conquest women writers to their
language, history and traditions and the contours and possibilities of their
literary culture are areas needing further investigation. We cannot confidently map our sense of the possibilities of medieval *translatio*, whether of
saints, *studii*, or *imperii*, without taking into account what evidence there
is from women, or without at least registering that, without such evidence
and more developed ways of evaluating it, our knowledge of post-
Conquest *translatio* must remain seriously incomplete.

NOTES

1. See for example, Carol Fewster, *Traditionality and Genre in Middle English
   Romance* (Cambridge: D.S. Brewer, 1987) esp. ch. 1.
2. See, however, the studies of Karl Uitti, *Story, Myth and Celebration in Old
   French Narrative Poetry, 1050–1200* (Princeton, New Jersey: Princeton
   University Press, 1973) ch. 1, and, especially, 'The Clerkly Narrator Figure in
   Old French Hagiography and Romance' *Medioeveo Romanzo* 2 (1975)
   pp. 394–408; Paul Jones, *Prologue and Epilogue in Old French Saints' Lives
   Before 1400*, University of Pennsylvania Publications in Romanic Languages

and Literatures 24 (Pennsylvania: University of Pennsylvania Press, 1933); A.B. Harden, 'The "Ubi Sunt" Theme in Three Anglo-Norman Saints' Lives' *Romance Notes* 1 (1959) pp. 53–5. On the general 'oral-literate' character of hagiography and its rhetorical stances, see Evelyn Birge Vitz, 'From the Oral to the Written in Medieval and Renaissance Saints' Lives' in Renate Blumenfeld-Kosinski and Timea Szell (eds) *Images of Sainthood in Medieval Europe* (Ithaca and London: Cornell University Press, 1992) pp. 97–114.

3. For a list of verse hagiography see J. Wogan-Browne, ' "Clerc u lai, muïne u dame": Women and Anglo-Norman Hagiography' in Carol Meale (ed.) *Women and Literature in Britain 1150–1500* (Cambridge: Cambridge University Press, 1993) pp. 75–8, n. 5.

4. See Ö. Södergaard (ed.) *La vie d'Edouard le confesseur, poème anglonormand du XIIe siècle* (Uppsala: Almqvist & Wiksell, 1948); W. MacBain (ed.) *The Life of Saint Catherine by Clemence of Barking* Anglo-Norman Text Society 18 (Oxford: Blackwell, 1964); Ö. Södergaard (ed.) *La vie sainte Audrée, poème anglo-normand du XIIIe siècle* (Uppsala: no publisher, 1955).

5. On the possibility of single authorship for the *Edouard* and *Catherine*, see W. MacBain, 'The Literary Apprenticeship of Clemence of Barking' *AUMLA* (1958) pp. 3–22.

6. The Benedictine nunnery of Chatteris is a possible (but not proven) provenance for the Life of St Audrey, first suggested by M. Dominica Legge, *Anglo-Norman Literature and its Background* (Oxford: Oxford University Press, 1963; repr. Greenwood Press, 1978) p. 264. On this point see further my 'Re-routing the Dower: The Female Voices of *La vie sainte Audrée*' in Sally-Beth MacLean and Jennifer Carpenter (eds) *Power of the Weak* (Champaign-Urbana: University of Illinois Press, forthcoming).

7. The post-Conquest abbesses of Barking (as of some other major female houses) were women of the royal family or from the nobility (see *Victoria County History of Essex* vol. II, p. 120). The exception is a rule-proving one: Henry II's appointment of the non-royal Mary Becket as abbess of Barking in reparation for her brother's murder.

8. See, for example, the continental fourteenth-century prose *remaniement* of Clemence of Barking's *Life of St Catherine*, made for the Saint-Pol family (P. Meyer (ed.) 'Notice du ms. Egerton 745 du Musée Britannique' *Romania* 39 (1910) pp. 532–69, 40 (1911) pp. 41–69). More generally, see the excellent account by John Frankis, 'The Social Context of Vernacular Writing in Thirteenth-Century England: the Evidence of the Manuscripts' in P.R. Coss and S.D. Lloyd (eds) *Thirteenth-Century England I: Proceedings of the Newcastle-upon-Tyne Conference, 1985* (Woodbridge, Suffolk: Boydell and Brewer, 1986) pp. 175–84.

9. 'The Clerkly Narrator . . .', *Medioevo Romanzo* 2 (1975) pp. 394–408.

10. Wace, prologue to *La vie de seint Nicolas*, quoted by Uitti, *Medioevo Romanzo* 2 p. 399, and see further n. 11 below.

11. Einar Ronsjö (ed.) *La vie de saint Nicolas par Wace* Etudes Romanes de Lund 5 (Lund and Copenhagen: Gleerup and Munksgaard, 1942):

> Li un sunt lai, li un lectré,
> Li un fol et li un senee,
> Li un petit et li un grant,
> Li un povre, li un manant.
> Si done Deus deversement

> Divers dons a diverse gent.
> Chescon deit mustrer sa bonté
> De ceo que Deus lui ad doné.
> Li chivaler et li burgeis
> Et li vilein et li corteis
> Deivent en Deu aver fiance
> Et honurer de lur substance.
> Bonement deivent esculter
> Quant il oient de Deu parler.
> Qui mels set mels deit enseigner
> Et qui plus poet plus deit aider.
> Qui plus est fort plus deit porter
> Et qui plus ad plus deit doner.
> Chascon deit mustrer son saver
> Et sa bonté et son poer
> Et Deu servir, son creatur,
> Et as barons sainz pur s'amur.
>
> (ll. 9–30)

12. Uitti, *Medioeveo Romanzo 2* p. 401.
13. André Vauchez, '*Beatu stirps*: Sainteté et lignage en occident aux xiiie et xive siècles' in Georges Duby and Jacques LeGoff (eds) *Famille et parenté dans l'Occident médiévale* (Paris, 1974; repr. Rome, 1977) pp. 397–406; Anita Guerreau-Jalabert, 'Sur les structures de parenté dans l'Europe médiévale' *Annales ESC* 36 (1981) pp. 1028–49; M.T. Clanchy, *From Memory to Written Record* (London: Arnold, 1979) esp. ch. 8, 'Hearing and Seeing'; Brian Stock, *The Implications of Literacy: Written Language and Models of Interpretation in the Eleventh and Twelfth Centuries* (Princeton, New Jersey: Princeton University Press, 1983) esp. Introduction and ch. 1.
14. See further Nancy Vine Durling, 'Hagiography and Lineage: the Example of the Old French *Vie de saint Alexis*' *Romance Philology* 40 (1986–7) pp. 451–69.
15. N.K. Willson (ed.) 'La vie de Clement pape' (University of Cambridge: PhD thesis, 1952) ll. 1–40:

> Li clerc de scole, ki apris unt
> Tant qu aukeus entendant sunt,
> Mult se peinent de livres faire
> E de sentences en lung traire,
> Que pur mustrer lur saveir,
> Que pur los del siecle aveir.
> Livres funt tut de nuvel,
> Sis adubbent asez bel;
> Bel escrivent e bel les ditent,
> Mès li lai poi i profitent,
> E clerc i sunt poi amendé
> Ki en lettrure ne sunt fundé.
> Li clerc meisme ki funt ces livres
> Prest ne sunt ne delivres
> De faire as nun lettrez aprendre
> E en vulgar cumun entendre
> Que ceo seit que il unt dit

En lur livres que unt escrit,
Kar ceo lur suffist asez
Que de autres clers seient loez
E que ceo peusse estre dit:
'Bons clers est ki si escrit.'
Pur ceo que fous est tel purpens
De si despendre en nient bon sens,
E pour ceo que livres sunt asez
Ki bien suffisent as lettrez,
Al mien avis mult mieuz serreit
E a plus grant pru turnereit
Si li livre de antiquité . . .
En tel language turné fussent
Que plusurs gent pru en eussent.
Ne sui pas de ces lettrez
Ki en clergie sunt fundez:
Nepurquant cel poi que sai
De si escrivre en purpos ai
Que clerc e lai qui l'orrunt
Bien entendre le porrunt.

I am grateful to the librarian of Trinity College, Cambridge, for permission to see Trinity College, Cambridge MS R.3.46, to the executors of Dr Willson's estate for permission to quote from this thesis and to Mr Louis Browne of Miller & Co., Cambridge, for his help in obtaining this permission.

16. R. Anthony Lodge (ed.) *Le Livre des Manières* (Genève: Droz, 1979) stanzas 244–313 (esp. 277–81) and stanzas 302–6.

17. Prof. W. MacBain argues this case in a forthcoming article rehabilitating these women translators of which he has very kindly given me the typescript.

18. Male authors who name themselves in the prologues to their texts include Benedeit (see Ian Short and Brian Merrilees (eds) *The Anglo-Norman Voyage of St Brendan* (Manchester: Manchester University Press, 1979)); Wace [at beginning and at end of Life] (see Ronsjö (ed.) *La vie de seint Nicolas* (1942)); Simund de Freine ('La vie seint George' in *Les oeuvres de Simund de Freine* Société des Anciens Textes Français (Paris, 1909)); Denis Piramus (*La vie Seint Edmund le Rei, poème anglo-normand du XIIème siècle par Denis Piramus* (Göteborg: Wettergren and Kerbor, 1935; repr. Geneva; Slatkine Reprints, 1974)); Angier of St Frideswide ('La vie de saint Grégoire le Grand traduite du latin par Frère Angier, religieux de Sainte-Frideswide' *Romania* (1883) pp. 145–208); Simon of Walsingham ('Vie anglo-normande de sainte Foy par Simon de Walsingham' *Romania* 66 (1940–1) pp. 49–84). Male authors named at the end of texts include Guernes de Pont St Maxence (E. Walberg (ed.) *La vie de saint Thomas Becket par Guernes de Pont-Saint-Maxence* (Lund: Glemp, 1922)); Wace (Hans-Erich Keller and Margaret Alison Stones (eds) *Wace: La vie de sainte Marguerite* Beihefte zur Zeitschrift für romanische Philologie 229 (Tübingen: Niemeyer, 1990)); Guillaume de Bernevile (G. Paris and A. Bos (eds) *La vie de saint Gilles* Société des Anciens Textes Français (Paris: Firmin Didot, 1881)); Guillaume de Ferrières (H. Petersen, 'Trois versions inédites de la légende de saint Eustache en vers français' *Romania* 51 (1925) pp. 363–96); Matthew Paris (A.T. Baker (ed.) 'La vie de saint Edmond, archêveque de Cantorbéry' *Romania* 55 (1929)

pp. 332–81); Peter of Pecham (A.T. Baker (ed.) 'Vie de saint Richard, évêque de Chichester' *Revue des Langues Romanes* 53 (1910) pp. 245–396); Bozon (M. Amelia Klenke (ed.) *Three Saints' Lives by Nicholas Bozon* Franciscan Institute Publications Historical Series I (St Bonaventure, NY; Franciscan Institute, 1947)); A.T. Baker (ed.) 'An Anglo-French Life of Saint Paul the Hermit' *MLR* 4 (1908–9) pp. 491–504). Matthew Paris and Bozon name themselves in the texts mentioned here, but not in their other hagiographic works. For the anonymous hagiographic lives see the list cited in n. 3 above.

19. See n. 8 above: the Barking *Edouard* also replaces Wace's account of the saint in one manuscript of Wace's *Brut*, see Södergaard (ed.) *La vie d'Edouard* (1948), pp. 46–9.

20. 'Jo ki sa vie ai translatee/Par nun sui Clemence numee./De Berkinge sui nunain,/Pur s'amur pris cest oevre en mein', MacBain (ed.) *The Life of St Catherine* (1964) ll. 2689–92. A translation of the Life (by G.S. Burgess and J. Wogan-Browne) is forthcoming.

21. Books dedicated to and/or owned by nuns from Barking survive sporadically from the seventh to the fifteenth century. On the history of the abbey see *Victoria County History of Essex* II pp. 117–21.

22.   Ele fud jadis translaté
           Sulunc le tens bien ordené
           Mais ne furent dunc si veisdus
           Les humes, ne si envius
           Cum il sunt al tens ki est ore
           Et aprés nus serrunt uncore.
           Pur ço que li tens est mué
           E des humes la qualité
           Est la rime vil tenue
           Car ele est asquans corrumpue.
           Pur ço si l'estuet amender
           E le tens selunc la gent user.

(MacBain (ed.) *The Life of St Catherine* (1964) ll. 35–46)

It is possible that the earlier vernacular text alluded to here is the fragmentary version of Catherine's Life preserved in Manchester, John Rylands Library, MS Rylands 6 (see E.C. Fawtier-Jones, 'Les vies de Sainte Catherine d'Alexandrie' *Romania* 56 (1930) pp. 80–104). Professor Ian Short of Birkbeck College, University of London, has pointed out to me that some lines in this text incorporate stage-directions; see also his 'Patrons and Polyglots: French Literature in Twelfth-century England' *Anglo-Norman Studies* 14 (1991) pp. 229–50, p. 236 n. 29. It is thus a text for semi-dramatic performance such as would fit with the milieu of a well-established nunnery: at Barking, for instance, under Katherine de Sutton (abbess from 1363–1376), liturgical ceremonies and dramas in Latin were reworked for performance: see Karl Young, *The Drama of the Medieval Church* (Oxford: Clarendon Press, 1934; repr. 1967) vol. I, pp. 164–7, 381–5.

23. The scriptural authority for this is I Cor.12:4, 8–11: Clemence however makes Christ rather than the Holy Spirit the central figure here.

24.   Car cil ki sul est bon de sei
           A nus dunad essample e lei;
           Sa bunté ne nus volt celer,
           Mais cumunement demustrer.
           De sun bien suffist chascun

Car il sul est a tuz commun.
De sa grant largesce nus paist
E tut nostre bien del suen naist.
(MacBain (ed.) *The Life of St Catherine* (1964) ll. 7–14)

25. See C. Walker Bynum, *Holy Feast and Holy Fast: the Religious Significance of Food for Medieval Women* (Cambridge: Cambridge University Press, 1987) *passim*.

26. For *Audrée*, see the study cited in n. 6 above. The Barking *Catherine* is studied in the fifth chapter of a work in progress for Oxford University Press, *Authorized Virgins: the Literature of Female Celibacy in Medieval England, 1150–1350*.

27. For a scriptural authority see II Peter 1:2–3. An influential Anselmian treatise on the custody of the soul contains a description of angels gazing at God in heaven, and is extant in a manuscript possibly belonging to Barking (see R.W. Southern and F.S. Schmitt (eds) *Memorials of St Anselm* Auctores Britannici Medii Aevi (Oxford: Clarendon Press, 1973) pp. 354–60; M.R. James, *Catalogue of the Western Manuscripts in the Library of Trinity College, Cambridge* (Cambridge: Cambridge University Press, 1902) vol. III, no. 1133, p. 122 (MS O.2.29, ff.175r–177r)). I am grateful to the authorities of Trinity College for permission to see this manuscript. For an account of the learning of enclosed women at this period, see Bella Millett, 'Women in No Man's Land: English Recluses and the Development of Vernacular Literature in the Twelfth and Thirteenth Centuries' in Meale (ed.) *Women and Literature in Britain 1150–1500* pp. 86–103.

28. For the original see Kathryn Young-Wallace (ed.) Matthew Paris, *La Estoire de Seint Aedward le Rei* Anglo-Norman Text Society 41 (London, 1983) p. 1, ll. 1–4.

29. For Anselm's Life of Edward the Confessor, see *Patrologia Latina* 195 pp. 737–90.

30. See M. Mollat, *The Poor in the Middle Ages: An Essay in Social History* trans. A. Goldhammer (New Haven and London: Yale University Press, 1986).

31. Mollat p. 111.

32. See esp. *Edouard* ll. 2373–432 (the king literally bears the burden of the poor and soils his royal vestments by carrying a cripple on his back).

33. See 'Women and Anglo-Norman Hagiography' in Meale (ed.) *Women and Literature* pp. 68–73.

34. See W. MacBain, 'Some Religious and Secular Uses of the Vocabulary of *fin'amor* in the Early Decades of the Northern French Narrative Poem' *French Forum* 13 (1988) pp. 261–76.

35. Catherine Batt, 'Clemence of Barking's Transformations of *Courtoisie* in *La Vie de Sainte Catherine d'Alexandrie*', *New Comparison* 12 (1991) pp. 102–23.

36. 'Medieval Women Writers: *aisthesis* and the Powers of Marginality' *Yale French Studies* 75 (1988) pp. 77–94.

37. See further Sheila Delany, 'Mothers to Think Back Through: Who Are They? The Ambiguous Example of Christine de Pisan' in her *Medieval Literary Politics: Shapes of Ideology* (Manchester: Manchester University Press, 1990) pp. 88–103.

38. To take one small example, the astonishing poem, 'Somer is comen & winter gon', in which a bloody child pursues a narrator along the hedgerows, reads very differently when its context in the tri-lingual nunnery manuscript, British Library MS Egerton 613, is remembered, and the possibility of a female

speaker of the lyric arises: see no. 54 in Carleton Brown (ed.) *English Lyrics of the Thirteenth Century* (Oxford: Clarendon Press, 1932).

39. See further Elisabeth M.C. van Houts, 'Latin Poetry and the Anglo-Norman Court 1066–1135: the *Carmen de Hastingae Proelio*' *Journal of Medieval History* 15 (1989) pp. 39–62; Therese Latzke, 'Die Fürstinnenpreis' *Mittellateinisches Jahrbuch* 14 (1979) pp. 22–65, esp. 48–65; Rita Lejeune, 'Role littéraire d'Aliénor d'Aquitaine et de sa famille' *Cultura Neolatina* 14 (1954) pp. 5–57; Suzanne Lewis, *The Art of Matthew Paris in the Chronica Majora* California Studies in the History of Art 21 (California and Aldershot: Scolar Press, 1987) pp. 5, 10, 447, 493 n. 75. John of Hoveden's *Rossignol* and Matthew Paris' Life of Edward the Confessor were dedicated to Eleanor of Provence, who took her granddaughter Princess Mary into retirement at Amesbury with her, where Trevet subsequently dedicated his *Chronicle* to the younger woman (see Legge, *Anglo-Norman Literature* pp. 233–5, 269, 299).

40. For a most fruitful approach to these problems in later medieval English culture, see Felicity Riddy, 'Women Talking About the Things of God: a Late Medieval Sub-Culture' in Meale (ed.) *Women and Literature* pp. 104–27.

41. The phrase is Germaine Greer's, quoted in Elaine Showalter, *A Literature of Their Own: British Women Novelists from Brontë to Lessing* (Princeton, New Jersey: Princeton University Press, 1977) p. 10.

42. The *Edouard* Life must be after 1163 and before 1189 (see Södergaard (ed.) *La vie d'Edouard* (1948) pp. 18–26; Legge, *Anglo-Norman Literature* p. 60); the *Catherine* Life must antedate its oldest extant manuscript of c.1200 but may be quite late in the twelfth century (MacBain (ed.) *Life of St Catherine* (1964) pp. xxiv–xxv), not necessarily very long before the *Audrée* Life. On Marie de France and the twelfth century, see G.S. Burgess and K. Busby, *The Lais of Marie de France* (Harmondsworth: Penguin Books, 1986) pp. 15–19. The extant manuscripts of the *Lais* are twelfth- and thirteenth-century (see A. Ewart, ed. *Marie de France Lais* (Oxford: Blackwell,1969) pp. xviii–xix). On the problems of internal chronology in the *Lais*, see G.S. Burgess, *Marie de France: Text and Context* (Manchester: Manchester University Press, 1987) ch. 1.

43. Ewart (ed.) *Marie de France Lais* p. 1, ll. 1–8, trans. Burgess and Busby, *The Lais of Marie de France* p. 41.

44. See A. Ewart and R.C. Johnston (eds) *Marie de France: Fables* (Blackwell: Oxford, 1966) Epilogue, p. 61, ll. 1–4. I am grateful to Dr Ann M. Hutchison of Toronto for first drawing to my attention the similarities between a miracle story in Marie [of Chatteris?] *La vie sainte Audrée* (see Södergaard (ed.) *La vie sainte Audrée* (1955) ll. 3470–3559) and Marie de France's *Eliduc*.

45. 'I, Marie, have translated the Book of Purgatory into French, so that it may be understood by lay people and the learned. Now let us pray to God that he cleanse us from our sins through his grace.' (Thomas A. Jenkins (ed.) *Marie de France: Espurgatoire Seint Patrice: An Old French Poem of the Twelfth Century* (Philadelphia, 1894: repr. Geneva, Slatkine, 1974).)

46. Widows often undertook less formal religious lives, such as that of the vowess. Patricia Cullum's paper 'Vowesses and Veiled Widows' at the 1990 University of York conference on 'Medieval Women: Work, Spirituality, Literacy and Patronage' first alerted me to the importance of this form of life for women in Britain. Vowesses have not been studied for the earlier period, but for the role of widows in Anglo-Norman monachism see Sally Thompson, *Women Religious: The Founding of English Nunneries After the Norman Conquest*

(Oxford: Clarendon Press, 1991) pp. 167–72, 177, 181, and, for a widow entering a monastic house after payment to avoid marrying against her will, p. 176. On continental practices see M-T Lorcin, 'Retraite des veuves et filles au couvent: quelques aspects de la condition féminine à la fin du Moyen Age' *Annales de démographie historique* (1975) pp. 187–204.

47. The extant manuscript of *Audrée* is a late thirteenth-century copy in the large collection of saints' lives once used in the convent of Campsey (MS Welbeck 1C1, now British Library MS Loan 29/61). On the problems of dating Marie de France's oeuvre, see the works cited in n. 42 above.

48. On the cultivation of Anglo-Saxon saints in the Anglo-Norman church, see Susan J. Ridyard, *The Royal Saints of Anglo-Saxon England* (Cambridge: Cambridge University Press, 1988); on Goscelin's hagiography, see Susan P. Millinger, 'Humility and Power: Anglo-Saxon Nuns in Anglo-Norman Hagiography' in *Distant Echoes*, Medieval Religious Women 1, Cistercian Studies Series no. 71 (Kalamazoo, Michigan: Kalamazoo Press, 1984) pp. 5–28.

49. For the suggestion that Christina knew an English version of the legend of St Cecilia, see Thomas Head, 'The Marriages of Christina of Markyate' *Viator* 21 (1990) p. 84. Manuscripts of Ælfric's Lives and homilies remained in circulation in the late twelfth century (see e.g. N.R. Ker, *Catalogue of Manuscripts Containing Anglo-Saxon* (Oxford: Clarendon Press, 1957) pp. 510–11).

50. For the Wintney rule see M. Arnold Schröer, *Die Wintney-Version der Regula S. Benedicti* (Halle, 1888): on the elaborate literary koiné in which *Ancrene Wisse* and the Katherine Group of saints' lives were produced for late twelfth- and early thirteenth-century audiences of women, see S.R.T.O. d'Ardenne (ed.) *Ðe Liflade ant te Passiun of Seinte Iuliene* (Liège, 1936; repr. Early English Text Society OS 248, London: Oxford University Press, 1961) pp. xxv–xxxiv, 177–180. For an example of late medieval nunnery ownership of French books, see A.I. Doyle, 'Books Connected with the Vere Family and Barking Abbey' *Transactions of the Essex Archaeological Society* (1955) p. 241, and for lists of religious houses and manuscripts, M. Dominica Legge, *Anglo-Norman in the Cloisters* (Edinburgh: Edinburgh University Press, 1950) pp. 111–16. In 1535 the canonesses of Lacock Abbey were said to 'have their rule, thinstitutes of their religion and ceremonies of the same writen in the frenche tonge which they understand well and are very parfite in the same, albeit that it varieth from the vulgar frenche that is now used and is moche like the frenche that the common Lawe is writen in' (*VCH Wilts* iii (1956) p. 309). I am not aware of any systematic study of the continuing use of French in late medieval English nunneries (where English evidence has unsurprisingly been the first concern of literary and other historians), but there is much incidental evidence to suggest it would be well worth making.

Chapter 2

Al-Ḥarīzī's *Maqāmāt:* A Tricultural Literary Product?[1]

RINA DRORY

Cultural contacts, particularly literary contacts, are generally assumed in traditional theories to consist of bilateral relations between two adjacent literatures, whereby one is considered to have 'influence' over the other. But very often we find cultural dynamics to be much more complex and elaborate, as literary contacts and relationships are often established among more than two literatures concurrently, and in ways more subtle and intricate than can be defined as the mere 'influence' of one literature over the other. Even what may appear to be a clear-cut case of the inspiration of one body of literature over another can turn out, upon close examination, to be a case of multiliterary contacts. It is not always easy to trace and account for such contacts, as they are not necessarily manifested in what are conventionally regarded by students of literature as the 'concrete data' of the field, namely, written texts. At times a whole cultural context has to be reconstructed in order to understand the actual circumstances that made possible the writing or production of a particular text, that is, the processes which dominated and manipulated a literary field at a given point in time, of which the written texts are only the final products. This can be particularly difficult for historians studying the past, who have virtually nothing but written texts to go by. Yet considering these final products, the written texts, as 'distinct facts', without taking into account the immediate context and circumstances of their production, can be quite misleading.

Al-ḤARĪZĪ'S *MAQĀMĀT*

This is the case with the famous Hebrew *Maqāmāt* by the Jewish author Judah al-Ḥarīzī (1170–1235) composed on the model of the Arabic

66

Maqāmāt by al-Qāsim b. 'Alī al-Ḥarīrī (1054–1122). The genre of *maqāmāt* (the closest in nature to the European picaresque novel) emerged in Arabic literature in an Eastern Islamic province towards the end of the tenth century, when al-Hamadhānī first composed his *maqāmāt* in 997, in Nishapur. But they hovered on the periphery of the canonized literature for about hundred years, until the *Maqāmāt* of al-Ḥarīrī appeared on the scene, and captured the literary taste of the period within a short time. The explicit praise of literary critics, the many commentaries written on his *Maqāmāt* almost from the time they were first published in Baghdad, and the testimonies of learned men who came from distant places, including Spain, to hear the authorized version of al-Ḥarīrī's *Maqāmāt* from his own mouth all provide ample evidence of an almost immediate prestige and popularity. Al-Ḥarīrī's *Maqāmāt* have become a symbol of Arabic eloquence and stylistic dexterity from its early history, and actually preserved this prominent status up until modern times.

Al-Ḥarīrī's *Maqāmāt* comprise a collection of fifty short independent narrations written in ornamental rhymed prose interspersed with verse, which share a common plot-scheme and two constant protagonists: the narrator and the hero. Each narration (*maqāma*) tells of an episode in which the hero, a vagrant and mendicant but also a man of letters and eloquence, appears in a certain public place (a market, a mosque, a cemetery, a public bath, a travelling caravan, etc.) in different postures, and tricks the people into donating him money by manipulating their feelings and beliefs. As Beeston recently put it,

> Despite his gifts of wit and eloquence, he is a hypocritical rascal—albeit a rather engaging one—and an unrestrained drunkard who, after a serious and moving religious homily, for example, which gains him alms from his auditory, dissipates the cash in low society at a tavern drinking wine; he himself is elderly, but occasionally has with him a youthful accomplice, whom he uses in playing crafty tricks for extracting money. (Beeston (1990) p. 133)

The narrator obviously witnesses the hero's adventures; and each episode ends with the narrator exposing the hero's identity, the hero justifying his behaviour, and their friendly departure.[2]

Al-Ḥarīzī's compilation of Hebrew *Maqāmāt* is traditionally regarded by scholars as a highly typical (perhaps *the* most typical) example of Arabic influence over Hebrew literature: the Arabic *Maqāmāt* were first translated by al-Ḥarīzī into Hebrew, and his own *Maqāmāt* were later composed on the same model. Moreover, he openly declared that he had been inspired by al-Ḥarīrī's *Maqāmāt*, discussing this in his preface. Yet an examination of the cultural circumstances within which this work was composed reveals that it cannot be understood solely in the light of the Arabic-Hebrew context. Rather, another cultural context has to be considered here, albeit one introduced into the Hebrew *Maqāmāt* in a far from simple way, but without which the very act of composing this work cannot be explained.

Al-Ḥarīzī, who was born in Toledo, was living in northern Spain during the second half of the twelfth century when an interest in Arabic texts began to flourish in Jewish as well as Christian circles. He became an Arabic-Hebrew translator and translated several Arabic and Judaeo-Arabic works, usually at the invitation of distinguished patrons or scholars of the Jewish communities of northern Spain and Provence, although he sometimes produced translations on his own initiative. Among his known translations are:

> Moses ibn Ezra's *Maqālat al-ḥadīqa fī ma'nā al-maǧāz wa'l-ḥaqīqa* (*The Treatise of the Garden on Figurative and Literal Expressions*), entitled *'Arugat ha-bosem* in Hebrew;[3]
> Maimonides' *Guide for the Perplexed* (*Moreh nebukhim*),[4] his *Introduction to the Mishnah* (*Hakdamot le-perush ha-mishna*),[5] his commentary on the first five tractates of the *Mishnah order Zera'im*[6] and his *Epistle on Resurrection* (*Ma 'amar teḥiyat ha-metim*);[7]
> 'Ali ibn Ruḍwan's *Epistle on Morals* (*Igeret 'alī ha-išmeelī*);[8]
> Ḥunayn ibn Isḥāq's *Adab al-falāsifa* (*Dicta of the Philosophers*), entitled *Musere ha-filosofim* in Hebrew;[9]
> Galen's *Dialogue on the Soul*.[10]

Between 1205 and 1215,[11] or between 1213 and 1216,[12] while still in northern Spain or in Provence, al-Ḥarīzī translated al-Ḥarīrī's *Maqāmāt*.[13] He then travelled to the East, where, sometime after 1216, he composed his own Hebrew *Maqāmāt*, entitled *Sefer taḥkemoni* and modelled on al-Ḥarīrī's Arabic *Maqāmāt*.[14] There, he also composed a Judaeo-Arabic *Maqāma*, describing his journey to the East.[15]

As mentioned earlier, this work is considered by any standard of the comparative literature approach to represent the most salient example of 'Arabic influence' over Hebrew literature in its Andalusian 'golden age'.[16] Its Arabic-Hebrew context has generally been regarded as so self-evident that it has been taken as plain fact, obvious enough to be passed by as common knowledge. The focus of literary research has thus been concentrated on the specific ways in which al-Ḥarīrī's *Maqāmāt* inspired *Sefer taḥkemoni*,[17] rather than on the cultural circumstances of its production. Yet it seems that a reexamination of those particular circumstances, overlooked, or taken for granted, may reveal that viewing this work exclusively from a general, unspecified 'Arabic-Hebrew' perspective[18] misses important evidence for the reconstruction of Hebrew literature in northern Spain and Provence by means of a new paradigm, quite different from the Arabic-Hebrew one of al-Andalus mentioned above.

The particular circumstances that led to the composition of *Sefer taḥkemoni* will be clarified if we try to reconstruct al-Ḥarīzī's literary awareness and his attitude toward cultural trends in Jewish society at the time. It is al-Ḥarīzī himself who gives us the key to this reconstruction, as he tends to present quite lengthy explanations of his motives, writing in the several introductions, or rather the dedications of this work to different patrons, and in the introductions to some of his Hebrew translations from the Arabic.

Following the contemporary custom among scholars to seek the patronage of distinguished figures in the community and support themselves by dedicating their written works to these figures (the same composition would often be dedicated to different patrons with only the dedication changed), al-Ḥarīzī dedicated his compilation of Hebrew *maqāmāt* to several different Jewish figures during the course of his travels in the Orient.[19] We can thus draw on more than one dedication of *Sefer Tahkemoni* in which al-Ḥarīzī takes great pains to explain—this too according to contemporary writing norms—how and why he decided to compose this work.

Al-Ḥarīzī addresses this subject in the work's two Hebrew dedications: one, to Shemuel ben al-Barqūlī, forms the introduction to the printed edition of *Sefer tahkemoni*;[20] the other, to Yoshiyahu ben Yishai, forms the first *maqāma* in the edition.[21] The same issue is also addressed in the Arabic dedication to Sadīd al-Dawla 'Abd al-Qādir of Aleppo and his son Abū Naṣr.[22] The Hebrew dedications are extended and written in a highly stylized rhymed prose that closely resembles the literary style of allegory (the first one in particular) or of the *maqāmāt* genre (the second one). The Arabic dedication is far more concise, and although it employs a rhetorical style reminiscent of Arabic-rhymed prose, it is still far clearer and more concrete than the rhetoric used in the Hebrew dedications.

The First Hebrew Dedication

In the first dedication, al-Ḥarīzī describes his state when he was prompted to compose the Hebrew *Maqāmāt* as a state of ordination. Intellect woke him from his sleep of folly and assigned him the task of reviving the Hebrew language. The holy tongue, he was informed, was fast deteriorating, having been abandoned by its people, who now favoured Arabic:

> They have enslaved the tongue of the Israelites to the tongue of Kedar [i.e., Arabic] and they said: 'Come and let us sell her to the Ishmaelites.' And they said to her: 'Bow down, that we may go over.' And they took her and cast her into the pit until she perished among them.

And the tongue of Kedar blackened her, and like a lion, tore her. An evil beast devoured her. All of them spurned the Hebrew tongue and made love to the tongue of Hagar [i.e. Arabic]. They embraced the bosom of an alien. They desired the wife of a stranger. They kissed her bosom, for stolen waters were sweet to them. Their hearts were seduced when they saw how excellent was the poetry that Hagar, Sarai's Egyptian handmaiden had borne. And Sarai was barren! (p. 32 [Hebrew: ed. Toporowsky (1952) pp. 9–10])

Bestirring himself, al-Ḥarīzī went to the fount of the Hebrew language to draw water from its sources of wisdom and awaited a sign of inspiration and instruction from God in the form of a young maiden who was to appear before him, rinsing him with drinking water from the flow of her sweet speech. A young maiden then indeed came forth, refreshed him with the honey of her lips, and identified herself as 'your mistress, the Holy Tongue.' He then 'betroth[ed] her unto him in righteousness and reverence without a [marriage]-contract or intercourse' (p. 34), and she later conceived and gave birth to their offspring, a literary composition. Al-Ḥarīzī then goes on to explain that the urge to compose his work had indeed come from al-Ḥarīrī's Arabic *Maqāmāt*, which was, to his mind, a fine illustration of the fact that there do exist other peoples who cherish their language and preserve it with care, unlike the people of Israel, who abandoned their native tongue and neglected it, at times even to the point of despising it. This, by the way, does not prevent al-Ḥarīzī from boasting that everything of real value and quality in this Arabic book is borrowed from the Hebrew. In composing the Hebrew *Maqāmāt* he wishes to show the people of Israel the beauty and resourcefulness of the Hebrew language and to convince them that it is appropriate for all types of literary expression, which he then lists. He stresses that many before him had tried to translate this work into Hebrew, but none had done so with much success. He himself had translated it at the request of 'some generous men [nobles] of Spain (Sefarad)'; but after travelling to the East he had realized that it was inappropriate, or even sinful, 'to translate a book of another people's goodly words as though the words of the living God were not among us' and that one would do best to write in one's native tongue.

The Second Hebrew Dedication

The second Hebrew dedication[23] is actually the first *maqāma* in the collection, which means that it draws on the narrative rather than the methodological discourse. Yet it serves the same purpose of elaborating on al-Ḥarīzī's reasons for composing the Hebrew *Maqāmāt*. In it the author, or rather his protagonist, finds himself in a literary encounter of

Jewish literati (literally, 'of the children of the Hebrews', which Reichert translates as 'of Jewish lineage'). Among them is a 'Hebrew lad', who advances the argument that Arabic is the most beautiful of all languages and that it would be virtually impossible to write a book such as al-Ḥarīrī's in a language other than Arabic. At this the author rises to the defence of the Hebrew language, stating that Arabic is indeed superior to all languages—except for Hebrew; unfortunately, since the Jews were exiled and began adopting the languages of their host nations, Hebrew has been gradually deteriorating; forsaken and forgotten, it has slowly wasted away.

Yet, he continues, even the little Hebrew that has survived is adequately equipped to ensure the composition of some splendid literary works; this, in its own right, attests to the language's superiority. Why, then, asks the young lad, have none of the children of Israel written any praiseworthy literary works in Hebrew that equal those written in Arabic, thereby highlighting the qualities of the Hebrew language? The author replies that, as for himself, he would find no difficulty in writing a praiseworthy book in Hebrew, but the real problem is that, with the lack of demand by the Eastern Jewish public for books of this nature, there is little point in producing them:

But the author, for whom shall he compose, and to the ears of whom shall he speak, while the ears are deaf and the hands are tight, and the times have shut up the eyes of creatures who are imprisoned in the house of passion, and have smitten the men that were at the door of the house with blindness? And there is not among them one who sees or who hears and no one takes it to heart and no one cares. And if you should search the communities of the world, from Egypt unto Babylon—you will not find one who loves wisdom or who honours its possessor or who requites it with good reward. And you know that as for precious books, their pearls are not composed except for those who understand them or for those who requite them with good reward. For they are not made for fools who deride them and scoff at them.

Now the secret of all delightful wisdom is laid bare through three conditions: when she finds a patron, or a sage, or a nobleman who longs for her. Then wisdom sells herself to him as a hand-maid and her light shines and is not withdrawn. And if one of these circumstances does not happen to her, then she goes out for nothing, without money.

Therefore, in our generation the hallowed stones are poured out and the most fine gold is changed, and poetry and rhetoric sell them-selves for bondmen and for bondwomen and there is none to buy them. And the generosity of patrons is like a staff of reed—upon tongues there is response to it, but in hearts there is no shelter for it. And in every place where I encamp, I call out: 'Ho! For a man of intellect!' But there is none who answers. And behold, the place is a

71

place for cattle. And in city after city we see every one of them asleep in the bosom of ignorance. And behold, there is no man there, neither voice of man, but a tied horse and a tied ass, tied and bound by the yoke of lust. And in this circumstance, how can the spirit be stirred up or the intellect soul long to compose any word of wisdom, or to speak of any theme of edification, or to set forth a lovely letter? Lo! Wisdom in the eyes of the children of our people is as one who puts a precious stone in a sling or as one who casts pearls at the feet of cattle. (pp. 49–50 [Hebrew: ed. Toporowsky (1952) pp. 22–23])

The young man agrees, but swayed by the author's valorization of the Hebrew language, he nevertheless urges him to ignore the folly of this generation and to write a book which will convince everyone (including other nations) of Hebrew's superiority. Promising to attend in every *maqāma*, and instruct the author as to what he should say, the 'Hebrew lad' also suggests that the book be dedicated to Yoshiyahu ben Yishai and to his two sons, David and Shelomo. The author accepts this suggestion and promptly composes fifty Hebrew *maqāmāt* which stylistically embody the beauty of the Hebrew language, yet are not too academic and are intended for a wide readership. The young man blesses the author, identifies himself as Ḥeber the Kenite—the hero common to all the *maqāmāt*—and promises to join the author in all his future *maqāmāt*.

The Arabic Dedication

Apart from the two Hebrew dedications, an Arabic one also appears in some of the manuscripts of *Sefer taḥkemoni*.[24]

As it was not included in the printed editions of the book, it seems to have escaped scholarly attention altogether. I think it would be worthwhile, therefore, to present the dedication in its entirety and in translation here:

[And so] I have noticed that most of the Israelite community in these lands of the East are devoid of the Hebrew language and denuded of its beautiful garments. If one of them were asked about a Hebrew word, it would seem as if he were being addressed in a foreign language. They are like those of whom it is said: 'For with stammering lips and with a strange tongue shall it be spoken to this people' (Isaiah 28:11).[25] I consider this to be one of the most terrible misfortunes to come upon our nation during our exile. This disease continues to spread among them, to the extent that most of them are never capable of putting the (Hebrew) letters together, and when they are, they are unable to understand or recognize what they have done, like those of whom it is said: 'and their children spoke half in the speech of

Ashdod, and could not speak in the Jews' language' (Nehemiah 13:24).

When I saw that virtue was held in the hand of contempt, and that the Holy Speech had been exchanged for ignorance and had come to be despised, I drew the swords of my determination (though their thoughts were notched) and begged the clouds of my creative imagination for rain (though they were empty of water). I then composed fifty Hebrew *maqāmāt*. I embellished them with pearls of the Prophets' words and studded them with precious stones of biblical phrases so that they turned out like embroidered gowns or well-ordered necklaces. Their pages shine with beauty, and their perfume is so strongly diffused that if the gardens once breathe it, they cannot but try to sniff it again. When the narrator tells his graceful stories, [even] the motionless mountains shake their shoulders (in astonishment). That is because I have included [in this collection] every amusing story and piquant tale; every enjoyable witticism and good joke(?) (lamḥa); every exhortation that moves to tears and every entertaining anecdote; and every brilliant epistle and skilful writing such as would turn the grieving lover to consolation, and the indifferent to the folly of passion. I have embellished it with a variety of light and serious words and with panegyrics, both those of good and bad effect; and I have followed the theme of obscenity to the limit. I have expressed the virtues and nobility of every generous man, and smitten the vile with the sword of mockery, now with the flat side of its blade, and now with its point.

And so this book became one of the most useful of all written books of its kind because its amusing anecdotes and charming stories are an incentive to ignorant souls and an encouragement to distracted hearts to study the Hebrew language and penetrate its wonderful secrets and extraordinary subtleties. For I have collected in it many words that are obscure and difficult to understand so that if the reader is able to understand those opaque expressions, he will have acquired a good deal of knowledge about the Hebrew language, understood many of its meanings, and erected a massive column of its structures. If he persists in reading these *maqāmāt*, Hebrew will run smoothly off the tip of his tongue, and the bridle of his eloquence and clear expression will be slackened. And with God's will we shall explain every phrase that seems difficult or opaque in this collection. [These are the titles of the *maqāmāt*, their number and the subject-matter of each and every one of them.[26]]

When the honorable head [of the community] Sadīd al-Dawla 'Abd al-Qādir, son of the heads of the Academy and the glory of the community of Aleppo, bestowed his generosity, charity, goodness and grace upon my tongue—even if my ink flowed from the oceans and if my pen were made out of trees, I would never have been able to express my thanks for his kindness—I thought it right to adorn this compilation with his name, unique as he is in his generation, and with the name of his honorable and precious son, Abu Naṣr. May the attention of God dwell with all its intensity upon their pure house, with its distinguished virtues. These are the titles of the maqāmāt according to their order. (Arabic: Drory (1991) pp. 18–19)[27]

The arguments of this dedication, which are advanced here in a rather straightforward way, can be summed up as follows: the majority of Eastern Jews have such a poor command of the Hebrew language that they can hardly join the letters together to form words, let alone understand the meaning of the words. In order to combat this ignorance, says the author, he has decided to compose fifty *maqāmāt* in Hebrew, the language of the Prophets, in a variety of enchanting literary forms (Arabic, by their description) that will attract readers and encourage them to learn the Hebrew language through reading the book. There are many awkward words and difficult expressions in it, which, when studied, will contribute to a good command of the structure and eloquence of Hebrew. The author also promises to provide a glossary of the difficult words in the *maqāmāt*.

What is so striking about these dedications is the fact that no admiration for Arabic literature, the peak of Arabic eloquence (to be expected in a work inspired by Arabic as much as this one), is expressed here, but rather discontent and unhappiness at the declining condition of the Hebrew language. Admiration for Arabic eloquence is mentioned as a seemingly popular, but nevertheless incorrect, sentiment. Al-Ḥarīzī is intrigued not so much by the idea of Arabic literary or linguistic superiority as by the Jewish cultural situation in the East, of which he became aware while visiting there and which he considered to be worrisome. In the East he discovered a Jewish public who were not as familiar with Hebrew as he expected them to be, who were uninterested in Hebrew writing and probably highly taken with Arabic culture.[28] Irritated by this situation, he raised his voice in protest; he wished to redirect the Eastern Jewish public back to their forsaken language by proving that Hebrew was no less suitable for literary and eloquent writing than Arabic and, perhaps, was even more suitable.

Why should al-Ḥarīzī have been so irritated and disturbed by this situation? Was it not common among Jews living within the Muslim culture (in the East as well as in Muslim Spain) to write more in Arabic than in Hebrew? In fact, it was customary to write in both languages while maintaining a very clear-cut division of functions between the two. Arabic served for all informative purposes, that is, the referential function of communication (to use Roman Jakobson's term in his well-known scheme)[29] while Hebrew was reserved for mainly literary-aesthetic and ceremonial functions (which were traditionally associated with one another in Jewish literature). Thus we find Jews writing (Judaeo-)Arabic Biblical and talmudic exegesis, law, theology, philosophy, linguistics, poetics, letters (official and private), but rarely poetry.[30] Poetic texts, be they liturgical or secular, in poetry or prose, were written in Hebrew, their poetic-aesthetic intention clearly marked by their highly ornamented rhetorical style and by their intensive play among semantic and non-semantic linguistic features. This division of functions was already established in Jewish writing by the first half of the tenth century, when Arabic models of writing first found their way into Jewish literature,[31] and was maintained practically throughout the entire Muslim period. The impact of this division on Jewish culture was so strong and at the same time so 'naturalized' that one could find in the same book poems written in Hebrew with introductory passages giving details of the circumstances under which each poem had been composed written in Arabic. It was therefore quite natural for Jews not to take much interest in the business of writing in Hebrew, which provided poetic registers only, when a full range of registers and literary forms was readily available in Arabic, comprising a tradition that had been viable for over two hundred years.

What was so irritating to al-Ḥarīzī, then, about such a well-established, venerable tradition of Jewish use of Arabic as the main written language? The reason for his attention will become clear only if we consider al-Ḥarīzī's cultural background and the ideological framework within which he worked during his earlier years in northern Spain and Provence. In the dedications cited above, al-Ḥarīzī addressed the poor command of Hebrew by Jews in the East. But, as already mentioned, he himself was not a native of the East but had travelled there from northern Spain, where Jewish writing was undergoing a complete revolution at the time. In northern Spain the traditional division of functions described above was in the process of breaking down, and Hebrew had begun to take over more and more functions which had traditionally been fulfilled by Arabic, gradually replacing Arabic as the major written language of Jewish literature. As a result, new literary genres were developing in Hebrew, either through translations from Arabic or in original forms of Hebrew writing.

The struggle between Hebrew and Arabic over written-language functions is clearly reflected in the prefaces added by contemporary northern Spanish Jewish authors to their Hebrew works, in which they argue that the Hebrew language is suitable for all literary purposes. In the preface to his *maqāmāt* collection, for example, Jacob Ben El'azar (late twelfth to early thirteenth century) places the argument for writing in Arabic in the mouths of 'Ishmaelite sages' who mock the Jews asking:

'Is there a language more suitable for praising or cursing, or for rousing love than the language of the Arabs? And for recounting wars and chronicles—are any words sweeter than our words?'

To which the author responds, addressing his own people:

You speak to me in beautiful words and say: 'Does not the Holy Tongue lag behind?'

75

'[Not at all!]—it puts song in the mouth of the dumb, so that he can sing fluently and not stumble, [You can] praise or curse in it, speak in rhyme[32] or tell a tale!'

And again in the following lines:

My people, what is it that you lack? / You can use my words to say whatever you want / and be sure that I will supply all your [literary] needs. / Speak with ease and do not fail, / 'put forth a riddle, and speak a parable' (Ezekiel 17:2), / read the book of tales [lit.: parables] which I have composed, / 'know therefore and discern.' (Daniel 9:25)[33]

Al-Ḥarīzī himself supplies, in the first dedication to *Sefer taḥkemoni*, a long list of literary forms which he included in his *maqāmāt*:

And I gathered together in this book many parables and sweet themes. Among them various poems and striking riddles, words of instruction, songs of friendship, proverbs of right things; words of admonition, events of the time and tidings of the years; the remembrance of death and the place of the shadow of death; words of repentance, and pardoning of guilt; the delights of love and songs of love; the betrothing of women, bridal canopy and marriage, and matters of divorce; the drunkenness of drunkards; the asceticism of ascetics; wars of heroes and events of kings; the adventures of the road; songs of praise, and supplications of prayers; ethics of the sages, and associations of the upright; the passion of lovers; gardens and hamlets; words of princes; the patter of children; the hunt of hunters; the treachery of deceivers, and the folly of fools; the slandering of scorners, the blaspheming of revilers; and wonderful songs and epistles written in a marvelous way, in order that this book may be as a garden in which are all manner of dainties and pleasant plantations. And in it each seeker will find his heart's desire and will attain of his longing sufficient for his need of that which he lacks. (pp. 36–37 [Hebrew: ed. Toporowsky (1952) p. 13])

There is, of course, an element of conventionality in this list of literary materials and forms, as it was customary among Arabic authors of the *adab* genre (and the *maqāmāt* authors followed suit)[34] to present such lists in the prefaces to their writings. Yet, put in this particular ideological setting, it is also meant to declare Hebrew an adequately literary language, in which one could, and should, address in writing any literary subject, using any literary form available. Declarations of this sort typically appeared at the time when Arabic was being displaced from its position as the main language for referential (informative) writing and Hebrew was taking over. In this particular case, the declaration prefaces a belletristic Hebrew text which actually signifies both the referential and the aesthetic functions of language. Such declarations, or even debates regarding Hebrew's adequacy as a scientific and informative language, are also found within texts actually written in Hebrew throughout the entire period.

But the most prominent sign of the breakdown of the traditional division of functions between Arabic and Hebrew is the abundance of translations into Hebrew that were produced in northern Spain and Provence during this period.[35]

Once again, it is the introductions to the translations, especially the earlier ones, which reflect a particular awareness of 'a new state' as regards the use of Hebrew for writing—an awareness different from the traditional one. The previous situation, whereby it had been customary to write virtually everything in Arabic, now seemed somewhat incomprehensible, even strange, with the result that some of the translators now felt the need to explain why previous generations of Jews had written in Arabic rather than in Hebrew. The main explanation given was that people in earlier times had failed to master Hebrew, so, if they wished to be understood, writers had no choice but to write in Arabic.

Moses Ben Ğiqaṭilla (mid-eleventh century) says in the introduction to his translation of Judah Ḥayyūğ's *Kitāb ḥurūf al-līn*:

> Forasmuch as a strange people bears rule over us, and we are swallowed up among nations of a deep speech and of a hard language [. . .], for these reasons therefore Jewish grammarians were obliged to compose their works in Arabic, this being current in the mouth of a powerful people and easy of comprehension, while Hebrew was obscure; the former clear and intelligible, the latter of doubtful meaning; as it was proper to explain the obscure by the clear, the difficult by the intelligible. The men of Zarephath, however, that dwell in the dominions of our brethren the children of Esau [i.e., the Christians], do not for the most part understand Arabic, while they dearly love and are accustomed to speak the holy tongue.[36]

Judah Ibn Tibbon (Granada 1120–Lunel 1190), in the introduction to his translation of *Farāiḏ al-qulūb* (*Duties of the Hearts*) by Baḥya Ibn Paqūda, says more bluntly:

> And after them [i.e. the sages of the Hellenistic and Byzantine periods, of the Mishnah and Talmud] most of the Geonim were in exile in the Ishmaelite kingdom [i.e. the Muslim kingdom] in Iraq, Palestine and Persia, and they spoke the Arabic language. All the Israelite communities in those places spoke that language. They composed all their commentaries on the biblical books, the orders of the Mishnah and the Talmud, in Arabic, as they did with most of their other works and with the responses to the queries that were asked of them. This is because all the people understood that language, and also because Arabic is an ample language that is adequate to every

77

subject and every speaker's and author's needs. Its idiom is
straightforward, clear, and capable of speaking to the point better on
any subject than is possible in Hebrew. For all we have of the Hebrew
language is that which is found in the books of the Bible, and this does
not suffice for all of a speaker's needs. Furthermore, they intended
their compositions to benefit the simple people, who did not have a
good command of the Holy Tongue. Therefore most of their compositions, on whatever subject they wrote, be it biblical or other studies,
were in Arabic.[37]

And in the introduction to his translation of *Sefer ha-riqma* by Ibn Ǧanāḥ,
he says:

He [Ibn Ǧanāḥ] wrote these books in Arabic, the language of the
people amongst whom he was living, because so were most of the
compositions of the Geonim and the sages in the Ishmaelite kingdom.
This is because Arabic is ample and eloquent, and its speaker finds
nothing lacking in it. But of the Holy Tongue we only have what is
found in the Bible, and that would not provide for all of a speaker's
needs. Also, most of the people do not understand Hebrew, but only
a few, and the rest of their contemporaries are familiar with Arabic,
and so they chose it for their writings. But the people of this exile of
the land of the Franks, and those of the Christian territories, do not
know Arabic; those works would be like a sealed book to them, and
would be inaccessible unless they were translated into Hebrew.[38]

In his translation of Maimonides' *Introduction to the Mishnah*, al-Ḥarīzī
voices, in an elegantly rhymed prose style, a more radical opinion:

When I understood what they [i.e. the Jews of Marseilles, who
ordered the translation from him] said, I hurried without waiting,
fulfilled their word, and translated the commentary of this master [i.e.
Maimonides] from Arabic into the Holy Tongue. I turned its lights
from the west (the direction of the setting sun) towards the east (the
direction of the rising sun). [. . .] I have translated it from the dark
language of Kedar [i.e. Arabic] into the language of gold and glory.
This is because I was jealous for the commentaries which the Torah
carried, which deserve the rights of the first born, and yet were born
on the knees of Hagar, Sarah's slave, while Sarah remained barren. In
wonderment, I asked: 'Can holiness and worldliness be joined? How
can light and darkness be united?' But the sage's [i.e. Maimonides']
intention was to give wisdom to the simple, so he wrote it in Arabic
for the sake of those who do not know the Holy Tongue but only
Hagarite [i.e. Arabic], and their language is 'half in the speech of
Ashdod and [they] could not speak in the Jews' language' (Nehemiah
13:24). So I made an effort, took courage and removed foreign
expressions from this holy treatise, so it left a prison to become a
king; it washed in pure water, took off its [old] clothes and put on
[new] ones. I translated its words into eloquent phrases and
sweetened it with the sweetness of the Holy Tongue.[39]

Al-Ḥarīzī no longer wishes to be understanding, or sympathetic, toward a practice so natural to Jewish literature in the East and in Muslim Spain, that is, using Arabic to write texts which bear upon the sacred scriptures or the Jewish codes of law. For him this practice is unacceptable, impossible, and obsolete and must be modified and corrected. By translating into Hebrew Jewish works originally written in Arabic al-Ḥarīzī feels that he is enabling these works to revert to their 'true' language, thus restoring the nation's lost treasures.

Judah al-Ḥarīzī as well as Judah Ibn Tibbon and his son Samuel (Provence, c.1160–c.1230), were among the first translators into Hebrew, as were also Abraham Bar Ḥiyya, Moses Ben Ǧiqaṭilla, Joseph Qimḥi, Jacob Ben El'azar, almost all of whom were emigrants to northern Spain and Provence. They translated mainly Jewish Arabic works, and sometimes the same work would be translated by more than one translator, as in the case of Maimonides' *Guide for the Perplexed*, which was translated by both al-Ḥarīzī and Samuel Ibn Tibbon. It may be typical of the vanguard to feel an (almost compulsive) need to comment frequently on their profession, thereby legitimizing it over and over again. Both al-Ḥarīzī and Judah Ibn Tibbon did so, as did Judah Ibn Tibbon's son Samuel, while at the same time they contested and criticized each other's work. We are thus afforded a fairly well-rounded view of how the translators themselves perceived the task of translating from Arabic into Hebrew at the time. This commentary reveals that al-Ḥarīzī and the Tibbons each viewed their mission quite differently: al-Ḥarīzī's overall attitude was one of unequivocal acceptance of the Hebrew-for-writing ideology, and he was in full accord with his mission. He seemed happy to convert into Hebrew any text he may have been asked to, convinced that by so doing he was simply reclaiming what had originally been there to begin with, but which had, over the ages, been lost or even 'stolen'. He sought to prove that the Hebrew language could be appropriately used in a wide range of written forms, so over and above translating, he also wrote his own *maqāmāt*, comprising a handbook of Hebrew styles intended to encourage Eastern Jews to use Hebrew as a written language. This is why he declares his intention to provide the reader of the *maqāmāt* with a glossary.

The Tibbons, on the other hand, regarded their work very differently. Judah Ibn Tibbon, for instance, expresses explicit doubts about the very possibility of translating into Hebrew and is sceptical about the quality of such translations (Zifroni 1949 [1928]:58). He addresses the difficulties facing the translator, discussing the fact that Arabic is an 'ample' language, while Hebrew is 'short' (i.e. limited) and sparse. His attitude movingly attests to the harsh difficulties facing an Andalusian newcomer to northern Spain who was accustomed to writing in Arabic and was forced to switch to Hebrew, undertaking to transform it into a language capable of accommodating topics for which in fact it had no working registers.[40]

Debates and discussions concerning the functions of Hebrew, its ability to supply a full range of literary modes of expression, and specific modes of translation, were all part of a single overall process: the creation of a new Jewish literature. Since Arabic literature still retained its high status in northern Spain and Provence, the construction of this new Jewish literature was accomplished mainly by borrowing from the Arabic literature. This is why northern Spanish Jewish literature resembles Andalusian literature up to a point and is usually regarded as a direct extension of it. But in fact the paradigm on which the new Jewish literature in Christian Spain was based was quite different from the dominant paradigm of Jewish literature during the Muslim period. The foremost innovation was the production of the new literature mainly (indeed, almost exclusively) in Hebrew. Writing in Hebrew was accompanied by ideological declarations which assigned to Hebrew writing the role of marking a particular collective or ethnic identity, that could be called 'national'.

What were the reasons for imposing this new role on Hebrew at this specific point in time and place? To what extent did the local environment motivate the use of vernacular languages (such as Castilian and Romance) in writing or the renaissance in Arabic-Latin translations introduce new literary practices into Jewish society, practices to be performed in Hebrew? These questions are still open and remain to be answered. Yet one thing does seem clear: if not for the prevailing cultural climate in northern Spain and Provence at the time, al-Ḥarīzī would most probably never have written his Hebrew *maqāmāt*. For although they seem so Arabic in character, as products of the Jewish-Arabic culture they would have been most unlikely, particularly in the East.[41] There would have been no reason to disturb the traditional Arabic-Hebrew division of functions prevalent during the Muslim period, thereby bringing about new forms of writing in Hebrew.[42] In other words, it took a non-Muslim and non-Arabic cultural atmosphere, that of Christian Spain, to produce a literary work so notably Arabic-Hebrew in nature.

NOTES

1. The present paper forms part of a project concerning Jewish-Arabic cultural contacts in twelfth- and thirteenth-century Christian Spain and Provence. A larger version of this study, entitled 'Literary Contacts and Where to Find Them: on Arabic Literary Models in Medieval Jewish Literature', will be published in *Poetics Today* 14:2 (1993).

   In the following notes, in cases where a book has been reprinted page numbers refer to the latest edition of that book unless otherwise stated.

2. For further information on the *maqāmāt* genre see (to mention only a few references out of quite ample literature) W.J. Prendergast, *The Maqāmāt of Badī' al-Zamān al-Hamadhānī* (London and Dublin: Curzon Press, 1915, repr. 1973); Régis Blachère et Pierre Masnou, *Al-Hamadhānī, Maqāmāt (Séances): choisies et traduites de l'arabe avec une étude sur le genre* (Paris: Librairie C. Klinsieck, 1957); Abdelfattah Kilito, *Les Séances* (Paris: Sinbad, 1983); James T. Monroe, *The Art of Badī' al-Zamān al-Hamadhānī as Picaresque Narrative* (Beirut: American University of Beirut, 1983); A.F.L. Beeston, 'al-Hamadhānī, al-Ḥarīrī and the *maqāmāt* Genre' in T.M. Johnstone *et al.* (eds) *The Cambridge History of Arabic Literature: 'Abbasid Belles-Lettres* (Cambridge: Cambridge University Press, 1990) pp. 125–35. On the *maqāma*'s fictional model, see R. Drory, 'Introducing Fictionality into Classical Arabic Literature: the *Maqāma*' *Studies in Arabic and Comparative Poetics* (forthcoming).

3. See Moshe Idel, 'Who was the translator of R. Moses ibn Ezra's *'Arugat ha-bosem?*' *Qiryat Sefer* 51 (1975–6) pp. 484–7 (Hebrew); Shraga Abramson, 'A Note on the Article by M. Idel (*Leshonenu* 34 p. 484) (Hebrew)' *Qiryat Sefer* 51 (1975–6) p. 712. (Hebrew).

4. L. Schlossberg and S. Scheyero (eds) Moses Maimonides, *Moreh Nebukim* (London 1851, repr. Warsaw 1904).

5. M.D. Rabinovitz (ed.) Moses Maimonides, *Hakdamot le-perush ha-mishna* trans. Judah al-Ḥarīzī (Jerusalem: Mossad ha-Rab Kuk, 1960).

6. According to al-Ḥarīzī's own testimony; see Y. Toporowsky (ed.) Judah al-Ḥarīzī, *Taḥkemoni* (Tel Aviv: Maḥbarot le-Sifrut, 1952) p. 406.

7. A.S. Halkin (ed.) Moses Maimonides, *Ma'amar teḥiyat ha-metim* trans. Judah al-Ḥarīzī, *Kobez Al Yad* (*Minora Manuscripta Hebraica*) 9 (1989) pp. 129–150.

8. M. Grossberg (ed.) 'Ali ibn Ruḍwan, *Igeret Ali Ha-Ishmaeli* (London, 1900).

9. A. Loewenthal (ed.) Ḥunayn Ibn Isḥāq, *Sefer musre haphilosophim* [*Sinnsprüche der Philosophen*], trans. Judah al-Ḥarīzī (Frankfurt am Main: J. Kauffmann, 1896).

10. A. Jellinek (ed.) Galenus, *Dialog über die Seele,* trans. Judah al-Ḥarīzī (Leipzig: C.L. Fritzsche, 1852).

11. Jefim (Ḥayyim) Schirmann, *Hebrew Poetry in Spain and in Provence* (Jerusalem: Mossad Biyalik and Tel Aviv: Devir, 1961) III, 98 (Hebrew).

12. See Abraham M. Habermann, '*Sefer Taḥkemoni* of rabbi Jehuda al-Ḥarīzī' *Sinai* 31 (1952) p. 113 (Hebrew).

13. The work, only part of which has survived, is called *Maḥberot itiel*. For modern editions, see Th. Chenery (ed.) al-Qāsim b. 'Ali al-Ḥarīrī, *Maḥberot itiel, trans. Judah al-Ḥarīzī* (London, 1872) and the edition of Y. Peretz (Tel Aviv: Maḥbarot le-Sifrut, 1951); cf. Samuel M. Stern, 'An unpublished *Maqāma* by al-Ḥarīzī' in J.G. Weiss (ed.) *Papers of the Institute of Jewish Studies, London* (Jerusalem: The Magnes Press, 1964) I, 186.

14. For modern editions, see S.I. Kaempf (ed.) Judah al-Ḥarīzī, *Die ersten Makamen aus dem Taḥkemoni oder Divan des Charisi nebst dessen Vorrede* (Berlin, 1845); P. de Lagarde (ed.) *Taḥkemoni* (Göttingen, 1883, repr. Hanover, 1924); and editions by A. Kaminka (Warsaw: Schuldberg, 1899) and Y. Toporowsky (Tel Aviv: Maḥbarot le-Sifrut, 1952), the last-cited used for quotation in this paper. For an English translation see: *The Taḥkemoni of Judah al-Ḥarīzī*, trans. V.E. Reichert (Jerusalem: V.E. Cohen's Press Publishers, 1965–73).

15. Hartwig Hirschfeld, 'Fragment of an Unknown Work by Judah al-Ḥarīzī' *Jewish Quarterly Review* 16 (1903) pp. 683–8, 693–7; Stern, 'An unpublished *Maqāma*', *Papers of the Institute of Jewish Studies, London* (1964) I, 186–201; *idem.*, 'A New Description by Judah al-Ḥarīzī of his Tour to Iraq' *Sefunot: Annual for Research on the Jewish Communities in the East* 8 (1964) pp. 145–56 (Hebrew); *idem.*, 'Rabbi Judah al-Ḥarīzī be Shivḥo Shel ha-Rambam' in M. Zohori and A. Tartakover (eds) *Hagut ivrit be-eropa* (*Studies on Jewish Themes by Contemporary European Scholars*) (Tel Aviv: Yavne, 1969) pp. 91–103; Yehuda Ratzaby, 'An Arabic Maqāma by al-Ḥarīzī' *Criticism and Interpretation* 15 (1980) pp. 5–51 (Hebrew); *idem.*, 'An Arabic *Maqāma* by al-Ḥarīzī' *Criticism and Interpretation* 23 (1988) pp. 51–5 (Hebrew).
16. This thesis is most prominently exemplified in Shlomo D. Goitein, 'Ha-Maqāma veha-Maḥberet' *Maḥbarot le-Sifrut* 5 [1] (1951) pp. 26–40.
17. See, for example, Jefim (Ḥayyim) Schirmann, *Die hebräische Übersetzung der Maqamen des Ḥarīrī* (Frankfurt am Main: J. Kaufmann, 1930); *idem.*, 'Le-ḥeqer meqorotav shel Sefer taḥkemoni li-Yehuda al-Ḥarīzī' *Studies in the History of Hebrew Poetry and Drama* (Jerusalem: Mossad Bialik, 1979) I, 369–74; Aisik Percikowitsch, *al-Ḥarīzī als Übersetzer der Makamen al-Ḥarīrīs* (Munich: B. Heller, 1932); Samuel M. Stern, 'Meqorah ha-'arabi shel maqāmat ha-tarnegol' *Tarbiz* 17 (1946) pp. 87–100; Abraham A. Lavi, 'Comparative Study of al-Ḥarīrī's Maqāmāt and Their Hebrew Translation by al-Ḥarīzī' (University of Michigan, Ann Arbor: PhD dissertation, 1984); Judith Dishon, 'On the Source of Judah al-Ḥarīzī's Twenty-First *Maqāma* in the Taḥkemoni' *Criticism and Interpretation* 13–14 (1979) pp. 9–26 (Hebrew); Joseph Dana, 'Concerning the Source of Taḥkemoni' *Tarbiz* 44 (1975) pp. 172–81 (Hebrew); *idem.*, 'Al-Hamaḏānī as a Source for Rabbi Judah al-Ḥarīzī' *Dappim* (*Research in Literature*) 1 (1984) pp. 79–89 (Hebrew); Yehuda Ratzaby, 'On the Source of Yehuda al-Ḥarīzī's Taḥkemoni' *Tarbiz* 26 (1957) pp. 424–39 (Hebrew).
18. Cf. Abraham S. Halkin, 'The Medieval Jewish Attitude Towards Hebrew' in A. Altmann *Biblical And Other Studies* (Cambridge Mass.: Harvard University Press, 1963) pp. 234–5.
19. In the Hebrew dedications of *Sefer taḥkemoni* the following names are mentioned: Shemuel ben al-Barqūlī and his brothers, Yosef and Ezra, of Wāsiṭ; Yoshiyahu ben Yishai of Damascus; Shemuel ben Nissim of Aleppo and Shemaryah ben David of Yemen. In the Arabic dedication Sadīd al-Dawla 'Abd al-Qādir of Aleppo and his son, Abū Naṣr, are named (see Abraham M. Habermann, '*Sefer Taḥkemoni* of rabbi Jehuda al-Ḥarīzī' *Sinai* 31 (1952) p. 114 (Hebrew); *idem.*, '*Sefer Taḥkemoni*'s Dedications and its List of Contents' *Maḥbarot le-Sifrut* 5 [2–3] (1953) pp. 39–46 (Hebrew).
20. Toporowsky (ed.) Judah al-Ḥarīzī, *Taḥkemoni* (1952) pp. 4–18; English translation: *The Taḥkemoni of Judah al-Ḥarīzī*, trans. Reichert (1965–1973) pp. 23–43, the latter used for quotation in the body of this paper and cited by page number alone.
21. *Ibid.* pp. 19–30; English translation: *ibid.* pp. 44–58.
22. Joshua Blau, 'The Arabic Introduction of "Sefer Taḥkemoni" and its Hebrew Translation' *Maḥbarot le-Sifrut* 5 (1953) pp. 47–9 (Hebrew); Rina Drory, 'The Hidden Context: on Literary Products of Tri-Cultural Contacts in the Middle Ages' *Pe'amin* (*Studies in Oriental Jewry*) 46–7 (1991) pp. 18–20 (Hebrew).
23. See n. 21 above.

24. This dedication was first published by Blau ('Arabic Introduction of "Sefer Taḥkemoni" *Maḥbarot le-Sifrut* 5 (1953) pp. 47–9) as an appendix to Habermann ('*Sefer Taḥkemoni*'s Dedications' *Maḥbarot le-Sifrut* 5 [2–3] (1953) pp. 39–46) from Bodley MS Poc. 192 (Adolf Neubauer, *Catalogue of the Hebrew Manuscripts in the Bodleian Library and in the College Libraries of Oxford* (Oxford: Clarendon Press, 1886) no. 1977), with a Hebrew translation. For a revised publication and Hebrew translation, see Drory (n. 22 above). Part of it is also to be found in Bodley MS Opp. Add. 4o, 156 (Neubauer, *Catalogue of Hebrew Manuscripts* no. 2517), where it is preceded by a Hebrew dedication to 'our master the Nagid Shemaryah' from 'the land of Yemen', and in Bodley Heb. MS d. 57 (Adolf Neubauer and Arthur E. Cowley, *Catalogue of the Hebrew Manuscripts in the Bodleian Library and in the College Libraries of Oxford* (Oxford: Clarendon Press, 1896–1906) no. 2745).

25. All of the English translations of Biblical verses are quoted from the *Jewish Publication Society of America* (*JPS*) edition of the English Bible.

26. This sentence clearly belongs at the end of the introduction, and indeed it is repeated there.

27. This translation, like all others in this paper, unless otherwise credited, is my own. I am most grateful to Professor Raymond Scheindlin, who was kind enough to read the draft translations of both the Arabic and the Hebrew texts and was extremely helpful in finding appropriate English equivalents for many phrases which were ambiguous and difficult in the original.

28. Testimony to the fact that Eastern Jews read also Arabic *maqāmāt* is provided by a Geniza fragment of Ibn Buṭlān's *Risālat da'wat al-aṭṭibā '*, found in the Taylor-Schechter collection in Cambridge. See Colin F. Baker, 'Medical Examination at the Dinner Table' *Geniza Fragments* 20 (1990) p. 2.

29. See Roman Jakobson 'Linguistics and Poetics' in *Selected Writings*, vol. 3 (The Hague: Mouton, 1981) pp. 18–51; here, pp. 21–8. Jakobson addresses the basic functions of verbal communication in general; his definition of the referential and the poetic functions are applied in my discussion to written texts only.

30. Poetry written by Jews in Arabic (using Arabic, not Hebrew, characters) was considered to be Muslim, not Jewish, literature. It thus survived mainly in Arabic literary anthologies, not in Jewish compilations. See Rina Drory, *The Emergence of Jewish-Arabic Literary Contacts at the Beginning of the Tenth Century* (Tel Aviv: Ha-kibutz Ha-meuḥad, 1988) (Hebrew) pp. 52–3; *idem*., '"Words Beautifully Put": Hebrew versus Arabic in Tenth-Century Jewish Literature' in J. Blau and S.C. Reif (eds) *Geniza Research after Ninety Years: The Case of Judaeo-Arabic* (Cambridge: Cambridge University Press, 1992) pp. 53–66.

31. Not without Hebrew competing with Arabic over the referential function; for a full discussion of this matter, see Drory, *Emergence of Jewish-Arabic Literary Contacts* (1988), pp. 41–54, and '"Words Beautifully Put"', *Geniza Research after Ninety Years: The Case of Judaeo-Arabic* (1992) pp. 53–66.

32. Literally, 'ask a riddle'; but judging by the medieval use of such phrases as *mašal ve-ḥidda* and *mašal u-melitza*, and by contemporary Biblical exegesis of such phrases, it seems that medieval Hebrew writers held the phrase to designate 'a (fictional) narrative, instructive or amusing', and used it in the sense of 'a tale', 'an anecdote', and quite often 'a rhymed piece of prose'.

33. Jefim (Ḥayyim) Schirmann, 'The Love Stories of Ja'aqob Ben El'azar' *Yedi'ot*

ha-Makhon le-Ḥeqer ha-Šira ha-'Ivrit (*Studies of the Research Institute for Hebrew Poetry in Jerusalem*) 5 (1939) pp. 216–17 (Hebrew); Yonah David, *The Love Stories of Jacob Ben Eleazar* (Tel Aviv: Ramot Publishing & Tel Aviv University, 1992–93) pp. 13–4 (Hebrew).

34. Cf. the introduction to al-Ḥarīrī's *Maqāmāt* (al-Qāsim b. 'Ali al-Ḥarīrī, *Maqāmāt* (Cairo, 1929) p. 6).

35. See Moritz Steinschneider, *Die hebräischen Übersetzungen des Mittelalter und die Juden als Dolmetscher* (Berlin: H. Itzkowski, 1893, repr. Gräz: Akademische Druck und Verlagsamstalt, 1956); Abraham S. Halkin, 'Translation and Translators (Medieval)' *Encyclopaedia Judaica* (Jerusalem: Keter Publishing House, 1971) vol. 15, pp. 1318–29.

36. J.W. Nutt (ed.) Judah Ḥayyūǧ, *Two Treatises on Verbs Containing Feeble and Double Letters by R. Jehuda Hayug of Fez, translated into Hebrew from the Original Arabic by R. Moses Gikatilia of Cordova; to which is added the Treatise on Punctuation by the same author, translated by Aben Ezra* (London and Berlin, 1870, repr. Jerusalem 1985) pp. 1–2 [English section]; p. 1 [Hebrew section].

37. A. Zifroni (ed.) Baḥya Ibn Paqūda, *Sefer ḥobot ha-lebabot* (*Farā'iḍ al-qulūb*), translated into Hebrew by Judah Ibn Tibbon (Jerusalem: J. Junovitch, 1928, repr. Tel Aviv: Maḥbarot le-Sifrut, 1949) pp. 56–57 (Hebrew).

38. M. Vilenski (ed.) Jonah Ibn Ǧanāḥ, *Sefer ha-riqma*, translated by Judah Ibn Tibbon, (Berlin, 1929, repr. Jerusalem: ha-Akademya la-Lashon ha-'Ibrit, 1964) p. 4 (Hebrew). Cf. on the same topic Joseph Qimḥi (c.1105–c.1170), who also explains that it was from their Muslim neighbours that the Jews learned the importance of being aware of one's own language and taking measures to preserve and cultivate it (H.J. Mathews (ed.) Joseph Kimhi [Kimchi], *Sefer ha-galuj* (Berlin: Mekize Nirdamin, 1887) p. 3); cf. Y. Rittenberg (ed.) David Kimhi, *Sefer mikhlol* (Lyck, 1862, repr. Jerusalem, 1952) p. 1. English translation and annotations: W. Chomsky, *David Kimhi's Hebrew Grammar 'Mikhlol'* (New York: Bloch Pub. Co., 1958).

39. M.D. Rabinovitz (ed.) Moses Maimonides, *Hakdamot le-perush ha-mishna*, trans. Judah al-Ḥarīzī (Jerusalem: Mossad ha-Rab Kuk, 1960) p. 4 (Hebrew).

40. Cf. Abraham S. Halkin, 'The Medieval Jewish Attitude Towards Hebrew' in A. Altmann (ed.) *Biblical And Other Studies* (Cambridge Mass.: Harvard University Press, 1963) pp. 239–41.

41. The different attitudes toward Hebrew writing found in northern Spain and the East are best illustrated by al-Ḥarīzī himself, who, in the preface to *Sefer taḥkemoni* describes how he was asked while still in Spain to translate al-Ḥarīrī's work into Hebrew: 'For the nobles of Spain, when they heard the words of the Arab's book [al-Ḥarīrī's *Maqāmāt*], marvelled at them. And they sought of me while I was still among them to translate this book for them and I was not able to turn them away' (p. 39). But when he composed his own Hebrew *Maqāmāt* in the East, he had to 'seek of the patrons of the world, from Egypt to Babylon, [for] one with whose name I might adorn the book and it would be sealed with his seal. I searched him among the leaders of the time, and sought for him but found him not, and no one answered me when I called' (p. 41), until at last a patron was found.

42. The fact that while still in the East, but apparently after he had composed *Sefer taḥkemoni* (Stern, 'An unpublished *Maqāma*', *Papers of the Institute of Jewish Studies, London* (1964) vol. 1, p. 199), al-Ḥarīzī also wrote a Judaeo-Arabic *Maqāma*, seems to indicate that he himself realized that there was no

84

great public for Hebrew writing there and that he would have to write in Arabic in order to make his voice heard. Explaining why he wrote in Arabic, he notes, 'When I visited Baghdad the Jewish community there turned its back on me and treated me rudely. I have therefore decided to compose a *Maqāma* in Arabic about them, in which I will expose some of their hidden feats . . .; let me quote here from this *Maqāma*, so that it serve to commemorate what they have done . . .' (*idem.*, 'A New Description by Judah al-Ḥarīzī of his Tour to Iraq' *Sefunot: Annual for Research on the Jewish Communities in the East* 8 (1964) pp. 150–1 (Hebrew)). His explanation clearly echoes the argument used about two hundred years earlier, when Arabic first began competing with Hebrew for the referential function of Jewish writing, namely that one should write in Arabic if one wanted the message to be clearly conveyed and understood by all (cf. Drory, *Emergence of Jewish-Arabic Literary Contacts* (1988), pp. 46–8, and Drory ' "Words Beautifully Put" ', *Geniza Research after Ninety Years: The Case of Judaeo-Arabic* (1992) pp. 53–66. Such an argument would accompany, needless to say, a refutation or a piece of satirical writing.

Chapter 3

The Complaint of Venus:
Chaucer and de Graunson

HELEN PHILLIPS

The so-called *Complaint of Venus* is a translation by Chaucer of three balades by Oton de Graunson (c.1340–1397).[1] Four of the ten textual authorities for Chaucer's poem have the title *The Compleynte of Venus*,[2] but there is no certainty that Chaucer intended any connection with Venus. Most of the authorities[3] place this work after the poem usually known as *The Complaint of Mars*,[4] often with rubrics which, albeit in a varying and confusing manner, present the two poems as a composite work, *The Complaint of Mars and Venus*.[5]

One manuscript, by John Shirley, states that the poem was linked to 'my lady of york' and 'my lord of huntyngdon',[6] and this was taken by some scholars, in the past, to indicate that *The Complaint of Venus* had some topical meaning in relation to a court love affair.[7]

All this provides problems for interpreting Chaucer's translation from de Graunson, and offers a variety of contexts in which the poem can be read. We do not know whether to take *The Complaint of Venus* as a counterpart to *The Complaint of Mars*, or as an independent poem whose title and speaker are unknown, or as a covert reference to a contemporary scandal. The various and contradictory statements that accompany it in different texts may be due to the fancy or confusion of fifteenth century scribes or editors, who had a liking for suggesting narrative contexts for lyrics.[8] If we take it as it stands, disregarding any titles or rubrics, the speaker is an unidentified woman who praises the man she loves and declares that she will persist in that love despite the unhappiness it brings. Four times Chaucer's poem mentions jealousy as a particular problem (whereas de Graunson only refers to it once), but there are no other clues to the lady's situation.

Among the many amorous complaints composed by de Graunson, there are five balades, all spoken by a male lover,[9] which in two of the four

86

extant manuscripts are presented together as a set. One manuscript entitles them: *Les cinq balades ensievans*.[10] Chaucer translates three of them, the first, fourth and fifth when they are presented as a set, and he changes the speaker to a woman. He also adds an *envoy*, in his own voice, addressed to 'princes' (or in two Shirley manuscripts to 'princesse'):[11]

> Princes, resseyueth this compleynt in gre,
> Vnto your excelent benignite
> Direct aftir my litel suffisaunce.
> For Elde, that in my spirit dulleth me,
> Hath of endyting al the subtilte
> Welnyghe bereft out of my remembraunce,
> And eke to me hit ys a grete penaunce
> Syth ryme in Englisshe hath such skarsete,
> To folowe worde by worde the curiosite
> Of Graunson, floure of hem that make in Fraunce.
>
> (ll. 73–82)

There are clearly some general questions about Chaucer's initial decision to translate these three balades. If *The Complaint of Mars* and *The Complaint of Venus* form a composite work, why did Chaucer choose to use a translation for the second part of that work? After all, de Graunson's three poems do not fit Venus in any particularly obvious way, and Chaucer showed himself quite ready to compose a complaint of his own for Mars. By using the translation Chaucer lost the opportunity to design a *Complaint of Venus* that was in style and content a true companion-piece to *Mars*, which is a complex poem, containing among other things an astrological allegory; *Venus* makes no reference to any of the more complex or idiosyncratic elements in *Mars*. Furthermore, why did Chaucer choose these three particular balades out of de Graunson's vast oeuvre of love lyrics or, indeed, out of the set of *cinq balades* (if it is a set), and why only three? Mars' complaint in *Mars* has fifteen stanzas, forming five sections, whereas *Venus* has only nine stanzas, forming three sections. Choosing to translate these balades also necessitated altering poems originally designed for a male speaker so that they could express the feelings of a woman.

There are further questions: was the decision to make the translation dependent on an occasion? An occasion when de Graunson was present? Who were the 'princes' mentioned in the *envoy*? Were the speakers in each of the *complaints* meant to represent a double identity: Mars and Venus but also the figures in some contemporary situation? Were the two poems intended for dramatic presentation, or as part of a dramatic, or semi-dramatic, performance (bearing in mind that the boundaries between dramatic and non-dramatic literature were less distinct than in modern literature)?

These are many questions. In this paper I would like to concentrate on examining, *worde by worde* at times,[12] the changes Chaucer made as translator. These changes may have something to do with *skarsete* of rhyme in English, but they appear to have at least as much to do with the process, for a male translator, of reconceiving what de Graunson had written for a male speaker as the expression of a woman's feelings. We may never know why Chaucer altered the speaker's sex, but one result is clear: by both translating and transposing the speaker's sex he entered doubly into a sphere of dependence and subservience.

One of the most oft-quoted comments in studies of translation is Hilaire Belloc's:

> The art of translation is a subsidiary art, and derivative. On this account it has never been granted the dignity of original work . . .[13]

Lori Chamberlain is one of several recent critics who have pursued the implications of this concept of translation (and there are many) for feminism. In 'Gender and the Metaphorics of Translation' (1988)[14] she sees traditional attitudes to translation and original work, and the language used to differentiate them, as parallels to, and agents of, patriarchal authority, power and legitimation. She examines 'the distinction between writing and translation—marking, that is, the one to be original and "masculine", the other to be derivative and "feminine"'.[15] The metaphors employed to describe translation frequently present it as an analogue to the unequal relations of male and female. Thus translation is dependent, obedient, subservient, faithful or unfaithful, artificial or potentially duplicitous, and essentially lacking creativity. On the other hand, the translator may exploit, invade or appropriate the source text.[16] (The metaphors may occasionally be mixed, just as the uneasy patriarchal perception of sexual and social relationships is multiple and often self-contradictory.)

Chaucer's decision to present a woman in love with a man in *The Complaint of Venus*, by translating and transposing an original designed for a male speaker in love with a woman, provides an opportunity to see how he approaches the differentiation of masculine and feminine, as well as the role of the translator in contrast to that of an original writer.

When we compare de Graunson's first stanza with Chaucer's,

> Il n'est confort qui tant de bien me face
> Quant je ne puis a ma dame parler
> Comme d'avoir temps, loizir, et espace
> De longuement en sa valour penser

5   Et ses doulz fais feminins recorder
    Dedans mon cuer, c'est ma vie par m'ame,
    Ne je ne truis nul homme qui m'en blasme,
    Car chascun a joye de li loer.

    Ther nys so high comfort to my plesaunce
    When that I am in eny heuynesse
    As for to haue leyser of remembraunce
    Vpon the manhod and the worthynesse
5   Vpon the trouthe and on the stidfastnesse
    Of him whos I am al while I may dure
    Ther oght blame me no creature
    For euery wight preiseth his gentilesse.

we notice de Graunson piling up nouns in l. 3 to represent the male speaker's own situation: 'temps, loizir, et espace'. A choice for him between two alternative states, 'puis . . . parler' l. 2, and '[puis] . . . penser' l. 4, is elaborated in ll. 3–4 by the insertion of 'de longuement' and the three nouns. In contrast, Chaucer gives his female speaker only one noun, 'leyser' l. 3, in the position corresponding to the three: 'leyser' corresponds to 'temps, loizir, et espace' and 'of remembraunce' corresponds to 'de longuement . . . penser'. As if to redistribute the lexical largesse withheld here from the female speaker, and to reinstate the syntactic structure of the repeated nouns, Chaucer gives her male beloved four analogously piled-up nouns: 'Vpon the manhod and the worthynesse,/Vpon the trouthe and on the stidfastnesse' in ll. 4–5, and adds a fifth, 'gentilesse', in l. 8.

In contrast, de Graunson's female beloved has only two attributive nouns, 'valour' and 'fais'. The latter noun, admittedly, is qualified by the adjectives 'doulz . . . feminins', but this is not merely a question of counting words; it is also a question of the type of words and their content. Both poets' language suggests it is possible to discern an interestingly wide range of attributes in a man, but only a narrow range in a woman. A man's state, whether he is the lover, in the French, or the beloved, in the English, is granted more attributes and more individual elements. The verbal structures suggest that a man has more distinct aspects—more nouns—than a woman.[17]

Similar things happen in stanza 2, but before looking at them it is worth noting that in the stylistic choices of stanza 1 de Graunson's male speaker is allowed more activity than Chaucer's female one. In lines 2 and 4 he has the alternatives of two contrasting actions, one of them powerful ('puis . . . parler') and the other not ('penser'); both verbs. Corresponding to this pair, Chaucer's woman has only two powerless states, and no alternatives: to be 'in heuynesse' and at the same time to have 'remembraunce';

both are states rather than actions, both nouns. To achieve this Chaucer destroys de Graunson's neat reference to those traditional twins of medieval love-language, 'douz penser' and 'douz parler'.[18] Even de Graunson's man's passive contemplation is couched in more active terms: he can 'recorder/Dedans mon cuer' the images. Though his state is one of enforced inactivity it is described in terms of more content-verbs than we find in Chaucer's translation: 'face', 'puis . . . parler', 'penser', 'recorder', 'truis', 'blasme', 'loer', versus 'may dure', 'oght blame', 'preiseth'.

Stanza 2:
Il a en lui beaute, bonte, et grace
10 Plus que nulz homs ne saroit deviser:
C'est grant eur quant en si po despace
Dieu a voulu tous les biens assambler;
Honneur la veult sur toutes honnorer;
Onques ne vy si plaisant jeune dame
15 De toutes gens avoir si noble fame,
Car chascun a joye de li loer.

In him ys bounte, wysdom, and governaunce,
10 Wel more than eny manes witte can gesse
For grace hath wolde so ferforthe hym avaunce
That of knyghthode he is parfite richesse.
Honour honoureth him for his noblesse.
Therto so well hath formed him Nature
15 That I am his for euer, I him assure;
For euery wight preysith his gentilesse.

In the first line de Graunson's lady has 'beaute', 'bonte', and 'grace'. Chaucer's man has 'bounte', 'wysdom', and 'governaunce'. The latter are more powerful qualities, and 'wysdom' and 'governaunce' denote social power and confer maturity and respect; and, whereas the trio 'beaute', 'bonte' and 'grace' is well suited to be advantageous to the lady's male wooer (they see her in terms of what he wants; though grammatically attributed to the lady they are psychologically more descriptive of his desire), 'wysdom' and 'governaunce' have their own spheres of power and extend outside the worlds of love and the lover's self-projection. (Note how the different triads alter the connotations of bonte/bounte.) Chaucer's man is accorded yet more words, in addition to 'bounte', 'wysdom', and 'governaunce'—words that suggest social power and dynamism: 'knyghthode', 'parfite richesse', 'noblesse', 'gentilesse', and 'wolde so ferforthe hym avaunce', introducing themes of volition and forward movement.

Corresponding to all these de Graunson's woman is 'plaisant', l. 14. In stanza 3 she is further identified through the qualities of being able to give entertainment and pleasure to others:

> Ou qu'elle soit bien fait et mal efface;
> Moult bien li siet le rire et le jouer;
> Son cuer esbat et les autres solace
> 20 Si liement qu'on ne le doit blasmer;
> De li veoir ne se puet nulz lasser;
> Son regart vault tous les biens d'un royaume;
> Il samble bien qu'elle est tresnoble femme,
> Car chascun a joye de li loer.

> And, notwithstondyng al his suffisaunce,
> His gentil hert ys of so grete humblesse
> To me in worde, in werk, in contenaunce,
> 20 And me to serue is al his besynesse
> That I am set in verrey sikirnesse,
> Thus oght I blesse wel myn aventure,
> Sith that him list me seruen and honoure;
> For euery wight preiseth his gentilesse.

Chaucer transposes the beloved's capacities to amuse and be pleasant into the far more powerful role of protecting. The man graciously chooses ('him list') to 'seruen and honoure'. The language of ll. 17–18 suggests a bending down from the great height: in a man of 'al his suffisaunce' this is 'so grete humblesse'. There is a curiously restrained response in the syntax of the woman he has thus deigned to honour: 'I am set . . .' l. 21, and 'Thus oght I . . .' l. 22. She, the 'I' in these constructions, is given very little room for manoeuvre, constricted by a passive and an 'oght'. She may be rapturous about this love, but it is a very constrained rapture.

The translation of the second balade involves fewer changes of this kind. This may be because of de Graunson's original wording is scarcely gender-specific at all. This balade is dominated by the expression of contrasts and reversals, as the refrain, 'Tout a rebours de ce qu'on veult trouver', says. Only ll. 43–4 express a specifically masculine point of view, and Chaucer omits this reference entirely:

> 41 Pour .j. court temps le geu est aggreable,
> Mais trop par est encombreux a user,
> Et, ja soit il a dames honnorable,
> 44 A leurs servans est trop grief a porter.

> 41 A lytel tyme his yift ys agreable
> But ful encombrouse is the vsynge
> For subtil Jelosie the deceyvable
> 44 Ful often tyme causeth desturbynge

There may be even something of a sense of potential ultimatum here from de Graunson's man: if this sort of thing went on it might become 'trop par . . . encombreux'. It may elevate women, but it is 'trop grief' for their 'servans' (variant 'amis') to bear.

Chaucer changed 'geu' to 'yift'. Perhaps he felt it was impossible to conceive a woman having the psychological complexity to enjoy, even briefly, an ambiguous pleasure, a game, in frustrated love. For the woman, rather than participation in an intriguing game, we have instead the metaphor of passive reception of a 'yift'. We seem to see the same inability to concede that a female heart could experience anything as interesting as a bitter-sweet emotion in stanza 8, where de Graunson's male lover experiences 'douloureuse' pain which is also 'joieuse' to him, but Chaucer's woman only experiences monotone pain, and puts up with it: 'for no peyn wille I not sey nay', l. 63. Even in a poem about frustrations—this second balade whose three stanzas are constructed on the idea of the frustration of what is desired—de Graunson's man is given language which accords him the excitement of mixed feelings, of alternatives and occasionally of the potentiality for independent volition, but Chaucer's woman is put into passive positions, has only dogged faithfulness, a stoic acceptance of what Love allots to her and no room for action: a single-toned experience.[19] Although for both poets this second balade is built on contrasts, Chaucer's woman still loses out on the range of varied experiences.

In l. 29 de Graunson lists, as one of the many reversals that love brings about,

Baissier les yeulx quant on voit regarder

He has to pay, temporarily, the high price ('cher comparer' l. 26, 'dons acheter' l. 37) for love, which includes the restriction of having to lower his eyes when others can look. Being free to 'regarder' when one wants has traditionally been the normal situation for a man. Only the unusual impositions of love mean that he has to accept being curbed, to lower his eyes. Chaucer cannot give his woman this line unchanged. For her there is no reference to any alternative. Instead there is simply a doubly expressed submissiveness:

29 And doun to caste visage and lokynge.

In l. 67 de Graunson's man hypothesizes that he might 'querir . . . royaume n'empire', but never find a better love, but Chaucer cannot give his woman so wide a horizon even in fancy: she surveys a much more narrow ambit: 'seche no ferthir, neythir wey ne went', l. 69, a far more restricted and humdrum landscape, from a kingdom or empire to a road or path.

Examples of this sort of change seem too consistent to be chance effects, or to be explained entirely by the technical problems of translating, or specifically of translating French balades with their tight rhyme-scheme into English. Through much of the text of *Venus* Chaucer's female lover is accorded a narrower and more monotone range of experience; her situation seems to have fewer distinct elements in it, and no power; the language is less active, more passive and static, less outward-directed. In contrast with the French female beloved, Chaucer's male beloved gets more attributes; there is no concern with physical charms or capacity to entertain other people, and in its place there is language which evokes social power, the potentiality for options and alternatives, activity, and self-determination.

It is sometimes said about Courtly Love, by those who believe in it, that it elevated women by putting them on a pedestal.[20] Here, when a man is put on a pedestal previously prepared for a female occupant the pedestal is widened. We see the converse when we turn to the treatment of the lover. Critics have written of the 'feminization' of the male lover in Courtly Love language, but Chaucer clearly found it in practice impossible to grant to a female lover the range of experience that de Graunson granted to a man.[21]

It may be objected that at the end de Graunson says of the lady (addressing his heart):

> Ne . . . si belle par mes yeulx ne verras.
> C'est jeunesse sachant et savoureuse
> Ja soit elle de m'amour desdaigneuse.
> (ll. 67–70)

So he does not entirely restrict his praise of her to vague or charming qualities. But the force of 'sachant et savoureuse' is weakened by 'jeunesse': it suggests a precocious child, and the context takes something from the praise, for l. 69 focuses the whole passage from the point of view of the male lover's amorous perception, and l. 70 ends by casting an eye ruefully back at his own state and success.

Briefly we should look at some other changes Chaucer makes. He increases the references to jealousy. (Jealousy is not, as it happens, a frequent theme in de Graunson.) Perhaps Chaucer was trying to adapt his version to the situation of Venus and Mars. Vulcan is a type of *le jaloux* in the *Roman de la Rose*,[22] and Phoebus in *The Complaint of Mars* is described as 'jelous', l. 140. It may, however, simply be a device to give greater unity to the English sequence of the three, originally more separate, balades.

It is interesting to notice that at two points Chaucer seems to have translated not the English semantic equivalent, but a word of similar appearance to the French. Perhaps 'yift', l. 41, was inspired by the visual image of forms like 'geu', 'gieu'[23] with their resemblance to Middle English forms *yifte, yefet, gift*, etc. 'gift',[24] and *yeve[n], geue[n]*, etc. 'give'. In l. 31 all ten authorities for Chaucer's poem have *pley*, though editors have emended to *pleyne*. 'Plaindre' may have reminded Chaucer of *pley[en]*,[25] and the near-homonym may, again, have inspired him to construct his own new patterning of ideas, rather than merely translating de Graunson's sense and structures: he creates the chiasmic contrast 'Pley in slepyng and dreme at the daunce', i.e. amusement in sleep and sleep in amusement. De Graunson had had a different contrast:

Plaindre en dormant et songier a la dance

i.e. misery in sleep and sleep in pleasure. There seems no reason to reject the reading 'pley'. After all, we have already seen Chaucer reworking de Graunson's neat antithesis of *parler* and *penser* in stanza 1, to create a different construction of ideas.

We find similar quasi-homonym translations in the Middle English *Romaunt of the Rose*, for example, 'reverye' for 'reverdie', 'warisoun' for 'guerredon', 'for a kyssyng' for 'por un ris', etc.[26]

Chaucer's envoy, though not corresponding to anything in de Graunson's five balades, must be considered in any examination of what Chaucer did to de Graunson. Elsewhere in his work, de Graunson has many envoys: to princes, singular and plural, as well as to a 'princesse'. Probably in *Venus* we should read 'princes', the reading of eight authorities. We may never know Chaucer's purpose in writing the envoy, nor the identity of its addressee(s). What is clear, however, are the multiple expressions of subordination in these ten concluding lines.

Here a voice representing the male author suddenly enters the poem. In *The Complaint of Mars* the concluding stanzas, addressing lovers, had been spoken in the voice of the fictional character, Mars. In *Venus* we end with a shift of point of view—not as striking and profound a shift as that which concludes the *Canterbury Tales* (if that is what the *Retraction* is) or the ending of *Troilus and Criseyde*, or even of the *Clerk's Tale*, but nonetheless a shift from the point of view of a character to a quasi-authorial voice. It is the kind of shift that in a typical *dit amoureux* manuscript would be marked as 'l'a[u]cteur' rather than 'l'amant';[27] a shift in the level of discourse, a shift from a statement by an intradiegetic to an extradiegetic figure.[28]

This extradiegetic, male, voice is itself being subordinate—to the princes whom he addresses, from his own 'litel suffisaunce'. He also lowers our estimation of himself as an author, as a creative protagonist: his creative powers and 'spirit' are dulled. His native language is itself inadequate. And he as translator can only 'folowe' de Graunson, the creative original, who is one of those who can 'make'.

All this might allow us to invoke the theory that as writers conceive of translation so they conceive of women. It is a theory that certainly seems worth considering in relation to this poem, even taking into account that all judgements about *Venus* must be regarded as provisional because so many questions about its purpose and reference remain unanswered.

With Chaucer, however, nothing is ever so single or simple. Apart from anything else, Chaucer is a poet *par excellence* of passivity, endurance, and suffering: his fascination with these states seems to be a central ingredient in his constant attraction to writing about oppressed women. Perhaps therefore we should widen our terms: from considering parallels between the translator and *women* to parallels between the role of translator and experiences of passivity, of suffering, of sensibility, and of *pacience* in all its senses. The parallels we have noted may not be simply gender-specific. It is worth looking elsewhere at Chaucer's presentation of himself, or his narrators, as translators.

The first thing we notice is that Chaucer does not always draw attention to his role as a translator. He does not, for example, tell us that the *ABC*, *Knight's Tale* or the *Man of Law's Tale* are translations or have sources; with *Melibee* he curiously obfuscates the issue; and—notoriously—where in *Troilus* he does claim the role of translator it is a fabrication, a fictional relationship between Chaucer in the translator's role and an original source, 'myn authour': a relationship with Lollius not with Boccaccio.[29] Where Chaucer refers to a source it is often for a purpose which is integral to his own work: in the *Parliament of Fowls* he cites Alain de Lille, but not Boccaccio, presumably because the former introduced ideas of plenitude which he wanted for his poem, whereas a reference to the latter would contribute nothing.

When we look at cases where Chaucer, as in *The Complaint of Venus*, presents a suffering, enduring, passive or *pacient* protagonist, female or feminized, we also often find that he also presents the narrator to us as a translator, or one who follows another writer: one whose own ego is in some way reduced, passive in relation to a source. We can see this in the proems to *Troilus and Criseyde*, as well as elsewhere in the narrator's self-presentation; in the references to Petrarch in the *Clerk's Tale*, the references to Statius and 'Corinne' in *Anelida*, and even in the *Second Nun's*

95

Tale. The last provides the simplest example. The Second Nun's Cecilia is a protagonist who endures all, strong through total self-emptying, filled with the power of the Other; she is God's 'thral', as her husband is God's 'lomb'. The narrator too presents herself (or himself?)[30] as totally dependent on the inspiration of an Other, the Virgin, submissive to her/his readers,[31] and in the role of translator:

> I have heer doon my feithful bisynesse
> After the legende in translacioun . . .
> (ll. 24–5)

> Yet preye I yow that reden that I write
> Foryeve me that I do no diligence
> This ilke storie subtilly to endite,
> For bothe have I the wordes and sentence
> Of hym that at the seintes reverence
> The storie wroot, and folwen hire legende,
> And pray yow that ye wole my werk amende.
> (ll. 77–84)

Troilus and *The Clerk's Tale* both shift points of view in their conclusions, having codas where a brisk, quasi-authorial voice is shafted in: as if the preceding narrative's passive, subordinate mood is felt to be unbalanced or incomplete. Within both texts, however, Chaucer while writing empathetically of passive protagonists had also adopted for his narrator the translator's role, that of dependent writer, following an 'original' who has fuller authority.

When we hear the voice of a translator in Chaucer, then, it seems often to be the dramatisation of a role rather than just the accurate documentation of a source (as the modern academic perhaps too readily assumes). It may be yet another strand in Chaucer's complex and highly idiosyncratic study of states that may be loosely summed up under the term *pacience*, which is one of the poet's most characteristic preoccupations.[32]

Whether *The Complaint of Venus* is the lament of Venus, another character, or an unnamed woman, it joins that long list of works in which Chaucer explores the pains, endurance, and passive vulnerability of women in love. The changes which he effects in switching the gender of lover and beloved as he translates de Graunson may offer us an unusually clear paradigm of literary stereotypes of male and female experience, and of the language of female dependence, but the addition in the envoy of an evocation of the role of the translator as an analogously dependent one makes the totality of the poem something rather more unusual. The voice representing the male author aligns his situation with the passive one of

96

the woman. What at first sight appears to be a depressing, and predictable, demonstration of a male author putting a female protagonist in her place ends by showing him putting himself into her place, or into a dependent and passive role very similar to hers.

NOTES

1. This paper arose from discussion with Alfred David, and I am very grateful to him for invaluable comments and suggestions on a draft version of this paper.
   Arthur Piaget (ed.) *Oton de Graunson, sa vie et ses poésies*, Mémoires et documents publiés par la Société d'histoire de la Suisse romande, series 3, vol. 1 (Lausanne: Librairie Payot, 1941) pp. 209–13 (balades I, IV, V, from the Paris manuscript); pp. 283, 308, 324 (from the Neuchatel manuscript); Amadée Pagès, *La Poésie française en Catalogne du XIIIe siècle à la fin du XVe siècle*, Bibliothèque méridionale, series 1, vol. 23 (Toulouse: E. Privat; Paris: H. Didier, 1936) (Barcelona MS); James I. Wimsatt, *Chaucer and the Poems of 'Ch' in the University of Pennsylvania MS French 15* (Cambridge: Boydell and Brewer, 1982) pp. 69–74 (Pennsylvania MS). All quotations here are from the Wimsatt text.
2. The authorities are listed in L.D. Benson (ed.) *The Riverside Chaucer* 3rd ed. (Oxford: Oxford University Press, 1988) p. 1187 (this edition is used for all quotations from Chaucer other than from *Venus*, for which see Appendix); the four are **F** (Bodleian MS Fairfax 16), **S2** (Bodleian MS Arch. Selden B. 24), **Th** (Thynne's edition), **JN** (Julian Notary's edition). In some other cases this title has been added later or may have been cropped.
3. Seven texts, plus **Pe** (Magdalene College, Cambridge, MS Pepys 2006, pp. 378–82) which lacks part of both poems, and British Library MS Add. 12524 which originally contained both.
4. Title in **L** (Longleat MS 258); three texts have *The Brooch of Thebes*; most have variants of *The [Love and] Complaint[s] [or Alliance] of [or between] Mars and Venus*.
5. Aage Brusendorff, *The Chaucer Tradition* (London: Oxford University Press; Copenhagen: V. Pio, 1925) pp. 261–8. Skeat opposed the idea of a link between the poems, and also the title *Complaint of Venus*; he also felt the second poem did not fit Venus and its three balades did not form a continuous complaint: W.W. Skeat (ed.) *Complete Works of Geoffrey Chaucer* (Oxford: Clarendon Press, 1894–9) I pp. 86–7.
6. Brusendorff, p. 263–8.
7. E.g. Skeat, I pp. 66–7; Haldeen Braddy, *Chaucer and the French Poet Graunson* (Baton Rouge: Louisiana State University Press, 1947) pp. 61–4, 71–85; George Williams, *A New View of Chaucer* (Durham, NC: Duke University Press, 1965) p. 165.
8. See Julia Boffey, 'The Manuscripts of English Courtly Love Lyrics in the Fifteenth Century' in Derek Pearsall (ed.) *Manuscripts and Readers in Fifteenth-Century England: The Literary Implications of Manuscript Study*, Essays from the 1981 Conference at the University of York (Woodbridge, Suffolk: D.S. Brewer, 1983) pp. 3–14, esp. 8–10.

9. Despite what Braddy believed, pp. 61–4, all five balades imply a male speaker.

10. Paris MS: Piaget, p. 209; these five in the same order also appear in the Pennsylvania MS: Wimsatt, pp. 69–74.

11. *Princes* could be 'princes' or 'princess', presumably royalty, though French lyricists sometimes address poems to the princes of *puys*.

12. Such an investigation is subject to a further problem: which extant French or English texts are closest to Chaucer's? Wimsatt (pp. 69–70) argues that the Pennsylvania de Graunson is closest to Chaucer's source-text.

13. Hilaire Belloc, *On Translation*, The Taylorian Lecture 1931 (Oxford: Clarendon Press, 1931) p. 3.

14. Lori Chamberlain, 'Gender and the Metaphorics of Translation' *Signs* 13:3 (1988) pp. 454–71, repr. in Venuti (ed.) *Rethinking Translation* pp. 57–74.

15. Chamberlain, *Signs* 13:3 (1988) p. 455.

16. Chamberlain, *Signs* 13:3 (1988) pp. 455–66; Chamberlain's examples of colonialist metaphors for translation seem less convincing than the sexist metaphors.

17. Admittedly, translation encourages nominalization (I am grateful to Michael McCarthy for discussions on this point); and the need for rhymes may have encouraged the use of nouns ending in *-aunce* and *-esse* (see Michio Masui, *The Structure of Chaucer's Rime Words: An Exploration into the Poetic Language of Chaucer* (Tokyo: Kenkyusha, 1964) pp. 12–27, which also cites *bisynesse, stedfastnesse, gentilesse, richesse, governaunce, remembraunce, benignitee,* and *aventure* as words which are more likely to appear in rhyming than in other positions); translation also often uses two or more words to render the sense of one word. Chaucer's multiple nouns, however, are not just trying to capture de Graunson's *sense*, but moving beyond it.

18. Familiar in *Roman de la Rose* and its descendants; Félix Lecoy (ed.) Guillaume de Lorris and Jean de Meun, *Le Roman de la Rose*, 3 vols. (Paris: Librairie Honoré Champion, 1962–70) ll. 2629–56 (*douz penser*); 2657–2700 (*douz parler*); 2701–48 (adds *douz regart*).

19. Dogged faithfulness: it is perhaps easy for a modern feminist to assume that when medieval defenders of women credit them with humble faithfulness they perpetuate an antifeminist stereotype, but the problems and prejudices that medieval women and their defenders faced were different from those that the post-Victorian world faces, and in the context of the traditional accusations of fickleness, obstreperousness and promiscuity from medieval misogyny, the assertion of their constancy and obedience is not unequivocally an antifeminist position.

20. C.S. Lewis, *The Allegory of Love* (Oxford: Oxford University Press, 1936) pp. 2–13, 20–32; see Sarah Kay, *Subjectivity in Troubadour Poetry* (Cambridge: Cambridge University Press, 1990) pp. 85–90.

21. Elaine Tuttle Hansen, 'The Feminization of Men in Chaucer's *Legend of Good Women*' in Sheila Fisher and Janet E. Halley (eds.) *Seeking the Woman in Late Medieval and Renaissance Writings: Essays in Feminist Contextual Criticism* (Knoxville: University of Tennessee Press, 1989) pp. 51–70; Kay *Subjectivity in Troubadour Poetry*, pp. 85–111.

22. *Roman* ll. 13793–838, 14136–72, 18029–99.

23. Variant spellings in the de Graunson texts.

24. Variant spellings in *Venus* texts.

25. A suggestion first made by George Pace, in unpublished notes on the text of *Venus*.
26. For these examples, see *Romaunt of the Rose* ll. 720 (*Roman* 708), 1537 (1506), 2338 (2221); other possible homonym translations include *Roman* 1031 sore (1015 sade), 2323 foote (2209 fleuter): for MS variants from the *Roman* see Pierre Langlois (ed.) *Le roman de la rose* Société des Anciens Textes Français II (Paris: Librairie de Firmin-Didot et Cie., 1920). Mary-Jo Arn has told me of similar homonym translations in Charles d'Orléans; see her 'Charles of Orleans as Translator/Adaptor: How a Poet Writes in Two Languages' *Target* (forthcoming, 1993), and her contribution to the present volume; see also Helen Phillips, 'Chaucer's French Translations' *Nottingham Medieval Studies* 37 (1993, forthcoming).
27. See Sylvia Huot, *From Song to Book: The Poetics of Writing in the Old French Lyric and Lyrical Narrative Poetry* (Ithaca and London: Cornell University Press, 1987) esp. pp. 90–6.
28. On the terms 'extradiegetic' and 'intradiegetic' see Gerard Genette, *Figures III* (Paris: Edition du Seuil, 1972) pp. 238–40.
29. *Troilus* I, 394, V, 1653; also II, 13–21, 48–9, etc. See also Bella Millett, 'Chaucer, Lollius and the Medieval Theories of Authorship' P. Strohm and T.J. Heffernan (eds) *Studies in the Age of Chaucer/Proceedings no.1, 1984: Reconstructing Chaucer* (Knoxville: New Chaucer Society, 1985) pp. 93–105.
30. The presentation of the narrator is not, generally, inappropriate to the fiction of a nun, speaking on horseback, but also represents him/her as 'sone of Eve', l. 62, as a translator, and as writing for readers.
31. *Second Nun's Tale* ll. 22–56.
32. See David Burnley, *Chaucer's Language and the Philosophers' Tradition* (Ipswich: Boydell Press, 1979) pp. 75–81; Jill Mann, *Geoffrey Chaucer* (Brighton: Harvester Wheatsheaf, 1991) pp. 87–164, esp. pp. 112–27, 153–4; Anna Baldwin, 'Patience in Chaucer' (forthcoming). There have been several recent studies of the theme, including studies of *Patience*, and recent work on Langland by Derek Pearsall, David Aers and Anna Baldwin, in Gerald J. Schiffhorst (ed.) *The Triumph of Patience* Medieval and Renaissance Studies (Orlando, Florida: University Presses of Florida, 1978).

APPENDIX

TEXTS

Oton de Graunson: three balades

Text: James I. Wimsatt, *Chaucer and the Poems of 'Ch' in the University of Pennsylvania MS French 15* (Cambridge: Boydell and Brewer, 1982) pp. 70–1, 73, 74.

Balade (I)

Il n'est confort qui tant de bien me face
Quant je ne puis a ma dame parler
Comme d'avoir temps, loizir, et espace
De longuement en sa valour penser

99

5　Et ses doulz fais feminins recorder
　　Dedans mon cuer, c'est ma vie par m'ame
　　Ne je ne truis nul homme qui m'en blasme
　　Car chascun a joye de li loer.

　　Il a en lui beaute, bonte, et grace
10　Plus que nulz homs ne saroit deviser:
　　C'est grant eur quant en si po despace
　　Dieu a voulu tous les biens assambler;
　　Honneur la veult sur toutes honnorer;
　　Onques ne vy si plaisant jeune dame
15　De toutes gens avoir si noble fame,
　　Car chascun etc.

　　Ou qu'elle soit bien fait et mal efface;
　　Moult bien li siet le rire et le jouer;
　　Son cuer esbat et les autres solace
20　Si liement qu'on ne le doit blasmer;
　　De li veoir ne se puet nulz lasser;
　　Son regart vault tous les biens d'un royaume;
　　Il samble bien qu'elle est tresnoble femme,
　　Car chascun etc.

　　Balade (IV)

25　Certes, Amour, c'est chose convenable
　　Que vos grans bien faciez cher comparer,
　　Veillier ou lit et jeuner a la table,
　　Rire en plorant et en plaignant chanter,
　　Baissier les yeulx quant on voit regarder,
30　Souvent changier couleur et contenaunce,
　　Plaindre en dormant et songier a la dance.
　　Tout a rebours de ce qu'on veult trouver.

　　Jalousie, c'est la mere du deable,
　　Elle veult tout veoir et escouter,
35　Ne nulz ne fait chose si raisonnable
　　Que tout a mal ne le veult tourner.
　　Amours, ainsi fault vos dons acheter,
　　Et vous donnez souvent sans ordonnance
　　Assez doulour et petit de plaisance,
40　Tout a rebours etc.

　　Pour .j. court temps le geu est aggreable,
　　Mais trop par est encombreux a user,
　　Et, ja soit il a dames honnorable,
　　A leurs servans est trop grief a porter.
45　Tousdiz convient souffrir et endurer,
　　Sans nul certain languir en esperance
　　Et recevoir mainte male meschance,
　　Tout a rebours etc.

Balade (V)

    Amours, sachiez que pas le veulz dire
50 Pour moy getter hors des amoureux las,
    Car a porte si long temps mon martire
    Qu'a mon vivant ne le geurpiray pas.
    Il me souffit d'avoir tant de soulas
    Que veoir puisse la belle gracieuse;
55 Combien qu'elle est envers moy dangereuse
    De li servir ne seray jamais las.

    Certes, Amours, quant bien a droit remire
    Les hauls estas, les moiens, et les bas,
    Vous m'avez fait de tous les liex eslire,
60 A mon advis, le meilleur en tous cas.
    Or ayme, Cuer, si fort com tu porras,
    Car ja n'avras paine si douloureuse
    Pour ma dame qui ne me soit joieuse
    De li servir etc.

65 Cuer, il te doit assez plus que souffire
    D'avoir choisi si bien que choisi as.
    Ne querir plus royaume n'empire,
    Car si belle par mes yeulx ne verras.
    C'est jeunesse sachant et savoureuse;
70 Ja soit elle de m'amour desdaigneuse
    De li servir etc.

Some variants from Paris MS (text in Arthur Piaget (ed.) *Oton de Graunson, sa vie et ses poésies*, Mémoires et documents publiés par la Société d'histoire de la Suisse romande, series 3, vol. 1 (Lausanne, 1941) pp. 209–13)
9. *bonte*: beaute; 14. *jeune*: om.; 26. *cher*: om.; 29. *voit*: doit; 33. *la mere*: l'amer; 44. *servans*: amis; 59. *liex*: bons.

Note: *lui* appears as a form of *li* in both MSS.

Chaucer, *The Complaint of Venus*

    Ther nys so high comfort, to my plesaunce,
    When that I am in eny heuynesse,
    As for to haue leyser of remembraunce
    Vpon the manhod, and the worthynesse,
5 Vpon the trouthe, and on the stidfastnesse,
    Of him whos I am al while I may dure.
    Ther oght blame me no creature,
    For euery wight preiseth his gentilesse.

In him ys bounte, wysdom, and governaunce,
10   Wel more then eny manes witte can gesse,
For grace hath wolde so ferforthe hym avaunce
That of knyghthode he is parfite richesse.
Honour honoureth him for his noblesse.
Therto so well hath formed him Nature
15   That I am his for euer, I him assure,
For euery wight preysith his gentilesse.

And, notwithstondyng al his suffisaunce,
His gentil hert ys of so grete humblesse
To me in worde, in werk, in contenaunce,
20   And me to serue is al his besynesse,
That I am set in verrey sikirnesse.
Thus oght I blesse wel myn aventure,
Sith that him list me seruen and honoure,
For euery wight preiseth his gentilesse.

25   Now, certis, Love, hit is right couenable
That men ful dere abye thi nobil thinge,
As wake abed and fasten at the table,
Wepinge to laugh and sing in compleynyge,
And doun to cast visage and lokynge,
30   Often to chaunge hewe and contenaunce,
Pley in slepyng and dreme at the daunce;
Al the reuerse of eny glad felynge.

Jelosie be hanged be a cable!
She wold al knowe thro her espyinge.
35   Ther dothe no wyght nothing so resonable
That al nys harme in her ymagenynge;
Thus dere abought is love in yevynge;
Which ofte he yifeth withoute ordynaunce,
As sorow ynogh and litel of plesaunce,
40   Al the reuerse of any glad felynge.

A lytel tyme his yift ys agreable,
But ful encombrouse is the vsynge,
For subtil Jelosie the deceyvable
Ful often tyme causeth desturbynge.
45   Thus be we euer in drede and suffrynge,
In nouncerteyne we langvisshe in penaunce,
And han wel ofte mony an harde meschaunce;
Al the reuerse of ony glad felynge.

But, certis, Love, I sey not in suche wise
50   That for t'escape out of your lace I ment;
For I so longe haue ben in your seruise
That for to let of wil I neuer assent;

No fors thogh Jelosie me turment.
Sufficeth me to se hym when I may,
55 And therfore certys to myn endying day
To loue hym best ne shal I neuer repent.

And, certis, Love, when I me wel avise
On eny estate that man may represent
Then haue ye made me through your fraunchise
60 Chese the best that euer on erthe went.
Now, love wel, Hert, and loke thou neuer stent,
And let the jelous put hit in assay
That for no peyn wille I not sey nay;
To love him best ne shal I neuer repent.

65 Hert, to the hit ought ynogh suffise
That Love so highe a grace to thee sent:
To chese the worthiest of al wise,
And most agreable vnto myn entent.
Seche no ferthir, neythir wey ne went,
70 Sithe I have suffisaunce vnto my pay.
Thus wol I ende this compleynt or this lay;
To love hym best ne shal I neuer repent.

Lenvoy

Princes, resseyueth this compleynt in gre,
Vnto your excelent benignite
75 Direct aftir my litel suffisaunce.
For Elde, that in my spirit dulleth me,
Hath of endyting al the subtilte
Welnyghe bereft out of my remembraunce;
And eke to me hit ys a grete penaunce,
80 Syth ryme in Englisshe hath such skarsete,
To folowe worde by worde the curiosite
Of Graunson, floure of hem that make in Fraunce.

Text: based on Fairfax MS, lightly emended and with modern punctuation.

Rejected readings from Fairfax MS
5. whiles; 26. bye the; 30. *hewe*: visage; 33. *be*: he; 44. derturbynge; 46. langvis-shen; 47. ful often; *meschaunce*: penaunce; 51. be; 56. *ne*: om. 62. Jelousie; 72. *ne*: om.; 77. subtilite; 80. hat; 82. maken.

Chapter 4

Tales of a True Translator: Medieval Literary Theory, Anecdote and Autobiography in Osbern Bokenham's *Legendys of Hooly Wummen*

IAN JOHNSON

1. THE MEDIEVAL PARATEXT

In a recent number of *New Literary History*, Marie Maclean, in the best medieval tradition, has provided a translation (plus commentary/ medita-tion) of Gérard Genette's 'Introduction to the Paratext'.[1] This is an attempt to theorize the so-called *paratext*, i.e. prefaces, commentaries, accompaniments, packagings, and in general the paraphernalia a text has 'to assure its presence in the world', the means by which a text 'makes a book of itself and proposes itself as such to its readers', as a zone of trans-action which attempts to ensure 'a better reception of the text and a more pertinent reading'.[2] In this stimulating article, which discusses the posi-tioning, temporal situation, status and pragmatics of paratextuality, Genette somewhat misrepresents the Middle Ages:

> . . . it is a recognized fact that a 'media dominated' period multiplies around texts a type of discourse unknown in the classical world, and a fortiori in antiquity and the Middle Ages, periods in which texts frequently circulated in their almost raw state, in the form of manu-scripts lacking any formula of presentation.[3]

This overlooks the fact that the medieval period was possibly The Age of Rampant Paratextuality, where commentaries, glossed texts, prologues, prayers and petitions, to say nothing of features of *ordinatio* and layout, proliferated at the commanding heights of literary culture. The self-refer-ring texts/paratexts of the mid-fifteenth century hagiographer, Osbern Bokenham, who is the subject of this paper, are at times analyzable in Genette's terms. For instance, Genette's distinction between public and private paratexts is reflected in Bokenham's public statements to all readers, his semi-private discourse aimed at patrons and dedicatees, and his privately-directed though publicly-recorded petitions to saints and the Divinity for his own spiritual benefit.[4]

However, this paper has a more historical, contextualizing, approach than that of Genette. Its main business is the confluence of vernacularized medieval literary theory and autoreferential and/or anecdotal materials written by an energetically orthodox translator not only about his experi-ence of translating but also about the intended reception and purposes of his work. Notable for theory-rich prefatory materials and other assorted commentary, especially self-exegetical or autobiographical, is Osbern Bokenham's *Legendys of Hooly Wummen*. His compilation of Saints' Lives, made in the 1440s, is loquaciously representative of the cultural mentality that engendered it.[5] This is particularly the case with the prologue at the very beginning of the collection.

2. BOKENHAM'S ANECDOTAL ARISTOTELIAN PROLOGUE

Before going on to consider its autoreferential features, something should be said about the theory-motivated structure and nature of Bokenham's prologue as part and parcel of a literary tradition of the academic prologue. The Latin and English traditions of the academic prologue have been discussed elsewhere. Suffice it to say that the traditional scholastic categories of *accessus*-tradition, under which a text of an *auctor* was appraised—*utilitas* (the utility/value of a work), *intentio* (intentionality), *nomen libri* (title), *modus agendi* (procedure/style), *ordinatio/forma trac-tatus* (structure and order of materials), *nomen auctoris* (name, life and status of the author), *materia* (sources/subject matter)—were vernacularized and significantly influenced the terminology and ideology of English translators' prologues.[6]

In the fourteenth century, the traditional terminology of the *accessus* was supplemented and sharpened up by an Aristotelian scheme based on the universal philosophical grid of the Four Causes. The efficient cause (*causa efficiens*) was the author; it could be *duplex*, e.g. God and Man, priest and Holy Ghost. The material cause (*causa materialis*) was the subject matter/sources of a work. The formal cause (*causa formalis*) was the form (structure, style and literary procedures). And, last but not least, the final cause (*causa finalis*) was the objective of the text and of the author, which combined the work of *utilitas* and *intentio* from the older scheme of the *accessus*.[7]

Most English prologues were not Aristotelian, but the prologue to Osbern Bokenham's *Legendys of Hooly Wummen* makes a display of its Four Causes. It is a typical medieval combination of artifice and flexibility. Although it is undoubtedly rather pedantic, it does not provide evidence that the life has gone out of the Aristotelian idiom, as has been claimed.[8] On the contrary, it is an energetic, discursive and sure-footed (if at times also flat-footed!) re-application of tradition, which fluently incorporates topical and anecdotal material into its theoretical structures. That a non-innovative and 'correct' writer like Bokenham is relying on such a tradition is high-quality evidence of its pervasive influence and life.

The prologue begins with a recapitulative explication of the Four Causes as applicable to literary works:

> Two thyngys owyth euery clerk
> To aduertysyn, begynnyng a werk,
> If he procedyn wyl ordeneelly:
> The fyrste is 'what', the secunde is 'why'.
> In wych two wurdys, as it semyth me,
> The foure causys comprehendyd be,
> Wych, as philosofyrs vs do teche,
> In the begynnyng men owe to seche
> Of euery book; and aftyr there entent
> The fyrst is clepyd cause efficyent,
> The secunde they clepe cause materyal,
> Formal the thrydde, the fourte fynal.
>
> (ll. 1–12)

The use of the word 'aduertysyn' reminds us that the function of theory, in any age, like that of a writer's self-presentation (and perhaps even like the way s/he may behave in real life), is as much to valorise a work as to explicate it. A properly executed work, says Bokenham, should have such a prologue as this one. By referring to 'clerks' as the makers of such works and as their philosophically-orientated theorists and judges, he displays the academic credentials which he believes to be necessary for the proper Englishing of Saints' Lives. The inter-relating of 'what' and 'why' with the Four Causes may symptomatise a harmonisation of the tradition of rhetorical *circumstantiae* with a cognate Aristotelian tradition.[9] The tradition of prologues structured according to a scheme of *circumstantiae* is associated in particular with Remigius of Auxerre and originated in ancient rhetoricians' belief that anything that was the subject of discussion could be appraised by means of a series of questions, 'who' (the author), 'what' (the text itself), 'why' (the text's objective), 'in what manner' (in what fashion the work was composed), 'where' (the place of composition), 'when' (the time of composition), and 'whence/by what means' (the matter from which the work was composed). Not all headings would necessarily be used. Bokenham's simplification provided by 'what' and 'why' is appropriate. Aristotelian discourse elaborates, explicates and amplifies the discourse of *circumstantiae*, which in its turn contains, recapitulates and distils the Aristotelian.

Fittingly, the procedure of this prologue is very like the common three-stage technique of the medieval commentator or translator, who may, firstly, gloss or simply quote the naked letter, then, second, paraphrase the literal sense/*sensus*; and finally extrapolate on the *sententia* and its teaching, thereby making theory the very matter, i.e. the material cause, of practice itself.[10] In the first section of this prologue, quoted above, he gives *ad verbum* literalistic gloss-translations of the Latin theoretical terminology. The second phase of the prologue deals with the literal-sense meaning of the terms, starting with the efficient cause:

> The efficyent cause is the auctour,
> Wych aftyr hys cunnyng doth hys labour
> To a-complyse the begunne matere,
> Wych cause is secunde; . . .
>
> (ll. 13–16)

The term 'auctour' is being used here in the most general sense. Bokenham is not claiming the authority of an evangelist or a Boethius. As if it were second nature and the obvious next step, he fluently runs the consideration of the material cause into the next, i.e. the formal, cause:

> . . . and the more clere
> That it [i.e. the 'matere'] may be, the formal cause
> Settyth in dew ordre clause be clause.
> And these thre thyngys longyn to 'what':
> Auctour, matere, and forme ordinat.
>
> (ll. 16–20)

The duty to elucidate, to make 'more clere', is twinned with the technique of rendering clause by clause, that is, *per cola et commata* in true Hieronymic fashion like a commentator-translator.[11] The re-imposition of the encapsulating question 'what' on the first three causes serves all the more to show that the members of the trio are natural conceptual partners. This also has the effect of highlighting the single member of the

107

'why' group, the final cause, i.e. the use and intentions of a work, which is set apart from the other theoretical terminology:

> The fynal cause declaryth pleynly
> Of the werk begunne the cause why;
> That is to seyne, what was the entent
> Of the auctour fynally, & what he ment.
> Lo! thus ye seen mown compendyously
> How in these two wurdys 'what' & 'why',
> Of eche werk the foure causys aspye
> Men mown, requyryd be philosophye.
> (ll. 21–28)

A distinction is apparently being made between, on the one hand, the ultimate value or utility of the work ('entent . . . fynally') and, on the other hand, what the author means ('& what he ment'). Such theoretical precision shows that academic literary theory did not affect such translators in broad generalities alone, but also at times in finer distinctions such as this.

The third phase of the prologue extrapolates on the Four Causes, and applies them copiously to the work in question. Bokenham's broader consideration of the efficient cause includes a refusal to mention his own name on account of his unworthiness, something of a modesty topos. What he does mention, though, is his priestly *officium*, as 'an austyn frere' (l. 32). The office holds an authority of its own, not unrelated to that of the *officium praedicatoris*, in which the priest/writer is the instrumental efficient cause, that is, a lesser, operative cause, with God the 'remote' moving and permissive cause. As such, a priestly writer was licensed and guided by God's grace. So it is not true to say that the fourteenth-century concept of the *duplex causa efficiens* has been lost from this work.[12] On the contrary, the work is studded with statements like this example:

> . . . I lowly beseche
> Hym that treuthe is & treuthe doth teche,
> The lord that syt a-boue the skye,
> That he in treuthe vouchesaf to gye. . .
> Bothe my wyt & eek my pen.
> (ll. 931–4, 937)

Later he commends God as authorial helper and invokes Christ instead of the Pagan Muses (ll. 5214–62).[13] Also, in that this is a compilation of Saints' Lives, Bokenham invokes their influence on his endeavour, as with St Margaret (ll. 329–36), and the Virgin Mary (ll. 1467–96). Such saints are prayed to for their intercession as part and parcel of the making and the reading of the work. Thus there is a meeting of efficient and final causality, of the work's motive power and its end.

The 'matere', summarised in a few cursory lines, is the 'lyf of blyssyd Margarete' (l. 75), the first of the Lives in the compilation. As for the formal cause, here called (l. 83) the 'forme of procedyng' (a conflation, so it would appear, of *forma tractandi* and *modus procedendi*, which shows that Bokenham was dealing with an ideological idiom rather than a ticklist of rigid terminology), it is discussed in the third phase not in terms of commentary-translation, for that has already been done, but with regard to Bokenham's inability as a *makere* or *rhetor* in the tradition of Geoffrey of Vinsauf ('after the scole of the crafty clerk . . . Galfridus anglicus, in hys newe poetrye' (ll. 85–88)). Instead he will translate as near as possible to the story of the legend. This is where theory and autobiography/ anecdote start to interpenetrate, because Bokenham goes into autobiographical detail about his *forme of procedyng*, for it seems that he himself copied and compiled his Latin sources with the express intention of Englishing them. He tells us that he went to Italy and, detained by rain at the Shrine of St Margaret, wrote down what he had read and heard there 'bothe be scripture and eek be mowthe' (l. 109):

> And al the processe I dede owt wryte
> Wych I purpose now to declare
> On ynglysh, & it brout wyth me to Clare.
>
> (ll. 120–2)

Such a degree of autobiographical detail in a passage ostensibly devoted to considering the formal cause, that is, how the work was made, is illuminating, not just because it tells us what the translator actually did, but also because it shows the spontaneous application of the theory to an anecdotal description of practice. Osbern's alleged *auctoritas* for the orally-transmitted material is its currency in that district of Italy round 'mownt Flask', where it 'is no-thyng vnkowthe' (ll. 110–11). Then, to give the story the ring of truth, he presents attached anecdotal circumstances about the distance of the shrine from Rome, the beguiling of pilgrims by the locals with Trebbiano wine rather than Muscadelle—a form of pseudo-logical or pseudo-authoritative proof in which false wine is adduced to validate the truth of Osbern's statement: *in vino veritas*:

> . . . who me not leue,
> Lete hym go thedyr & he shal it preue—
> On thys half Rome ful fyfty myle
> Or ellys more, where men begyle
> The wery pylgrymys kun ful wel
> Wyth Trybyan in stede of Muskadel . . .
>
> (ll. 111–16)

This attempted valorisation by alleged associated circumstances which strictly in themselves prove little or nothing—authentication through specificity that cannot be refuted—turns out to be a hallmark of Bokenham, who, it seems, is attempting to treat of 'where' in a manner akin to the tradition of prefatory *circumstantiae*. Anyhow, the very process of translation is valorised by physical association with the shrine and the power of the saint.

Significantly, the story of Osbern's Italian travels is split between philosophical causes; for whereas the previous passage concerning the area round 'mownt Flask' was part of the consideration of the formal cause, Osbern's Venetian travels are incorporated into his discussion of the final cause. And so, autobiography is bisected and presented through/by theory. For this Aristotelian tourist, his discussion of final causality has an urgently personal touch, for Bokenham tells the tale of the origin of his special veneration for St Margaret, this being a further, personal, final cause behind the final cause of stirring others to devotion. Chased out of a barge into a Venetian fen, he was saved (we are not told how) from a 'cruel tyraunth' by a ring with which he had touched the saint's bare foot (kept in a shrine back home), which is credited with the power of saving from danger people who touch it with a brooch/ring. This stirred him all the more 'Hyr lyf to translate' (ll. 133–74). A personal final cause of his literary activity is the additional spiritual benefit to be won from the saint he serves.

That Bokenham provides all this autobiographical information and yet also wishes not to reveal his name is not so much a symptom of immodest feigned modesty as might at first appear. The question of immodesty is not really the issue here anyway, because the personal details are unconnected with self-aggrandisement. Instead they witness to a 'real-life' experience of the saint's power, which may be 'shewyd/ Bothe on lernyd & eek on lewyd' (ll. 145–6).[14] Bokenham is a Christian witness, not just to his sources but also to the reality of the power of the saint. So, even though he is liberally conventional in the use of modesty topoi, his piety, pure intention and respect for St Margaret and his *matere*, which are what actually count, all have the ring of extreme sincerity.

A general, final cause is also described, that of exciting 'mennys affeccyoun' to devotion. 'Mennys' presumably means humanity in general because his *Legendys* are frequently dedicated to women like Kathryn Denston (ll. 1466, 6366, 7363–4), Elizabeth Vere, Countess of Oxford (ll. 5054–5, 9536, 10613), Kathryn Howard (ll. 6365, 7363–4), Isabel Bourchier, Countess of Eu (ll. 5004–117, 5356), and Agatha Fleg (l. 8340):

> But who-so wyl aske me fynally
> Of thys translacyoun the cause why
> In to oure language, I sey causys two

Most pryncypally me meuyd ther-to.
The fyrst cause is for to excyte
Mennys affeccyoun to haue delyte
Thys blyssyd virgyne to loue & serue,
From alle myscheuys hem to preserue.

(ll. 123–30)

Captious Wits

Further personal final causality is discussed, again at length. He was moved to translate by the request of a named friend, Thomas Borgh. Bokenham asks Thomas to protect him and his work from sneering Cambridge wits. In this restrictive phase of his paratext, such evasiveness is arguably a literary role in itself. Not that he was by any means the first Middle English writer to identify those for whom his work is not intended. The *Cloud* author, for instance, indicates the unsuitability of his work for those in the Active Life.[15] Bokenham, however, goes much further. His audience-avoiding modesty topos is tied up with a real-life ploy to avoid personal hurt and embarrassment. However valuable his *Legendys* might be, he was aware that they were relatively unspectacular as fine writing. To protect himself, Bokenham will not express his name in his work (normally a modesty topos), but, rather differently, he asks for it to be kept safe from the Cantabrigians:

And yet I sore feryd me of enuye,
Wych is euere besy and eek diligent
To depraue priuyly others trewe entent;
Wherfore, hyr malyhs to represse,
My name I wil not here expresse,
As toforn is seyd; wherfore I preye
And requere eek, if I it dare seye,
Yow, sone and fadyr, to whom I dyrecte
This symple tretyhs, that ye detecte
It in no wyse wher that vylany
It myht haue, and pryncypally
At hoom at Caunbrygge in your hows,
Where wyttys be manye ryht capcyows
And subtyl, wych sone my lewydnesse
Shuld aspye; wherfore, of ientylnesse,
Kepyth it as cloos as ye best kan
A lytyl whyle . . .

(ll. 196–212)

This sounds too worried to be mere rehearsal of convention. Perhaps he fears that the captious Cantabrigians, possibly looming in his imagination as ghastly clerical misogynists and intellectual snobs to a man, would pounce on his hagiography in Suffolk speech as faulty, lowbrow,

111

provincial, and mere women's work to boot. At this point, Bokenhamian topical *inventio* takes a new twist: the deflection of detractors, i.e. putting them off his scent by confusing the issue with a smokescreen of more anecdotal circumstance, for he beseeches Thomas:

> . . . and not-for-than
> If ye algate shul it owth lete go,
> Be not aknowe whom it comyth fro,
> But seyth, as ye doon vndyrstand,
> It was you sent owt of Ageland
> From a frend of yourys that vsyth to selle
> Goode hors at feyrys, & doth dwelle
> A lytyl fro the Castel of Bolyngbrok,
> In a good town wher ye fyrst tok
> The name of Thomas, & clepyd is Borgh
> In al that cuntre euene thorgh & thorgh;
> And thus ye shul me weel excuse,
> And make that men shul not muse
> To haue of me ony suspycyoun.
>
> (ll. 212–25)

A captious wit might hold his tongue, not wishing to insult a personal friend of Thomas, a fellow-Agelander (which Osbern probably was not— more smokescreen?[16]) who may have sent this as a sincere gift, and who, after all, *surely must be* a decent fellow, because he's an *honest* horse-seller (the medieval stereotypical equivalent of the second-hand car-dealer). The seemingly paranoid inventiveness of these lines develops, elaborates and anxiously chews the convention it invokes. Moreover, Bokenham's behaviour squares somewhat with Genette's invocation of the distinction between *official* and *officious* statements:

> Any paratextual message for which the author . . . assumes a responsibility which he cannot escape is official . . . On the other hand, the greater part of the authorial epitext—interviews, conversations and confidences—is officious, because the author can always more or less get rid of his responsibilities by denials such as . . . 'It was not intended for publication.'[17]

It would appear here that Osbern, through the official peritext of his prologue, is trying to engineer an officious epitext that would consign his whole work to the very 'angle of oblyuyoun' (l. 40) he seeks to avoid in respect of his other, intended, readers.[18] On the other side of the coin, Bokenham, as we shall see next, shows himself willing and able to exert a comparable degree of officious energy, not to keep his text from an unintended readership, but this time emphatically to bestow or foist it on a targeted readership.

3. BOKENHAM'S TWELFTH NIGHT: *THE PROLOCUTORYE IN-TO MARYE MAWDELEYNS LYF*

Even before the prologue proper to Mary Magdalen's Life, there is a so-called *Prolocutorye*, a highly rhetoricized, autobiographical, anecdotal, decorous overture to the following work (ll. 4981–5262). A long, florid, and dramatically self-interrupted astrological opening passage dates the events of a tale which, for its characteristic paratextual garrulity, might be described as 'proloquacious', to coin a term. Bokenham tells us how he was at a Twelfth Night revel, held in the presence of Isabel Bourchier, Countess of Eu, whose lineage is then iterated at some length. (Not only should this appeal to her, it should appeal to others, who can therefore regard this work as good enough for anyone.) While her four sons danced, the Countess and Bokenham, we are told, talked of the Saints' Lives he had Englished to date, and she requested from him an English Life of Mary Magdalen. Bokenham's praise of her sons, reinforced by the undeniable fact that they danced, serves to imply an equally undeniable factuality in Isabel's 'request' to Bokenham to translate. ('Þis ladyis foure sonys . . . daunsyng,/And oþere mo in þere most fressh aray/Dysgysyd' are compared to the month of May—their garments may have been woven by a Ovidian Minerva, and so on (ll. 5023–34)). The flattering presentation of Isabel's piety at revel would make it awkward for her to refuse Osbern now that he has taken the trouble to render *this, her* work:

> I seye, whyl þei þus daunsyng dede walke
> Aboute þe chaumbyr, wyth me to talke
> It lykyd my lady of hyr ientylnesse
> Of dyuers legendys, wych my rudnesse
> From latyn had turnyd in-to our language,
> Of hooly wummen . . .
>
> (ll. 5035–40)

Bokenham then lists, somewhat self-publicisingly, a number of his Lives, and reveals that he 'newly had begunne to ryme' (ll. 5050) St Elizabeth's Life for the spiritual benefit of the Countess of Oxford, Elizabeth Vere. Perhaps to keep up with the Veres, Isabel makes her request. What the Countess of Eu is alleged to have said is dignified by 'translation' into rhyme:

> 'I haue,' quod she, 'of pure affeccyoun
> Ful longe tym had a synguler deuocyoun
> To þat holy wumman, wych, as I gesse,
> Is clepyd of apostyls þe apostyllesse;
> Blyssyd Mary mawdelyn y mene,

Whom cryste from syn made pure & clene,
As þe clerkys seyn, ful mercyfully,
Whos lyf in englysshe I desyre sothly
To han maad, & for my sake
If ye lykyd þe labour to take,
& for reuerence of hyr, I wold you preye.'
(ll. 5065–75)

Presumably, she is meant to be flattered by the celebrity of appearing in verse as a devout character in eloquent command of the threshold into a hagiographical text (initiated by herself): one who shows a laudable appreciation of the 'apostyllesse'. Such a request 'of þe poete is a myhty comaundement' (l. 5084), so he agrees, on condition that she lets him go first on a pilgrimage to 'seynt Iamys' to get an indulgence for a year's worth of remission, as it is a special 'yere of grace' (ll. 5085–5111). 'She me pardonyd' (l. 5110), he says, transferring the language of penance to a secular noblewoman, thereby displaying his humility and her graciousness. Such a delay bespeaks an obedience higher than that due to Isabel but he nevertheless humbly allows the Countess the power of yea or nay. She can bathe in the reflected virtue of his peregrination. After gaining his indulgence he should be spiritually purer and more illumined with the grace necessary for the devotional task of translating.

To strengthen his position yet further, he presents himself as a humble instrumental efficient cause replicating but outdoing the pagans' own invocation of their deities. Following the *auctoritas* of a Church Father, he cites Augustine's citation of Plato, thereby getting on his side both pagan antiquity and patristic authority:

But fyrst I wyl wyth an humble entent
Me conform to þe sage counsel
Of a phylosofyr, wych, as Austyn doth tel,
The prynce is of phylosofyrs alle,
Wurthyly whom men Plate calle,
Wych in hys book of hy Phylosofye
That he entytlyt vn-to Thymye,
Hys dyscyple, seyis on þis wyse:
'To al men,' quod he, 'it is a guyse,
A cerymonye aryit, & a custom
Obseruyd & kept as a relygyoun,
In alle her werkys both more & lesse,
At þe begynnyng wyth humbylnesse
To beseche þe souereyn dyuynyte
In here werk begunne here help to be,
That þei not erre ner do amys'.
(ll. 5118–33)

As in the prologue to the whole work, Bokenham, an inveterate invoker of theory, turns to philosophy and philosophers, suitably patristically-filtered, to guide and valorise what he does. He intends to perform an act of *translatio studii* or *translatio auctoritatis* to outdo the pagans with superior Christian prayer:[19]

> Syth þan paynyms obseruyd þis,
> Mych more me þinkyth awt we
> It to perform wych crystyn be,
> And of owr-self mowe no þing do,
> In alle oure werkys recours haue to
> Our souereyn god wyth humble preyere;
> Wherfore, er ferther in þis matere
> I do procede, wyth hert & thought
> To hym I þus preye þat me made of nought.
> O souereyn & most blyssyd trynyte . . .
>
> (ll. 5134–43)

Thus begins a long prayer (ll. 5143–262), towards the end of which, in a manner reminiscent of Walton in his Boethius preface, he spurns the Muses for Christ (ll. 5214–24). He then rejects the insincere eloquence of profane contemporary courtly poets, who deceive their ladies into thinking they are near a lovesick death with conceitful language so decorated that it has the colours of May or of a peacock's tail, which is hardly appropriate to their professed morbid subject matter (ll. 5225–43). Bokenham, on the other hand, has a 'humble entent & hert entere' (l. 5247) to serve God and the 'entent' of Isabel's devotion, and of any other readers (ll. 5246–58). He intends to 'translate' properly, despite his inability, 'in wurdys pleyne/In-to oure langwage oute of latyn' (ll. 5252–3). *Fidus interpres* indeed.[20]

4. INTERLUDE

We can now move on from Bokenham the translator at revel to Bokenham the translator on holiday. Whereas Twelfth Night gave him an opportunity to start a new translation, Michaelmas provides the occasion for abandoning his translating for a recreational break.

The medieval notion of literature as recreation for those who read it, and even for those who wrote it, is well-known. Even the mighty *De Consolatione Philosophiae*, Walton tells us, was written as a 'recreacioun'.[21] For the sake of refreshment, however, Bokenham takes a break from literature, for half-way through the Legend of St Margaret, he decides to be anything other than a translator for nine days:

And now of you I aske leyser & space
Of reste a whyle, for certeynly
Euene as a pilgrym so fare now y . . .
(ll. 878–80)

This translator-pilgrim is tired, hungry and needs refreshment, so that he will be 'More strong to performyn his iourne' (l. 893). His self-presentation is particularly appropriate, for his translating is a journey of devotion through textual labour. It is framed by petitionary prayer, with Bokenham hoping to draw on the merits of the saints through whose Lives he progresses, almost as if he were visiting their shrines. This ties in nicely with his weaving of a real-life pilgrimage to St James into the fabric of the Mary Magdalen *Prolocutorye*, and his working-in of the story of his Italian pilgrimage into the prologue that opens the whole work. Moreover, it is not inconceivable that he was attempting in some corrective way to produce a moralized complement to, or effacement of, the most famous piece of pilgrimage literature in English, the *Canterbury Tales* (he knew the works of Chaucer well enough to draw on the *Second Nun's Tale* for his version of the Life of St Cecilia).[22] Perhaps we have here a one-man moralized hagiographical response to, or *translatio* of, not just the *Legend of Good Women* but also, perhaps, the *Canterbury Tales*, for in the *Legendys of Hooly Wummen* all the faithfully-rehearsed tales are about women who were not merely good but historically holy. Repetitively similar, the *Legendys* are told by the same non-fictional pilgrim-compiler. To be sure, all the tales suit the teller.

Such speculation aside, Osbern's hands, wits, eyes and pen are giving out:

Ryht so, as I seyde, it faryth be me;
For sykyr myn handys gynne to feynte,
My wyt to dullyn, and myn eyne bleynte
Shuld be, ner helpe of a spectacle;
My penne also gynnyth make obstacle,
And lyst no lengere on paper to renne,
For I so ofte haue maad to grenne
Hys snowte vp-on my thombys ende,
That he ful ny is waxyn vnthende;
For euere as he goth he doth blot,
And in my book makyth many a spot,
Menyng therby that for the beste
Were for vs bothe a whyle to reste,
Til that my wyt and also he
Myht be sum craft reparyd be.
(ll. 894–908)

116

He then asks for a break till Michaelmas, which is 'not longe' (l. 911), only nine days away. Taking what he asks for, he signs off cheerfully, and starts again—not, as promised, at Michaelmas, but *after*:

> For lengere leyser I nyl aske ywys.
> This grauntyd, fare-weel! now am I free
> Nyne dayes heraftyr for to pleye me.
>
> Now myhilmesse day is come & past,
> To acomplyse I wyl me hast
> The promys wych that I behyht.
> (ll. 918–23)

To the twentieth-century reader, raised on the conventions of novelistic and dramatic illusion, and schooled in the preoccupation of some modern critics with showing that writing is about writing, this gap may look opportune. But to discourse at this point on frame-breaking or the work laying bare the conditions of its production, reflexivity, etc., is, we might think, possibly to make more of this than need be. In short, Osbern took a break, and was garrulous about it, as usual: he re-iterates what he has so far done (ll. 869–75), and gives details of the date, circumstances, and intention, in all playfully advertising himself and his work by telling us that he is doing his best with his hard literary labours. Interestingly, it looks as if the *circumstantiae* of academic tradition which we encountered in the prologue inform his re-introduction to the remainder of the legend:

> . . . whow & whan,
> Fro whens, & wheder, & be what man,
> And also fyrst be what occasyoun,
> Of seynt Margarete the translacyoun
> From Antyoche was maad into Itayle.
> (ll. 925–9)

Such snappy interrogativeness indicates a successful holiday.

5. TRANSLATIO *AUCTRICITATIS*: PROLOQUACITY, PETITION AND SELF-COMMENTARY

So, what are some of the key features in Bokenham's autoreferential paratextuality, and what is their motivation?

Firstly, though at times a little like the eagle in Chaucer's *House of Fame*, Osbern does not betray or stultify the Aristotelian idiom, counter to what has been argued elsewhere.[23] The energy of his use of it and the discursive diversity of materials and postures he works into the Four

117

Causes prologue show the tradition to be alive and serviceable. It would be wrong to expect him to show the same imagination in procedure and playing with theoretical tradition that we see in Chaucer or Gower, for he is writing serious hagiography, not a mock-*compilatio* with fictional pilgrim-*auctores* (*Canterbury Tales*), or tales of love within a moral framework (and complete with moralizing glosses) like the *Confessio Amantis*.

Turning to the more autobiographical elements of his work, it can be seen that theory, literary convention and 'real life' (and its tales) were by no means mutually exclusive. His literary transactions seem to have a real social dimension, however affectedly conventional at least some of them may seem. Though we cannot be certain of the factuality or details of his own 'circumstances', i.e. what/how things really happened, it seems reasonable to conclude that Bokenham uses theory and rhetorical convention to construct his claims about what happened in 'real life'. Moreover, he seems, or at least claims, to have followed and utilized convention in his conduct, as anyone might. The confluence of autobiography, theory and rhetoricizing—which might be termed his 'proloquacity'—witnesses to the shareable affectivity of the familiar and authoritative, and the rehearsible plenitude and flexibility of convention.

Something might at this point be said about the *private*, i.e. *petitionary*, paratext and motivation for his activity. We must not and cannot ever forget that Bokenham's perpetually petitionary disposition, which was made possible and buttressed by his translating of the Lives of holy women, is intended to get favour from those saints and prayers from patrons and readers. Given Osbern's vital personal interest in this function, it could perhaps be said that the hagiographical matter is a paratextual enablement to the text of prayer, thereby inverting the text/paratext relationship. Such a quality was by no means unusual in medieval literature. Just as the *Legendys of Hooly Wummen* are studded with prayers and petitions, so the fifteenth-century meditative Life of Christ, the *Speculum Devotorum*, has a petitionary frame and centrepiece, for the translator requests the reader to say three Aves, three Pater Nosters and a Creed at the beginning, middle and end of the text, not only for the grace that is necessary for the reading of the work, but also for the forgiveness of the writer's own sins.[24] Divine favour, however, is not just to be had through prayer but through literary labour itself: to translate a saint's life is effectively to serve that saint, who has powers to guide the pen of the hagiographer. Therefore Bokenham asks for the saints' and the Holy Ghost's intercession on his behalf at the beginnings and/or ends of legends. Take, for example, his request to Borgh to pray to St Margaret for a pardon for him (ll. 226–40), or his closing prayer in the legend of St Feyth:

> And specyaly, lady, for þi passyoun,
> Shewe hem þe grace of singulere fauour
> Wych in-to ynglyssh of pure deuocyoun
> Of þi legend was þe translatour.
> Graunth hym, lady, in hys last our
> Of lyuyng, so to be clensyd fro synne
> Wych on þi day to lyuyn fyrst dyde begyn.
>
> (ll. 4028–34)

(Incidentally, Bokenham seems to be an unusual petitioner in not registering his name; but then, the saints, God and his female patrons should know him.[25])

Petitionary prayer and disposition went hand-in-hand with the humble instrumental efficient causality of Bokenham's literary activity, as presented by himself. Thus, St Margaret's gracious causality is invoked in prayer:

> Vouchesaf of thy singuler grace, lady,
> My wyt and my penne so to enlumyne
> Wyth kunnyng & eloquence that suffycyently
> Thy legende begunne I may termyne.
>
> (ll. 333–6)

Likewise, as well as asking for help from Agnes, he initially asks her to purchase not so much a saving pardon as literary competence (though he does not tell us which of the two he believes to be the taller order):

> Me wyt purchace, lady, & language
> Thy lyf begunne wyth to termyne.
>
> (ll. 4097–8)

It is only after performing his task that he asks for his heavenly reward:

> Gramercy also, o blyssyd virgyne,
> Most gracyous anneys, & martyr also,
> Wych vouchyddyst-saf þine erys inclyne
> To prohemyal preyer wych I þe made to.
> Gramercy, lady, for now I haue alle do,
> And for my guardoun, lady, purches þou me
> The aftyr þis mysery in blysse to se.
>
> (ll. 4729–35)

A highly personal affectionate devotion permeates such requests. A measure of just how pressingly real for Bokenham were his relationships with his saints is the fact that three of them, Cycyle, Feyth and Barbara (ll. 8272–84), are 'hys valentyns'. To him, celestially sentient and alive, they are more than mere literary *materiae*, and more, even, than remote efficient causes. Just as they are able to intercede on the basis of earthly-acquired sanctity, so also are they registered as still, in a way, in possession of their legends ('thy legende/lyf') as their self-conscious chief actants and effective *auctores*, or rather *auctrices*. This distinctive active authority, proper to 'hooly wummen' who cause (one might say 'engender') and graciously tend the mediation of their 'legendys', might perhaps be described not so much as *auctoritas* but rather as *auctricitas*, to coin another term. In their *Vitae* the women saints are presented, or present themselves, as in control and comprehension of what they do and why they do it. No mere passive victims, they ordain narrative events and construct themselves with free will and formulaic predictability. They know their own exemplariness, and are even given to self-commentary. As Lucy says of herself when boiling oil is thrown on her:

> In þe myddys stondyng of þe leye,
> Lucye stedefastly þus dede seye:
> 'I haue besowt my lord Ihesu
> That þis feer mow no vertu
> Or power haue to touche me,
> For two causys: oon ys þat þe
> The more anguysshyd I myht make,
> Anothyr ys of deth to take
> Awey from crystene men þe fere,
> And to suffraunce of passyoun þe myhtyer.'
> (ll. 9393–402)

From legend to legend, much the same woes and joys happen in the same ways for the same reasons to rather indistinguishable saints, who can still exert influence on the re-iteration of their formulaic histories: it is the translator's duty to follow saint and story faithfully. Bokenham's repetition of such 'fixed' narratives is cognate with his rehearsal of another formulaic discourse, the discourse of petition and prayer, for his petitions and prayers, on one hand, and his translating, on the other, are both forms of devotional recitation.

But sometimes in his paratext, Osbern seems to be going his own way, displaying himself as a writer. This, however, is not so much a display of self, in terms of name, honour and reputation, as of self as correct, exemplary and trustworthy. He does this to justify his matter and manner, and to win prayer or ghostly favour, an objective much more important and pressing than recognition either as a *rhetor* after the manner of Geoffrey of Vinsauf, or, still less, as an *auctor*. After all, he could scarcely appropriate, like a would-be *auctor*, the rightful and inalienable eternal property of a saint. For instance, if we think of Bokenham alongside those seriously egoistic Italian writers, Dante and Boccaccio—who, knowing all too well that the works of the classical *auctores* were accompanied by commentary-tradition, tried to canonise themselves as *auctores* by producing loftily academic commentaries on their own works—what we find is not comparability but illuminating contrast.[26] Where Dante in the *Convivio* and Boccaccio in his *chiose* on the *Teseida* try to make vernacular *auctores* of themselves by providing their own works with commentaries similar to those which academic tradition had produced for classical auctores, Bokenham, in his paratextual self-commentary, is a supplicant and compiler. Perhaps he could not conceive of the possibility of a vernacular *auctor* as such, for he regarded his superior English contemporaries like Gower, Chaucer and Lydgate, however wonderful, as *rhetores* of colours, not *auctores* (ll. 413–20). Though Bokenham draws on terms and idioms born of commentary-tradition, he does not produce the chasm of interpretative distance between paratext and text created by the Italians, who, in the depersonalized voice of the medieval exegete, extracted allegorical meanings and moralizations from their works. On the contrary, in his autoexegesis Osbern is wrapped up in an intimate petitionary deference to his Saints and the *matere* of their Lives. His paratext serves to protect and advertise the material's inherent utility in its transmission from Latin to vernacular culture.

The self-exegesis of Boccaccio's *chiose* and Dante's *Convivio* is different from that of Bokenham in putting reverent, i.e. moralizing, interpretations on texts which are frequently irreverent in their amorous subject matter. Hagiography, being already reverent, needs no moralizing. This is not to say that Bokenham does not present a moralized self, seeming to do the right thing by his patrons and saints. Unlike Dante and Boccaccio, who opt for the 'impersonal' voice of the commentator diverging from that of the *auctor*, Bokenham's unmistakeable voice, however obedient, is always audible in text and self-commentary alike.[27]

To be sure, Bokenham does not attempt by his paratextual autoexegesis to accord himself the status of an *auctor*, but his paratextual prayers and petitions, aided by his apparently genuine humility, would, if successful, have a different but nonetheless formidable power, for he believed that the prayers with which he besought the saints to help his work really could gain access to the grace desirable for him and his task. In his prayers grace is a signified, with the intention that it become a reality (*res*) informing the work. A comparable phenomenon occurs in medieval meditative Lives of Christ when the act of imagining Christ brings the reality of Christ Himself into a dialogue with the soul. Both petitionary prayer and meditation, in a sense, can help to bring what they signify to reality. Thus it may be said that Bokenham's paratext has an intended 'efficient' role in the production of the text. Moreover, in that Bokenham's prayers frequently praise God and His Saints they can be thought of as having the 'performa-tive force' of accomplishing what they describe, and as thus constituting a self-valorising advertisement of spirituality, 'since it is sufficient to say it in order to do it', as Genette says in a comparable context.[28] This prayerful aspect of the paratext, at first sight, has little ostensible function (unlike the literary-theoretical materials of the prologue) in producing, regulating or explicating the text. Yet both aspects, prayerful and self-exegetical, bestow value, for writer and reader, and an appreciation of this may help to explain the motivation and nature of the theory-invoking autoreferential paratext of the *Legendys of Hooly Wummen* and its ines-capably Bokenhamian *proloquacity*. For not only could the medieval paratext be the threshold between outside world and text, it could also be the threshold between humanity and heaven.

ACKNOWLEDGEMENTS

I would like to thank Alastair Minnis, John Burrow, Margaret Connolly, Michael Alexander and Roger Ellis for their helpful comments during the preparation of this article.

NOTES

1. See Gérard Genette, 'Introduction to the Paratext' *New Literary History* 22 (1991) pp. 261–72, and, in the same issue, Marie Maclean, 'Pretexts and Para-texts: The Art of the Peripheral' pp. 273–9.
2. Genette, 'Introduction to the Paratext' pp. 261–2.
3. *Ibid.* pp. 262–3.
4. *Ibid.* p. 267.
5. Osbern Bokenham, *Legendys of Hooly Wummen* ed. Mary S. Serjeantson, Early English Text Society OS 206 (London: Oxford University Press, 1938). See Serjeantson's introduction, pp. i–xxx, for basic information about Bokenham and his work. See also the following studies of autoreferential poetry by J.A. Burrow: 'The Poet as Petitioner' *Studies in the Age of Chaucer* 3 (1981) pp. 61–75; 'Autobiographical Poetry in the Middle Ages: The Case of Thomas Hoccleve' *Proceedings of the British Academy* 68 (1982) pp. 389–412; and 'Hoccleve's *Series*: Experience and Books' in Robert F. Yeager (ed.) *Fifteenth-Century Studies: Recent Essays* (Hamden, Conn.: Archon, 1984) pp. 259–73. See also A.J. Minnis on scholastic and vernacular Italian aspects of medieval autoexegesis: '*Amor* and *Auctoritas* in the Self-commentary of Dante and Francesco da Barberino' *Poetica* 32 (1990) pp. 25–42. I am grateful for access to a typescript draft of Professor Minnis's unpublished paper, entitled 'Medieval Autoexegesis: Authority and the Divided Self', delivered at Konstanz in 1991, which concentrated on Boccac-cio's *chiose* on his own *Teseida*, and on which I draw later in the paper.

122

6. For more detailed discussion and examples of the academic literary prologue, see Minnis, *Medieval Theory of Authorship* pp. 9–39; R.W. Hunt, 'The Introductions to the "Artes" in the Twelfth Century' in G. Bursill-Hall (ed.) *The History of Grammar in the Middle Ages* Amsterdam Studies in the Theory and History of Linguistic Science, Series III—Studies in the History of Linguistics (Amsterdam: John Benjamins, 1980) vol. 5 pp. 117–44; A.J. Minnis and A.B. Scott (eds) with the assistance of David Wallace *Medieval Literary Theory and Criticism c.1100–c.1375: The Commentary Tradition* (Oxford: Clarendon Press, 1988) pp. 12–36; Ian Johnson, 'Prologue and practice: Middle English lives of Christ' in Ellis (ed.) *The Medieval Translator* (1989) pp. 69–85, and also my dissertation, 'The Late-Medieval Theory and Practice of Translation with special reference to some Middle English Lives of Christ' (University of Bristol: PhD thesis, 1990), esp. pp. 104–59.

7. See Minnis *Medieval Theory of Authorship* pp. 28–9, 75–84, 91–4, 160–5.

8. Minnis *Medieval Theory of Authorship* pp. 164–5.

9. Minnis *Medieval Theory of Authorship* pp. 16–7, 19. See also Copeland *Rhetoric, Hermeneutics, and Translation* pp. 66–73, 161–6.

10. This refers to Hugh of St Victor's famous distinction of three levels of textual meaning, whereby the 'letter' involved linguistic construction, the 'sense' involved straightforward, open meaning, and the *sententia* was a deeper level of understanding which required an interpretative effort of exposition: see C.H. Buttimer (ed.) *Didascalicon* iii.8, Studies in Medieval and Renaissance Latin 10 (Washington: Catholic University of America, 1939) p. 58. See further the important article by M.B. Parkes, 'Punctuation, or Pause and Effect' in J.J. Murphy (ed.) *Medieval Eloquence: Studies in the Theory and Practice of Medieval Rhetoric* (Berkeley and Los Angeles: University of California Press, 1978) pp. 127–42, p. 131.

11. Kelly *The True Interpreter* p. 121.

12. See Minnis *Medieval Theory of Authorship* p. 164, where it is stated that, with Bokenham, 'the fourteenth-century belief in the idea of the *duplex causa efficiens* as a means whereby writers could decorously describe themselves as mere instruments of the divine will, has now been lost'.

13. For discussion of another late-medieval translator of authoritative materials who also draws on theoretical tradition and spurns the Muses for Christ, see I.R. Johnson, 'Walton's Sapient Orpheus' in A.J. Minnis (ed.) *The Medieval Boethius: Studies in the Vernacular Translations of* De Consolatione Philosophiae (Woodbridge, Suffolk: Boydell and Brewer, 1987) pp. 139–68, esp. pp. 160–2.

14. See Minnis *Medieval Theory of Authorship* pp. 164–5, who takes Bokenham to task: 'Bokenham gives himself all the credit for his work. His refusal to reveal his name in the "Aristotelian prologue" does not strike one as a particularly modest gesture, in view of the amount of autobiographical detail.' But it could also be said that it is fair enough for Osbern to seek spiritual credit through his work, and that this quest is buttressed rather than hindered by the autobiographical material.

15. Phyllis Hodgson (ed.) *The Cloud of Unknowing and the Book of Privy Counselling* Early English Text Society OS 218 (London: Oxford University Press, 1944) pp. 1–3.

16. See Serjeantson's introduction (EETS OS 206) p. i, and the note to l. 216 on p. 291.

17. Genette, *New Literary History* 22 (1991) p. 267.

18. For the terms 'epitext' and 'peritext', *ibid.*, pp. 263–4.
19. For discussion of these Latin terms, see Alastair J. Minnis, 'Commentary as Criticism: A Chapter in the History of Medieval Literary Theory' in Marianne Børch, Andreas Haarder and Julia McGrew (eds) *The Medieval Text: Editors and Critics: A Symposium: Proceedings of the Fourteenth International Symposium organized by the Centre for the Study of Vernacular Literature in the Middle Ages held at Odense University on 20–21 November 1989* (Odense: Odense University Press, 1990) pp. 13–30, esp. pp. 14–19.
20. The historical context of the varied topic of the *fidus interpres* and of attitudes to adequacy and faithfulness in translation is illuminated in Rita Copeland, 'The Fortunes of "Non Verbum Pro Verbo": or Why Jerome is Not a Ciceronian' in *The Medieval Translator* (1989) pp. 15–35.
21. See Mark Science (ed.) *Boethius: De Consolatione Philosophiae Translated by John Walton Canon of Oseney* Early English Text Society OS 170 (London: Oxford University Press, 1927), Prologus, stanza 10; and Glending Olson, *Literature as Recreation in the Middle Ages* (Ithaca: Cornell University Press, 1982).
22. I understand that Professor A.S.G. Edwards has projected a study of Bokenham's use of Chaucer in his version of St Cecilia's Life.
23. Minnis *Medieval Theory of Authorship* pp. 164–5.
24. James Hogg (ed.) *The Speculum Devotorum of an Anonymous Carthusian of Sheen* Analecta Cartusiana 12–13 (Salzburg: Universität Salzburg, Institut für Anglistik und Amerikanistik, 1973–4) pp. 10–11.
25. Burrow 'Poet as Petitioner' *Studies in the Age of Chaucer* 3 (1981) pp. 61–6.
26. Minnis '*Amor* and *Auctoritas*' *Poetica* 32 (1990) pp. 28–34, 40–1.
27. Minnis '*Amor* and *Auctoritas*' pp. 28–34, 40–1.
28. Genette, *New Literary History* 22 (1991) pp. 268–9. See also Nicholas Watson, 'Translation and Self-Canonization in Richard Rolle's *Melos Amoris*' in *The Medieval Translator* (1989), pp. 167–80: 'Praise is always in a sense about itself as much as its ostensible subject, since it can usually be reduced to a single and self-reflexive injunction: praise is telling oneself and others to "praise"' (p. 177).

Chapter 5

Charles of Orleans: Translator?

MARY-JO ARN

Most medieval translations that have come down to us were made at one or several removes (both linguistic and cultural) from the original texts. These cultural and linguistic differences make the translator's access to the author's range of meanings for his or her specific audience difficult. Medieval translators at times understood their authors' meanings and intentions well, but more often only partially. In addition, their intentions may well have differed from those of the authors of their texts, and so they may have felt compelled, either for their own reasons or because of the audiences they were writing for, to augment, shorten, clarify, or otherwise vary the text they were translating.[1] For the French and English poems of Charles of Orleans, however, these conditions do not hold. The English poems contained in London, British Library MS Harley 682, were made in most cases soon after and directly from their French counterparts, for private reasons, by a translator who knew the author as well as he knew himself. Indeed, translator and author were one and the same: Charles, Duke of Orleans, prince of the house of Valois and poet.[2]

Many of the resulting poems are hardly translations at all in the ordinary sense, however, and treating them as such removes them from consideration as original works of art. Charles's manipulation of his own work allowed him to exercise the (French) translator's art but also the (English) author's control. This unusual freedom produced some remarkable and intriguing results: after an extremely short novitiate, Charles not only felt unconstrained to translate his French poems accurately (either the text or the tone), but went so far as to play clever games with sound correspondences between the two languages that have nothing to do with translating the meaning of the French texts into English.

If fate had been kinder to the duke, he would never have considered translating a poem he had written in French into English. The son of

Louis of Orleans (brother of Charles VI) and Valentina of Milan, Charles was captured by the English at the battle of Agincourt in 1415 and held prisoner in England for twenty-five years. He was twenty-one years old when he was captured, forty-six when he returned home to France. French was a language of status in England in the fifteenth century, but the reverse was not true. Frenchmen may sometimes have spoken English because they were involved in diplomacy or trade with the English or because they had lived in areas of France occupied by the English (sometimes for decades or even centuries), but no Frenchman wrote poetry in English for aesthetic or social reasons, and Charles's first attempts to 'translate' his own poems into the language of his captors were probably born of a combination of boredom and the challenge of a new kind of word game. Charles was not breaking new ground, for others (beginning with Chaucer in the late fourteenth century) had translated courtly lyrics into English from French, establishing in the process a series of linguistic correspondences for names, terms, themes, and ideas. Nor was he rewriting his poetry for an audience of a status very different from his French one. His minute English audience, made up of himself and a few members of the households where he was held prisoner, was in many ways as similar to his French audience (his peers and members of his household) as any could be.

Charles certainly began writing poetry in English by translating work he had written in French, so it ought to be easy to trace the development of the poet's skills in his new language from fumbling beginnings to accurate, clear translations, but it is not. At some point he simply decided to put away his French poetry and begin writing directly in English. He even tried his hand at Chaucerian-style narrative verse—with brilliant success. But it is very difficult to say, on the basis of linguistic proficiency and accuracy of translation, which are earlier and which later poems (though other kinds of evidence make some understanding of the order of composition possible),[3] and the reasons why it is so difficult to date Charles's English compositions are interesting. Because his reach always exceeded his grasp, experimentation marks every phase of Charles's development as an English poet, and thus occasional difficulties keep pace with his progress in writing English verse. From the beginning, for instance, he was not inclined to re-use his French rhymes, in spite of the fact that many of them could easily have been transposed into English rhyme-sets, heavily gallicized as the language of English courtly poetry had become. What is more, the duke never felt constrained to produce a literal translation of his own poetry—or of anyone else's, as his remarkably loose English translation of a poem by Christine de Pisan (English Ballade 59) demonstrates.

He did not labour under the constraints that respect for the original author or material placed on other medieval translators—those, say, of the Wycliffite Bible—nor was he limited by any *auctoritas* or intention in the original text that was important to transmit accurately.[4] There was no message he felt compelled to convey to a particular audience, no audience he had to please. He was not dealing with (interpreting, commenting on) texts fraught with political, historical, or religious truth,[5] but with love poems, and with a fictional narrator who lives through two love affairs—each propelled by narrative verse and fleshed out with numerous ballades and roundels, all of them composed from the narrator's point of view. It is unsurprising, therefore, to find Charles 'playing a different tune' in his English poems from the start; nor, since he was writing primarily for his own amusement, should it surprise us that he seldom takes the easy way out when faced with translation problems.[6] As a result, his English poems sometimes look like translations, but the closer one looks the more the English poems seem to defy simple inclusion in that category.[7]

Though he frequently wrote octosyllabic verse in French, he nearly always opted for a ten-syllable line in English. On the one hand this required regular metrical adjustments to fill the longer line; on the other, it gave the poet more space in which to get out of rephrasing difficulties.[8]

> N'a pas long temps qu'alay parler
> A mon cueur, tout secrettement,
> Et lui conseillay de s'oster
> Hors de l'amoureux pensement;
> 5 Mais [il] me dist bien fellement:
> 'Ne m'en parlez plus, je vous prie;
> J'ameray tousjours, se m'aist Dieux,
> Car j'ay la plus belle choisie.
> Ainsi m'ont raporté mes yeulx.'
>   (*Ballade* VI, ll. 1–9)

> Not long agoo I hyed me apase
> In secret wise myn hert forto counsayle
> Himsilf forto withdrawe *as for a space*
> Out of Loves painfull thought *and trauayle*,
> 5 To which he seide [to] me, 'Nay, sett there a nayle!
> Speke [to] me no more therof, y hertly pray,
> For, God wot, to love *I shall me payne*,
> For I haue chose the fayrist *that be may*,
> As me reportid hath myn eyen *twayne*.'
>   (Ballade 6, ll. 1–9)

This is one of the earliest of the poems that survive in both versions (French and English).[9] The translation is generally line by line (ll. 2–3 are disposed somewhat differently), but the poet does not attempt to preserve the French rhymes. His techniques for filling out the English lines to ten syllables are obvious. In line 5 he replaces the adverb *fellement* with 'Nay, sett there a nayle!' The resulting line is both longer and more dramatic— an effect common in the English poems (a week in the French becomes a year in the English, etc.). In a second language, it is easier to write in concrete, narrative, or dramatic modes than in abstract ones, and thereby to be more certain that you have said what you meant to say.

The poet's problem in the following example is, unusually, too great economy in his English:

> Humblement vous en vueil prier,
> En le [i.e., my heart] gardant en loyauté
> Soubz clef de Bonne Voulenté,
> Comme j'ay fait . . .
> > (*Ballade* XXXII)

> In my most humbil wise y yow requere
> To kepe [my heart] in trouthe—how? in an holow tre?
> Nay, vndir kay of Faithfull Volunte
> As y haue yowris doon . . .
> > (Ballade 32)

He polishes off the meaning of the second (8-syllable) line in four syllables of English (*to kepe in trouthe*). In order to fill out the line and maintain the rhyme he inserts two rhetorical questions (*How? in an holow tre?*) that make the English more lively and colourful than the French, and give evidence that the poet did not hesitate (as a translator might have) to alter his tone and imagery when he felt he needed to. Roundel 19 provides a good example of the poet's wandering off from the meaning of his French original; the opening lines of the English version (about which I will have more to say) are a fairly close translation of the French, but the middle of the final stanza of the English version takes a turn and returns only at the end to parallel the French, necessitated by the use of a refrain.

> Puis qu'Amour veult que banny soye
> De son hostel, sans revenir,
> Je voy bien qu'il m'en fault partir,
> 4 Effacé du livre de Joye. . . .
> De confort ay perdu la voye,
> Et ne me veult on plus ouvrir
> La barriere de Doulx Plaisir,
> Par Desespoir qui me guerroye,
> 13 Puis qu'Amour veult que banny soye.
> > (*Chanson* XXIII, ll. 1–4, 9–13)

128

Syn love hath cast me banysshe everydell
Out of his hous, for now and evermore,
I must depart unto my grevous sore,
4 With face delyverid from all joy and weel.
    . . .

For of Comfort the way it fro me fell
Thorugh Mysfortune that hath me so fortore
That my lady hath my deth yswore—
With dubbil sorow thus I entirmell,
13 Syn love hath cast me banysshe everydell.[10]
(Roundel 19, ll. 1–4, 9–13)

Charles's earliest attempts to translate poems he composed in French into English are not much more literal than his later ones. A good example is the very first ballade in both manuscripts (composed, if not actually first, then nearly so). The French poem begins,

Belle, bonne, nompareille, plaisant
Je vous suppli, vueilliez me pardonner.

His English version begins,

Most goodly fayre aboue alle those lyuyng
I yow biseche that ye lust pardone me.

The first line of the French poem is indeed difficult to render word by word, since English tends to use phrases whereas French can use individual adjectival descriptors. Charles therefore uses a different rhetorical strategy in English: he translates only the first word (*belle/fayre*), picks up the meaning of *nompareille* and reshapes it into the superlative plus intensifier *most goodly*, adding for good measure the comparison to all other ladies (*aboue alle those lyuyng*). The second line is a reasonable translation of the meaning of the French line, though it is not elegant Middle English.

But that is not all. The word *bonne* reappears as the adjective *goodly*. However much we would like *goodly* to carry overtones of *good*, it does not carry that meaning in its adjectival form in the fifteenth century (or thereafter). Here, it is simply an intensifier, strengthening (as if it needed strengthening) the meaning of *most*.[11] The rhyme of the second line is also interesting. His transposition of the two final words in the line might be simply his translation of one syntactical grouping into another, or it may (and more likely does) represent a similar perceptual quirk to that involved in transposing *bonne* into *goodly*. Charles was not simply translating *me pardonner* into *pardone me*, but in a quite different sense, he was translating—or I would say transposing—the sound, the cadence, of

129

the three-syllable word *pardonner* into *pardone me*. There is abundant evidence of Charles's fascination with sound correspondences between the two languages, for instance in the opening line of the second stanza of this same ballade:

> Se si *a plain* vous vois mes maulx disant
> Force d'Amours me fait ainsi parler.

When he turned to English, Charles wrote,

> My greef *to playne* albe y not konnyng
> Loue causith this my nakid wordis fle.
> (Ballade 1)

The meaning is the same in both versions: 'If I cannot tell you clearly the source of my pain, it's the God of Love's fault.' But notice how the poet plays on *sound* correspondences in order to arrive at the English version. The verb *to playne* translates the meaning of *disant* (to say), but the sound of *a plain* (clearly). Charles used this same kind of sound-play in the first example, cited above, where '*N'a pas long temps qu'alay parler/ A mon cueur*' becomes '*Not long agoo I hyed me apase/. . . myn hert forto counsayle.*' Here he has picked up *[N]a pas* and reproduced it as *apase*. There is no possibility here of translation (or mistranslation) of meaning— only of a play on spelling and sound.

Charles wrote poems in English for his own pleasure. They were (especially at first) purely personal productions, though he surely showed them or read them to those around him.[12] His writing in English began as attempts to translate his French poems, but he never felt constrained to translate them as literally as, say, Richard Ros did when he translated Chartier's *La Belle Dame* or Quixley when he translated Gower's *Cinkante Ballade*.[13] For Charles, sound-play was as much a pleasure in writing in English as was the hunt for rhymes and their arrangement, or the wit of the verse itself. Some of the sound-play is internal, echoing and repeating and playing on earlier passages or poems (this is true both of the French and of the English poems), but this bilingual echo and repetition is perhaps harder for us to understand. Indeed such sound-play has been mistaken in Charles's case as evidence of *mis*translation by another person and used by more than one scholar in recent years as evidence that the English poems were not written by Charles at all, despite the narrator's identification of himself in the English poems as 'Charlis, duk of Orlians'.[14] These scholars are convinced that the English poet did not know French well enough to translate correctly, but many other examples have convinced me that the author of the English poems could not have translated from French at all if he had not known a word like *agree*, which he transposed into *in gre*:

> Recevez le, s'il vous plaist et agree
> (*Chanson* XXVI)

> And him in gre [willingly] take as yowre servaunt swore
> (Roundel 26).

Even more unlikely as a mistranslation is the second line of Roundel 19 (quoted above):

> Je voy bien qu'il m'en fault partir,
> *Effacé du livre* de Joye
> (*Chanson* XXIII)

> I must depart unto my grevous sore,
> *With face delyverid* from all joy and weel.
> (Roundel 19)

The French *effacé du livre* is rendered (or appears transposed into) *with face delyverid*, but that the translator could have thought that the one meant the other in English exceeds the bounds of probability.

Charles was perhaps not alone in indulging in this kind of wordplay in English, however. Helen Phillips has discerned a similar sort of play, which she terms 'homonym translation', in works by Geoffrey Chaucer. In comparing *The Complaint of Venus* to its source in the work of Oton de Graunson, she discovered 'translations' like *plaindre/pley[en]*, and she notes further a series of 'quasi-homonym translations' in the *Romaunt of the Rose*.[15]

To most modern speakers of English this kind of sound-play is unfamiliar.[16] Cockney rhyming slang, however, works something like this, where 'tit for tat' means 'hat', or 'dog and bone', 'telephone'. In rhyming slang there is no link in meaning between the words that stand for an object and the object itself; the only link is one of sound. This is exactly the kind of 'code' Charles is indulging in, except that in his case he apparently produces it for an audience of one. The French, on the other hand, may recognize this sort of sound-play more easily. In fact it enjoyed a certain vogue in medieval French poetry from as early as the twelfth century.

> Lasse, lasse, maleureuse et *dolente*!
> *Lente* me voy, fors de soupirs et *plains*.
> *Plains* sont mes jours d'ennuy . . .
> (Deschamps, 'Balade équivoque, retrograde et léonine')

Alas! Alas! unhappy and *full of woe.*
Slow do I see myself, save in sighs and *complaints,*
Full are my days of torment . . .[17]

The final syllable (plus -e) of the final word of each line is repeated at the opening of the following line, but in each case, with a quite different sense. Christine de Pisan, Deschamps, and many others indulged in this kind of wordplay on occasion, and although Charles never, to my knowledge, wrote a poem using exactly this technique, he was surely aware of it. Though I doubt that the technique as his compatriots had used it was very attractive to Charles, who seldom indulged in such obvious patterning, he rang the changes on it by playing the rather private game of matching sounds in his mother tongue to those in the language of his enemy, the English. For a poet who wrote macaronic verse in Latin-and-French and Italian-and-French and even incorporated the sounds a baby makes into one of his French poems,[18] such wordplay was only one of a hundred techniques for displaying his wit and indulging his fancy as he waited year after year for his return to France.

For a century and a half, scholars have been referring to Charles's 'English translations' of his French poems.[19] If we are searching for a better, more accurate word to describe the relationship between the two bodies of poetry, it makes more sense to refer to a given French poem as having an English 'version' than an English 'translation', and his work in English is best described as consisting in part of 'reworkings' or 'rewritings' of his French poetry (he composes many envoys for English versions of ballades that lack them in the French, for instance). Nor are we talking merely about systematic changes (though there are some) in tone or style. In many passages he does not attempt to say the same thing he had in the French version of a lyric. His are not simply loose translations, but variations (of many different kinds) on his French poems. To borrow terms Roger Ellis used in introducing the essays in the first volume of *The Medieval Translator* (1989, p. 2), Charles's English versions *neither* 'displace' nor 'replicate' the corresponding French poems. They are simply new poems. He is not attempting to 'make plain the implied meanings of an original' (p. 3).

Did Charles of Orleans think of himself as a translator or as a poet working over some of his older material? I doubt that he would have made any distinction between the two activities, and, if he had, I suspect that he could not have cared less which role he was playing. Charles was composing English poetry even when he was working from another poem lying before him, a poem that he had composed in French. In order to appreciate his poetic skills fully, in fact, it is useful (as well as entertaining) to read one of his French poems, then its English

132

counterpart, and finally to explore the space between the two; only then is it possible to understand how this most musical of poets heard each language sing.[20]

NOTES

1. On the various degrees of variation from a source text, see especially the articles by Copeland, Johnson, and Burnley, in Ellis (ed.) *The Medieval Translator* (1989).
2. According to Pierre Champion, who edited the French poems, a few of the French poems under discussion were written before Agincourt, the rest were written during the duke's captivity in England between 1415 and 1440 (*Charles d'Orléans: Poésies* 2 vols. (Paris: H. Champion, 1921–27, repr. 1971) pp. xxiii–xxv and 551, 407n). The English poems that correspond to them were all written during Charles's years in England. On the authorship of the poems, see my article, 'Charles of Orleans and the Poems of BL MS, Harley 682', *English Studies* 74 (1993) pp. 222–35.
3. For information about the order of composition, see the introduction to my edition, *Fortunes Stabilnes: A Critical Edition of Charles of Orleans' English Book of Love* Medieval & Renaissance Texts & Studies (Binghamton, New York, forthcoming).
4. Roger Ellis writes '. . . the translator [of a Bible-commentary] reveals an understanding that, however active a role he may play in bringing an authoritative interpretation of the Bible story to his readers, he is still the servant of that story, not the master: scribe-compiler, not author' (*Medieval Translator* (1989) p. 6).
5. This is not to say that translators of such texts always produced accurate, close translations; such translators often 'improved' their texts by augmenting them, or they tailored them for a particular audience in the target language by abbreviating or otherwise selecting or slanting the material found in the source text. In these reworkings, however, that kind of purposeful tailoring is not to be found.
6. Though it is reasonable to expect that he might have shown or read his poems to the members of the noble households where he was held captive and perhaps their guests (his captivity was not so restricted as to make this unlikely), discussion of his 'audience' is actually not very useful, since there is no evidence that his poetry was known beyond the households of his captors.
7. I recognize that the term is a fluid one, especially as students of medieval translation use it (see, for example, Burnley in *Medieval Translator* (1989)).
8. In itself, the use of a longer line generally marks the work of a translator of poetry. Hans H. Meier discusses Charles's use of the longer line (one of the kinds of evidence which established *Elckerlijk* as the original and *Everyman* as a translation of it) in his article, 'Middle English Styles in Translation: The Case of Chaucer and Charles' (in Michael Benskin and M.L. Samuels (eds) *So Meny People Longages and Tonges: Philological Essays in Scots and Mediaeval English Presented to Angus McIntosh* (Edinburgh: M. Benskin and M.L. Samuels, 1981) pp. 367–76).
9. The French is quoted from the edition of Pierre Champion, based on Paris, B.N. MS fr. 25458. The English text, slightly normalised, is from my edition

of the English poems (see n. 3 above). The English poems were edited previously by Robert Steele and Mabel Day for the Early English Text Society, OS 215, 220 (London: Humphrey Milford, Oxford University Press, 1941, 1946, repr. 1970).

10. Chaucer had provided English equivalents for many French courtly concepts, figures, and terms; these were taken as models by later English poets (translation of *loyauté* into *trouthe* in the previous passage is one example, though *Bonne Voulenté* in the same example is not). Note the echo in the English version of this example of the *dubbil sorow* of Chaucer's Troilus (to replace the *Desespoir* of the French). During his years in England Charles certainly read not only the *Troilus*, but Chaucer's *Complaint unto Pity*, the *Book of the Duchess*, and perhaps the *House of Fame* (see my edition, cited above n. 3). Those interested in comparing passages that diverge radically (all of them in the midst of 'translations' of lyrics) may consult the following sampling: English Ballade 5, stanza 3 and French *Ballade* 5; E B 11, st. 3 and *B* 11; E B 14, sts. 2, 3, & envoy and *B* 14.

11. Charles uses the phrase seven times in this way. He also uses the adjective form *goodly* to mean 'beautiful' and 'opportune' and 'excellent' and 'large' and 'kind' (the adjective phrase *more goodly* to mean 'greater'); the adjective *ingoodly* to mean 'very beautiful'; the adverb *goodly* to mean 'graciously' or 'willingly'; and the noun forms *goodlihed* and *goodlynes* to mean 'beauty' and 'graciousness'; *goodlyon* to mean 'fair one' (cf. the relevant entries of the *Oxford English Dictionary* and the *Middle English Dictionary*).

12. The name Anne Molins occurs in an English poem found, not in Harley 682, but in the (partially) autograph manuscript of his French poems (Paris, B.N. f. fr. 25458 p. 311, no. 120). A number of the poems in the Harleian manuscript point to similar 'uses', for example, Roundel 20, which begins, '*As for the gift ye have vnto me geve,/I thanke you, lo, in all that in me is*'. For further information, see my edition (above, n. 3).

13. Richard Ros, 'La Belle Dame sans Mercy,' in W.W. Skeat (ed.) *Chaucerian and Other Pieces, The Complete Works of Geoffrey Chaucer* (Oxford: Clarendon Press, 1894–9), vol. VII pp. 299–326; Henry Noble MacCracken, 'Quixley's Ballades Royal (?1402)' *Yorkshire Archaeological Journal* 20 (1909) pp. 35–50. We have ample evidence that Charles was capable of literal translation, for example in the letter patent that opens the extant English work (ll. 1–55).

14. See, for example, Daniel Poirion, 'Création poétique et composition romanesque dans les premiers poèmes de Charles d'Orléans' *Revue de Sciences Humaines* nouv. série 90 (1958) pp. 185–211, and Theo Stemmler, 'Zur Verfasserfrage der Charles d'Orleans zugeschriebenen englischen Gedichte' *Anglia* 82 (1964) pp. 458–73. Their arguments were countered by John Fox in his article, 'Charles d'Orléans, poète anglais?' *Romania* 86 (1965) pp. 433–62. See also my article (*English Studies* 74 (1993) pp. 222–35.

15. 'The *Complaint of Venus*: Chaucer and de Graunson' in this volume, esp. her n. 26. See further her article 'Chaucer's French Translations', *Nottingham Medieval Studies* (forthcoming). Isolated examples from known translators must be judged case by case; I am not suggesting that every mistranslation is a case of intentional wordplay. What I am suggesting is that the regular use of such 'sound translations' in the hands of someone who is obviously competent in both languages suggests that something other than error is at work.

16. Students of translation may well recognize the phenomenon, however. There are many examples of modern translators (who were not the authors of the source text) employing sound-play. For examples see Gideon Toury, *In Search of a Theory of Translation* (Tel Aviv: Porter Institute, 1980) pp. 42–5. James Joyce is said to have authorized readings, in translations of *Ulysses*, 'that involved sound equivalences or sound correspondences in preference to the retention of sense correspondences' (private correspondence; I am grateful to Prof. Maria Tymoczko for this information). This is, of course, quite different from the authorial use of such sound-play.
17. John Fox, *A Literary History of France: The Middle Ages* (London: Benn; New York: Barnes and Noble Books, 1974) p. 325 (italics mine).
18. For example, *Ballade* CIV; *Chansons* LXXXVI and LXXXVII; *Rondeaux* CLXV and CLXXI (Latin); *Rondeau* CCLVI (Italian); see also *Rondeau* CCXI, *Chanson* LXXX (Champion edition).
19. Some people have called Chaucer's *Troilus* a translation, too, and the term is probably about as accurately applied to the one as to the other (see Burnley's discussion of *translacioun* and *enditing* in *Medieval Translator* (1989) pp. 38–9).
20. Research for this article was completed during a fellowship year at the Netherlands Institute for Advanced Study, 1987–8.

Chapter 6

Richard Whitford and Translation

VERONICA LAWRENCE

The early sixteenth-century Bridgettine Father, Richard Whitford (c.1475–1542?), is known primarily for his original works. These devotional writings, which include the popular *Work for Householders*, are increasingly attracting scholarly interest among researchers in history, theology and English literature. Whitford wrote in English, often for a lay audience; he sought to defend and explain the faith on the eve of the Reformation. His translations, however, which amount to a sizeable body of works, have largely been ignored. A closer examination of Whitford's practice of translation, of the ways in which he expressed and modified his source text in the target language may be helpful for the assessment of the authenticity of works attributed to Whitford where authorship is in doubt.

Although he was writing at the time of the English Renaissance and Reformation, the subjects about which Whitford wrote and his manner of expressing himself reflect a continuity with the medieval past. His writings include translations of St Bernard's *De Praecepto et Dispensatione*,[1] the Rule of St Augustine,[2] the martyrology used at Syon,[3] *De Cura Rei Famuliaris* attributed to Bernard Sylvester,[4] a homily of St John Chrysostom on the subject of detraction[5] and a translation of the *Epistola de perfectione vitae*, attributed to St Bernard.[6] They also include translations of a number of works which Whitford ascribed to various authors but which have not been identified: two alphabets or crossrows attributed to St Bonaventure[7] and an instruction to avoid and eschew vices and follow good manners attributed to St Isidore.[8] Whitford also translated a Latin treatise, the authorship of which was unknown to him, and entitled it *A worke of dyuers impedimentes and lettes of perfection*.[9] In addition to these larger scale, formal translations, Whitford also engaged in the practice of translation in his original works by incorporating into them translations of passages from the Bible and the Fathers.

136

Finally, Whitford also indicates in his writings that he embarked upon the translation of at least three works, none of which has been indisputably identified. One of these is a translation of the *Scala Paradisi* of St John Climacus,[10] begun by John Fewterer, Confessor-General at Syon, and completed by Whitford.[11] The second is a work by one 'Mapheus' on the subject of perseverance.[12] The third is a translation of one of the writings of Jean Gerson but Whitford does not give the title of the work. This translation has mistakenly been identified with an early sixteenth-century translation of the *Imitatio Christi*, also attributed in its preface to Gerson.[13] The attribution to Whitford of the *Imitatio Christi* translation was challenged by Professor Glanmor Williams in 1961 on both stylistic and bibliographical grounds and his arguments are considered to be authoritative.[14] Indeed, one of the editions of Whitford's *Work of Preparation . . . vnto Communion* even contains a reference to the translation of the *Imitatio* in question but makes no suggestion as to the translator's identity. Whenever Whitford makes a reference to one of his own writings, he is at pains to associate the work with himself.[15] If, therefore, Whitford had been the author of the *Imitatio Christi* translation, it seems unlikely that he would not have mentioned the fact.

Two other translations have also mistakenly been attributed to Whitford. These are *The Four Revelations of St Bridget*[16] and *The Myroure of Oure Ladye*.[17] Perhaps the Bridgettine associations of both works may, to some extent, explain why they came to be attributed to Whitford. On its own, however, this cannot be considered sufficient grounds for attribution. Whitford refers infrequently to St Bridget or her writings in his works. Other bibliographical, thematic and biographical discrepancies[18] also make Whitford's authorship of these works highly unlikely.

This paper will only examine authentic surviving Whitford translations. Within this group, we will limit ourselves to a discussion of those translations where some comparison can be made between the translation and the source text. In the case of Whitford's *Worke of dyuers impediments and lettes of perfection*, for instance, we know that the work is a translation. However, the Latin treatise from which it was translated appears never to have been satisfactorily identified. The same is true of the alphabets and crossrows attributed to St Bonaventure and the instruction to avoid and eschew vices and follow good manners attributed to St Isidore. In the case of the translation of the St John Chrysostom homily on detraction, there arises the question whether Whitford translated from the Greek[19] or whether his work is a translation of a translation. This leaves us with a much smaller body of works: the Rule of St Augustine, the martyrology used at Syon, the *Epistola de perfectione vitae* attributed to St Bernard, St Bernard's *De Praecepto et Dispensatione* and the *De*

Cura Rei Famuliaris attributed to Bernard Sylvester. We have chosen to concentrate on the latter two works, although the others certainly merit further study.

The focus of the discussion of Whitford's translation of these works will be the way in which he shapes or changes his original. What does he add to his source text and what does he leave out? Does he give the reader any indication that he is making changes to the text that he is translating? Are any idiosyncracies to be noted in his practice of translation and have they any parallels in the composition of his original works?

In addition to an examination of Whitford's translation of St Bernard's *De Praecepto et Dispensatione* and the *De Cura Rei Famuliaris* attributed to Bernard Sylvester, this paper will also look at Whitford's translation of certain Biblical passages. In his original writings, the source from which he quotes most frequently is the Bible.[20] He usually makes reference to passages from the Bible in order to emphasise or illustrate the point that he is making. He incorporates these short translations into his text, indicating the source of his translation in the margins. These translations of Biblical texts will be examined in order to see whether they exhibit similar features to his translations of St Bernard and the *De Cura Rei Famuliaris*. Finally, Whitford's own comments on his practice of translation will be discussed in the light of his actual method of translation.

First, a few works need to be said about the two Whitford translations that will be discussed. The *De Cura Rei Famuliaris* is a short work of approximately only twelve hundred words.[21] Whitford's translation of the work may be found in all editions of his *Work for Householders* except the first,[22] and occupies only about eight pages. The Latin work is attributed to St Bernard and takes the form of a letter addressed to a knight, Raymund, who is described as 'castri Ambrosii' and, in some versions, as 'castri Sancti Angeli Dominus'.[23] Nothing further is known about Raymund's identity. Whitford, in his translation, makes no mention at all of Raymund. Instead, he addresses the letter to 'good deuoute christians'.[24] By doing this, he is implicitly suggesting that the work which he is translating ought not to be considered merely as a document of historical interest, but as a treatise of practical value to a wide readership. He does, however, translate the opening sentence of the treatise, explaining that the work, attributed to St Bernard, is by Bernard Sylvester whom he describes as 'a greate lerned man' (*'vir eruditissimus'*).[25] That Whitford should include such information is hardly surprising. In his other translations, he often includes details about the authorship of his source text. In his translation of the *Epistola de perfectione vitae*, for instance, Whitford states that the work has been attributed to St Bernard. He casts some doubts on the authenticity of the piece, but does not name his candidate for the actual author of the work:

A Good holsome lesson and profytable vnto all christyanes/ascrybed vnto saynt Bernard/& put among his warkes (I thynke) by some good man that wolde it shulde therby haue the more authoryte/& the rather be red & better be borne awaye.[26]

The *De Cura Rei Famuliaris* is a treatise on domestic economy. It advises the householder on how best to govern his servants, wife, children and purse. It is a relevant appendix to Whitford's *Work for Householders* which offers advice on the spiritual governance of a household.

St Bernard's *De Praecepto et Dispensatione* is a much longer work. Whitford's translation covers eighty-eight pages and may be found in the middle of one of his original works, *The Pype . . . of perfection. The Pype, or tonne of the lyfe of perfection* is the longest original and only polemical work that Whitford wrote. The only surviving edition appeared in 1532, two years after the earliest extant dated edition of *A Work for Householders*. The work concerns the three vows of the religious life and is a defence of the life of perfection against the attacks made upon it by the followers of Luther.

The work is divided into five parts. The first part concerns Whitford's defence of monasticism against the attack of the Lutherans and discusses the ceremonies of religion. The second part concerns the various religious Rules and is very brief because, as Whitford explains, the subject matter that it concerns has already been discussed fully and in detail in his translation of the Rule of St Augustine.[27] The third part concerns the three essential vows and is divided into three members. The first deals with obedience and is followed by Whitford's translation of St Bernard's *De Praecepto et Dispensatione*, the second concerns wilful poverty and the third chastity. In the fourth part, Whitford discusses religion and, in the fifth, the life of perfection.

De Praecepto et Dispensatione takes the form of a letter. St Bernard indicates that he is writing the work in answer to the request of two monks for a treatise on the subject of commandment and dispensation. He begins by asking whether everything enjoined by the monastic Rule ought to be considered as a commandment to be kept under pain of deadly sin, or whether it should be considered merely as a counsel, or whether the Rule ought to be considered as a combination of precepts and counsels. He then turns his attention to the subject of obedience, the chief precept of any monastic Rule. He enquires into the nature of monastic obedience and into the degrees into which it may be divided.

Whitford's translation of the work is introduced by a 'preface of the translatour as argument vnto the worke that foloweth'.[28] He gives the context of the work for the benefit of his readership so that 'the matter that folowethe may be vnto you the more open & playne':

> . . . you shall vnderstande that two religious men, monkes of saynt
> Bennettes rule: made instance meane and requeste (by wrytyng of
> diuerse epistles) vnto saynt Bernarde/to haue knowlege and exposi-
> cion or declaracion (for theyr conscience) of certeyne poyntes of theyr
> sayd rule. And he (to satisfie theyr deuoute mynde) made this boke
> or worke for an answere. And dyd dedycate/directe/and sende forth
> the same worke vnto a father of religion/the abotte of Columbens/and
> by hym to be sende vnto hym that was abbotte and souereyne vnto the
> sayd religious brethren.[29]

This short preface reflects an interest of Whitford's that has already been
seen, namely his concern with the background details of the work that he
has translated.

Probably the first thing to be noticed in Whitford's translations of St
Bernard and the *De Cura Rei Famuliaris* is his use of gemination, sets of
two or more words approximately synonymous, in his translation of a
single Latin word. As Valerie Worth has noted in her recent study of
translation from Latin into French in the sixteenth century, this practice
was common.[30] In Whitford's case, it was particularly pronounced.
Examples are numerous. Some examples of the translation of verbs are as
follows: 'prodere' becomes 'to betraye/disclose & shewe forth'[31] and
'exponendo' becomes 'in discussynge/exponing and assoiling'.[32] Adjectives frequently receive a similar treatment: 'vilis' becomes 'vyle: fylty and
stynkyng'[33] and 'ungues teneri' becomes 'soft and tender nayles'.[34]
Examples of the use of gemination in Whitford's translation of nouns are
'imperitia' as 'foly or ignoraunce';[35] and 'epistolae' as 'epistles/writynges
or letters'.[36] Even some adverbs are translated in this way: 'quomodo' is
translated as 'howe/or vnder what fourme or maner'[37] and 'quatenus' as
'how ferre/or howe depely'.[38] Combinations of adjectives and nouns are
also subject to such amplification. 'Magna providentia' becomes 'great
providence/and good foresyght'[39] and 'nuptiae sumptuosae' becomes
'sumptuous and costly weddyngs or bridales'.[40] One should note here the
difference in the above two examples of translation: in the first case, the
adjective-noun combination is translated twice; in the second, the combination is broken up with the two elements translated separately.

Whitford's extensive use of gemination in his translations goes hand-in-
hand with a characteristically heavy reliance on synonyms in his original
writings:

> *Swonynge* also or *talmynge*/is (in maner) a dethe/syth the body (for
> that tyme) is *destytute*/and *voyde* of all the wyttes and some in such
> *swones*, *talmes*, done *expyre*, *dye*, and *departe* this lyfe, yet those that
> done *suruyue*/*recouer*, and *lyue* agayne/done euydently shewe what

peyne they *had*, or *suffred*/that so departed in theyr *swone*, or *talme*/
but they *confesse*/and *say playnly*: they felte no manner of payne/but
rather a greate ease of all peynes: ergo in dethe is no peyne.[41]

Frequently Whitford's use of synonyms in his original writings is accompanied by alliteration; for instance, 'stubburne and styffe herted' and
'peyne and the punysshement of god'.[42] One finds this use of alliteration
in combination with gemination in Whitford's translations as well: 'red-
ditus' is translated as 'gaynes/gettynges/or rentes';[43] 'revidere' becomes 'to
count and compare'[44] and 'comperi' becomes 'I perceyued and proued'.[45]
Sometimes one can even see the way in which Whitford carefully chooses
the words of his translation in order to incorporate alliteration. He translates 'abyssum ingredior quaestionum' as 'I shal entre this depe see of
subtyle questions'.[46] Another example of modifications made to the
source text in order to incorporate alliteration may be found in Whitford's
translation of the phrase 'liquare culicem et camelum glutare'. 'Liquare'
is translated as 'melt or mince' and the entire phrase becomes 'melt or
mince a gnat/and swalowe a Camell hole'.[47] At this stage, Whitford even
decides to add a phrase not found in the source text, simply for the
purpose of enhancing the alliterative effect of his translation: 'to stumble
at a strawe and leape ouer a blocke'.[48]

What was Whitford's purpose behind his heavy use of gemination in his
translations? It was probably two-fold. He saw himself primarily as a
clarifier of the faith to those who were at risk of slipping into the error of
heretical belief. Thus, the act of clarification is intertwined with his
practice of translation. He was also very conscious of the cadence of his
compositions, as he certainly intended some of them to be read aloud.
Thus, clarification of the source text and sonority of the translation may
well be the reasons for Whitford's reliance on the stylistic feature of
gemination.

To what extent does Whitford stray from his source text? Does he make
any additions or omissions? Does he ever change the meaning of his
source text? On the whole, he tends to be very faithful to the text that he
is translating. When he makes additions to his text, they tend to be of an
explanatory nature, in order to clarify the text for the reader. Whitford
translates 'hoc ultimum' as 'this last distinction' and then, in case his
reader has forgotten what that was, he proceeds to explain: 'that is to say:
that some of the sayd poyntes of the rule: ben counsayles onely/and some
commaundementes'.[49] On another occasion, Whitford departs from his
source text in order to explain the meaning of the term 'voluntary': 'that
is to say: a thyng to be receyued of fre wyll at libertie/& nat of any neces-
site/notwithstandyng that same thyng that nowe I shall call voluntarie.'[50]
He also departs from the source text, especially in *De Cura Rei*

Famuliaris, to add some words of advice of his own to those of his source text; for instance, when *De Cura Rei Famuliaris* advises frugality and caution in domestic management, Whitford adds, 'It is also good policy: to haue one yeres rente/or a yeres gaynes in store for chaunces/whiche is nat contrary vnto christianyte: where extreme or very strayte nede is nat perceyued in the neighbour.'[51] This advice may have been informed by Whitford's bursarial responsibilities at Queens' College, Cambridge. Whitford's departures from the source text are not surprising in view of the later medieval perception of the existence of a kinship between translation and commentary.[52]

Whitford also has a tendency to incorporate into the translation of his source text a timely proverb or adage not found in his source. When Bernard Sylvester recommends that his reader live according to his means, Whitford adds: 'Then (after the commune proverbe) cute your thonges: after/or accordynge vnto youre ledder.'[53] In the same context, Whitford adds a Latin proverb and then provides a translation: 'An olde prouerbe. Qui plus expendit quam rerum copia tendit. Non admiretur si paupertate grauetur. That is. who so done spende beyonde theyr faculte/No meruayle thoughe with nede they greued be.'[54] This love of proverbs is reflected in Whitford's original writings where he quite frequently interjects a maxim or old saying to help him make his point.

Whitford leaves out sections of his source text less often than he makes additions to it. Sometimes when he runs into a rhetorical passage, the sense of which is repeated further on in the source text, he will not provide a translation. When the *De Cura Rei Famuliaris* declaims, 'Quid est avarus? Homicida. Quid est avaritia?',[55] Whitford does not bother to translate word for word presumably because the nature of avarice and the similarities between the miser and the manslayer are explored further on in the source text.

Only very rarely will Whitford abbreviate his source text in his translation. Usually the transformation of source text will involve the movement from a single word to a word-pair or word-group of roughly the same meaning. Only very occasionally does one find the reverse occurring. On one occasion, one finds St Bernard's 'consilia tantum vel monita' translated rather surprisingly simply as 'only counsayles'.[56]

Finally, Whitford will occasionally slightly change the emphasis of the source text in his translation. In *De Cura Rei Famuliaris*, one finds: 'Sumptus pro militiam honorabilis est', which Whitford translates as: 'Expences done vpon warre bene more honourable/than profytable.' Whitford then adds a sentence that does not appear in the source text: 'Better to suffre some wronge/and to bye peace than to make warre/or to keep warre',[57] making his own views on the matter perfectly clear.

Whitford does not always follow his source text sentence for sentence. He will frequently break up a sentence or phrase in his source text to form two sentences in his translation. This happens most often in his translation of St Bernard, who is notoriously difficult to translate and whose sentences tend to be quite lengthy. The following is an example of the way in which Whitford turns a phrase of St Bernard into two sentences of his own.

> sine nutu abbatis sicut dare, ita et accipere datas prohibentur epistolas.

> they ben prohibitte and forboden to sende forth any epistles/writynges or letters: without knowlege and lycence of theyr abbotte. So ben they (lyke maner) prohibite & forboden any thyng to receiue.[58]

Whether Whitford could have provided a more economical translation is debatable. It is clear that Whitford's main aim in providing a translation of his source text is the provision of the text in an understandable form to an audience that had no Latin and no formal training in theology. He had no intention of failing in this aim through lack of sufficient explanation of the concepts and teachings contained in his source.

Let us now turn to Whitford's translation of Biblical passages in his original works. There can be no doubt that there were certain verses of the Bible that Whitford was particularly fond of quoting. A favourite was, for example, Hebrews 13:14, which he quotes on four separate occasions and in three different works.[59]

If one examines the four times that he quotes this passage, one finds that he renders it into English slightly differently on each occasion. The first reference to this passage in *A dayly exercyse and experyence of dethe* is given by Whitford in both Latin and English: 'non habemus hic ciuitatem manentem . . . we haue nat here (sayth he [St Paul]) any cytie or dwellynge place.'[60] The final reference to this passage in *A dayly exercyse and experyence of dethe* also appears in both Latin and English. The English is rendered as: 'we haue here (sayeth he [St Paul]) no dwellyng place/but we do seke and serche for an other place.'[61] In *A werke of preparacion . . . vnto communion*, he translates the passage as follows:

> The seruauntes of Christe haue here nothynge in suerty, for they haue here no city ne dwellynge place of suerty to byde in: but done seke for an other lodgyng, where the [sic] shall be (as is sayd) in full surety and certaynty/neuer to chaunge, ne to be mynysshed of theyr ioy in any parte: but euer to remayn in one perfect and most ioyfull state/blessed euer of our lorde god and moost swete sauyour Iesu whyder he brynge vs that bought vs.[62]

The *Of Patience* translation reads as follows and includes the Hebrews reference almost as an aside:

> In tokyn wherof: euery man when he is fyrste borne, and receyued into the hospitall and ynnes of this worlde (for we haue here no dwellynge place) he begynneth thys lyfe with teres and wepynge.[63]

The fact that Whitford translates 'ciuitatem manentem' sometimes as 'city or dwelling place' and sometimes simply as 'dwelling place' and that he translates 'aliam' sometimes as 'an other lodging' and sometimes as 'an other place' suggests that Whitford's translation of the passage is a free one. It also indicates a reappearance of his fondness for replacing one Latin word with two or more English words of roughly the same sense.

These observations are borne out by his translation of some of his other favourite Biblical passages. For instance, in *The Pype . . . of perfection* and *Of Patience*, he quotes Matthew 11:12 four times. In *Of Patience*, Whitford renders the passage in both Latin and English: 'Regnum coelorum vim patitur. &c' and 'The kyngdome of heuen doeth suffre violence, and the violent persous [sic]: do rauysh, and wynne it.'[64] The first reference to this passage in *The Pype . . . of perfection* reads: 'The religion of christe dothe require violence punisshemente and constreynte of the flesshe.'[65] The second reference reads: 'The state and perfection of Christes religion/dothe requyre violence and stryfe.'[66] The final quotation of the passage reads: 'The perfection of Christes lawe & religion: dothe require violence & force/and those persones that ben violent/and quicke: done revishe & cayche it.'[67] Once again, Whitford has translated the Latin in a variety of ways. For 'regnum caelorum', Whitford has 'the kingdom of heaven', 'the religion of Christ', 'the state and perfection of Christ's religion' and 'the perfection of Christ's law and religion'. For 'vim patitur', Whitford has 'doth suffer violence', 'doth require violence and strife' and 'doth require violence and force'. For 'et violenti rapiunt illud', he has 'and the violent persons do ravish and win it' and 'and those persons that are violent and quick do ravish and catch it'. Thus, it is evident that Whitford translates his Biblical passages as he goes, in the manner that best suits the context in which he makes the quotation. Perhaps these texts were so familiar in his mind that he embroidered them perfectly naturally.

Eight other favourite Biblical passages of Whitford's will be given. All of his 'translations' of these passages will be shown so that the reader may compare them with one another and with the Latin text.

A Gospel passage that Whitford likes to quote in *The Pype . . . of perfection* is part of Matthew 8:20: 'Filius autem hominis non habet ubi caput reclinet.' He translates this as 'The sone of the virgine . . . hathe nat (as they say) an hole: to hyd his hed in',[68] 'The sone of man hathe nat where to hyd his hed & take reste in',[69] and 'For (as he [Christ] sayd himselfe) he had nat (as they say) an hol to hyde in his had/ne any thynge proper as his owne.'[70] The repetition of the phrase 'as they say' is interesting and may be significant. Whitford also quotes Luke 9:62 a number of times in *The Pype . . . of perfection*: 'Nemo mittens manum suam ad aratrum, et respiciens retro, aptus est regno Dei', from a passage that appears also in Matthew, though without this verse, only a few verses after the previous one. Whitford translates the Latin as follows: 'Here of I take of the wordes of our sauiour as in the places byfore rehersed/where he sayd that no persone puttynge his hande vnto the ploughe/& lokynge backe: is apte for the kyngdome of heuen',[71] 'No maner of persone that hath bounde hymselfe: by full consent of soule: vnto any diuine or godly werke/& after doth loke backe/& forsake that enterprise: can be apte/or mete for the kyngdome of heuen'[72] and:

> And where they [present-day religious] promysed at theyr entre: nat only to forsake the worlde/and all the pleasures therof: but also to bere paciently the yoke of Christ/& mekely to suffre the peines/& laboures of religion: now they loke back from the plogh/or plowe/ whervnto they put theyr hande/and dyd promyse by solempne vowe: to folowe the same continually with diligence . . ./vnto the ende of theyr lyfe.[73]

The last is a good example of Whitford's use of the Biblical passage in the context of his chosen subject of discussion. One final verse from the Gospels that appears fairly frequently in Whitford's writings is Luke 17:10: '. . . cum feceritis omnia quae praecepta sunt vobis, dicite: Servi inutiles sumus: quod debuimus facere, fecimus.' Whitford translates this passage in *The Pype . . . of perfection* as:

> Syth our sauiour sayth. whan you haue done all that you can:[74] yet may you say you ben but bounde seruauntes vnprofitable bycause you haue done that was your duety and bonde and no more[75]

and

> That is: whan you haue done all maner of thynges that were commaunded you: say you (vnto your selfe) we bene vnprofytable seruauntes. For we haue done nothynge: but that was our duete. And wo & vengeaunce shulde haue come vnto vs: if we had nat done it.[76]

The passage also appears in *Of Patience* as follows:

> For (as our sauiour sayde) we may iustly say when we haue done all
> that was commaunded vs: yet be we but vnprofytable seruauntes, and
> haue deserued no rewarde.[77]

Two of the Biblical passages that Whitford often quotes are taken from
the Pauline Epistles. One comes from St Paul's Letter to the Philippians
2:8: 'Humiliavit semetipsum factus obediens usque ad mortem, mortem
autem crucis.'[78] Whitford refers to the passage a number of times in *The
Pype . . . of perfection*, for instance: '. . . that is to meane by the obedience of our lorde and sauiour Iesu/that was rendred obedient vnto deth
and that deith [sic] moste shameful the deth of the crosse.'[79] Whitford also
makes considerable use of a passage from St Paul's Second Letter to
Timothy 2:5: '. . . non coronatur nisi legittime certaverit.' Whitford
quotes this passage once in *The Pype . . . of perfection* and twice in *Of
Patience*. His translation of the verse in *The Pype . . . of perfection*, for
instance, reads: 'No persone shall haue the croune of euerlastynge
rewarde but he that hathe foghten/wrastled/stryuen & duely laboured
therfore.'[80]

Finally, two passages in the First Epistle of St John recur a number of
times in Whitford's writings. One is 'Omnis qui odit fratrem suum,
homicida est' (1 John 3:15). In *The Pype . . . of perfection*, Whitford
translates this verse as 'Who so euer . . . dothe hate his brother is an
homicide or mansleer'[81] and in *A werke for housholders* as 'For who so
euer so doth [hates another person]: is an homicide and mansleer'[82] and
'For (as scripture sayth) who so euer dothe bere in the harte or mynde any
hatered, malyce, euyll wyll, or stomacke agaynste any christian, is an
homicide . . .'[83] The other passage from the First Epistle of St John of
which Whitford makes frequent use is part of 1 John 4:20: 'Qui enim non
diliget fratrem suum quem videt, Deum, quem non videt, quodmodo
potest diligere?' Whitford quotes this passage twice in *A werke for
housholders*: '(For he that loueth nat his neyghbour) whom he may se
with his bodyly eye or syght (sayth saynt Iohn) howe may he loue god
(whome he can nat so se) so in lyke maner the offence of the neyghbour
is forth with the offence of god'[84] and 'And sure it is, that who so euer
doeth not hooly and fully loue his neyghbore, whome he may se & behold
with his bodyly syght, he cane neuer loue god/whome he cane not se, nor
so beholde.'[85] He also quotes this passage in *The Pype . . . of perfection*:
'For saynt Iohan sayth/he that loueth nat his neghboure: whome he may
se & perceyue with his bodely syght: howe can he loue god whome he can
neuer so se ne perceyue . . .'[86]

Whitford's translation of Biblical passages, therefore, tends to be free, varying according to the context in which he is quoting them. He reasserts his love of synonyms in these translations. The most striking example of this is his translation of the word 'odit' as 'whosoever doth bere in the harte or mynde any hatered, malice, euyll wyll or stomache'.

One final feature of the Biblical verses that Whitford translates most frequently is especially worthy of note. Seven of the ten quotations that he uses most frequently encourage persistence in the faith in spite of adversity: 'the Son of man has nowhere to lay his head' (Matthew 8:20), 'the kingdom of heaven has suffered violence and men of violence take it by force' (Matthew 11:12), 'No one who puts his hand to the plough and looks back is fit for the kingdom of God' (Luke 9:62), 'when you have done all that is commanded you, say "We are unworthy servants; we have only done what was our duty"' (Luke 17:10), 'he humbled himself and became obedient unto death, even death on a cross' (Philippians 2:8), 'An athlete is not crowned unless he competes according to the rules' (2 Timothy 2:5) and 'For here we have no lasting city, but we seek the city which is to come' (Hebrews 13:14). This is consonant with Whitford's reason for writing. He never denies the difficulties and risks that his audience must face in living Christian lives; his main aim is rather to encourage his readers in their times of trouble and to instil them with hope and inspiration to struggle on. It should not be surprising that the Biblical passages that seem to stick in Whitford's mind and recur in his writings in translated form reflect the message that underlies all of his literary endeavours.

Finally, something needs to be said about Whitford's comments about his own practice of translation. He frequently gives his readers some indication of his methods of translation. In his translation of the cross-rows, he indicates to his readership that he has attempted to render the second crossrow as close to the original as possible: 'Thus haue we rendered the Latin in sentence/after the same metre/in maner and measure.'[87] Whitford also gives the reader an insight into his method of translating *An instrucyon to auoyde and eschewe vices*. He self-consciously chose to adopt a mode of translation that was not strictly literal: 'more after the sens and meanyng of the auctour: then after the letter.'[88] He adds that he has included in his translation not only the entire effect of his Latin source but also has mingled with his translation certain relevant insights of his own: '. . . and somewhere I haue added vnto the auctour, rather than minushed any thynge.'[89] Whitford also adopted an abbreviation, 'a.l.', in the margins of *The Martiloge*, an abbreviation that he also used in his translation of *The Rule of St Augustyne*. He used it in order to indicate that his translation had consciously strayed from the Latin because he had deemed the Latin to be faulty.[90] He explains his use of this abbreviation in the preface to *The Rule*:

> And where in ony place this comyn edicyon doth dyffre from the origynall: we haue noted the same in the margende with these letters. a.l. id est alia littera. that is/an other lettre.[91]

Although Whitford was concerned about the integrity of his translation, communication with his reader was always his main concern. This may in part explain his amplification of the source text through the use of gemination.

It has been shown that Whitford's translations comprise a substantial proportion of his *corpus*. Although many of these are difficult to study from the perspective of Whitford's practice of translation because the source text cannot be identified, an examination of those which are based on a known source text has proved very valuable. It has highlighted characteristic features not only of Whitford's translations but also features which his translations share with his original works. These include his use of gemination and alliteration, often in combination with one another, and his love of proverbs. In both his translations and his original works, he is concerned to make himself understood to his readers. He has a tendency to diverge from his translation in order to provide a short commentary on it for the benefit of his reader. In the material that he chooses to translate, especially the Biblical passages, he is anxious to impart a spirit of hopefulness to his readers, a feeling which permeates all of his original writings.

Translations of two important works of spirituality, Thomas à Kempis' *Imitatio Christi*[92] (mentioned above) and the *Speculum Monachorum* of Louis of Blois,[93] have been attributed to Whitford but his authorship of these translations remains in dispute. When questions of authorship arise in relation to the canon of Whitford's writings, it is therefore valuable to compare the work of questionable authenticity with his translations as well as with his original works. Are there certain word pairs that Whitford uses over and over again which help to put his signature on his writings? Two examples of this have been noted. On one occasion in St Bernard's *De Praecepto et Dispensatione*, Whitford translates 'victus' as 'vanquisshed and ouercommen'.[94] In *De Cura Rei Famuliaris*, he translates 'vincitur' as 'vaynquisshed and ouercomen'.[95] In the same work, Whitford translates 'homicida' as 'homycide & mansleer'.[96] When translating 1 John 3:15 in both *The Pype . . . of perfection* and *A werke for housholders*, he again translates 'homicida' as 'homycide & mansleer'. It would be very useful to know which other word-pairs or word-groups recur in this way in Whitford's writings.[97]

We also need to explore the extent to which Whitford's efforts as a translator reflect the translation activities of Syon as a whole. Syon's reputation for a fervent and orthodox spirituality manifested itself, in part, in its literary productions, in the form of both original works and translations. Can one justifiably refer to a school of translation at Syon not unlike that at Vadstena, albeit on a smaller scale? Certainly Syon was active in the field of translation, but the extent of its activity and the part that Whitford played in this context still needs to be fully explored.

NOTES

1. J. Hogg (ed.) Richard Whitford, *The Pype or Tonne of the Lyfe of Perfection* vol. 3, Salzburg Studies in English Literature, Elizabethan and Renaissance Studies 89 (Salzburg: Institut für Anglistik und Amerikanistik, 1979) pp. 225–320 (ff. cxii^r–clxx^v) (hereafter *Pype.*)
2. See Whitford, *The rule of saynt Augustyne* (de Worde, 1525); see also W.A. Jackson, F.S. Ferguson and K.F. Pantzer (eds) *Revised Short-Title Catalogue, 1475–1640* (London: Bibliographical Society, 1976–86) (hereafter *RSTC*) 922.3.
3. F. Proctor and E.S. Dewick (eds) Whitford, *The Martiloge in Englysshe after the vse of the chirche of Salisbury and as it is redde in Syon with addicyons*, Henry Bradshaw Society, vol. III (London: Harrison & Sons, 1893).
4. See Whitford, *A werke for housholders* (Redman, 1537) Fiv^v–Giv^r (*RSTC* 25425).
5. Whitford, *Here foloweth dyuers holy instrucyons and teachynges very necessarye for the helth of mannes soule* (W. Myddylton, 1541) ff.Yii^r–Yv^v (*RSTC* 25420) (hereafter *Dyuers holy instrucyons*).
6. See Whitford, *A dialoge or communicacion . . . For preparacion vnto howselynge* (Waylande, 1537) Kvii^v–Lix^r (*RSTC* 25413.5).
7. *Ibid.* Iii^r–Kvii^r.
8. Whitford, *Dyuers holy instrucyons* (Myddylton, 1541) ff.66^r–86^r (*RSTC* 25420).
9. *Ibid.* ff.49^r–65^v.
10. See St John Climacus, *Scala Paradisi* in J.-P. Migne (ed.) *Patrologia Cursus Completus . . . Series Graeca* (Paris, 1864) 88, 631–1164.
11. Whitford, *Dyuers holy instrucyons* (Myddylton, 1541) f.47^r. (*RSTC* 25420).
12. Whitford, *Pype* vol. 2, p. 174 (f.lxxxvi^v).
13. *Ibid.* vol. 4, p. 452 (f.ccxxxvii^v); Thomas à Kempis, *The folowing of Christ* (Cawood, 1556) Ai^v (*RSTC* 23967).
14. G. Williams, 'Two Neglected London Welsh Clerics: Richard Whitford and Richard Gwent' *The Transactions of the Honorable Society of Cymmrodorion* (1961) vol. I pp. 30–2; David Knowles *Bare Ruined Choirs: The Dissolution of the English Monasteries* (Cambridge: Cambridge University Press, 1976) p. 103n, although James Hogg still regards the question as open. (Whitford, *Pype* vol. 1, part 2, pp. iii, 79–99.)
15. Whitford, *A werke of preparacion* (Redman, 1531?) Bii^b (*RSTC* 25412); V.J. Lawrence, 'The Life and Writings of Richard Whitford' (University of St Andrews: PhD thesis, 1987) ch. 2.

16. *The Four Revelations of St Bridget* (Godfray, n.d.) (*RSTC* 1915).
17. J.H. Blunt (ed.) *The Myroure of oure Ladye* Early English Text Society ES xix (London: N. Trübner & Co., 1873).
18. Lawrence, 'Life and Writings of Whitford' pp. 104–6, 121–32; Whitford, *Pype* vol. 1, part 2, pp. 72–9.
19. Whitford's contemporary at Syon, the martyr Richard Reynolds, was known to have been adept in Greek; see D. Knowles, *Religious Orders in England* vol. 3 (Cambridge: Cambridge University Press, 1959) p. 215.
20. Lawrence,'Life and Writings of Richard Whitford' p. 212.
21. See J. Rawson Lumby (ed.) *Bernardus de cura rei famuliaris, with some Early Scottish Prophecies, etc.* Early English Text Society OS 42 (London: Trübner & Co., 1870) (hereafter *Bernardus de cura rei famuliaris*) pp. vi–ix. See also *RSTC* 1967.3.
22. That is, *RSTC* 25421.8.
23. *Bernardus de cura rei famuliaris* pp. vi, 1.
24. Whitford, *A werke for housholders* (Redman, 1537) Fiv^v.
25. *Loc. cit.*
26. Whitford, *A dialoge or communication . . . For preparacion vnto howselynge* (Waylande, 1537) Kvii^v–Kviii^r (*RSTC* 25413.5). The *Epistola de perfectione vitae* had previously been translated by Thomas Betson in his *Ryght profytable treatyse* of 1500. This may have been the translation that Whitford considered reworking, but he ultimately abandoned the project in favour of a complete retranslation. See A.I. Doyle, 'Thomas Betson of Syon Abbey', *The Library* 5th ser. xi (1956) pp. 117–8.
27. Whitford, *Pype* vol. 2, p. 123 (f.lxii^r).
28. Ibid. vol. 3, p. 225 (f.cxii^r).
29. *Loc. cit.* Contracted forms have been expanded silently in quotations.
30. Valerie Worth, *Practising Translation in Renaissance France: The Example of Etienne Dolet* (Oxford: Clarendon Press, 1988) p. 18.
31. St Bernard, *Sancti Bernardi Opera, Vol. 3: Tractatus et Opuscula*, J. Leclercq and H.M. Rochais (eds) (Rome: Editiones Cistercienses, 1966) p. 254 (hereafter Leclercq and Rochais); Whitford *Pype* vol. 3, p. 227 (f.cxiii^r).
32. Leclercq and Rochais, p. 254; Whitford, *Pype* vol. 3, p. 228 (f.cxiii^v).
33. *Bernardus de cura rei famuliaris*, p. vi; Whitford, *A werke for housholders* (Redman, 1537) Fv^v (*RSTC* 25425).
34. Leclercq and Rochais, p. 254; Whitford, *Pype* vol. 3, p. 228 (f.cxiii^v).
35. Leclercq and Rochais, p. 254; Whitford, *Pype* vol. 3, p. 227 (f.cxiii^r).
36. Leclercq and Rochais, p. 253; Whitford, *Pype* vol. 3, p. 227 (f.cxii^v).
37. Leclercq and Rochais, p. 254; Whitford, *Pype* vol. 3, p. 229 (f.cxii^v).
38. *Loc. cit.*
39. *Bernardus de cura rei famuliaris*, p. vi; Whitford, *A werke for housholders* (Redman, 1537) Fv^b (*RSTC* 25425).
40. *Loc. cit.*
41. Whitford, *A dayly exercyse and experyence of dethe* (hereafter *Dethe*) (Waylande, 1537) Aviir– ^{v} (*RSTC* 25413.5). See also Whitford, *Pype* vol. 5 (Appendices, including a transcript of the 1537 Waylande edition of *Dethe*) p. 71. Note Whitford's frequent use of triplets in this extract (italics mine) from one of his original works.
42. Whitford, *A werke for housholders* (de Worde, 1530) Diii^r (*RSTC* 25422). See also, Whitford, *Pype* vol. 5 (Appendices, including a transcript of the 1530 de Worde edition of *A werke for housholders*) p. 32.

43. *Bernardus de cura rei famuliaris* p. vi; Whitford, *A werke for housholders* (Redman, 1537) Fvʳ (*RSTC* 25425).
44. *Bernardus de cura rei famuliaris*, p. vi; Whitford, *A werke for housholders* (Redman, 1537) Fvᵛ (*RSTC* 25425).
45. Leclercq and Rochais, p. 253; Whitford, *Pype* vol. 3, p. 227 (f.cxiiiʳ).
46. Leclercq and Rochais, p. 254; Whitford, *Pype* vol. 3, p. 228 (f.cxiiiᵛ).
47. Leclercq and Rochais, p. 255; Whitford, *Pype* vol. 3, p. 230 (f.cxiiiᵛ).
48. Whitford, *Pype* vol. 3, p. 230 (f.cxiiiiᵛ).
49. Leclercq and Rochais, p. 255; Whitford, *Pype* vol. 3, p. 229 (f.cxiiiiʳ).
50. Whitford, *Pype* vol. 3, p. 230 (f.cxiiiiᵛ).
51. Whitford, *A werke for housholders* (Redman, 1537) Fvʳ (*RSTC* 25425).
52. See Johnson, 'Prologue and Practice: Middle English Lives of Christ' in Ellis (ed.) *The Medieval Translator* (1989) pp. 71–2.
53. Whitford, *A werke for housholders* (Redman, 1537) Fvʳ (*RSTC* 25425).
54. *Ibid*. Fvʳ–Fvᵛ.
55. *Bernardus de cura rei famuliaris* p. vii.
56. Leclercq and Rochais, p. 254; Whitford, *Pype* vol. 3, p. 226 (f.cxiiᵛ).
57. *Bernardus de cura rei famuliaris* p. vi; Whitford, *A werke for housholders* (Redman, 1537) Fvᵛ (*RSTC* 25425).
58. Leclercq and Rochais, p. 253; Whitford, *Pype* vol. 3, p. 226 (f.cxiiᵛ).
59. The passage is quoted in *A dayly exercyse and experyence of dethe*, *Of Patience* (see *RSTC* 25420) and *A werke of preparacion, vnto communion*.
60. Whitford, *Dethe* (Waylande, 1537) Aviᵛ (*RSTC* 25414). See also Whitford, *Pype* vol. 5, p. 70.
61. Whitford, *Dethe* (Waylande, 1537) Dvʳ (*RSTC* 25414); Whitford, *Pype* vol. 5, p. 97.
62. Whitford, *A dialoge or communicacion* . . . (Waylande, 1537) Eiiiᵛ–Eiiiiʳ (*RSTC* 25413.5).
63. Whitford, *Dyuers holy instrucyons* (Myddylton, 1541) f.40ᵛ (*RSTC* 25420).
64. *Ibid*. f.3ᵛ.
65. Whitford, *Pype* vol. 2, p. 28 (f.xiiiiᵛ).
66. *Ibid*. vol. 2, p. 82 (f.xliᵛ).
67. *Ibid*. vol. 4, p. 367 (f.cxcviiʳ).
68. *Ibid*. vol. 2, p. 42 (f.xxiᵛ).
69. *Ibid*. vol. 2, p. 53 (f.xxviiʳ).
70. *Ibid*. vol. 4, p. 326 (f.clxxiiiᵛ).
71. *Ibid*. vol. 2, p. 65 (f.xxxiiiʳ).
72. *Ibid*. vol. 2, p. 78 (f.xxxixᵛ).
73. *Ibid*. vol. 4, p. 361 (f.cxciiiiʳ).
74. 'All that you can' is an interesting point of translation, expanding the more limited 'omnia quae praecepta sunt vobis'.
75. Whitford, *Pype* vol. 2, pp. 39–40 (f.xxʳ–xxᵛ).
76. *Ibid*. vol. 2, p. 171 (f.lxxxvʳ).
77. Whitford, *Dyuers holy instrucyons* (Myddylton, 1541) f.45ᵛ (*RSTC* 25420).
78. Note that this verse is also frequently repeated in the *Jesus Psalter*, a work often attributed to Whitford.
79. Whitford, *Pype* vol. 2, p. 53 (f.xxviiʳ).
80. *Ibid*. vol. 2, pp. 82–3 (f.xliᵛ–xliiʳ).
81. *Ibid*. vol. 2, p. 35 (f.xviiiʳ).
82. Whitford, *A werke for housholders* (Waylande, 1537) Ciiiʳ.
83. *Ibid*. Eviiʳ.

84. *Ibid.* Aviii[r].
85. *Ibid.* Evii[r]–Evii[v].
86. Whitford, *Pype* vol. 3, p. 185 (f.xcii[r]).
87. Whitford, *A dialoge or communicacion* . . . (Waylande, 1537) Kvii[r] (*RSTC* 25413.5).
88. Whitford, *Dyuers holy instrucyons* (Myddylton, 1541) f.66[r] (*RSTC* 25420).
89. *Loc. cit.*
90. Whitford, *Martiloge*, p. 8.
91. Whitford, *The rule* (de Worde, 1525) Ai[v] (*RSTC* 922.3).
92. *RSTC* 23963–23968.
93. Syon MS. 18.
94. Leclercq and Rochais, p. 254; Whitford, *Pype* vol. 3, p. 228 (f.cxiii[v]).
95. *Bernardus de cura rei famuliaris*, p. vii; Whitford, *A werke for housholders* (Redman, 1537) Fvi[r] (*RSTC* 25425).
96. *Loc. cit.*
97. An examination of Whitford's use of cadence and an exploration of possible connections between it and that of the Latin *cursus* would also be valuable. For the relationship between cadence in the Latin *cursus* and the Book of Common Prayer, see the paper of Morris W. Croll in J. Max Patrick and Robert O. Evans (eds) *Style, Rhetoric and Rhythm* (Princeton: Princeton University Press, 1966) pp. 303–59.

Chapter 7

A Medieval Travel Book's Editors and Translators: Managing Style and Accommodating Dialect in Johannes Witte de Hese's *Itinerarius*

SCOTT D. WESTREM

Daniel Defoe, in one of the more curious anecdotes recorded in his *Tour Thro' the Whole Island of Great Britain*, describes a puzzling experience he had in the Somerset town of Martock, where, while visiting a school in the mid-1720s, he happened upon an extraordinary tutorial in session. As Defoe recalls the event:

> I observ'd one of the lowest Scholars was reading his Lesson to the Usher, which Lesson it seems was a Chapter in the Bible, so I sat down by the Master, till the Boy had read out his Chapter: I observ'd the Boy read a little oddly in the Tone of the Country, which made me the more attentive, because on Enquiry, I found that the Words were the same, and the Orthography the same as in all our Bibles. I observ'd also the Boy read it out with his Eyes still on the Book, and his Head like a meer Boy, moving from Side to Side, as the Lines reach'd cross the Colums of the Book; his Lesson was in the *Cant.* 5.3. of [which] the Words [were] these, 'I have put off my Coat, how shall I put it on, I have wash'd my Feet, how shall I Defile them?' The Boy read thus, with his Eyes, as I say full on the Text. 'Chav a Doffed my Cooat, how shall I Don't, Chav a wash'd my Veet, how shall I Moil'em?'

> How the dexterous Dunce could form his Mouth to Express so
> readily the Words, (which stood right printed in the Book) in his
> Country Jargon, I could not but admire.[1]

Defoe's wonder at what he assumes must be a kind of oral disfigurement
blinds him to the young boy's singular achievement. What is remarkable
about the Martock school lesson is not the 'Dunce's' physical ability to
produce bizarre diphthongs and palatalizations but his dexterity at sight
translation, automatically turning a passage of Authorized text in an
authorized dialect into a phonologically and semantically different form of
the same language.[2]

This phenomenon—receiving a text in one dialect and transforming it
with little effort into another—bears directly on the complex issues
surrounding medieval literary translations. It is a key factor, for example,
in mapping out the evolution of a peculiar travel book that purports to
relate the adventures of a priest from the diocese of Utrecht on a 'pilgrimage' during the late 1300s to the Holy Land, to India, and, he says, past
the very walls of Eden. The book survives in Latin in seven fifteenth-
century manuscripts, the earliest of which dates from 1424, and eleven
early printed editions, seven of them incunables and all but one produced
before 1510. These texts identify the author as Johannes [Witte] de Hese
and call the work the *Itinerarius*, a name and title that will be used here.
In addition, records survive of three versions of the same narrative in late-
medieval Dutch; these are untitled, attributed to Jan (or Johan) Voet, and
probably date from (or can be traced to) the second half of the fifteenth
century.

A careful study of the Latin manuscripts and early printings reveals
deliberate manipulations of the text by scribes and/or editors as they
sought to enhance the simple—even rather puerile—language of the original; over the course of four distinct revisions, the *Itinerarius* in its Latin
form acquired greater stylistic sophistication, although the actual
substance of Witte's travel claims and observations went nearly
unchanged. By contrast, the Dutch texts of the *Itinerarius* seem at first to
be so discrepant as to represent three separate translations. I believe,
however, that they can all be traced to a single rendering of the earliest
state of the Latin text into Dutch—possibly the dialect employed around
1450 in Holland (now a province in the western Netherlands)—and that
variants in the surviving Dutch texts result from 'translations' into eastern
dialects (Gelderland/Overijssel). Despite these orthographic and semantic
differences, however, the Dutch translation experienced less editorial
intervention than did the Latin original.[3] Witte's *Itinerarius*, in other
words, provides an intriguing, conservative case study for modern scholars
who are attempting to understand the medieval translator as scribe and

compiler with 'reference to the translator as author/interpreter'.[4] It also reminds us that contemporaneous (and sometimes competing) dialects constitute yet another factor that must be considered in assessments of textual production and evolution during the later Middle Ages, when people of all classes were 'multilingual, the borders between literature and functional literacy were not clearly defined, the cult of authorial personality was only just emerging, and the formulation of literary values had not such a grip as they do upon modern scholars.'[5]

Before examining in detail the Latin and medieval Dutch textual traditions of Witte's *Itinerarius*, I want first to summarize the book's content and to place it in the framework of other late-medieval travel accounts by Europeans who claim to have visited Asia: these works were frequently translated but the textual interrelationships have not received ample attention. Scholars interested in translation theory can thus find considerable material in the fascinating world of late-medieval travel literature. Against this background, my delineation of the textual history of the *Itinerarius* will acquire greater clarity, especially as I consider both the editorial freedom exhibited by fifteenth-century scribes of the Latin text and the different strategies employed by a medieval book's scribal editors over against its translator.

Johannes Witte de Hese's *Itinerarius* is a digest of miracles, danger, opulence, terror, disorientation, unexpected hospitality—in short, the full range of travel adventure. According to the treatise's opening sentence, the narrator was visiting '*sancta loca*' in Jerusalem when he decided to continue his pilgrimage toward the Jordan, making his way from there to Egypt. He crossed the Red Sea and ate some of its grotesquely-shaped flying fish; he crossed the Sinai desert and watched a unicorn detoxify a stream poisoned by venomous animals about a mile from the dwelling of a hermit fed daily with manna from heaven. Even in territory that was relatively familiar to medieval Europeans from Holy Land pilgrimage books, Witte's experiences are exotic. Without declaring his destination, Witte boards a ship in Egypt and sails past Ethiopia, through perilous seas, and into the arms of soldiers loyal to the Great Khan, who throw him in prison. At this juncture we learn that he and a group of companions (who enter the story unannounced) are in fact on their way to the shrine of St Thomas, the apostle to whom Christian tradition ascribes the evangelization of India, a saint so revered and feared that the Khan releases Witte instantly when he announces his devotional goal. Witte's route leads him through three expansive regions that are styled Lower, Middle, and Upper India; he encounters giant cannibals who prey on sailors, Oriental cities whose towering buildings dazzle his European eyes, and, in Edissa, which he reckons to be twenty-four times larger than Cologne, a magnificent palace whose architecture mirrors the wealth and piety of its most important resident, Prester John. The building is both a bizarre behemoth and an upside-down ziggurat—two German miles on a side, supported by 900 columns, and arranged in seven levels, each reserved for a segment of Prester John's population, and each larger than the last, reflecting the hierarchically increasing sanctity of its inhabitants.

Nearby, on the island of Hulna, is Witte's stated goal. In a great church, to which pilgrims cross dry-shod when the sea parts in its annual miraculous recognition of the apostle's feast day, he views the well-preserved remains of St Thomas. Witte demonstrates his sacerdotal vocation by carefully describing the Eucharistic liturgy, in which the Indian patriarch and two archbishops distribute the Host using Thomas's hand, which opens to worthy communicants and withdraws from sinners; indeed, Witte testifies that the omniscient hand rejected three people when he was there in 1391, but that after many prayers of intercession they eventually warranted the saint's approval.

Although he has attained his spiritual goal, Witte is still far from home and his adventures far from over. After receiving Prester John's permission to depart, he and his companions continue to sail 'in the remotest parts of the sea', changing course once to the north but tending otherwise to the east. He witnesses a spectacular sunset reflecting 'like a shining star' on the walls of the Earthly Paradise, nearly drowns when an island on which he is cooking dinner turns out to be an inhospitable whale, successfully gains the release of three souls from gloomy Purgatory, and avoids both Gog and Magog. His return to Jerusalem completes what appears to be the circumnavigation of an Earth with three continents, but of the Holy City he has nothing to report because, as he states flatly in his concluding sentence, 'Many people know what things there look like. The end.'

It goes without saying that the modern reader, like Johannes Witte de Hese himself, finds much that is incredible on this itinerary. While the work cannot be regarded as reliable history or deeply satisfying literature, it warrants attention as a literary phenomenon and a textual artifact. The *Itinerarius* stands as evidence, for example, that by 1400, the very motion of travelling could propel a narrative; here the journey is the plot and not simply a plot device, as the travel book in its infancy explores new ways for literature to instruct and to please.[6] Furthermore, Witte, whose historicity cannot be proved, establishes himself as the voice of a trustworthy traveller, claiming to have seen much but also admitting lapses in his observation and memory, thus echoing the voices of other fourteenth-century pilgrims, including the controversial John Mandeville. Like *Mandeville's Travels*, the *Itinerarius* acquires much of its information, albeit less carefully, from earlier texts, such as 'The Letter of Prester John' and some version of the St Brendan legend.[7] Finally, and perhaps most significant in terms of European cultural history, Witte's book

156

represents a shift—a translation—of the focus in conventional medieval itineraries from holy places in Palestine, territory that pilgrims had measured obsessively, to the fantastic Orient.

Because the *Itinerarius* bears a formal resemblance to other late-medieval pilgrimage accounts and because it no doubt catered to growing interest in the East during the 1400s, it is unsurprising to discover that the book, despite the wildness of many of its claims, enjoyed a moderate popularity in Latin and that it was translated not long after its composition. Many narratives about travel to Jerusalem, usually written in Latin by clerics, circulated in at least one vernacular simultaneously with the original version.[8] That the *Itinerarius* appeared in Dutch soon after its composition around 1400 is almost to be expected, given Walter Hoffmann's study of an increasing preference for writing in (Low) German among the scribally literate of the Lower Rhine region during the late 1300s. The magistrates of Boechout (East Flanders), in fact, stopped using Latin in 1249. Hartmut Beckers has pointed out that works in German about Oriental geography and culture were particularly popular in the vicinity of Cologne after around 1350.[9] The interrelationship between Latin and vernacular versions of books about travel, pilgrimage, and geography has received little attention, which is unfortunate given what such an analysis could tell us about the readership and function of a variety of texts. Most fourteenth- and fifteenth-century pilgrims did not read, and fewer still knew Latin. Vernacular translations of descriptions of the Holy Land expanded the usefulness of such texts as guide books for lay people who received spiritual merit for piously visiting shrines in actual Jerusalem or in recreations of its holiest places, such as the Church of the Holy Sepulchre, 'rebuilt' at Bruges, and, even more frequently, the Tomb itself (the Anastasis Rotunda), medieval copies of which may still be seen at Fulda, Constance, and Paderborn (and many other sites throughout Europe).[10]

The *Descriptio de Terra Sancta*, by Burchard of Mount Zion, is perhaps the exemplar of a meticulous pilgrimage account. Compiled in the 1280s by a Dominican who had spent several years in the Middle East, the book is a masterpiece of keen observation and judicious inquiry, one of Burchard's principal tasks being to arbitrate between rival claims identifying the site of a single event in Judaeo-Christian history (a dispute that had profound economic as well as spiritual consequences). The *Descriptio*'s virtues were not lost on its European readers: it survives in at least 110 manuscripts, two of which are in French and two in German; three sixteenth-century German printings are also known.[11]

Ricold of Monte Croce asserts that he travelled as far east as Baghdad in the 1290s, and his *Liber peregrinationis* offers an opinionated assessment of the inhabitants of the Middle East—Muslims, Jews, and

Christians (many of them schismatics according to the Roman church). His book survives in at least 15 medieval manuscripts: seven in Latin, six in French, and two in Italian.[12] One of the first European pilgrimage accounts to appear in the fourteenth century is William of Boldensele's *Liber de quibusdam ultramarinis partibus*, completed by 1336, and noteworthy in part because of its bold claims: William alleges that he charmed the sultan of Egypt into affording him many favours that enabled him to write an insightful, if not especially humble, guidebook. Records exist of 29 surviving manuscript copies, 23 of which are Latin; the remaining six preserve a French translation made by Jean le Long, a Benedictine at Ypres who produced a vernacular anthology of books related to travel and geography in 1351. In addition, Hartmut Beckers has reconstructed part of a Low German translation of the *Liber* from fragments of a fourteenth-century manuscript that was cut up and used to bind another text in the 1500s.[13] While it has few students today, William's book attracted at least two significant readers within a generation of its composition. It was the source of some of the information included in a pilgrimage narrative written around 1350 by Ludolph von Suchem (or Suchen), a parish priest from the diocese of Paderborn, who claims to have been in the Holy Land from 1336 to 1341, and whose account is one of the liveliest and most personal (despite its borrowings) of the Middle Ages. At least 54 manuscripts of Ludolph's book are known or recorded, 40 in Latin and 14 in a Low German translation.[14]

William's better-known reader, of course, was the compiler of the encyclopedic *Travels of Sir John Mandeville*, undoubtedly the most successful medieval book related to travel and a relatively untapped source for information about the processes of medieval translation.[15] More than 275 manuscripts preserve the text in its French original and at least nine other medieval languages: during the 150 years following its composition around 1360, the *Travels* appeared in Italian, Spanish (Aragonese and Castilian), Czech, Danish, and Irish; in addition, it was rendered twice into German, twice into Latin, four times into Dutch, and into Middle English (the 44 extant Middle English manuscript versions constitute six discrete recensions—four in prose, one metrical, and one stanzaic fragment).[16] Of these versions, only the German has been carefully investigated; no reliable edition exists of the original French, nor has any scholar ventured to explore thoroughly the interrelationships among the book's translations.[17]

Although they did not enjoy the extraordinary popularity or wide dissemination of *Mandeville's Travels*, two other medieval books deserve mention here; both survive in around 100 manuscript copies and both extend the reader's horizon, as Johannes Witte de Hese does, into the Far East. The first of these is the *Divisament dou monde*, a description of the world written around 1295, originally in French, by Rustichello of Pisa, supposedly based on information he obtained from his prison cellmate Marco Polo. The book, which offers an unusually trustworthy account of mercantile affairs in China but makes claims for Polo, its putative protagonist, that should be taken *cum grano salis mediaevalis*, has an extremely complicated but reliably investigated textual history, including translations into Latin, Italian, and German before 1450.[18] A generation later, in 1330, Odoric of Pordenone, a Franciscan from Friuli, dictated an account of his sojourn in the Orient, which may have lasted from 1307 to 1321. Like Johannes Witte de Hese, Odoric was far more concerned about peculiar wonders than quotidian life—or even the work of his fellow missionaries in China—but this may be the key to the success of his *Relatio*. Recent tallies put the number of existing manuscripts from 93 to 137, recording as many as three distinct Latin versions and translations into Italian, French, German, and Spanish. Of these, Latin, French, and German texts have been edited.[19]

As a story and as an artifact, then, Johannes Witte de Hese's *Itinerarius* forms part of an important literary tradition; the significance of its history as an edited and translated text will be the focus of the rest of this study. As noted above, the *Itinerarius* survives in Latin in seven manuscripts, seven incunables, and four other early printed editions. Over the course of its copying and printing history, the text underwent stylistic changes— but almost no substantive alterations—that make it possible to identify five distinct Latin versions of Witte's account: one that must be fairly close to the autograph copy, and four revisions, each rhetorically more sophisticated than the last. In addition, records exist of three versions of the *Itinerarius* in medieval Dutch that, despite differences in spelling, syntax, and even vocabulary, must all derive from a single ancestor. Pertinent information about these texts, including abbreviations that will be used for them during the remainder of this study and a register of the phases of the Latin text's development, is found in Table 1, overleaf.

Although the autograph version of Witte's book is lost, it was probably very similar to the nearly identical texts preserved by the earliest known manuscripts, both of which originated in the Rhineland: M (copied almost certainly in 1424 at Bonn by Johannes of Purmereynde) and Be (copied around 1460). The Latin in this first phase of the *Itinerarius* is rudimentary and unadorned: mostly simple, declarative sentences linked by coordinating conjunctions uneasily bear the weight of a narrative about journeying to the ends of the world. With the exception of Prester John's palace and the shrine of St Thomas, descriptions of which together comprise nearly half the book, the cities and lands Witte visits seldom keep his attention for more than one sentence; his vocabulary rises above the pedestrian only when he recounts liturgical matters, which suggests that if

Table 1

Latin Manuscripts

Be	MS lat.fol. 245	Staatsbibliothek zu Berlin, Preußischer Kulturbesitz 2; Potsdamerstr. 33, Berlin
G	MS 718	Universitätsbibliothek, Giessen
Gt	MS 13	Universiteitsbibliotheek, Gent (see Printed Edition 5, below)
S	1424/Co	James Ford Bell Library, University of Minnesota, Minneapolis, Minnesota [Phillipps MS 6650]
P	MS VI. E. 21	Státny Knihovna, Prague (see Printed Edition 1, below)
T	Cod. lat. 18770	Bayerische Staatsbibliothek, Munich [Tegernsee MS 770]
W	Cod. lat. 4758	Österreichische Nationalbibliothek, Vienna (see Printed Edition 1, below)

Dutch Manuscripts

A		MS once in library of Dr J.F.M. Sterck of Aardenhout; last recorded seen 26 October 1961
B	MS Phill.1981	Staatsbibliothek zu Berlin (1; Unter den Linden 8) [Meerman MS 1055]
H		Manuscript once in the library of Abraham de Vries of Haarlem; published in 1845; sold at auction March 1864

Latin Printed Editions

1	Cologne: Johann Guldenschaff, c.1490 (copy text for P and W)
2, 3, 4	Cologne: Cornelius de Zyrickzee, c.1496–99 (all ultimately based on #1)
5	Antwerp: Govaert Bac, after July 1496 (copied from #3) (copy text for Gt)
6, 8	Deventer: Jacob de Breda, after 10 April 1497 (#6), 24 January 1504 (#8); both copied from #4
7, 9	Deventer: Richard Pafraet, 1499 (#7), 1505 (#9); both copied from #6
10	Paris: Robert Gourmont for Oliver Senant, after 1506; copied from #8
11	Antwerp: Johannes Withagius, 1565 (ed. Nicholas Mameranus); copied from #11

Table 1 (continued)

Phases in the Development of the Latin Text

Phase 1:	M, Be
Phase 2:	G, T
Phase 3:	1 (P, W), 2*
Phase 4:	3–10 (Gt)
Phase 5:	11

* Printed edition 2, of which very few copies are known, is a transitional text with many typographical errors, several of which set up variant readings preserved in subsequent printed editions.

Father Witte is a complete fiction, his creator was nevertheless a cleric. No editor was able to overcome completely these weaknesses at the level of composition.

The earliest known state of the text had undergone revision by the mid-1400s, as is demonstrated in two manuscripts—G and T (the latter was almost certainly in the great library of the Benedictine monastery at Tegernsee by 1473).[20] This second phase of the Latin text removes its autobiographical quality by shifting into the third-person; what the scribal editor hoped to achieve by this move is a riddle. Clearly, however, G and T represent a text that has been revised by someone with an ear for storytelling: the passage that describes the liturgy of the Feast of St Thomas, clumsily arranged in phase one, is here restructured so that its dramatic climax—when the Apostle's hand refuses to distribute the Host to three sinful communicants until they are brought to a full confession—comes at the conclusion rather than in the middle of the narration. G and T also contain revisions that seem more serendipitous than selective; little is gained in clarity or grace by the replacement in phase two of *relique* with *alie*, *gubernando* with *regendo*, and *largiter* with *optime*, but this kind of verbal manipulation characterizes every later version of the Latin.[21]

The text's most significant metamorphosis had occurred by the time it appeared, around 1490, off the press of Johann Guldenschaff at Cologne.[22] It is impossible to say whether the revisions were found in a manuscript (now lost) he used to prepare the first printed edition of the *Itinerarius*, or whether they were made principally in his workshop; in any event, this third phase of the book shows marked stylistic improvement. Redundancies that characterize the beginnings of sentences in the original text disappear here: the editor of phase three simply omits *item* fourteen times; he rewords the initial *et*, ubiquitous in M and Be, over 100 times, often turning one of two independent clauses into a participial phrase or a gerundive, or employing a different connective, such as *vero*, *namque*, *autem*, or *siquidem*. Altogether some 140 sentences start off in a revised—

arguably more polished—manner. There is a marked preference for passive voice constructions, which presumably carry an air of greater formality. In addition, this editor makes several changes in substance, almost all of them reducing Witte's numerical extravagance. Thus, the number of rooms that revolve atop the imperial residence at Edissa is reduced from 24 to nine, and Prester John's retinue of vassal kings is cut from 72 to 18.

No major substantive changes occur in the fourth or fifth phases of the *Itinerarius*'s textual history, but both continue the pattern of stylistic revisions. Cornelius de Zyrickzee, whose press was also at Cologne, clearly used Guldenschaff's incunable edition to produce three of his own. His most significant alteration returns the narrative to the first person, a perspective maintained in all subsequent printings, which are based directly or indirectly on one of Zyrickzee's. Each printing reveals minor tinkering with the text; sometimes this habitual fiddling with participial phrases and clauses linked by coordinating conjunctions ironically ends up restoring the wording of Witte's original. The most elegant version of the *Itinerarius* was printed in 1565 by Johannes Withagius at Antwerp; in the editor's introduction, Nicholas Mameranus, a well-known man of letters in his day, claims to have found an old manuscript whose antiquated Latin he decided to cast in the pleasant language of the sixteenth-century humanists. Mameranus, who succeeded in this venture, is the only editor who both admits to revising the *Itinerarius* and claims credit for it.[23]

Table 2 registers a very moderate example of the changes that the Latin text underwent over the course of its five phases.[24]

In this passage, Witte reports seeing grotesque fish—with round, feline heads and aquiline beaks—flying over the surface of the Red Sea as far as one can shoot a bolt from a crossbow. He claims to have sampled the fish, which he says must be boiled a long time before serving; he also saw other animals but can no longer remember them. Characteristics of the text's stylistic development are evident here: the narrative shifts into the third person in phases two and three (in edition 1, this leads to a blurring of the distinction between Johannes Witte de Hese and Prester John [lines 3–4], a confusion that is cleared up in the fourth phase with edition 3). The initial *et*, with which sentences in phase one habitually begin, is deleted in lines 1 and 3 (end); midway in line 3, however, an *et* creeps into the second phase and remains. In phase three, the deletion of *super aquas* from line 1 eliminates a practical redundancy (where else can fish fly but over the water?), and the shift in lines 3–4 of several nouns to the plural ('heads', 'cats', and 'beaks') makes for a more consistent comparison (the singular 'eagle' remains anomalous). Other changes are less clearly improvements in style: word transpositions in lines 1, 3, and 6 show no syntactical preference (indeed, the editor appears determined to reverse

Table 2

M,Be	Et in	mari rubro predicto vidi	pisces volantes super aquas ad spacium tantum
G,T	Et in	mari rubro predicto vidit	pisces volantes super aquas ad spacium tantum
1		In mari namque rubro vidit	pisces volantes	ad tantum spacium
3		In mari namque rubro vidi	pisces volantes	ad tantum spacium
11		In mari autem rubro vidi	pisces volantes	ad tantum spacium

M,Be	quantum	balista posset sagittari. Et illi pisces sunt rubei coloris, habentes in
G,T	quantum cum balista posset sagittari. Et illi pisces sunt rubei coloris, habentes in
1,3,11	quantum	balista posset sagittare. Et illi pisces sunt rubei coloris, habentes in

M,Be	longitudine ultra duos pedes, habentes eciam caput rotundum ut cattus, et
G,T	longitudine ultra duos pedes, et habentes	rotunda capita sicut cattus, et
1,3	longitudine ultra duos pedes, et habent	rotunda capita sicut catti,
11	longitudine ultra duos pedes, et habent	rotunda capita sicut catti:

M,Be	rostrum ut	aquila. De quibus piscibus
G	habentes rostra velut	aquila. De quibus piscibus Johannes presbyter
T	habentes rostra sicut	aquila. De quibus piscibus Johannes presbyter
1	rostra autem velut	aquila. De quibus piscibus Iohannes presbiter
3	rostra autem velut	aquila. De quibus piscibus ego Iohannes
11	rostra autem velut	aquila: de quibus piscibus ego Ioannes

M,Be	comedi. Et sunt pisces grossi propterea	oportet ipsos diu
G,T	predictus de Hese comedit. Et sunt pisces grossi propterea	oportet ipsos diu
1	predictus	comedit. Et sunt pisces grossi propter quod oportet eos diu
3	Hese predictus	comedi. Et sunt pisces grossi propter quod oportet eos diu
11	Heseus	comedi. Et sunt pisces grossi propter quod oportet eos diu

M,Be	bulire. Et vidi	plura alia rara animalia de quibus non habeo memoriam (Be *trsp* rara animalia).
G,T	bulire. Et vidit	plura animalia alia rara, quibus non habuit memoriam.
1	bulliri. Et vidit ibidem	plura animalia	rara,	quorum non habuit memoriam.
3	bulliri. Et vidi ibidem	plura animalia	rara,	quorum non habui notitiam.
11	bulliri. Et vidi ibidem	multa animalia	rara,	quorum non habui notitiam

whatever adjective/noun order exists in the copy text), and little is gained in semantic content by altering *plura* to *multa* or *memoriam* to *notitiam* in line 6, which seem to be compulsive rather than considered revisions.

A Dutch text of Witte's *Itinerarius* cannot yet be reliably established. Transcriptions exist of all or part of three manuscripts, all of them probably from the fifteenth (or early-sixteenth) century, but these originals are, at least for the moment, unlocated. The exemplar most likely to resurface is manuscript A, which was owned by Dr J.F.M. Sterck of Aardenhout and was described carefully on two sheets of paper by Willem de Vreese, a paleographer at the University of Leiden, on 10 July 1936. De Vreese's notes record the manuscript's incipit and explicit, from which we may assume that the text was more or less complete; he hesitated to date it definitively (writing 'circa' and leaving a blank). G.I. Lieftinck, another distinguished paleographer and de Vreese's successor at Leiden, examined this manuscript on 26 October 1961, possibly in answer to a request made through the agency of Beijers, an antiquarian firm at Utrecht; he noted that it 'now has on the fly leaf' as a mark of ownership 'ex libris Dr. A.J. Henneman (Nijmegen)'. Beijers' catalogues from the 1960s and accessible records (some were destroyed when the house moved in 1969) offer no clue in tracing this manuscript.[25]

The only surviving manuscript copy of the medieval Dutch translation is B, which is a late-seventeenth-century transcription by Antonius Maittaire (1635–1710), a professor of law at the University of Leiden who published capacious works on prominent figures in Dutch history and on travellers to the Holy Land. Maittaire's transcription appears to be careful: the orthography of B varies considerably and shows no sign of normalization, even when a word appears more than once in the same sentence.[26] At one juncture, where a reader might expect the relatively common medieval Dutch word *wyde* instead of the unusual dialectalism *syde*, Maittaire has written the latter word with 'sic' in the adjacent margin. A colophon identifies the scribe of the copy text for B as Hendrik van Rhemen and dates his work 14 February 1373. This is certainly an error (but *whose* is unclear): the opening sentence in B has Witte (styled 'Iohan Voet') begin his travels in 1398. Maittaire appears not to have noticed this inconsistency, one that introduces a further problem since all Latin manuscripts record Witte as having set out for India in 1389—a date consistently given in Roman numerals, which would seem to preclude a simple transposition of numerals in the Dutch. A possible explanation is that the original translation was completed in 1398.[27]

The third record of the *Itinerarius* in a medieval Dutch translation is text H, the edition of an incomplete manuscript—it ends mid-sentence around two-thirds of the way into the narrative—published in 1845 by Matthias [Matthijs] de Vries. Then only 25 years old, de Vries went on to enjoy a prolific career as an editor, linguist, and lexicographer. He claims to have produced the text faithfully from five sheets of paper, written in a hand 'clearly of the early 15th century', which he discovered at the back of an incunable (Werner Rolewinck's *Fasciculus temporum* in both Latin [Louvain: Veldenar, *recte* 1475] and the Dutch translation [Utrecht:

Veldenar, 1480]) owned by his father, the city librarian at Haarlem. (The book—including the manuscript—was sold in 1864 to H.W. Willems but its location is now unknown.) De Vries's printed edition (H), like Maittaire's transcription (B), appears to be fairly trustworthy: the erratic spelling shows no sign of normalization and footnotes justify readings that might be taken for mistakes. At the same time, its medieval Dutch is 'standard' and dialectally unspecific enough to suggest some editorial manipulation.[28]

Although no actual medieval manuscript preserving the Dutch text of the *Itinerarius* is known today, the surviving records indicate, despite considerable variation among A, B, and H, that only one Dutch translation was made, that it was rendered from a Latin manuscript in phase one (but neither M nor Be), and that the variants among the Dutch texts can be attributed somewhat to editorial intervention on the part of scribes (as is more profoundly evident in the Latin manuscript tradition) but much more so to the often-ignored phenomenon of dialect. In the Dutch texts, most orthographic, syntactic, and semantic differences arise as a result of a scribe's own linguistic history rather than his editorial predilections. On the other hand, intriguing characteristics of some medieval translators do not surface here: whoever rendered the *Itinerarius* into Dutch had little trouble understanding the subject matter, did not feel a need to defend or to challenge Witte's more remarkable claims (of having seen Prester John, for example), and omitted no material in an obviously programmatic way.[29] One difference in the Dutch text is its expansion of Witte's description of a hermit he witnessed in the Sinai desert: to the Latin list of rather generic characteristics (the hermit sleeps on a stone, wears a hair shirt, and receives manna from heaven daily), the translation adds a miraculous account of saints Paul and Anthony, who once lived at this same site, and of their encounter with a devoted she-wolf. The addition has the quality of a marginal gloss.[30]

The she-wolf interpolation is not an indication that the *Itinerarius* was composed in Dutch and then rendered into Latin (with the passage omitted), even though vernacular-to-Latin translations are hardly unusual, especially after 1400, and even though A, B, and H make no reference to a Latin original, name no translator, and do not identify Jan (Johan) Voet with Johannes Witte de Hese. That Witte's *Itinerarius* must in fact have been composed in Latin and translated into medieval Dutch is demonstrated by the passage in Table 3 overleaf, which records in parallel text part of a Latin sentence in M (phase one; the earliest known Latin manuscript) and its vernacular equivalent as recorded in B and H.

This passage describes how the Virgin Mary, on the Holy Family's flight into Egypt, entered a temple of idols, causing them all to crash immediately to the ground. That it takes between 43 and 49 Dutch words

Table 3 (ll. 30-33 [Latin]; 28-32 [Dutch])

B	Ende die kercke plach in voertyden
H	Ende die kerke plach in voertyden
M	. . . *que* *prius*

B   te wesen een tempel der afgaden; mer doe onser   lieve vrouwe quam in den
                                                     tempel,

H   te wesen een tempel der afgode;   maer doen onse lieve vrouwe quam in den
                                                     tempel,

M   *fuerat*   *templum ydolorum, in quod, cum*   *beata virgo primo*
                                                       [p'o] venit,

B   doe si vloen was om Herodes willen mit hoeren kinde, doe vloen alle

H   doen sy mit hoeren lieven kijnde ghevloen was om Herodes wille, doe vloen
                                                     daer alle

M   *ex metu Herodis in Egiptum fugiendo,*

B	de duvels uit	ende ruemden hoer alle den tempel.
H	die duvelen uyt den beelden	ende ruymden den tempel, als men daer seghet.
M	*demones fugierunt*	*et ceciderunt ydola in templo, ut dicitur ibidem.*

to render 28 Latin words results from the grammatical sophistication that makes the latter language so efficient, but it also reflects the translator's intention to clarify all verbal relationships: thus, *que* in line 1 is identified more closely as *die kercke* ('the church') and *quod*, in line 2, is specified as the *tempel*. The translator makes no attempt to improve the text's style. In fact, the translation suffers from redundancy and an occasional vagueness that may indicate misunderstanding: in the Latin, the Virgin flees *ex metu Herodis*, 'for fear of Herod', but in the Dutch she flees on account of his *wille*, his 'will', 'purposing', or even 'desires'. In the Latin, moreover, the idols crash 'as soon as' the Virgin enters the temple (*primo venit*), whereas in the Dutch she enters, without adverb but *mit hoeren kinde*, 'with her child'.[31]

Other markers indicate that Latin was the language of composition for the *Itinerarius*. Table 4 offers a representative (but not comprehensive) list of readings demonstrating that Dutch cannot be the text's original language given the preponderance in B and H of synonymic pairs, Latinisms, and strained syntax that can best be attributed to a translator's difficulties with a foreign text.[32] Latin words and phrases, given in italics, correspond to Dutch renderings in B and H (the surviving text of A is too limited).[33]

Compared in this way, the Dutch texts of Witte's *Itinerarius* clearly complement each other. Collated, however, they may appear to be separate translations. The opening lines of the narrative, shown in

Table 4

SYNONYMIC PAIRS

VERBS

ardentes	bernen unde luchten (B); bernende ende luchtende (H) 40 [41–2]
stillare	uit te lopen (B); uyt te lopen ende te vlieten (H) 48 [52]
intoxicant	valschen unde to fenynen (B); velschen ende te fenijnen (H) 67 [81–2]
expellendo	suveren ende to gansen (B); suveren ende te gansen (H) 70 [85–6]
pugnant	te stryden ende te vechten (B); te striden ende te vechten (H) 91 [120–1]
pereclitando naves	die schepen toe hinderen ende toe verderven (B); die schepe te hijnderen ende te verderven (H) 102 [136]
custoditur	gewaert (B); ghehuet ende ghewaernt (H) 187 [210]

NOUNS AND NOUN/ADJECTIVE PHRASES

animalia nociva	schadelike serpenten ende dieren (B); schadeliker serpenten ende quader dieren (H) 46–7 [49–50]
ramos	twyge ende rysen (B); twigen ende riser (H) 51 [58]
emunitatem claustri	op den hof des cloesters (B); op die veste off opten hof des cloesters (H) 51–2 [59–60]
victoriam	saghe ende winninghe (B); seghe ende verwin[n]inghe (H) 61 [73–74]
laycorum	weerliker ende leeker luyde (B); waerliker luden ende leker luden (H) 212 [240–1] (see also *animalia nociva*, above)
pulchritudinis	sierheyden ende schoenten (B); sierheyden ende schoenheyden (H) 218 [247]
cursus	circulen unde gengen (B); cirkelen ende ghenghen (H) 267 [307]

ADVERB

velocissime	snel ende gerade (B); sneel ende gheringhe (H) 156 [196]

LATINISMS IN DUTCH

gradu[s]	graden (B); grade[n] (H) 192, 193, 200, 211 [216, 217, 227, 238]
liberia	liberye (B); liberie (H) 209 [236]
dormitorium	dormiter (B); dormter (H) 216, 240 [244, 273]
chorus	choer (B); c[h]oer (H) 217, 241, 251 [245, 275, 286]

STRAINED PHRASEOLOGY DUE TO DIFFICULTY UNDERSTANDING ORIGINAL

que regio dicitur inferior India	genoemt dat uterste eylant off dat uterste eynde (B); ghenoemt dat nederste eylant of dat nederste Indyen (H) 83 [108–09]

Table 5, offer a good example of the semantic variety that promotes this appearance.

Apparent differences among A, B, and H should not obscure their notable parallels: unlike any Latin text, they all identify the traveller as Jan [Johan] Voet and place him in the Holy Land in 1398. The change in name may itself be a translation, an unnecessary—even inaccurate—one, since Witte was already an established surname in the Utrecht area by 1400. Close inspection of the texts reveals such continuity in syntax and semantics that they can only be the product of a single translation; their variants stem from transposition, omission, and orthographical difference.

Transposition, as was evident in the Latin text of Table 2, frequently can be attributed to minor, unprogrammatic editorializing. Omissions in the three Dutch texts, obvious in Table 5, constitute a more significant issue. To be sure, many are minor and offer parallels to the history of the Latin text: B lacks the transitional *item*, brought over verbatim 14 times in H, as well as many coordinating conjunctions ('and', 'but'), adverbs ('there'), and conventional pieties ('blessed', 'holy', 'our dear Lord'—13 such usages). As has already been observed, B occasionally deletes half of a synonymic pair found in H.[34] But in at least 29 instances, four or more words conveying a substantial idea in H are missing in B. Of these, six passages run to considerable length and include descriptions of poisonous animals in the Sinai (72 words), man-eating cyclopes in the Ethiopian Sea (65 words), the astronomy tower at Adrianopolis (152 words), statuary outside Prester John's palace (214 words), Prester John's magic mirror (59 words), and the palace's revolving towers (69 words).[35] Omissions in B reveal no specific editorial policy—they are neither the most nor the least exaggerated of Witte's claims—but they do suggest that at least one scribe (or, less likely, the transcriber Maittaire) did not take the *Itinerarius* very seriously.

The surviving records of Witte's *Itinerarius* in translation display differences that are far more intriguing than matters of transposition and omission, however. Most of the variants found in the texts of A, B, and H

Table 5

A	In dem namen ons heeren ende indeniaer ons heeren 1398
B	In den jaer ons Heeren MCCC ende XCVIII
H	Inden jaer ons heren dusent driehondert ende XCVIII

A	jc er Jan	voet	van vtert	heb ghewest	te
B	ick Heer Iohan Voet		van Utrecht	heb geweest	toe
H	ic Johan Voet, priester uten ghesticht	van Utrecht,	heb gheweest	tot

Table 5 (continued)

A jherüsalem jnden mere om   te visenteren daer de heÿlighen steden
B Iherusalem in den Mey, umme   daer te visiteren die hillige stede.
H Jherusalem inden Mey toe vanden eynde te visiteren daer die heylige sted

A ende oec voert tot mÿnder bedeuaert totter jordanen ende voert
B Ende oick tat   mynre bedevaert ter   Iordanen,   voert
H Ende oeck voert mijn   bedevaert totter Jordanen;   voert

A totten roden mere aen dat lant van egipten tot eender stat gheheten
B toe den roeden meer an dat lant van Egypten, tot eynre stadt geheyten
H toe den roden meer aen dat lant van Egipten, tot eenre stat gheheiten stad

A hermopolus datz i   hoeffstat van egipten jn dier stat woende onse
B Hermopolis. Dat is eyn hovetstadt van Egypten. In der stadt woende onse
H Hermoplois. Dat is een hoeft stad van Egipten. Inder stat woende onse

A   vrouwe   met hoeren   lieüen   kinde
B lieve vrouwen   met hoeren   lieven   kynde
H lieve vrouwe seven jaer mit hoeren ghebe[ne]diden kynde,

A   ihum   ende in den roeden mere daer de stat
B   Iesum Cristum. Ende inden roeden meer, daer die stadt
H onsen lieven here Jhesu Christo. Ende in den roeden meer, daer die stat

A bÿ lÿt   daer sach ic in vÿschen   de roet waren van varwen
B by licht, daer sach ick ynne vissche, die weren roet van verwen,
H by leghet, daer sach ick in vissche,   die waren roet van verwen

A   ende vlieghen boeüen dat water wel so veer
B   ende vlogen boven   water wal so veer
H ende waren meer dan twe voet lanck. Die vische vlogen boeven den meer

A als men mit j boghe mocht schÿten   ende daer
B als men mit enen boghe sceten mochte   ende daer van
H alsoe verre alsmen myt enen boeghe scieten mach; ende si

H hadden een ront hoeft, recht als een vat, ende enen beck als een aer;

A   heb ic aff gheten
B   heb ick   gegeten.
H ende desen visch heb ic af gheten, ende sijn al hart, ende daer om moet

A   voert so heb ic daer ghesÿen vele wonderliker dieren [A ends]
B   Voert heb ick daer gesien vele seltsame dieren ende fenyne
                                                          dieren . . .
H langhe siden. Voert soe heb ick daer ghesien vele selsenre dieren. . .

have probably come about as a result of copying by scribes who were speakers of different dialects of Dutch from the second half of the 1400s.[36] The incipit and explicit of A give only a fragmentary sense of the missing manuscript's linguistic character, but its dialect is clearly eastern Netherlandic, probably from Gelderland.[37] Strong markers from the northeastern area of the Dutch linguistic region characterize B, while H may originate in the western province of Holland, although, as noted above, its language is so standard that a specific source is difficult to identify. Table 6 shows phonological and grammatical markers of these two dialects and their locations in B and H. Orthography varies considerably even *within* each of the three versions of the work, but these phenomena are quite consistent throughout the respective text.[38]

Variants in B and H are not restricted to orthographical and grammatical differences. At least 34 significant semantic discrepancies exist, many of which apparently result from scribal revision or confusion.[39] Several do not, however, and they may be useful in trying to determine which text—

Table 6

PHONETICS

oo and o	u and o
[een]hoorn (B); [een]horen (H) 84	druncken (B); droncken (H) 80
woonen (B); wonen (H) 114, 126, 145, 158	wulfinne (B); wolfinnen (H) 91
dooden (B); doden (H)121–22	gewulft (B) ghewolft (H) 279, 295, 305
groote/n/r (B); groten/r (H) 141, 143, 162	runt (B); ront (H) 280
165, 187, 209, 236, 246	sunne (B); sonne (H) 282

oo and oe	a and e
door (B); doer (H) 64, 101	wasset (B); west (H) 24
clooster (B); cloester (H) 154	saghe (B); seghe (H) 73
schoon (B); schoen (H) 239, 244, 287, 288	valschen (B); velschen (H) 81

a and ae	e and ee
an (B); aen (H) 16, 65, 89, 103, 108, 128	belden (B); beelde (H) 212, 251, 313
wal (B); wael (H) 176, 185, 193, 207, 252	gewest (B); gheweest (H) 214
pallas (B); palaes (H) 206, 211, 216, 224	heft (B); heeft (H) 254
anbedt (B); aenbedet (H) 319	

l before a dental	s and sc
golde (B); gout/goude (H) 254, 314	sloech (B); scloech (H) 56, 78
solde (B); soude (H) 256, 324	slept (B); scleept (H) 98
ho[e]lden (B); houden (H) 279, 307, 317	slo[e]t (B); sclo[e]t (H) 163, 169
olders (B); ouders (H) 316	slangen (B); sclanghen (H) 184, 187
coelt (B); cout (H) 322	slaen (B); sclaen (H) 324

Table 6 (continued)

GRAMMAR

Third-pers. sg. verb endings in e/en

Moses leyde (B); Moeyses leyden (H) 14–15
Paulus woende (B); Paulus woenden (H) 92

Third-pers. sg. verb endings in t/n

sint (B); sijn (H) passim (28 instances)
gaet (B); ghaen (H) 221

Adjective endings in e/er

IV groote steyne (B); vier groter steen (H) 15
van wonderlicke grootte (B); van wonderliker groetten (H) 26–27
vele guede crude (B); vele goeder crude (H) 76

Adjective endings: uninflected/en

hoechlick und oetmoedelick (B); hoechliken ende oetmoedeliken (H) 277
suverlick/ wonderlick/ verveerlick (B) 230; suverliken/ wonderliken/
ververliken (H) 32

Noun Plurals

kinderen (B); kijnder (H) 14, 80, 121
dick (B); dinghen (H) 20
duvels (B); duvelen (H) 31
broeders (B); brueder (H) 40, 154–55
droppels (B); droppen (H) 54
vogels (B); voghele (H) 58, 61
rysen (B); riser (H)58
loeven (B); lover (H) 117
husen (B); huse (H) 149
berg[h]en (B); berghe (H) 183, 189
cooplieden (B); coeplude (H) 200–01
belden (B); beelde (H) 212, 251, 313
graden (B); grade (H) 216
wormen (B); worme (H) 262
coningen (B); coninghe (H) 312
sanghen (B); sanghe (H) 31

Contracted Syllables in H

wasset (B); west/wast (H) 24, 183
bernet (B); bernt (H) 47
gevestet (B); ghevest (H) 49
hovet/hoofet (B); hoeft (H) 5, 62, 203
rusteden (B); rusten (H) 68
soeticheit (B); suetheyt (H) 79
steket (B); steecht (H) 84
gecledet (B); ghecleet (H) 98, 100
alre langesten (B); alre lansten (H) 119
seygelen (B); seylen (H) 138
lopet (B); loept (H) 194

Contracted Words in B

omt (B); om dat (H) 62
int (B) in dat (H) 84
dats (B); dat is (H) 109

B or H (too little is known of A for it to be considered here)—represents the *Itinerarius* in its dialect of composition. Two such discrepancies may be seen in the passage in Table 7.

Witte here describes a perilous voyage through a long, cave-like tunnel on the Indian coast, recalling the terrifying darkness of the passage and, particularly, its exit, where the ship and its frightened passengers plunged 20 cubits in returning to the open sea. Two translators could not separately have arrived at such nearly identical passages, and yet the semantic variations are curious. In the third line, for the Latin word *foramen* 'open-

Table 7 (ll. 141–9 [Latin]; 172–82 [Dutch])

B	Ende daer sloegen wy voert toe schepe unde voeren by geleyde
H	Ende daer scloeghen wij voert in een scip ende voeren by gheleide
M	*Et ibidem intravimus navem navigando sub ducatu*
B	des grooten Caens, ende quamen tot eynen groten steynberch gelegen
H	des groten Caens voersz., ende quamen tot enen groten steenberch, gheleghen
M	*Grandicanis predicti viii diebus, veniendo ad unum montem altissimum*
B	in den mere. Die berch heft onder eyn gat,
H	inden mer. Die berch heeft onder een gat,
M	*petrosum iacentem in mari habentem subtus unum foramen per spacium*
B	wal eynre mylen lanck; daer mosten wy doer varen. Meer dat gat is
H	wael drie milen lanck; daer moesten wy doer varen; mer dit hol is also
M	*trium miliarium per quod nos transnavigare oportuit. Et illud foramen est*
B	duyster, dat wy altyt bernde kersen by ons hebben mosten.
H	also duyster, dat wy alle weghe bernende keersen by ons hebben moesten.
M	*ita tenebrosum quod semper oportebat habere candelas ardentes.*
B	Ende in den uitganck des gates most dat schip mit ons nedergaen
H	Ende inden uut ganc des hols moest dat schip mit ons neder gaen,
M	*Et in exitu foraminis oportebat navem descendere nobiscum*
B	XX cubiten lanck, so dat dat meer daer sonderlinge syde is und licht
H	wael XX cubitus lanc, alsoe dat dat meer daer sunderlinghen neder is
M	*bene ad spacium viginti cubitorum, quia ibidem mare*
B	umme des gates willen, dat daer so vele te hoghe uytgiet.
H	om des hols wil, daer soe voele te hoghe uyt gheet.
M	*respectu foraminis est ita bassum.*
B	Ende in den gat hadden wy grooten anxt.
H	Ende inden hol hadden wij sunderlinghen groeten anxt.
M	*Et maxime ibidem timebamus.*

ing, hole, cave', both B and H read *gat*, which has a wide range of meanings including all those listed for *foramen*. In lines 4, 6, 8, and 9, however, where *gat* is repeated in B, the text of H reads *hol*. The difference may arise out of the dialectal identity of individual scribes. While usage of *gat* is recorded throughout the medieval Dutch linguistic territory, *hol* is somewhat more common in the west; it may also result from the H-scribe's desire to avoid repetition. In his next anecdote (lines 191–8), Witte mentions a wild river that runs through a *foramen* in the region where pepper is cultivated, a phenomenon described in H as *daer gaet een hoel doer* but in B as *daer geit under een hol ende gat door*, a synonymic pair that may enter the text as a double translation—of the Latin *and* of a Dutch dialectalism. As an example of how automatic such linguistic conversion could be, in the eighth line of Table 7, the Latin word *bassum* is rendered *neder* in H and *syde* in B, the latter being peculiar to the territory of Oostnederlandsch. It would thus appear that B—with its omissions and signs of minor editorializing—is not only a (slightly) later version of the *Itinerarius* in its single translation into Dutch, but it also represents a translation from a western to an eastern dialect of the language.

Ultimately, it is less important to identify the earliest state of Witte's *Itinerarius* in medieval Dutch or to determine its textual history than it is to recognize, with its aid, the linguistic freedom of the scribes whose labours helped to preserve both the book and their own words. The orthographical, grammatical, and semantic variation evident in Table 6 and throughout this discussion underscores the ability of medieval people to manoeuvre among vernacular dialects with relative ease. In fact, such intellectual activity appears to have been as uncontemplated as was the recitation from the Bible of Defoe's amazing dunce. Working with medieval translations may frustrate and exhaust modern scholars: because scribes worked so freely in and through their resilient dialects, devising a critical edition of a vernacular text recorded in more than two manuscripts can be a nightmare. At the same time, methodical examination of these texts can teach us much about the vitality of language and the complications of literacy during the late Middle Ages.

NOTES

1. *A Tour Thro' the whole Island of Great Britain* 4 vols. (London: G. Strahan, 1724–27) 1, p. 78.
2. I have often witnessed this skill among my relatives in western Norway. There, in a sliver between towering mountains that is still difficult of access, I listened in amazement the first time that my great-uncle, a gnarled goat

farmer and autodidact, took up a Bible, printed with the grammatical revisions prescribed by Norwegian parliamentary acts since the country's independence in 1905, and read it in a dialect (Oppstrynsk, in the Nordfjord region) that preserves the inflected nouns, now-archaic vocabulary, and staccato pronunciation of late-medieval Norse.

3. A much fuller account of the *Itinerarius*—including its relationship to late medieval travel books, textual history, and meaning—can be found in my book-length study, scheduled for publication by the Medieval Academy of America, *Johannes Witte de Hese's* Itinerarius: *A Fourteenth-Century Extension of the Medieval Pilgrim's Horizon*. This is an extensive revision of part of my dissertation, 'A Critical Edition of Johannes Witte de Hese's *Itinerarius*, the Middle Dutch Text, an English Translation, and Commentary, Together with an Introduction to European Accounts of Travel to the East (1240–1400)' (Northwestern University, 1985) pp. 249–640. As I note in passing below, three of the surviving Latin manuscripts are copies of printed editions; the eleventh and final printed edition appeared in 1565; and I have not yet succeeded in locating an actual fifteenth-century Dutch manuscript, which is why I refer to surviving 'records' of this translation.

4. The observation is Roger Ellis's in his introduction to *The Medieval Translator* (1989) p. 4. Other students of translation theory have formulated similar arguments, including Frantisek Miko's blanket assertion: 'Le traducteur prend inévitablement pour point de départ l'interprétation du texte'; see 'La théorie de l'expression et la traduction' in James S. Holmes (ed.) *The Nature of Translation: Essays on the Theory and Practice of Literary Translation* (Bratislava: The Hague, Mouton, 1970) p. 74. Miko is echoed in the same volume by Holmes himself, in 'Verse Translation and Verse Form' p. 93. Rita Copeland more specifically analyzes the medieval translator as an interpreter in 'Rhetoric and Vernacular Translation in the Middle Ages' in T.J. Heffernan (ed.) *Studies in the Age of Chaucer* (Knoxville: New Chaucer Society 1987) p. 43.

5. J.D. Burnley, 'Late Medieval English Translation: Types and Reflections' in *The Medieval Translator* (1989) p. 53. In this passage, Burnley is specifically describing medieval England, but his sensible observation may be applied to medieval European culture in general.

6. I discuss this at greater length in 'Two Routes to Pleasant Instruction in Late-Fourteenth-Century Literature' in David G. Allen and Robert A. White (eds) *The Work of Dissimilitude* (Newark, Del.: University of Delaware Press, 1992) pp. 67–80.

7. Modern scholars often use a medieval writer's dependence on earlier authorities for their own convenient purposes. 'Borrowings' by the author of *Mandeville's Travels*, for example, constitute the stick of alleged plagiarism with which the book, its narrator, and its author have been beaten for the past century. Among the Mandeville-author's contemporaries, Marino Sanudo takes much of his information from the *Descriptio* of Burchard of Mount Zion, and Ludolph of Suchem lifts whole passages from William of Boldensele, but no one has questioned the integrity of their accounts (these writers are discussed below, except for Sanudo, whose *Liber secretorum fidelium Crucis* is known only in Latin).

8. For an overview of some accounts and their content, see J.R.S. Phillips, *The Medieval Expansion of Europe* (Oxford: Oxford University Press, 1988); Donald Howard, *Writers and Pilgrims: Medieval Pilgrimage Narratives and*

Their Posterity (Berkeley: University of California Press, 1980) pp. 11–32; and the first part of my dissertation, pp. 1–248 (n. 3 above). In my summary here, I focus on medieval manuscript transmission and vernacular translation.

9. Walter Hoffmann, 'Deutsch und Latein im spätmittelalterlichen Köln' *Rheinisches Vierteljahrblatt* 44 (1980) pp. 117–47; Pierre Brachin, *The Dutch Language: A Survey* trans. Paul Vincent (Cheltenham: S. Thornes, 1985), p. 11 (originally published as *La langue néerlandaise* [Brussels, 1977]); and Hartmut Beckers, 'Der Orientreisebericht Wilhelms von Boldensele in einer ripuarischen Überlieferung des 14. Jahrhunderts' *Rheinisches Vierteljahrblatt* 44 (1980) p. 150 n. 7. Brachin points out that the move from Latin to Dutch took place over a long period of time; courts in Mechelen were not using the vernacular until 1465 (p. 11).

10. See Robert Ousterhout, 'Loca Sancta and the Architectural Response to Pilgrimage' in Robert Ousterhout (ed.) *The Blessings of Pilgrimage* Illinois Byzantine Studies 1 (Urbana: University of Illinois Press, 1990) pp. 108–24.

11. For manuscript tallies throughout this article, I am depending on my own research and on two invaluable bibliographies: Titus Tobler, *Bibliographia Geographica Palaestinae* (Leipzig: S. Hirzel, 1867) and Reinhold Röhricht, *Bibliotheca Geographica Palaestinae: Chronologisches Verzeichnis der von 333 bis 1878 verfassten Literatur über das Heilige Land mit dem Versuch einer Kartographie* (Berlin: H. Reuther, 1890, repr. [expanded by David H.K. Amiran] Jerusalem, 1963). Amiram makes no attempt to update Röhricht's register, which, after more than a century of political upheavals, seriously needs revision. For information cited here, see Tobler, *Bibliographia*, pp. 27–30; Röhricht, *Bibliotheca*, pp. 56–60. No critical edition of the *Descriptio* exists; one Latin manuscript text was edited by J.C.M. Laurent in *Peregrinatores Medii Aevi Quatuor* (Leipzig: J.C. Hinrichs, 1864) pp. 3–99; this edition, in turn, was the basis for the English translation by Aubrey Stewart, *A Description of the Holy Land, by Burchard of Mount Sion*, Palestine Pilgrims' Text Society 12 (London, 1896, repr. New York, 1971).

   The large number of manuscript texts of the *Descriptio* may reflect the fact that within a decade of the book's completion, the Egyptian sultan conquered the last European stronghold in the Levant (1291), bringing to a virtual standstill European pilgrim traffic to the East. At the same time, it testifies to Burchard's enduring abilities as an observer and arbiter: the book remained a standard source of information about the Holy Land into the 1500s, when it was published in Latin at least thirteen times.

12. Tobler, *Bibliographia*, pp. 30–1; Röhricht, *Bibliotheca*, pp. 61–2. Only one 'modern' version of Ricold's book exists: one Latin manuscript was edited by Laurent in *Peregrinatores Medii Aevi Quatuor* pp. 103–41 (see n. 11 above).

13. Tobler, *Bibliographia* pp. 35–6; Röhricht, *Bibliotheca* pp. 73–4. C.L. Grotefend's edition of William's book is included in his article 'Die Edelherren von Boldensele oder Boldensen' *Zeitschrift des historischen Vereins für Niedersachsen* (1855 [for 1852]) pp. 209–86 (esp. pp. 237–86). The journal is rare; moreover, Grotefend based his edition on an extremely inferior Latin manuscript, as Christiane Deluz has demonstrated in her Sorbonne thesis, '*Liber de Quibusdam Ultramarinis Partibus et Praecipue de Terra Sancta* de Guillaume de Boldensele (1336) suivi de la traduction de Frère Jean le Long (1351)' (n.d. [1972]). Jean le Long's French translation is cited by Louis de Backer [Baecker] in *L'extrême Orient au moyen âge d'après les manuscrits d'un flamand de Belgique Moine de Saint-Bertin à Saint-Omer et d'un Prince*

d'Armenie Moine de Prémontré à Poitiers (Paris: E. Leroux, 1877); this work includes Jean's translations of Ricold of Monte Croce and Odoric of Pordenone (see n. 19 below). I am preparing a complete critical edition and the first English translation of the Latin text. The textual history of William's *Liber*—in Latin and in the French translation—is exceedingly important, in my opinion, because it will provide specific information about the composing habits of the author of *Mandeville's Travels*. On the German translation, see Beckers, 'Der Orientreisebericht' pp. 148–66 (full reference n. 9 above).

14. Tobler, *Bibliographia* pp. 39–41; Röhricht, *Bibliotheca* pp. 76–9. No critical edition of the work exists in either Latin or Low German. Two separate and quite different Latin manuscript versions have been published: Ferdinand Deycks (ed.) 'De Itinere Terræ Sanctæ Liber' in *Bibliothek des Litterarischen Vereins in Stuttgart* 25 (1851); and G.A. Neumann (ed.) 'Ludolphus de Sudheim. De Itinere Terre Sancte' in *Archives de l'Orient Latin* vol. 2 (Paris: E. Leroux, 1884, repr. New York, 1978), Documents pp. 305–77. For an edition of one manuscript in Low German, see J[ohann] G[ottfried] L[udwig] Kosegarten, *Ludolph von Suchen. Reisebuch in das Heilige Land, in Niederdeutscher Mundart* (Greifswald: C.A. Kock, 1861). Neumann contends that the text of the two manuscripts in his edition represents a Latin compilation by Nicolas de Hude made from a German original: 'Ces constructions étranges et barbares ne peuvent s'expliquer que si l'on suppose le texte original écrit en allemand' (p. 309); de Hude's German source, however, seems to have been itself a translation from the Latin. Deycks's edition is the basis for the only modern English translation of the book, by Aubrey Stewart: *Ludolph von Suchem's Description of the Holy Land, and of the Way Thither* Palestine Pilgrims' Text Society 12 (London, 1895, repr. New York, 1971).

15. The Mandeville-author's borrowings from William of Boldensele (and other sources) were not nearly so slavish as his detractors assert; see C.W.R.D. Moseley, Intro., *The Travels of Sir John Mandeville* (Harmondsworth: Penguin Books, 1983) pp. 18–22; and my 'Two Routes' pp. 72–4 (n. 6 above).

16. See Josephine Waters Bennett, *The Rediscovery of Sir John Mandeville* The Modern Language Association of America Monograph Series 19 (New York, 1954) Appendices 1 and 2; Christian K. Zacher, 'Travel and Geographical Writings' in Albert E. Hartung (gen. ed.) *A Manual of the Writings in Middle English 1050–1500* (New Haven: Academy of Arts and Sciences, 1986) vol. 7: 2235–54, 2449–66; and Iain Higgins, 'Imagining Christendom: Asia in *Mandeville's Travels*' in Scott D. Westrem (ed.) *Discovering New Worlds: Essays on Medieval Exploration and Imagination* (New York: Garland, 1991) pp. 95–6 and 108–10, nn. 11–12.

17. For an excellent critical edition of Michael Velser's late-fourteenth-century translation of the *Travels*, see Eric John Morrall (ed.) *Sir John Mandevilles Reisebeschreibung* Deutsche Texte des Mittelalters 66 (Berlin, 1974). Christiane Deluz explores but does not edit the French original in: Le Livre de Jehan de Mandeville: *une 'géographie' au XIVe siècle* Publications de l'Institut d'Études Médiévales—Université Catholique de Louvain 8 (Louvain, 1988). Malcolm Letts made a preliminary study of the *Travels* in its several translations in *Sir John Mandeville: The Man and His Book* (London, 1949); Letts' preference for the title *The Book* (rather than *The Travels*) of Sir John Mandeville deserves consideration in light of the work's encyclopedic character. Iain Higgins promises to provide a more perceptive analysis of all extant versions of the book in chapter one ('Texts and Versions') of his book-in-

progress, tentatively entitled *Writing East: The Fourteenth-Century Travels of Sir John Mandeville.*

18. On the French and Latin texts, see the magisterial critical edition by Luigi Foscolo Benedetto, *Marco Polo: Il Milione* (Florence, 1929); and A.C. Moule and Paul Pelliot (eds and trans.) *Marco Polo: The Description of the World* 2 vols. (London, 1938). For the German translation, see Horst von Tscharner (ed.) *Der Mitteldeutsche Marco Polo* Deutsche Texte des Mittelalters 40 (Berlin, 1935). The best modern English translation of the book (although its title is a mistranslation) is Ronald Latham's *The Travels of Marco Polo* (Harmondsworth: Penguin Books, 1958, repr. 1979).

19. Tobler, *Bibliographia* p. 34; Röhricht, *Bibliotheca* pp. 69–71; and Reinhold Jandesek, *Der Bericht des Odoric da Pordenone über seine Reise nach Asien* Bamberger Schriften zur Kulturgeschichte 1 (Bamberg, 1987) pp. 4–5 (and n. 10). A Latin edition is by Anastasius van den Wyngaert, *Itinera et Relationes Fratrum Minorum Saeculi XIII et XIV, Sinica Franciscana* vol. 1 (Florence, 1929); distinguished work with the German translation is by Gilbert Strasmann, *Konrad Steckels Deutsche Übertragung der Reise nach China des Odorico de Pordenone* Texte des Späten Mittelalters und der Frühen Neuzeit 20 (Berlin, 1968). A version of the French translation by Jean le Long is in Backer, *L'Extrême Orient* (see n. 13 above). The only available modern English translation is in vol. 2 of Henry Yule's *Cathay and the Way Thither, Being a Collection of Medieval Notices of China* 2nd edn., rev. by Henri Cordier, Hakluyt Society, 2nd ser. 33 (London, 1913).

20. An inscription on the manuscript spine reads 'Tegernsee 1473'; Ambrosius Schwerzenbeck's library inventory of 2 August 1484 includes mention of 'Iohannis Hess presbiteri Narraciones eius de transmarinis partibus'; see Günter Glauche, *Mittelalterliche Bibliothekskataloge Deutschlands und der Schweiz* vol. 4[2] (Munich, 1981) pp. 751–3, 812 (lines 1943–4).

21. A few variants in the Dutch texts that might at first seem to support two or more independent translations are also probably owing to a scribe's whimsy. Examples include these clusters of readings found below in Table 5: *om te visenteren daer* (A), *umme daer te visiteren* (B), and *toe vanden eynde te visiteren daer* (H) in line 3; and *boeüen dat water wel so veer* (A), *boven water wal so veer* (B), and *boeven den meer alsoe verre* (H) in line 10. For the Latin original of this second example, see Table 2, line 1.

22. As noted in Table 1, manuscripts P and W are copies of this first incunable edition.

23. Edition 11 is definitely based on de Breda's second Deventer printing (#8), but Mameranus may have come across a hand-written copy of this book (see n. 22 above, and Table 1, Latin Printed Editions 1 and 5).

24. Latin- and Dutch-text line numbers given in Table headings and in discussions below correspond to the critical editions of both texts in my dissertation (see n. 3 above). In referring to passages reproduced in the Tables, however, I give the number, within the Table and beginning with 1, of the relevant line cluster.

25. I am indebted to Mr Edgar Franco at Beijers, and especially to Dr Pieter Obbema, at the University of Leiden, for his many courtesies and bibliographical lessons. Through him I gained access to archival material at the University of Leiden relating to Dr Sterck's library, including de Vreese's notes (he died in 1938) and a letter from Sterck, dated 22 February 1941 (a few weeks before his death), in which he states 'I still own the Reisverhaal.'

There too is an auction catalogue from 1936 in which the Voet/Witte de Hese manuscript is dated 'ca. 1540' (but on unstated authority) and listed as 'withdrawn' from sale.

The antiquarian firm of Gilhofer and Ranschburg advertised manuscript A in a catalogue that described it as a 'Low German manuscript of the XV century' containing a '[v]ery interesting narration of Jerusalem and other Holy Places, which has never been in print' by Jan Voet van Utrecht; see *An important Collection of Incunabula and XVI Century Books partly from a Monastery Library and in their original Gothic Bindings*, Catalog 190 (Vienna, n.d. [11 March 1926]) p. 116 (Item 227). Additional details in this listing, albeit confused, indicate that A is a more-or-less complete medieval Dutch text of the *Itinerarius*. For more information, see my study of the *Itinerarius* (n. 3 above) pp. 103–8.

26. For example, the word 'and' appears as *ende* 243 times, *und* 76 times, *unde* 49 times, *end* twice, and *ande* once. One reading is uncertain, and twice *en*, from the context, must mean 'and'. The same is true of frequently employed words such as *comet* (spelled seven different ways), *oick* (which has four spellings), and *maer* and *giet* (both of which appear in three forms).

27. Latin manuscripts M and Be and Dutch manuscript B include a sentence, near the end of the narrative, placing Witte/Voet at the Shrine of St Thomas in 1391; the date is also in the Gilhofer and Ranschburg advertisement for A (see n. 25 above); H, a fragment, has already broken off at this point (see my discussion, below). Thus, a departure date of 1398 is inconsistent even within the Dutch text.

28. 'Fragment eener Nederlandsche Vertaling van het Reisverhaal van Joannes de Hese' *Verslagen en Berigten Uitgegeven door de Vereeniging ter Bevordering der Oude Nederlandsche Letterkunde* 2 (1845) pp. 5–32. De Vries's article appeared while he was working on a three-volume edition, *Jan van Boendale's* Der leken spieghel *(1330)* (Leiden, 1844–1848). One passage of this lengthy poem (III. 15) invokes Lady Grammar to teach her cleric-servants how 'to write and spell correctly' and exactly from a text. De Vries's other editorial work, for which original manuscripts survive, appears to be unintrusive.

The Rolewinck incunable, with the manuscript inserted, was auctioned 16–26 March 1864 by the antiquarian firm of Frederik Muller of Amsterdam; see *Catalogus der . . . Bibliotheek . . . Ds. Abr. de Vries* (Amsterdam, 1864), pp. ix, 89 (entry 1895); the sale to Willems is noted in an annotated catalogue now at the Vereeninging der Bevordering van den Belangen des Boekhandels in Amsterdam. H.W. Willems owned a bookstore at Konigsplein 7 in Amsterdam; he died on 9 May 1881.

29. On the ways in which medieval translators might manipulate a text in order to represent plausibly to their readers a distant place or time, to make subject matter suitable for a Christian audience (by omitting objectionable passages or by introducing subjunctive/conditional verb forms), and to finesse dubious claims by emphatically asserting their truthfulness, see two studies by Jeanette M.A. Beer: *Li Fet des Romains: A Medieval Caesar* Études de Philologie et d'Histoire 30 (Geneva: Droz, 1976) pp. 93–127; and *Narrative Conventions of Truth in the Middle Ages* Études de Philologie et d'Histoire 38 (Geneva: Droz, 1981) pp. 48–55 *passim*, and 69–71 (the last of these includes an analysis of Marie de France's translation, *L'Espurgatoire Seint Patriz*, and Sir Owein's putative journey to Purgatory and the Terrestrial Paradise, to both of which Witte's book may be compared).

30. I have been unable to determine if the she-wolf ('wulfinne') anecdote has a peculiarly Dutch history, one that supplants the more familiar lions of the hagiography of St Anthony. The textual expansion, which amounts to some 40 words, is in B and H; de Vreese's notes on A do not extend to this section of text.
31. Hypothetical explanations for these discrepancies are readings in the Latin copy-text of *motu* for *metu* and *p'o* as an abbreviation for *primo* but mistakenly read as *puero*.
32. By 'synonymic pairs' I mean a translator's use of two words or phrases to render one in the original language, a phenomenon also called 'doubling'. I borrow the label from Leslie C. Brook, who believes that synonymic pairs 'enrich the prose' of an original—indeed, that a 'translator gives good value to his reader . . . by using two terms to translate one Latin one'; see 'The Translator and His Reader: Jean de Meun and the Abelard-Heloise Correspondence' in Ellis (ed.) *The Medieval Translator II* (1991) p. 110. I would not argue so enthusiastically about verbal pairing in the Dutch version of the *Itinerarius*. In my list of Latinisms, I have included some words from the ecclesiastical register, but only those for which a Germanic alternative existed. For the first example, *gradus*, MS B employs a synonymic pair at line 221 [Latin 195]—*trappen of graden*—*trappen* having a Germanic etymology.
33. B occasionally omits half of a synonymic pair found in H (see the last entry under sub-heading 'Verbs' and the first and third under 'Nouns'). This may result from a later scribe's editorializing attempt to omit a redundancy (see my comment on omissions in B, below). Line numbers are for the Latin and [in brackets] Dutch texts from the editions in my dissertation (see nn. 3 and 24 above).
34. See n. 33 above, and the last line of Table 3 (B typically omits the translated phrase *als men daer seghet* 'as people there say'). Willem de Vreese's notes suggest that the text of A resembles B with regard to omissions. B also occasionally offers a more economical reading than does H: see line 3 of Table 5.
35. As noted above, H ends abruptly some two-thirds of the way into the narrative; the remainder of the text in B omits another 15 passages of five or more words that are found in the Latin text of phase one.

    For its part, H omits six passages of five or more words found in B: three of these are brief phrases that convey information of substance, two are almost certainly eye-slips triggered by word repetition (a scribe—or perhaps the editor Matthias de Vries—overlooks 17 words about the port at Damietta and 16 words on the topography of the pepper fields), and one is a sentence of 19 words elaborating on the lions that guard Prester John's palace and their prescient ability to kill 'Jews and other heathens' who approach (this is not part of any surviving Latin text and may well be an interpolation in B). In addition, H pares down at least two synonymic pairs in B (*rijcks* for *landes ende rykes* [204] and *verblinden* for *verdunckeren noch verblinden* [302–03]), and omits the piety *hilliger* once (286).
36. For the analysis below, I rely on several important studies: Ludger Kremer, *Mundartforschung im ostniederländisch-westfälischen Grenzgebiet* Beschreibende Bibliographien 7 (Amsterdam, 1977); K. Heeroma, 'De Taalgeschiedenis van het Oosten' *Driemaandelijkse Bladen* NS 2 (1950) pp. 21–32; Heeroma, 'Hauptlinien der Ostniederländischen Sprachgeschichte' *Niederdeutsches Jahrbuch* 80 (1957) pp. 51–65; Willy L. Braekman, *Medische en*

Technische Middelnederlandse Recepten (Gent, 1975); and Norbert Richard Wolf, *Regionale und überregionale Norm im späten Mittelalter* (Innsbruck, 1975), especially pp. 18–20 (manuscript descriptions), 77–100 (parallel texts), and 241–67 (philological study). In Wolf's study of dialectally different versions of Francis of Assisi's *Regula bullata* in Low German/Dutch, the text of MS Br (Biblioteka Uniwersytecka we Wroclawiu IV. D. 5 [dated 1486; provenance eastern Netherlands]) closely resembles text B here (in orthography, uncontracted syllables, and the persistent *l* before a dental); the dialect of his MS Hg (The Hague, Koninklijke Bibliotheek Cod. 75 G 63) is similar to H here. See also Table 6, below. I have also profited much from correspondence with Dr Hartmut Beckers of the University of Münster.

37. De Vreese's transcription of A's incipit is given fully in Table 5; according to his notes, the explicit reads: 'binnen j quartier van j jare quamen wÿ weder tot jerüsalem ende hoe dat daer ghestelt is dat weten wel veel goeder lüden etc.' The manuscript also included a short penitential text written by the same scribe for which de Vreese gives an incipit and explicit that show linguistic features similar to the *Itinerarius*.

38. See n. 26 above. I am particularly cautious about these findings since, as I noted above, no actual medieval exemplar of this Dutch translation is currently available, and for texts A, B, and H we must rely on the skill and care of transcribers whose attention may not have focused on issues of language and dialect.

39. Editorial interference probably explains such variants as *kinderen van Israel* in B versus *volck van Israel* in H (69; both texts read *kinderen/kijnder* at line 14 and *volcke/volck* at line 54) and *beduyt* in B versus *beteykent* in H (197). Mistaken readings probably account for discrepancies such as *manieren* in B and *meren* in H (137). That B is a later version of the text than H is suggested by several readings that indicate revision: the Latinism *hoerlodium* in H (for *orlogium* in the Latin of MS M) is given the more Dutch equivalent of *orgel* in B (231); similarly, *ghepaveydt* in H (for *pavimentata*) is *geschieert* in B (296); and a rather formal reference to the Great Khan's return to his court in H (*doen [hi] quam int lant*) is, more colloquially, *doe [hy] to huys quam* in B (165). These are 'one-way translations'—that is, one can see how the readings in H could become B but not the reverse.

Chapter 8

The Translation of the Feminine: Untranslatable Dimensions of the Anchoritic Works

Anne Savage

This paper grew out of translating the anchoritic texts for *The Classics of Western Spirituality*, an introduction to the anchoritic material for an anthology called *The English Mystical Tradition*, edited by W. Pollard (University of Florida Press: forthcoming), and a paper on the translation process itself presented at the Third Cardiff Conference on The Medieval Translator: Theory and Practice of Translation in the Middle Ages (Cardiff, 1991). This version of the conference paper has been restructured and rewritten as a result of discussions with people attending the conference, in order to focus more strikingly on the ambivalence which figures so markedly in the perceptions and beliefs about feminine experience displayed by the writer(s) of those anchoritic texts, how the anchoress herself is involved in a process of *translatio*, and how these aspects of the anchoritic material as it will now be read have also filtered through the ambivalences of a particular modern translator, also a woman.

The early thirteenth-century anchoritic material—*Ancrene Wisse* (*A Guide for Anchoresses*), *Hali Meiðhad* (*Holy Maidenhood*), *Sawles Warde* (*Soul's Keeping*), the Passions of the virgin martyrs Katherine, Margaret and Juliana, *þe Wohunge of Ure Lauerd* (*The Wooing of Our Lord*), and the prayers in the Wooing group—provide any translator with a wide array of linguistic problems on all levels from basic word-meaning to style and tone; but by the time I had finally translated the last Passion of the third virgin martyr in the group to be stripped, tortured and decapitated,

181

I somewhat belatedly admitted real defeat on other than linguistic grounds. And the experience of translating a virginity treatise so *methodically* convincing as *Holy Maidenhood* throughout my pregnancy and the birth of my son was startling. I had never found the gap between my own time and the time I study so great; the apparently familiar was painfully familiar, and what was strange seemed irreconcilably strange. I was not sure what could be recuperated in a translation for the modern reader, whose religious experience or lack or rejection of it is in the context of an extremely different world. How much would actually need cultural translation, and how much would be simply carried along silently with the translated language like so much baggage, that is, unquestioned assumptions about women, women's bodies, their normal ranges of behaviour, and of course about what constitutes unusual feminine behaviour? Was a translator to provide an apologetic introduction, to attempt the explanation of cultural differences—and, if so, which ones? The more I framed my apology, the fewer clear cultural differences I found. What has often been seen as the ultimate goal of translators, to reproduce in the target audience the same responses as the original language did for its contemporary one, was clearly impossible not only because of the age of the texts, but also the specificity of their original audience, whose extreme way of life prepared them for the content. The more I understood about how, exactly, those responses were elusive, the more I discovered that I had no desire to reproduce them, whatever they might have been, precisely because of that indeterminate amount of silently-carried baggage.[1]

What I focus on in this paper is ambivalence: the writers', the anchoritic audience's, and the translators'. The writers are many, even if the immediate author of some of the anchoritic texts were only one male cleric.[2] Many different sources are employed, and they may appear in straightforward quotation or paraphrase, recontextualized to the point of profound reinterpretation, subversively or ironically rewritten, etc.[3] I include the audience as an honorary author, participants in the composition of the text, since the writer addresses them personally as anchoresses in the course of *Ancrene Wisse*, generically as virgins in *Holy Maidenhood*, and, in course of the life of St Margaret, as 'widows along with the wedded! And maidens especially . . .' (p. 288);[4] they are *designed* for women, and in this paper I will attempt to illustrate something of what that means. Generally speaking, I believe that the anchoritic works show us highly refined attitudes to the feminine experience, although synthesized in a social context that could hardly be more specific and rarified.[5]

In these texts we find that the anchoritic experience is defined in many ways as an essentializing of feminine experience: the woman is refined by the process of *translatio* from the ordinary spheres of sexual identification in rape, seduction and marriage, pregnancy and childcare, into the anchoritic cell, where she becomes the betrothed, lover and bride of Christ, mother to her own eternal soul, and determiner of its fate.

Many of the writer's sources and images are firmly grounded in the traditional hatred and suspicion of the human body in general and the female body in particular which has been common to Christian writings on sex, marriage, women, and both feminine and masculine virginity.[6] Yet in *Ancrene Wisse*, for example, the overt and undeniably sincere attitude of the writer is love for his readers, and not only does he love them but he has a profound respect for, if not awe of, their role as warriors in an endless battle of which he himself is something of a spectator.[7] His desire in assimilating and adding to his material is to provide practical help for women who have engaged in this fight. The other anchoritic texts I discuss here represent efforts in the same direction, even at their most severe.

The anchoritic war is conducted at the most basic levels of experience— obtaining even minimal nourishment, through the senses, during thought about anything:

> . . . sometimes a bird alights on the earth, to seek its food as its flesh requires; but while it stays on the earth, it is never secure, but often turns round, and keeps looking intently about. In the same way, the good anchoress, fly she ever so high, must at some times alight down on the earth of her body to eat, drink, sleep, work, speak and hear about what she needs to of earthly things. But then she must look carefully about her as a bird does, keep watch on every side, so that she does no kind of wrong—lest she be caught by some of the devil's snares, or hurt in some way, during the time she stays so low. (*Ancrene Wisse* Part III, 'The Inner Feelings', p. 98)[8]

Of course medieval attitudes to the human body in general can seem obsessively negative to modern readers; but negative attitudes to sex, whether in texts for men or women, have focussed on the female rather than the male body as the primary source of the problem.[9] This is somewhat grounded in the ancient and apparently modern medical misunderstanding of female anatomy as imperfect or lesser male anatomy[10]— and an imperfection in substance as a result of having been second on the agenda in creation, taken from Adam instead of being the *direct* result of divine action on primeval slime.[11]

There are several currents of thought and feeling in the anchoritic works about these subjects: in the Passions, the virgin martyrs must remain virgin so as not to be devalued as Christ's brides; on the other hand, feminine sexuality is happily disposed of in *Holy Maidenhood* as something every woman would be glad to be rid of if she could; and *Ancrene Wisse* deals with sexuality as temptation—part of the battle, the cross—as a kind of suffering which women experience in a particular way all their lives, and which anchoresses refine in their solitude.

In the Passions of the virgin martyrs we see a shift of the focus of violence from rape, specifically, to torture and martyrdom—sexual assault is *somewhat* displaced to become overall assault on the female flesh. From the anchoress's point of view, the female flesh *is* the object of assault, constantly, by fantasies of sexual fulfilment, marriage and children, and by any other appetites—by any force that might motivate her to leave her enclosure. The extremely negative exemplary fantasies of sex, marriage and children in *Holy Maidenhood* focus the anchoress's attention on these as violence and bondage, as in the Passions.

> . . . In bed she has to put up with all his crudities and indecent fooling, however filthy they turn out to be, whether she wants to or not. Christ shield every maiden from asking or wanting to know what these are, for those who experience them find them most hateful, and call those who never know what it is lucky indeed, and they hate what they do. (*Holy Maidenhood*, p. 237)

Though the ostensible subject of *Holy Maidenhood* is virginity, there is a curious way in which martyrdom is also a theme: marriage as unsuccessful martyrdom, a kind of imprisonment and suffering which is to be avoided at all costs, since it drags the soul into a mire which is only barely to be escaped by widowhood and almsgiving (*ibid*. p. 232), and for which even the best possible reward is far less than that of the spiritually successful virgin. The vision presented to the anchoritic reader by these two works, then, is of one kind of martyrdom or another, both specifically expressed in terms of sexual assault and its effects on the female body.

Idiosyncrasies of the anchoritic allegorical viewpoint provide some convolutions in the narrative line of the Passions, not as Passions *per se*, but as narratives of masculine abduction and/or attempted seduction of female virgins. Some aspects of the narrative, however, are distinctly non-allegorical; that is, they seem to stand immovably rooted in an idea of the female body as a literal element which it is impossible to interpret further. The virgin martyrs all remain virgin; though immersed in boiling brass, dismembered and burnt till they crackle, they are never sexually assaulted, let alone violated, though the sole reason for their troubles, at least initially, is saying no to sex. It is clear that the depreciation of the virgin's real value which would occur if she were actually raped could not safely be assumed to be spiritually replaceable, and she would inevitably be seen as a less fitting bride of Christ, if a fitting one at all:

> . . . Those who are under the law of marriage, thanking God and praising him that he prepared for them, when they wished to leave the sublimity of maidenhood, at least such a place to alight in that they

were not hurt—though they were degraded . . . Whoever so falls from maidenhood's honour that marriage's woven bed does not catch them, they plunge down to the earth so rapidly that they are all torn apart, both flesh and limb. (*Holy Maidenhood*, p. 232)

In the Passions, rape is introduced as a subject then dropped, suspending it indefinitely over the narrative. It is replaced by the symbolic rape of torture and decapitation, when the virgins have declared themselves as brides of Christ; then it is their Christianity, their inviolable spirituality, which the male torturers unsuccessfully assault through the female body.

This displacement has some powerful implications. Most obviously, it means that the writer and readers are able to concentrate on and draw out the assault on the woman's body without the problems which an equally-protracted rape scene would necessarily introduce. Not the least of these would be the fact that rape in medieval literature is often presented as a non-crime if not a joke, a fate which it shares with much literature since then.[12] However, it also makes explicit a paradigm of rape, precisely *because* the rape is transformed into the most general violence on the whole body: what drives the male assault is feminine resistance, feminine inviolability itself. The fact that 'no', however extremely expressed from intellectual debate to a preference for being immersed in boiling brass, is never an acceptable answer to the man who wants a woman's body, is one of the most parodied aspects of masculinity in the Passions. Abductors, suitors, and fathers (Juliana's is interested at first in the mercantile aspects of his daughter's body—giving her to a high-status son-in-law against her will, who is consequently driven by rage at her refusal) do not come off at all well here.

Applications to the anchoress's situation are several: she is clearly in potential physical danger as well as spiritual, and the threat is sexual contact or even the *rumour* of any kind of sexual misbehaviour. The most dire aspect of this is the depth of the anchoress's responsibility. If the sexual contact is initiated by a man, she is as responsible as the man in Exodus 21:33–34 who digs a pit and leaves it uncovered, so that his neighbour's beast falls in (*Ancrene Wisse*, Part II, 'The Outer Senses', p. 69). Even if the contact is not initiated by her, she may come to harm through it by gossip, by desiring it or even thinking of it; but she is made to realize that because her body itself is potentially detrimental to the spiritual well-being of men, she must take responsibility for having it to the extent that

if he is tempted so that he sins mortally in any way, even if it is not with you but with desire toward you, or if he tries to fulfill with someone else the temptation which has been awakened by you, be quite sure of the judgment. (*Ancrene Wisse*, Part II, 'The Outer Senses', p. 69)

185

The traditional notion that whatever happens is the woman's fault because she is a woman—it is in the order of nature for her to be responsible for men's sin—is followed here by a contemptuous dismissal of the entire male animal: 'A dog will happily enter wherever he finds an opening' (*ibid.*). This dismissiveness is minimal, however, and rather privileges the dog in such a situation, just as the beast in Exodus 21:33–34 is not expected to be responsible for its actions. Satire against and parody of masculine *attitudes* occasionally have a presence in the anchoritic literature (see below), but certainly not enough of a presence to undermine the authority of the author, the misogynistic sources he employs, or that great patriarchal establishment, the church.

Other anchoritic parallels with the virgin martyrs are not, perhaps, immediately obvious. The anchoresses' high spiritual status apparently made them objects of curiosity to many; they are warned in particular about religious men in *Ancrene Wisse*:

> Now, here comes a weak man—though he holds himself estimable if he has a wide hood and a closed cloak—and he wants to see some young anchoresses. And he just has to see whether her looks please him, she whose face has not been burnt by the sun—as if he was a stone! . . . Yes, my dear sisters, if anyone is eager to see you, never believe good of it, but trust him the less. I would not have it that anyone see you unless he has special leave from your director. (*Ancrene Wisse*, Part II, 'The Outer Senses' pp. 68–9)

On the other hand, as spiritual athletes somewhat on display, they are required at times to martyr themselves—to expose themselves or the inner sanctum of their cell to the male eye—in the service of the spiritual needs of men:

> Do not bid any man to look in at your altar *unless his devotion requires it and he has your leave*. Draw well inside and draw the veil down over your breast, and quickly do up the cloth again and fasten it very tightly. If he looks towards your bed, or asks where you lie, answer lightly, 'Sir, it doesn't matter', and keep silent. ([Emphasis mine] *Ancrene Wisse* pp. 71–2)

Enough men 'had leave' to look to warrant advice; surely there were sometimes cases in which it was unclear to the anchoress whether a particular man had permission or not. While she is advised to *request* a bishop not to look at her, if he insists she should allow him a short look. The author then recounts the anecdote of the anchoress who would not grant St Martin permission to look at her, for which he honoured her greatly (*ibid.* p. 72). Perhaps some male religious were willing to live up to his example, but the stripping of the virgin martyrs by their masculine torturers, and the scornful endurance of exposure by Katherine, Margaret and Juliana, would have provided a model of inspiration in the cases of men who chose to look if they could, placing the anchoress at risk if men then sinned because of having looked. In spite of the praise given the anchoress who refused St Martin, the writer advises them not to be like her if the bishop is insistent, but to uncover if asked, even if it would be praiseworthy to refuse. 'To a woman who desires it, open, for God's sake' (*ibid*. p. 71), even though 'Some have been tempted by their own sisters' (*ibid*.). Whatever kinds of temptation are meant or implied here, they are clearly not on the same scale.

On the one hand, the anchoress is to hold herself responsible for any spiritual damage done to a man who looks at her, even if he does so against her will; on the other hand, she herself is made susceptible to damage by any contact with him. The degree and kind of fear is illustrated by an incident in the Passion of St Margaret: when the virgin, guarding her foster-mother's sheep, is approached by the wicked sheriff's henchmen and seized, her prayer is not to be delivered from rape, but to be delivered from carnal temptation, even though Olibrius is about as unattractive a sexual abductor as could be. The later long debate with the demon focuses on sexual temptation, and is punctuated by the demon's efforts to seduce her. His language is pleading and flattering, like that of Eleusius (Juliana's suitor), a parody of the passionate love-language elsewhere given to the anchoress herself or to Christ.[13] The anchoress must needs be even more watchful of her own body than of men who want to see her; she is alone with her own body, and its prisoner. She is inside the 'castle wall' (see below, p. 196), which replicates her virginity, sealing her away from men; but because she is inside, she is susceptible to temptations to leave it—the anchorage, and her virginity.

The lives of the virgin martyrs Katherine, Margaret and Juliana also provide the feminine anchoritic audience with inspiring models of women dramatically cut off from their families: orphaned, or rejected by their fathers after refusing to be brides. The anchoress, by her own profession, is cut off from her family and undergoes a ritual death. Her enclosure is represented as burial in a grave after the administration of Extreme Unction and the recitation of the prayers for the dying.[14]

There is only one mention made anywhere of how to conduct oneself with family members, in *Ancrene Wisse*, Part VIII:

> As for other things, how often you should receive friends or family, and how long keep them with you: family feeling is not proper for an anchoress. There was once a religious man, and his natural brother came to him for help, and he referred him to his third brother, who was dead and buried. The brother answered wonderingly. 'No!' he

said. 'Is he not dead?' 'And so am I,' said the holy man: 'Dead in the spiritual sense. Let no fleshly friend ask me for fleshly comfort.' (*Ancrene Wisse*, Part VIII, 'The Outer Rule', p. 203)

So advice about family is rare in the anchoritic literature, probably because once the anchoress had been enclosed she was inaccessible to family pressure to advance the family interest by marriage. Yet the anchoritic ideal, like any ideal, grows in a rich social soil: investment in a dowry large enough to attract a high-status bridegroom would be socially as well as financially beneficial to a family.[15]

On the other hand, daughters could be encumbrances. A poor family might be obliged to spend more than they could afford on a dowry, as *Holy Maidenhood* mentions (p. 227), and a woman might well find herself and her children in poverty. David Herlihy has noted that 'at least from 1200, the sums paid as dowries entered an inflationary spiral',[16] so that if a daughter could find a patron to support her as an anchoress parents might be relieved of an expense.[17] While none of the factors just mentioned could produce a *successful* anchoress,[18] they would certainly have served the purpose assigned them by *Holy Maidenhood* as powerful inducements for the anchoress to continue in the way of life she had already chosen. *Holy Maidenhood* is explicit about everything, from disadvantages to horrors, that the options of marriage, sex and childbearing were likely to involve even for the woman lucky enough to have found economic security and a husband she loved. The relative freedom of virginity, however poor in the economic sense, is *per se* attractive; and if that is not enough, which it certainly would be for some, *Holy Maidenhood* is lavish in its descriptions of the *future* joys virginity could bring.

Saints Katherine, Margaret and Juliana are *exempla* of a heroic feminine spirituality dramatically and publicly expressing anchoritic ideals: virginity; absolute fidelity to Christ their bridegroom; the rejection of marriage, which, in return for material wealth, would give their husbands the right to determine completely their feminine roles. Maxentius (*Katherine*), Olibrius (*Margaret*) and Eleusius (*Juliana*) urge and threaten the virgins with wealthy, high-status pagan marriages; Katherine is offered political and religious authority as well. The three men become increasingly vindictive as their frustrations increase, the torture is intensified, and the virgins respond with more and more fortitude. For the anchoress, along with the idea that marriage *is*, in her terms at least, a pagan institution, the virgin martyrs' situation is presently her own, in which even the committed fiancée of Christ will sometimes be tortured—not necessarily by literal abductors or suitors, but certainly by what Maxentius, Olibrius and Eleusius, represent to her—by temptation in the form of desire for a husband, children and an establishment. The renunciation of these is clearly foreseen as a penance she will often require superhuman strength to endure. The fantasies of marriage which *Holy Maidenhood* produces and destroys in detail are introduced uncompromisingly as follows:

> But let us demonstrate more plainly still . . . what the wedded endure: so that you, maiden, may know by this how cheerfully you could live in your maidenhood, quite apart from the joy and honor in heaven that mouth cannot tell. Now you are wedded, and come down so low from so high—from the likeness of the angels, of Jesus Christ's beloved, of a lady in heaven, into flesh's filth, into the way of a beast, into man's slavery, and into the world's woe . . . 'No,' you will say, '. . . From a wife's and a husband's coming together awakens the world's prosperity, and a wealth of beautiful children, who greatly gladden their parents.' You have said this, and think now that you speak the truth; but I will show you that it is all smoothed over with lies. (*Holy Maidenhood* p. 234)

In spite of the invisibility of the anchoress to the community in which she lives, she too has made a dramatic and public renunciation of the world by her enclosure. In some ways the anchoritic life in the cell attached to the church represents the invisibility of an ideal, an inviolate femininity heroically maintained. Whatever the anchoress does escape in the form of marriage and all its woes, she certainly never escapes the carnal suffering of her femininity. In the privacy of her cell, though, she has the opportunity to translate that suffering into a different locus, to identify it as Christ's suffering.

The specifically feminine interpretation of images of enclosure found in these works—the translation of virginity from a masculine sphere of significance into a feminine—occurs in the focus on the anchoritic life itself, and also on the woman in society and the whole issue manifested by the desired/despised, exalted/blameworthy female body. In *Ancrene Wisse* the crucifixion is inverted into a feminine image: an enclosure, a prison, a narrow womb, that aspect of their humanity which makes them imprisoned in the particular way they are, whether they are sexual partners, mothers or virgins in a garden enclosed until their immaculate wedding at death, which is both a sexual union and a birth.

> And was he not himself a recluse in Mary's womb? These two things belong to the anchoress: narrowness and bitterness. For the womb is a narrow dwelling, where our Lord was a recluse; and this word 'Mary', as I have often said, means 'bitterness'. If you then suffer bitterness in a narrow place, you are his fellows, recluse as he was in

189

Mary's womb. Are you imprisoned within four wide walls?—And he
in a narrow cradle, nailed on the cross, enclosed tight in a stone tomb.
Mary's womb and this tomb were his anchorhouses. In neither was he
a worldly man, but like one out of the world, to show anchoresses that
they must not have anything in common with the world. 'Yes,' you
answer me, 'But he went out of both.' Yes, and you too will go out
of both your anchorhouses as he did, without a break, and leave them
both whole. That will be when the spirit goes out in the end, without
break or blemish, from its two houses. One of them is the body, the
other is the outer house, which is like the wall around a castle.
(*Ancrene Wisse*, Part VI, 'Penance' pp. 186–7)

I believe these unusual interpretations are to some indefinable degree
reflections of the writer's closeness to the women he wrote for, and they
are in many ways fighting with the inherited literary tradition. The writer
and his audience are much preoccupied by the practical feminine neces-
sities of physical liberation which must precede spiritual liberation:
freedom from financial dependence on a spouse concerning her own needs
and those of children; independence from the danger, pain and fear
involved in bearing children; independence from sex with a partner she
did not choose for herself and has no right to refuse. We are *aware of*
changes to women's rights in the workforce, medical practice and the
availability of contraception, and changes to the laws of marriage and
divorce which have given some women in the western/northern world
some degree of these things in a way not possible to envision in the early
thirteenth century, but this does not mean that we can easily read ourselves back into these texts by trying to imagine life without these
developments. Our own alternatives will make it difficult to see the
anchoritic one as the writer does and his readers are encouraged to do: as
freedom.

There is another kind of *difference* which will render that vision alien to
us, even as we recognize domestic stereotypes which have remained pretty
constant, like The Wife In Tears In The Kitchen, The Grumbling
Husband, The Brute and The Brutalized.[19] While we *expect* the distant
past to be inaccessible, what is often most alien to us is an extremely
recent past we have rejected but are not yet clear of—those things we
have only recently defined as unacceptable, for example genocide. It is
not really the things we need a cultural anthropologist to understand, but
the things we desire no longer to understand, which we try to alienate as
we read.[20] What is alien in the anchoritic texts is an overall acceptance of
the discourse of masculine sexual authority, for example the way the
anchoress is definitely told that she must open up to a peeping bishop
even when she is simultaneously told that it would be praiseworthy to tell
him to get lost. Many of the topoi I have discussed in this paper are now

190

recognized as political issues to an extent, but are still popularly defined (in the media, for example, and in the thousands of novels people buy at newsstands, in airports and bus stops, as comedy, tragedy, etc.) as the language of women grumbling among themselves about men and trying to make the best out of an inescapably bad situation.[21] And this language is often poised on the edge of an admission which is painful and damaging to any person's concept of self: that one is a victim. The surreal insistence of the virgin martyrs that their victimization is an illusion of their torturers is haunting and troubling.

Recuperative translation of the anchoritic works is further complicated not only by a translator's desire for alienation, but by a desire to find something positive in these texts. These polarities were forcefully illustrated by a conversation between two academics which occurred at the 23rd International Congress on Medieval Studies at Kalamazoo: 'I read these texts with a lot of anger,' said one woman; 'I read them with a lot of love,' said another. 'I'm glad there's someone who can do that,' was the reply. The angry reader is a nun, and the loving reader a mother of three. The author of the thirteenth-century texts write lovingly, respectfully and admiringly, but his attitudes are still enthroned within a discourse about women which is largely or totally unacceptable to many; love, respect and admiration in such a discourse are confusing when we cannot simply reject them as hatred in disguise. The affection of the clerical writer for his readers is a complicated phenomenon. Even at his most severe, for example when he advises that confession be naked—'Sir, God's mercy, I am a foul stud-mare, a stinking whore'[22]—he cannot easily be accused of hatred of women; and even when he subverts traditionally misogynistic sources to help his female readers, parodies and satirizes masculine attitudes and pretensions for the purpose of entertaining and supporting women, he clearly does not mean to undermine a masculine power structure. As a translator I am startled to find that translating the texts has not really exposed them, that even the intensified essentializing and isolation of the feminine experience which occurs there is not necessarily visible to a modern reader; it was hardly if at all visible to the nexus of composers—sources, interactive audience, and author.

Perhaps one of the most difficult aspects for a modern audience to see is how any of this could be conceived as increased spiritual freedom—how liberation of the anchoress in any sense proceeds from her 'translation' as a feminine body within the slavery of earthly marriage to a feminine body within the joy and eternal life of heavenly marriage. Both are, after all, marriage, and we are reminded graphically quite often that real marriage to a real man is slavery; yet heavenly marriage is modelled on the earthly and its positive features are ultimately derived from the earthly as an experience, and so the image of sexual union constantly vacillates between negative and positive. In both kinds of marriage the anchoress is married to and remains subordinate to a masculine figure, be it a repulsive idiot, a desired but unloving man, or the infinitely preferable Christ.

> Reflect, innocent woman: once the knot of marriage has been knit, you have to stay with him, be he an idiot or a cripple—be he anything whatsoever. (*Holy Maidenhood* p. 237)

> 'Get her, right now. If she's a free woman, I'll have her and keep her as a wife; if she's a slave, I choose her for a concubine . . .' 'Tell me,' he said, 'whether you're the child of a free parent or a slave-woman.' The blessed maiden Margaret answered him at once, and said, 'I'm a free woman, but God's slave'. (*St Margaret* p. 289)

Marriage to Christ seems to be posited on a courtly model to the extent that within this union all courtly love promises in the way of devotion, fidelity and ecstatic reward is given by Christ to the anchoress; and yet courtly love (however slippery a subject to define), with its emphasis on the ecstatic suffering of restraint and at the same time sensuality, is most often a literary model for fulfilling sex and love *outside* marriage. It may be that its appropriateness as a model for the anchoress's relationship to Christ resides in that very notion—its disassociation from the model of marriage in which the woman's body is a complex unit of currency and her spiritual state is irrelevant. It seems that the feminine body as the primary unit of exchange in the bourgeois marriage must simply be rejected by author and audience as an arena for spiritual attainment, activity, or domain, while the body and sex remain their battlefield.[23]

A 'courtly' kind of love, in which a man serves a woman, is at least often *expressed* in terms of the freedom it offers a woman over her own affairs, and particularly over her body, however much that freedom seems conventionally to have suffered from a final resort to force by the male lover.[24] Criseyde tells herself that she has no interest in marriage for this reason[25], and it is one of the reasons the subject of marriage never arises in *Troilus and Criseyde* though it would solve the problem of Criseyde's having to leave Troy. An anchoritic context for love in which the man is in the woman's service has an unusual dimension: the absence of a real male lover except as she imagines him to be. This places her in charge of both sides of the love-dialogue; she is wholly responsible for what happens in the dramatic meditations, wooings, and their after-effects in her continued solitude. Her male confessor does not have the authority to take this freedom from her, and it certainly seems from the testimony of *Ancrene Wisse* that he encourages rather than interferes with her inner dialogue.

There are several ways of looking at this phenomenon as a process of translation: as with all spiritual writings, there is no attainment posited for the reader without the translation of the text, in which spiritual experience is described or directed, into some form of experience for the reader; the translation of this material into the specifically feminine experience of the audience, however, requires the reader to have the force of character to take charge of the situation entirely, and often to reverse the standard male-female power-relations, even when enclosed in a cell and under the guidance of a male spiritual director. Certainly in the process of translating these texts I have found myself to be involved in a much larger web of consequences than I ever imagined, not the least of which is the awareness that both feminine experience as presented in literature, and the experience of women themselves, are still under the pressure of translation, both within the academy and without. Feminine experience as presented in the anchoritic texts was conceived by the writer to be translatable into Christ's experience, a translation from the worldly female body, in which the battle for spiritual attainment is already lost, into a female body poised on the edge of the highest spiritual reward:

> But the maiden's song is [unlike all others in heaven] . . . , shared with the angels', music over all the music in heaven . . . For this is forever their song: to thank God and praise him that he gave them so much grace from himself that they forsook every earthly man for him, and kept themselves always clean of fleshly filth in body and in heart, and instead of a man of clay took the Lord of life, the king of sublime happiness; for which reason he honours them so much above all the others, as the bridegroom does his wedded spouse. This song none but they can sing. (*Holy Maidenhood* p. 233)

However, then as now, currents of ambivalence about what is defined as feminine experience and its relationship to spirituality continue to flow in many different directions for any reader, woman or man; this makes it impossible to know at what point the text needs no further translation.

NOTES

1. I am extremely grateful to Ruth Evans for her reading of and suggestions concerning the revision of this paper, especially where questions of translation and gender meet. I would also like to thank Jocelyn Wogan-Browne for her suggestions and support.

'In treating the content of a message, one must often distinguish clearly between the discourse itself and its temporal-spatial setting. That is to say, what happened in a narrative may constitute one series of problems, but the cultural setting of the narrative itself may introduce quite a different series of difficulties. When the circumstantial setting of a source-language text is widely divergent from any corresponding setting in a receptor language, serious problems may be involved in providing a meaningful equivalent text': Eugene Nida, 'A Framework for the Analysis and Evaluation of Theories of Translation' in Richard W. Brislin (ed.) *Translation Applications and Research* (New York: Gardner Press, 1976) p. 49; the question of 'the best translation' is considered on pp. 64–5. One of the complexities of translation as an act is that on the one hand the linguistic feat seems transparent, something we do all the time; on the other hand, that act itself is the focus of a deep theoretical uncertainty as to nature and even possibility—see, for example, Paul de Man, '"Conclusions": Walter Benjamin's "The Task of the Translator"' in his *The Resistance to Theory* (Minneapolis: University of Minnesota Press, 1986) pp. 73–105, and Joseph Graham (ed.) *Difference in Translation* (Ithaca: Cornell University Press, 1985). The essays in Lawrence Venuti (ed.) *Rethinking Translation: Discourse, Subjectivity and Ideology* (London and New York: Routledge, 1992) investigate, among other things, relationships between gender, creativity and translation (e.g. Lori Chamberlain, 'Gender and the Metaphorics of Translation' pp. 57–74).

2. E.J. Dobson investigated this question in *The Origins of Ancrene Wisse* (Oxford: Oxford University Press, 1976); for a very brief summary of the reasons why a single writer may have been responsible for the anchoritic material or at least most of it, see Nicholas Watson's and my introduction to *Anchoritic Spirituality: Ancrene Wisse and Associated Works* (Mahwah, New Jersey: Paulist Press, 1991) pp. 8–15; see also my paper, 'The Solitary Heroine: Aspects of Meditation and Mysticism in *Ancrene Wisse*, *Hali Meiðhad*, the Katherine Group and the Wooing Group' (in W. Pollard (ed.) *The English Mystical Tradition*, forthcoming).

3. The sources of the anchoritic material have been heavily investigated as to identity, though not as to particular application in the anchoritic works. In *Anchoritic Spirituality* our footnotes attempt to do this at least superficially; for a general breakdown of source material, see the introductions to the individual works.

4. While this literature eventually had a more general application than just to the anchoritic life, and became in its turn source material, its original intention seems to have been for an anchoritic audience. See *Anchoritic Spirituality*, Introduction pp. 7–8 for a summary of the reasons behind this assumption. I use the term 'audience' as inclusive of 'readership', since the anchoresses are encouraged to read parts of *Ancrene Wisse* at least to their maidens—who sometimes may have become anchoresses themselves.

5. For an analysis of numbers and gender ratios of English anchoresses and anchorites between 1100 and 1539, see Ann K. Warren, *Anchorites and Their Patrons in Medieval England* (Berkeley: University of California Press, 1985) pp. 18–29. The largest total number is given as being during the fourteenth century: two hundred and fourteen. Estimates for the twelfth and thirteenth centuries are ninety-six and one hundred and ninety-eight respectively, with female recluses in the majority at five to three and four to one in these centuries.

6. *Ancrene Wisse* Part II ('The Outer Senses') opens with material drawn from traditional misogynistic, pro-virginity writing (Jerome's *Epistola ad Eustochium*, XXII, 21 and 25, *CSEL* 54, pp. 173, 179): interpretations of the loose woman—Eve, Dinah, Bathsheba—and her destructive effects, all in the

service of illustrating why an anchoress should especially guard her sense of sight and stay away from her window. Commentaries on these women as types helped to frame the definition of feminine nature as inferior, contact with it polluting. Jerome did indeed defend religious women, but by denaturizing them, in some sense removing them from their wicked bodies. It is this *removal* from the feminine body which makes them equal to men:

> *Quamdiu mulier partui servit et liberis, hanc habet ad virum differentiam, quam corpus ad animam. Sin autem Christo magis voluerit servire quam saeculo, mulier esse cessabit, et dicetur vir.*

> While a woman serves for birth and children, she is different from man as body is from soul. But when she wants to serve Christ more than the world, then she shall cease to be woman and will be called man. (*Commentarium in Epistolam ad Ephesios Libri III, PL* 26, 533)

St Ambrose likewise finds that a woman *occurrit in virum perfectum* ('progresses to perfect manhood') if she is a believer, doing without *nomine saeculi, corporis sexu, lubrico juventutis, multiloquio senectutis* ('a worldly name, a sexed body, youthful deceitfulness, elderly gabbling'), sins of worldly pride, inconstancy and garrulousness being, in this discourse, particularly strong in women. Only unbelieving women should be *designated* as women: *Quae non credit, mulier est, et adhuc corporei sexus appellatione signatur* (Ambrose, *Expositio Evangelii secundam Lucam, PL* 15.1844). Vern L. Bullough discusses these and other notions in 'Medieval Medical Views of Women' *Viator* 4 (1973) pp. 485–91.

7. Nicholas Watson and I have disagreed with the fairly-frequently expressed assumption, in both past and recent readings of these texts, that the writer is condescending to his readers, and views them as mere spiritual beginners. See *Anchoritic Spirituality*, pp. 19–28; and I have also considered this question in 'The Solitary Heroine' (full reference, n. 2 above).

8. All quotations from the anchoritic texts being discussed in this paper are from Nicholas Watson's and my translations in *Anchoritic Spirituality*.

9. E.g. *Tu es diaboli ianua; tu es arboris illius resignatrix; tu es diuinae legis prima desertrix; tu es quae eum suasisti, quem diabolus aggredi non valuit; tu imaginem Die, hominem, tam facile elisisti; propter tuum meritum, id est mortem, etiam filius Dei mori habuit* (Tertullian, *De Cultu Feminarum*, 1.2): 'You are the Devil's gateway. You are the unsealer of that forbidden tree. You are the first deserter of the divine Law. You are she who persuaded him whom the devil was not valiant enough to attack. You destroyed so easily God's image man. On account of your desert, that is death, even the Son of God had to die' (translated by Rosemary Radford Ruether in 'Mysogynism and Virginal Feminism in the Fathers of the Church' Rosemary Ruether (ed.) *Religion and Sexism* (New York: Simon and Schuster, 1974) pp. 150–83). Ruether summarizes: '. . . [P]atristic theology makes use of the same assumptions [as Augustine's] of woman's subordination to man in the order of nature, and her special "carnality" in the disorder of sin, which imply the same attitudes, however unjustified by the contrary assumption of the equivalence of male and female in the original creation [Genesis 1:27: "God created man in his own image; in the image of God he created him; male and female he

195

created them"]. This definition of femaleness as a body decrees a natural subordination of female to male, *as flesh must be subject to spirit in the right ordering of nature* [quoting from Augustine, *De Contin.* I. 23]' p. 157.

10. I am extremely grateful to Jocelyn Wogan-Browne for drawing my attention to this, and for making available to me her paper entitled 'What Medicine Makes of Women or, A Brief History of the Hymen' delivered at The University of Liverpool's Women's Studies Seminars on 'Women in Medicine . . . Women in Maths'. While it seems incredible to me, I find that I am no more amazed by the following—extracted from a longer passage she quotes—than I am by the more extreme parts of, say, *Holy Maidenhood*:

> [On the female urogenital triangle:] All the *male* formations and structures are present in the female, but *modified* greatly for *functional reasons*. The essential difference is the *failure* in the female of midline fusion of the genital folds . . . *Lacking* the *rigid* support of the *complete* perineal membrane of the male, the perineal body is more mobile in the female . . . The female urethra [has] *a few poorly-developed* pit-like glands, *said to be homologous with the prostate but bearing no resemblance to the structure of that gland* . . . (R.J. Last, *Last's Anatomy, Regional and Applied* 7th edn (Edinburgh: Churchill Livingstone, 1984) pp. 354–6; I have left in Wogan-Browne's emphases.)

For an analysis of Galen's 'reading' of the female sex organs as inverted male ones, see Thomas Laqueur, *Making Sex: Body and Gender from the Greeks to Freud* (Cambridge, Mass.: Harvard University Press, 1990) pp. 25–33.

11. Genesis 1:27, quoted in n. 9, notwithstanding. It is an interesting oversight in the neoplatonic scheme of things that the idea of a copy being less perfect than its original did not inevitably produce, as it does if the logic is a carried through, a notion of feminine superiority, since, of course, every man *since* Adam at least has come from a woman.

12. I am indebted for some of these ideas to a session at the 1992 Kalamazoo conference on medieval studies entitled 'Rape in the Middle Ages', with papers by Anne Schotter, Heather Seagroatt, Helene Scheck and Greta Austin, and to Kathryn Gravdal as respondent. Gravdal's comic-serious comment that she and other feminist interpreters of medieval texts had been criticized for 'planting rape scenes in the major literature of the Western world' was more important than I immediately grasped. Rape was *legally defined* as a crime in the Middle Ages as now; but if in both practice and literature it is redefined during or after the fact as seduction, it is not 'really' a crime. If at some later time the act is *socially* as well as legally defined as a crime, of course it is retrospectively 'reinvented' in many situations and texts where it did not exist as such before. Anne Schotter pointed out that in the Latin comedies she had examined, rape from the point of view of the clerical audience was seen as a property crime against the husband, and hence a satisfying subject for clerical parody. I felt that the exception she mentioned, *Pamphilus* (F. Pittaluga (ed.) *Pamphilus* in *Commedie latine del XII e XIII secolo* Vol. 3, Istituto de filologia classica e medioevale (Genoa: Università di Genova, 1980); see also T.J. Garbaty, *'Pamphilus: De Amore, an Introduction and Translation' Chaucer Review* 2 (1967) pp. 108–34), which can certainly be read as portraying rape as a crime against the woman herself, a

betrayal of love, proved the rule. Parody in the Passions of the virgin martyrs is entirely at the expense of men, and in *Ancrene Wisse* also the sexual pretensions of men, especially religious men, are parodied. Gravdal's book will be of interest to many: *Ravishing Maidens: Writing Rape in Medieval French Literature and Law* (Philadelphia: University of Pennsylvania Press, 1991).

13. See, e.g. Christ as the warrior-lover begging the haughty woman he loves to be allowed to die delivering her from her enemies, *Ancrene Wisse*, Part VII, 'Love' p. 191, and the anchoress praising Christ's beauty in 'The Wooing of Our Lord', p. 248.

14. See Ann K. Warren, *Anchorites and Their Patrons* pp. 97–8; Henry A. Wilson (ed.) *The Pontifical of Magdalen College* Henry Bradshaw Society 39 (1910) pp. 243–4.

15. The life of Christina of Markyate illustrates the trials of a young woman heroically resisting her family's determination to force her into a particular marriage. Inwardly committed to a religious life but without episcopal sanction, Christina preferred to hide for four years in the anchoritic cell of her friend Roger, in a cupboard so small she could not wear clothes enough to keep warm. See Charles H. Talbot (ed. and trans.) *The Life of Christina of Markyate: A Twelfth-Century Recluse* (Oxford: Clarendon Press, 1959).

16. See David Herlihy, 'Life Expectancies for Women' in Rosmarie Thee Morewedge (ed.) *The Role of Woman in the Middle Ages* (Albany: State University of New York Press, 1975) p. 12. Herlihy comments finally, 'There remains, however, this paradox: as her hopes of surviving improved, as her relative numbers grew, so the social position of the medieval woman seems in some ways to have deteriorated . . . Many women in late medieval society, especially in the cities, were economically superfluous and regarded as a burden by their own families. Many understandably grew alienated from the institutions and the values of society. This surely is why irregular religious movements, such as the Beguines, had a powerful appeal for women', p. 16.

17. 'Ask these queens, these rich countesses, these proud ladies of their way of life. Truly, if they consider it rightly and acknowledge the truth, I have them to witness that they lick honey off thorns . . . When it is like this with the rich, what do you expect with the poor, who are unworthily dowered in marriage, and ill-provided for? Like almost all gentlewomen now in the world, who do not have the wherewithal to buy a bridegroom of the same rank as themselves, and give themselves into the slavery of a less worthy man with all that they have' *(Holy Maidenhood* p. 227).

18. Candidates for the anchoritic life were examined by the bishop for their fitness, both personal and economic. Such vetting would likely have weeded out women *merely* looking for an escape from marriage. See Warren, pp. 53–91.

19. The following are all from *Holy Maidenhood*: '. . . the woman who, when she comes in, hears her children screaming, sees the cat at the bacon and the dog at the rind, her cake burning on the hearth and her calf sucking spilt milk— and the lout grumbles away . . .' (p. 239); 'When he is out, you are painfully anxious and frightened about his coming home. When he is at home, all your wide house seems too small; his glaring terrifies you; his ugly noise and crude grumbling fill you with horror. He rebukes you, rails at you and humiliates you disgracefully, he takes you shamefully as a lecher his whore, strikes you and beats you as his bought slave and born serf. Your bones ache and your

flesh pains you, your heart swells in bitter anger within you, and outwardly
your face is inflamed with fury' (pp. 236–7).

20. I am grateful to Nicholas Watson for discussing these aspects of this section
with me, and particularly for his anecdotes about teaching these texts: the way
students return over and over again to the question of whether the anchoritic
texts are decisively positive or negative about women, even when it is clear
whichever answer they find is not the only one. Perhaps also illustrative here
is the way in which a very large proportion of my youngest female students are
horrified or offended by the idea that they themselves might have suffered
under any kind of sexual stereotyping or sexual discrimination; even though
they walk home in organized bands escorted by a stalwart male to protect
themselves against rape and murder on the campus and in its environs, they
consider sexual discrimination as a thing of the distant past—a 'medieval'
phenomenon. Their attitude is, I think, a result of not being burdened by
childcare and economic responsibility (see next note).

21. I am generally indebted to Judith Levine's *My Enemy, My Love: Man-Hating
and Ambivalence in Women's Lives* (New York: Doubleday, 1992) for her
careful listening to the many women she talked to and whose voices she
records, as well as her lucid analysis of so difficult a topic; it is hard to say
exactly how it helped in rewriting a paper on thirteenth-century anchoritic
texts, but it did. It certainly requires any reader to realize that even the political rights women now have legally are for a great majority of women simply
invisible, unacknowledged, or simply layered on top of their Other role of
childbearer, childkeeper and domestic, without any sense of incongruity or
irony by partners and fathers—sometimes not even by themselves. Both this
note and the previous one point, I hope, to the way in which modern readers
of these texts will find themselves caught in the necessity of believing the
medieval texts extremely foreign while recognizing more than they want to.

22. *Ancrene Wisse*, Part V, 'Confession' p. 164.

23. In 'The Solitary Heroine' I have used the term *incarnational mysticism* for the
particular kind of mysticism posited by the anchoritic life, which is grounded
in the experience of a daily life of suffering in the body with Christ, a daily
martyrdom. The fact that I have found this idea to be instantly rejected by
some male academics in the field of mysticism points to several features of the
academy past and present: the intellectualization of religious experience by
the male clerical institution, the rejection of the body entirely by mystics like
Bernard of Clairvaux, even as they insist, for example, on the heavily physical, erotic literary vehicle of the Song of Songs as the ideal expression of
mystical experience; the association of femininity in particular with the body,
and hence with an inferior spirituality (an often unspoken feature of the
debate about women in the priesthood); and simply a resistance to redefini-
tion by discovery in texts which are marginally considered canonical if only for
the purpose of source-hunting.

24. Ovid's advice is probably the most well-known:

> Vim licet appelles: grata est vis ista puellis:
> Quod iuvat, invitae saepe dedisse volunt.
> Quaecumque est veneris subita violata rapina,
> Gaudet, et inprobitas muneris instar habet.
> At quae cum posset cogi, non tacta recesset,
> Ut simulet vultu gaudia, tristis erit.

You may use force; women like you to use it; they often wish to give unwillingly what they like to give. She whom a sudden assault has taken by storm is pleased, and counts the audacity as a compliment. But she who, when she might have been compelled, departs untouched, though her looks feign joy, will yet be sad.
(J.H. Mozley (ed. and trans.) *The Art of Love, and Other Poems* Loeb Classical Library (London: William Heinemann, 1929).

Force is advised by Andreas Capellanus in the love of women of the peasant class, at least (*De arte honeste amandi* ch. 11). The ambiguous situation in *Troilus and Criseyde* is an extremely familiar one:

> What myghte or may the sely larke seye,
> Whan that the sperhauk hath it in his foot? . . .
> This Troilus in armes gan hire streyne,
> And seyde, 'O swete, as euere mot I gon,
> Now be ʒe kaught, now is ther but we tweyne,
> Now ʒeldeth ʒow, for other bote is non.'
> To that Criseyde answerede thus anon,
> 'Ne hadde I er now, my swete herte deere,
> Ben ʒolde, i-wis, I were now nought heere.'

(B.A. Windeatt (ed.) *Troilus and Criseyde* (London & New York: Longman, 1984) Book III. 1191–2, 1205–11.)
25. *Troilus and Criseyde*, II. 604–9, 750–805.

Chapter 9

Encoding and Decoding: Metaphorical Discourse of Love in Richard Rolle's Commentary on the First Verses of the Song of Songs[1]

DENIS RENEVEY

In *Ego Dormio*, a Middle English epistle written for the spiritual direction of a nun of Yedingham, the first of the great Middle English mystics Richard Rolle (ob. 1349) writes in his prologue:

> Ego dormio et cor meum vigilat. The þat lust loue, hold þyn ere and hyre of loue. In þe songe of loue I fynd hit written þat I haue set at þe begennynge of my writynge: 'I slepe and my hert waketh.' Mich loue he sheweth þat neuer is wery to loue, bot euer, standynge, sittynge, goynge, or any oþer dede doynge, is euer his loue þynkynge, and oft sithe þerof dremynge. Forþi þat I loue þe, I wowe þe, þat I myght haue þe as I wold, nat to me, bot to my Lord. I wil becum a messager to brynge þe to his bed þat hath mad þe and boght þe, Crist, þe kynges son of heuyn, for he wil wed þe if thou wil loue hym.[2]

Not only the Song of Songs' verse (Cant. 5:2) which begins the first line of the epistle and gives the work its name, but the direct reference to the Song of Songs ('þe songe of loue') in the third sentence, as well as other borrowings elsewhere in the epistle, all testify to the importance of this Biblical book in the making of the epistle.[3] Thus, the role of 'messager' which Rolle ascribes to himself in the above quotation is the result and product of his knowledge and practice of the commentary tradition that had grown up around the Song of Songs, as well as his experiential knowl-edge of the relationship between the soul and God.[4] In fact, the 'mes-sager' embodies the whole of the definition which Isidore of Seville had given to the word *interpres* in his *Etymologiae*:

> Interpres, quod inter partes medius sit duarum linguarum, dum trans-feret. Sed et qui Deum [quem] interpretatur et hominum quibus divina indicat mysteria, interpres vocatur [quia inter eam quam trans-feret].

> [Interpreter: because one is between the parts, midway between two languages, when one translates. But he is also called an interpreter who is placed between God, whom he interprets, and men, to whom he reveals the divine mysteries, because that which he carries over is between.][5]

The evidence gathered here, as well as the results conveyed on a larger scale by the work of Nicholas Watson on the chronology of Rolle's writ-ings, indicate that the access to *Latinitas* and the practice of vernacular translation were momentous in the shaping of the role of spiritual director which Rolle took on in the last stages of his life.[6] Many people are familiar with Rolle as translator in his last works—the idea of 'messenger', and the fact that he actually includes translated material in them.[7] The process by which Rolle came to this understanding of his own function is perhaps less well known, notwithstanding Watson's recent study, and I should like to show how Rolle's idea of translation is working very diffe-rently in an earlier work, commonly called *Super Canticum Canticorum*.[8] My concern in this paper is with the textual practices of Rolle as a medieval *interpres*, and especially as a commentator of the Song of Songs.

Rolle's commentary deals only with the first two-and-a-half verses of the Song of Songs.[9] The most accurate title given to the commentary is that copied by the scribe of MS. Trinity College, Dublin, 153: *Incipit Exposicio Super Primum Versiculum Canticum Canticorum Secundum Ricardum Heremitam* (hereafter *Super Cant.*).[10] In view of the length of the existing commentary, it is quite clear that Rolle never intended to write a commentary on the whole of the Song of Songs.[11] Nevertheless, *Super Cant.* is arguably a finished piece, in which the triad of *calor*, *dulcor* and *canor*, characteristic of Rolle's mysticism, appears prominently. It could be argued that Rolle uses the commentary genre as a flashy wrapping to give greater credit to his mystical experience. On the other hand, and more probably, literary competence, necessary for the crea-tion of the affective and metaphorical discourse which takes place as Rolle peruses the verses of the Song of Songs, is part and parcel of his mysticism.

The interest shown in the spiritual experience, and the occurrences of the terms *experientia* and *experire*, increase in proportion as medieval commentators devote their writing—as most of them do—to the tropological sense of Scripture.[12] With Rolle, the spiritual experience is translated into the metaphorical language. The interpreter of Scripture becomes translator of his spiritual experience, appropriating to himself the imagery, displacing the textual practices of the commentary and accommodating them to his effusive prose. Rolle uses the verbal signs of the Song of Songs to encode the mystical experience.

In this respect we may observe an instructive contrast with Rolle's vernacular translation of and gloss on the *Psalter*.[13] Manifestly dependent on the Latin original, which precedes both translation and gloss, the translation is designed to function as textual facilitator to allow the audience access to *Latinitas*.[14] This is Rolle's justification for the use of simple English words and for his word-for-word translation:

> In this werke .i. seke na straunge ynglis, bot lyghtest and comonest. and swilk that is mast lyke til the latyn. swa that thai that knawes noght latyn. by the ynglis may com til mony latyn wordis. In the translacioun .i. folow the lettere als mykyll as .i. may. And thare .i. fynd na propire ynglis .i. folow the wit of the worde, swa that thai that sall red it thaim there noght dred errynge.[15]

In *Super Cant.* and other texts equally replete with the imagery of the Song of Songs, by contrast, Rolle moves away from the role of textual interpreter and liberates himself from the notion of service to an authoritative text.[16] If in the *Psalter* Rolle indicates in the prologue that 'In expounynge .i. fologh haly doctours',[17] in this work he uses the textual strategies of the commentary genre to constitute himself as *auctor*. The recuperation, and replacement, of the *auctoritas* by a text which claims to be authoritative, allows Rolle to build up a textual tissue ideal for the encoding of his spiritual experience. Rolle's concern has moved away from the one exposed in his prologue to his *English Psalter*: the notion of service of the *interpres* towards the *auctoritas* has disappeared.[18] The *interpres*, transmuted into an *auctor*, uses *Latinitas* as a means of consolidating his standing among the fathers of the church.[19]

Most commentators of the Song of Songs reflect in their prologues on the difficulty of unveiling the mystery hidden in this book. St Bernard of Clairvaux refers to individual experience as the only means of understanding the message of the text.[20] William of St Thierry addresses the holy spirit and asks to be filled with love in order to take part in the conversation of the bride and the bridegroom.[21] Their approach is cautious and reflects the concerns of the *interpres* before divine *auctoritas*. Rolle instead does without a prologue and embraces the Song affectively to project himself as the bride.[22] The effect of such a personal apprehension implies a radical transformation of the contextual setting of the Song. Rolle may be the most extreme in the ways the authorial text is subject to displacement, but he follows a long tradition which set some of its verses in a variety of contexts, such as mariological commentaries or various liturgical offices.[23] Commentators of this particular book are unable to accept the literal meaning in the Biblical context. The overt sensuality of the vocabulary of love challenges any simple view on the divine origins of this Biblical book. William of St Thierry believes that God placed it with the other books in a condescending gesture to man's frailty, as a compound of both the material and the spiritual. Richard of St Victor regards the silliness of the literal sense as a means for the contemplative to look beyond the literal horizon.[24] Commentators resort themselves to explanation and interpretation to justify the position of the Song in the Bible. The necessity for a constant reappraisal of its place within the Bible provides clear evidence of the difficulty of making sense of the vocabulary of love within the Biblical context. A literal understanding, that is, is not appropriate within this special context. The task of the commentators is to create a new context for the text which allows for new conditions of reading.[25]

The depiction of *caritas* is an important element of those new conditions.[26] *De IV Gradibus Violentae Charitatis* (hereafter *De IV Grad.*) of Richard of St Victor offers a detailed and systematic study of this virtue. Some of the major ideas and images of this important work are echoed in *Super Cant.* and *Melos Amoris.*[27] The metaphor of love as fire, with its strong physical basis,[28] as well as the degrees of love, called *insuperabilis*, *inseparabilis*, *singularis* and *insatiabilis*—with the omission in Rolle of the final degree, are without doubt borrowed from the Victorine treatise.[29] Moreover, Richard of St Victor defines further his four degrees as first, the love of the heart, second, the love of the whole heart, third, the love of the soul, and fourth, the love of all the virtues.[30] For each degree, the articulation of the relationship of the individual with God is couched in a distinct affective mould:

> Forte adhuc David in primo gradu erat, sed jam de secundo presumebat quando psallens dicebat: *Confitebor tibi, Domine, in toto corde meo.* Qui in secundo gradu est fiducialiter psallere potest: *In toto corde meo exquisivi te.* Qui tertium gradum obtinet profecto ejusmodi jam dicere valet: *Concupivit anima mea, Domine, desiderare justificationes tuas in omni tempore.* Qui quartum gradum ascendit, et Deum ex tota virtute diligit, dicere potest profecto: *Non timebo quid faciat michi homo*, eo quod sit *paratum cor* ejus *sperare in Domino; confirmatum est cor* ejus, *non commovebitur in eternum, donec despiciat inimicos suos.*[31]

[Maybe David was still in this first degree, while ruminating about the second, when he was saying in his psalm: *I will praise thee, the Lord, with my whole heart*. The one who is at the second degree can sing confidently: *With my whole heart have I sought you*. The one who obtains the third can already say: *My soul has desired with longing your ordinances at all times*. The one who has ascended to the fourth degree and who loves God with all his strength can say in all security: *I will not fear what man can do unto me*, because *his heart is disposed to trust in the Lord. His heart is strengthened, he shall not be moved until he looks down upon his enemies.*]

Richard of St Victor also qualifies the degrees of charity according to the model of natural love. The first degree celebrates the betrothal, the second the wedding, the third the consummation of the marriage, and the fourth the childbirth.[32] In many ways, *Super Cant.* stands as the expression by Rolle of the third degree described by Richard of St Victor.[33] The *jubilatio* theme, also an important feature of *De IV Gradibus*, reaches in *Super Cant.* a climax in the *Encomium Nominis Jesu*, which makes the fourth section of the commentary.[34] The *jubilatio* theme, the *incendium amoris*, the *Quia amore langueo*, the liquefaction image, and, above all, the notion of *caritas*, all present in *De IV Gradibus*, are important elements of Rolle's mysticism, assimilated into his own mystical system through reflection and meditation.[35] The Victorine presentation of the contemplative life by means of the fusion of the carnal and spiritual senses had an immediate appeal to Rolle.[36]

The conflation of those traditions with Rolle's more idiosyncratic characteristics creates a context suitable for the articulation of more daring utterances. Rolle needs to secure the meaning of the terms of love by stressing their metaphorical potential. The Biblical narrative of the wise and the foolish virgins (Math. 25:1–13) allows him to define the spiritual lover against a background which depicts the behaviour and attire of the carnal lover:

Amodo igitur O virgines celo suspicite; ibi sponsum querite; cum amatoribus mundi nolite vos inquinare. Fatuas enim virgines Christus se non cogniturum asserit, quas mundialis amore vanitatis ab illo nunc expellit. Ille utique iam pompose muliercule in tortis crinibus, cornibus elatis incedentes, solo amore carnali decorari appetunt. Illam solam viam que Christo ducit odiunt et abhorrent, quia autem formam et substanciam a deo datam frustra et nequiter non curant effundere.[37]

[Henceforth accordingly look up to heaven, o virgins; there seek the bridegroom; don't corrupt yourselves with the lovers of the world. Indeed Christ declares he will not recognize the foolish virgins, whom he expels for their love of wordly vanity. In any case at present those pompous little women with their curled hair, going (about) with

204

elevated horns, strive to be adorned only for carnal love. They hate
and abhor this only way which leads to Christ, because they don't care
that they are pouring out the form and substance given by God in
deception and worthlessly.]

The importance of the Song of Songs is crucial to his habilitation as a
psychologically confident hermit. Moreover, his mysticism, both in its
formulation and perception, relies heavily on the linguistic implications of
the metaphorical discourse of love.[38] The transfer of the terms of love into
a new semantic field belongs to the process of spiritual purgation.

The vehemence with which Rolle opposes two sets of meaning for the
whole range of the vocabulary of love supports the view that Rolle
charges his metaphorical utterances with more than an ornamental or
affective value. As with Hildegard of Bingen, and most of the mystics, the
metaphorical meaning of Rolle's lexical terms of love conveys the
contemplative experience.[39] As a concept taken from the domain of the
affectiones, love, as *eros* or as *caritas*, has a basis in bodily experience.[40]
The process of interiorization of the external language of love marks out
Rolle's most mystical pages. The interiorized language of love comes out
as metaphorical discourse. In the course of the process, Rolle operates the
transfer of meaning from the semantic field of carnal love to that of the
conceptual domain of God by attempting to assign the latter with a series
of defining terms. The terms of love lead to the understanding of some of
God's attributes as the eternal light, *caritas*, the celestial melody, *dulcor*,
the fire and its heat. In one of his long condemnations of the carnal lovers,
Rolle argues that it is not possible to play with the world and still rejoice
with Christ in the future life. In his crude language, he asserts: 'Venter
saturatus venerem pocius quam Christum amplexatur' [A full stomach
embraces more easily Venus than Christ].[41] The terms of love in Rolle's
mind retain the double meaning expressed by metaphorical discourse.
Because of his propensity for feminine beauty and his desire for concupiscence, Rolle refrains from exploring too daringly the cognitive
possibilities of metaphorical discourse in a loose context.[42] As the terms
of love convey simultaneously two meanings, the commentators of the
Song have to build up a context for the vocabulary of love to limit their
literal meaning. Some of Rolle's passages reflect his psychological difficulties in using the material taken from the semantic field of love to express
his contemplative experience. The frantic tension prompted by the
encounter or visualization of enticing women forces Rolle to effect a
drastic transfer of the sexual desire, which serves instead to establish the
loving relationship of the soul with God. In the spiritual state which he
claims to have reached, Rolle maintains: 'eciam inter feminas possumus
vivere et delectacionem femineam in animo nullam sentire' [we are indeed

able to live among women and feel no delight of women in the soul].[43] In theory, the sexual desire has lost power to seduce and invade the soul by means of the imagination. The use of women as a gauge to measure spiritual progress is a remarkable feature of Rolle's idiosyncratic mysticism. This sexual inhibition could account for the use by Rolle of his three personal concepts of *calor*, *canor*, and *dulcor*, whose literal contexts, although not necessarily devoid of possible links with the semantic field of love, do not relate to it strictly.[44] But the metaphorical language needs its literal referent to convey meaning. By trying to block it, Rolle also puts at stake the metaphorical meaning, which is always in need of its original primary sense in order to exist. *Super Cant.* is mostly concerned with the use of textual commentary practices to fix the metaphorical meaning of the terms of love as a translation and gloss of a mystical experience. The Song of Songs as such is not Rolle's principal concern. His concern indeed consists in using the imagery of the Song to encode his own relationship with God.[45]

The oddity in delineating the essence of God, and the relationship of the soul to Him, is caused by the impossibility of the mystic's expressing it in the discursive mode.[46] For that reason, Rolle resorts to, and counts on, both traditional vehicles and made-up terms as cognitive tools expressing the conceptual reality of the mystical experience, without saturating his commentary with a list of symbols. Instead, Rolle's preference for metaphorical meaning implies the resurgence and the interplay of two distinct components: on the one hand that of the world of love and courtship, and on the other that of the field of contemplation. The notion of transference of meaning from one component to another does not imply the rejection of the meaning given in the first semantic field. This fact is supported by the mystical texts and the experience which they provide, as well as by the nature of metaphorical meaning itself. Moreover, the cognitive force of metaphorical meaning depends largely on the virtuosity with which the writer organizes his utterances according to the relations of affinities and contrasts which the terms bear with one another.[47] *Super Cant.* demonstrates the difficulties with which Rolle, like most commentators, maintains those relations. If the Song of Songs provides most of its vocabulary of love to define the contemplative experience, it does not however unfold itself according to the natural progression of a human love relationship. Furthermore, the displacement of the text in the commentary form makes it vulnerable to the intentions of its interpreters. As the human *auctor* becomes more inquisitive before the divinely inspired texts, he acquires the techniques to set them in his own chosen context, at his own pace.[48] Commentators are startled, for instance, by the first line of the Song: *Osculetur me osculo oris sui.* Bernard of Clairvaux develops a theory of contemplative progression from this first verse. The kissing of Christ's feet, hands and face symbolize the different stages of the contemplative life, from a love of Christ in his humanity to the love of his Godhead. From a lexical term borrowed from the semantic field of love, Bernard creates a new set of functions for the kiss, unrelated to the originating field.[49] This is the manner by which Bernard slackens the pace of his commentary, in order to affix a theory of contemplation upon it. The interpretation of Bernard in this case is symbolic. Rolle instead maintains the double meaning of the term of love, and clearly interprets the gesture of kissing with regard to both the semantic field of love and the conceptual domain of God. In relation to other love attitudes, the kiss denotes an advanced stage of the love relationship. It bears the same position with respect to the contemplative experience, as no other term can possibly articulate it in as explicit a manner. Rolle evaluates the position of the utterer of the first half verse with respect to the contemplative life:

> Nimirum immundicie amatores in hiis verbis nequaquam placuerunt Christum. Rapitur autem divine contemplacionis dulcedine, ardorem incircumscripti luminis presentit veraciter, qui in hiis verbis, *Osculetur me osculo oris sui* deum recte glorificat.[50]

> [Surely the lovers of filth in those words by no means have pleased Christ. On the other hand she is ravished by the sweetness of divine contemplation, truly she feels beforehand the flame of the infinite light, who in those words, 'That he may kiss me with the kiss of his mouth', glorifies God properly.]

Rolle's view of carnal love is expressed here in strikingly negative terms. Those performing and enjoying fornication and impurity (*amatores immundicie*) will certainly not be able to understand and learn inwardly from the metaphorical meaning of those terms. The ways by which Rolle ponders on the language of love reflect an important aspect of his psychology which is responsible for the effective way in which his spiritual experience is encoded at the metaphorical level. As Rita Copeland has pointed out, the use of metaphorical terms in Rolle's writing is not arbitrary and conventional, but is the essence of the experience itself.[51]

Super Cant. is structured around a series of discussions on the sinful nature of carnal love, so as to establish a contrast with the most elevating passages using the same vocabulary of love. This textual practice protects the text from intrusion by readers whose assumptions and expectations would not be those of a lover of God. Unlike the monastic and scholastic commentaries which were aimed at a certain milieu, the circulation of Rolle's work was not circumscribed by any social or religious barriers. Rolle alludes only once to possible audiences for *Super Cant.*: thus he distinguishes a primary audience made up of hermits like himself, and a secondary audience of laymen. This important allusion is set right after a passage dealing with the meaning of the breasts in comparison with the kiss. Rolle has come to make this comparison by joining the verse *Osculetur me osculo oris sui* to the *Quia meliora sunt ubera tua vino fragrancia unguentis optimis*:

> Set et ideo languet ad osculum *quia meliora sunt ubera tua vino*. Nam si ubera Christi meliora vino non intelligeret, profecto querere osculum non auderet. Quia nisi in divinis doctrinis delectari satagimus proculdubio ad suavitatem eterne dulcedinis veraciter non suspiramus. Hoc manifestum est quandoquidem et laicus, quam cito divino amore se tactum senserit, ad audiendum et loquendum de deo, secularibus curis postpositis, vehementer inardescit. Quanto eciam magis nos qui eciam, iuvante deo, scripturas sacras intelligere possumus ad legendum et audiendum verbum dei ac aliis scribendis et docendis nos accingere debemus.[52]

> [Yet and on that account she languishes for the kiss 'because your breasts are better than wine'. For if she did not understand that the breasts of Christ were better than wine, certainly she would not dare ask for a kiss. Because if we are not busy to be pleased in divine instructions, without doubt we do not truly long for the pleasantness of the eternal sweetness. This is plain seeing that even the layman, as soon as he has experienced himself touched by divine love, impetuously burns to hear and to talk about God, neglecting secular concerns. Hence much more we who, with the help of God, can understand sacred scriptures, we must gird ourselves to read and hear the word of God and for other things which are to be written and taught.]

Being a lover of God implies an understanding and knowledge of the religious background, as well as the ability to trace the different layers of discourse. Rolle assumes that lovers of God will read his text with a set of inbuilt assumptions helping them to understand the terms of love spiritually.[53] Yet at some point Rolle reminds his audience to interpret what they read in the spiritual light:

> Hic igitur ab hac proteccione dei reprobus excluditur qui instabilis in prosperis cadens in adversis a demone deportatur. Sicut enim beata sunt ubera que sancti suxerunt, sic maledicta sunt ubera que peccatores nutrierunt. Set volo ut hic nichil carnale intelligas, set totum spirituale. Cum diabolus inventor sit primus et pater peccati, mali cum peccant quasi ab eo nati sunt. Illos eius ubera nutriunt, dum ad gulam et luxuriam et ad cetera vicia letantes vadunt.[54]

[Then the reprobate is excluded from this godly protection, who, unstable in prosperity, falling in mischief, is carried away by the demon. So indeed blessed are the breasts which the saints sucked, but accursed are the breasts which nourished the sinners. But I want you to understand nothing here carnally, but everything spiritually. As the devil is first the inventor and the father of sin, so the evil ones are as if they were born from him when they sin. His breasts nourish them, while rejoicing they rush towards gluttony, lust and other vices.]

In *Super Cant.*, the authorial voice becomes the mouthpiece for the soul, whereas previous commentators took an objective standpoint in their description of the bride and the bridegroom according to an exposition of the four senses of Scripture.[55] If Richard of St Victor shares a strong interest in the metaphorical meaning of the terms of love, he refrains nevertheless from narrating from the bride's point of view. Rolle however strongly identifies with it in his narration: the Song thus becomes expressive of his effusive voice.[56] No other commentator appropriates the Song of Songs in such a drastic way. While being a pure expression of the mystical state, this kind of commentary defies the genre in which the text is couched: the narrative voice loses the flexibility which would allow it to pass from an interpretation based on one of the four senses to another sense, as is the practice in traditional commentaries. The mystical commentary of Rolle bears witness to a strong tradition, necessary to its making, but one which filters through to the individual declamations of the narrative voice.

Thus, *Super Cant.* is replete with a substantial number of terms from the semantic field of love which have been interpreted metaphorically numerous times. Yet the new context in which they are set demands a reinterpretation of their metaphorical meaning. In fact, each mystical text demands to be decoded by the reader, regardless of the tradition from which it emerged. As the reader apprehends the text, he will have to solve the incongruities of the metaphorical meaning individually, according to his spiritual needs. *Ruminatio*[57] on the Bible and other mystical texts allows readers to measure their spiritual progress by checking the gap which separates the literal meaning of the lexical terms from their understanding of the term's metaphorical meaning. Rolle in fact actualizes this process textually, when he opposes the two senses of the vocabulary of love. Whether this process is didactically oriented is unclear, but it inevitably leads readers to compare their own understanding with that of the narrative voice, which becomes a matrix against which a measurement and a comparison are possible. Seductive as it may be, the process implies an acceptance of a form of contemplative experience which is circumscribed by the assumptions of the narrative voice. Nevertheless, if the opposition of the different meanings of the vocabulary of love throws light on the different layers of interpretation of the lexical terms, it does not explicate the nature of the higher meaning. Metaphors force the audience to rethink accepted concepts, to extend them, or to invent new conceptualizations.

The ways by which the narrative voice moves from the effusive tone inspired by the anagogical sense to an interpretation of carnal love support the argument for a metaphorical interpretation of the conventional terms of love. Conceptually, the domain of God has no set pattern, is discursively non-expressible, visually non-describable. It therefore needs metaphorical utterances to have existence and meaning. Thus the function of metaphorical language is far from being only ornamental. Metaphors are essential components of the expressive capacity of language, which is not devoid of cognitive import. Rolle has no interest in constructing a mystical theology. Unlike Bernard, who systematizes through the use of symbols, Rolle sticks closely to the metaphorical interpretation. The ways by which both treat the term of the kiss for the contemplative life are significant. Bernard elaborates an entire system around this term, whereas Rolle uses the terms *osculum* and *osculare* in their different forms thirty-nine times in *Super Cant*. He combines the kiss metaphor with other terms to enhance its expressive capacity, or alters its meaning by setting it in new contexts. Thus Rolle's concern with the vocabulary of love is poetical, expressive and cognitive, as he tries to improve its strategic force within the contemplative field by widening the meaning of its metaphorical sense. The more often a term, like *osculum* for instance, is combined with words from other semantic fields, the greater the informational content conveyed by the metaphorical utterance will become. In his quest for a pure language that is a channel through which communication and fusion between the soul and God may be achieved perfectly, Rolle posits his high style, rich in metaphors and metonymies, as a potential solution. His incessant warnings against a carnal understanding of the terms of love may be accounted for, not only as the result of a personal sexual inhibition, but also as the fear of seeing his pure language mistranslated.[58] The most difficult task for Rolle consists in his reconciling of two original texts: on one hand, the spiritual text, not within ordinary human reach, sacred and untouchable, and on the other hand, the carnal and erotic vocabulary, available to all and highly effective in awakening an emotional response.

Metaphors of love are alive as long as they convey simultaneously the two contents; one originating from the field of courtship and carnal love, and the other, the field of mystical love, which is organized with reference to the originating field. Without the metaphorical utterance, Rolle's mystical experiences could not be conveyed. The literary theories and textual practices which emerged from the commentaries of the Song of

Songs are echoed in the sophisticated use of the metaphorical discourse of love by Rolle.[59] That discourse rests on a tissue of Biblical analogies which were woven already in the early days of the commentary tradition. The vocabulary of love translates best the mystical phenomena, and the relations the terms of love bear with one another in the originating field serve to guide the relations which they continue to share with one another in the new field. Ideally speaking, the contemplative experience can be scanned in an epistemic way by defining the relations each term bears with the other. The terms of love delineate most precisely the mystical experience. Their high-powered emotional potential can affect the audience when the terms are used in a strategically effective way. The position of the terms of love in their new context is essential to the development of the new affective strategies of the text.[60] Terms like *osculum* and *amplexio* each convey a certain aspect of physical love which, transposed to a mystical context, express also a notion of the contemplative experience. However, those two terms keep the same relation with one another. As the embrace and the kiss are often used jointly in the description of a love scene, so is it when they are transferred to the field of contemplation. Rolle uses the terms together three times, first at the beginning of his exposition:

Amplectitur igitur sponsas suas, que omnes una sunt sponsa, et melli-fluo amoris osculo omnes et singulas saciat, eternisque amplexibus confortat.[61]

[He embraces then his brides, who are all one bride, and he satisfies all and each one with the honey-dropping kiss of love, and comforts with eternal embraces.]

The two terms are joined again towards the middle of the exposition, in a passage dealing with the maidens and their love for Jesus:

Est itaque verus amor, castus, sanctus, voluntarius amatum pro seipso non pro suis amans, in amato se totum figens, nil extra se querens, de se contentus, flagrans, estuans, ex amato inardescens, vehemens, se in se ligans, impetuosus miro modo, omnem modum excedens, ad solum amatum se extendens, cuncta alia contempnens set et obliviscens, in amato canens, illum cogitans, illum incessanter meminens, ascendens desiderio, pergens in amato, ruens in amplexibus, absortus in osculis, totus liquescens igne ardentis amoris, ut tibi, O bone Ihesu, merito dicatur: *Adolescentule dilexerunt te nimis.*[62]

[And accordingly it is true love, chaste, sacred, loving freely the beloved for himself, not for his goods, setting itself completely in the beloved, seeking nothing outside of him, contented about himself, blazing, being inflamed, taking fire from the lover, ardent, binding

211

itself to him, impetuous in a marvelous way, exceeding all measure, stretching out to the only beloved, despising and also forgetting all other things, singing in the beloved, thinking him, remembering him constantly, increasing in desire, proceeding in the beloved, rushing towards embraces, absorbed in kisses, melting completely in the fire of ardent love, so that to you, O good Jesus, it is said justly: 'The young maidens loved you exceedingly'.]

They appear again in the last fourth of the *Super Cant.*:

Et dum a priori rigore et nocivo frigore liquescit, ad amplectendum, ad osculandum dilectum eciam aliquando nec tracta nec vocata currit.[63]

[And when she melts by the prior chilliness and the hurtful cold, neither dragged along nor called, she runs to the beloved sometimes to embrace and kiss.]

Terms of love create a tension between vehicle and topic as the latter, while not being discursively definable, needs physical imagery to be expressed.[64] The use of the vocabulary of love to define the domain of God differs significantly from its use to define the domain of Jesus in his humanity. As the latter can find some articulation outside the sphere of metaphorical expressions, the conceptual domain evades a clear delineation by means of those expressions. Without an appropriate and moderate application of the terms of love, the depiction of the relationship of the soul with Jesus in his humanity resounds with powerful and explicit sexual allusions.[65] But the conceptualization of the godhead necessitates metaphorical meaning as a means to give it cognitive strength. The special resourcefulness of the language of love in conveying metaphorical meaning to express different aspects of the contemplative life is due to the essential similarities of the two fields. Indeed, the notions of desire and love expressed by the terms of love also define the contemplative experience. Those notions constitute the common boundary of the two fields, which is exploited by the mystics and other religious writers to persuade the audience to accept a metaphorical transposition of relations. Rolle works with the Latin language to carry out the encoding of his mystical experience. After this first translation stage, once the terms have been solidly grounded in their new context, the second translation stage, from Latin to the vernacular, may take place. Rolle preserves his characteristic high style when he describes the third degree of love in his Middle English epistles. He however needs to provide a sort of *accessus* to that highest degree of love in the form of a description of the first and second degrees. Rolle expects the English audience to be as able as the clerical one at decoding and construing meaning from the metaphorical discourse of love. However, in the epistles, the 'messager' is more negotiator between God and man than expositor of his own *auctoritas*. The careful and well-explained didactic programme of the epistles reflects a new attitude. The epistles invitingly offer themselves as practical exercises and systems for the audience to use according to its needs. Having invented a language in which his inner world may translate itself, Rolle preserves that language and its style in the vernacular with the provision of a new contextual apparatus that still shows the language to be characteristically his own, but also potentially that of his audience.

NOTES

1. My thanks are due to Vincent Gillespie, Fellow of St Anne's College, Oxford, and Roger Ellis, whose numerous valuable suggestions I have incorporated into this paper. I am also grateful to Frank McGovern for suggesting improvements to the English. Any inconsistencies, of course, are my sole responsibility. Without the support of the Berrow Foundation, it would not have been possible to pursue my DPhil research at the University of Oxford.
2. S.J. Ogilvie-Thomson (ed.) Richard Rolle, *Prose and Verse* Early English Text Society 293 (Oxford: Oxford University Press, 1988) p. 26, ll. 6–10. I have not reproduced all of Ogilvie-Thomson's editorial diacritics.
3. Some parts of the first meditative lyric included in the *Ego Dormio* derive from a fragment of a Latin meditation, the *Respice in Faciem Christi*, ascribed in the Middle Ages to Augustine. Other parts of the same lyric are free translations of Rolle's own *Incendium Amoris*. Another Latin poem, the *Candet Nudatum Pectus*, already translated into the vernacular in the early thirteenth century, also finds its way in the *Ego Dormio* lyric, albeit as a free translation; see Ogilvie-Thomson (ed.) R. Rolle, *Prose and Verse* p. 205; see also Carleton Brown (ed.) *Religious Lyrics of the Fourteenth Century* (Oxford: The Clarendon Press, 1924, revised 1957) pp. 1–2.
4. For an introduction to the commentary tradition, see Minnis, *Medieval Theory of Authorship*: see also Minnis and Scott (eds) *Medieval Literary Theory and Criticism c.1100–c.1375*; for a study of the Song of Songs tradition, see E. Ann Matter, *The Voice of My Beloved: The Song of Songs in Western Medieval Christianity* (Philadelphia: University of Pennsylvania Press, 1990); see also Ann W. Astell, *The Song of Songs in the Middle Ages* (Ithaca and London: Cornell University Press, 1990).
5. See W.M. Lindsay (ed.) *Isidori Hispalensis Episcopi Etymologiarum Sive Originum Libri XX* 2 vols. (Oxford: The Clarendon Press, 1911, repr. 1962) 10. 123; quoted in Copeland, *Rhetoric, Hermeneutics, and Translation* pp. 89–90 (translation by Copeland).
6. See Nicholas Watson, *Richard Rolle and the Invention of Authority*, Cambridge Studies in Medieval Literature 13 (Cambridge: Cambridge University Press, 1991); see esp. Excursus I, 'The Chronology of Rolle's Writings', pp. 273–94; for alternative chronologies, see Hope Emily Allen, *Writings*

Ascribed to Richard Rolle, and Material for his Biography Modern Language
Association Monograph Series 3 (New York: D.C. Heath and Co.; London:
Oxford University Press, 1927); see also J.P.H. Clark, 'Richard Rolle as a
Biblical Commentator', *Downside Review* 104 (1986), pp. 165–213.

7. Of related interest to this point, see Watson, *Richard Rolle*, pp. 226–32; see
also my own discussion of the 'messager' role in ch. 6 of my dissertation, 'The
Moving of the Soul: the Functions of Metaphors of Love in the Writings of
Richard Rolle and Antecedent Texts of the Medieval Mystical Tradition'
(University of Oxford: DPhil, 1993).

8. See Nicholas Watson, 'Translation and Self-Canonization in Richard Rolle's
Melos Amoris' in Ellis (ed.) *Medieval Translator* (1989) pp. 167–180.

9. All references to the Bible are to A.C. Fillion (ed.) *Biblia Sacra Juxta
Vulgatae* (Paris: Librairie Letouzey et Ané, 1887).

10. See Elizabeth Murray, 'Richard Rolle's Commentary on the Canticles Edited
from MS. Trinity College, Dublin, 153' (Fordham Diss., 1958) (hereafter
Rolle, *Super Cant.*); see also Yves Madon, 'Le *Commentaire* de Richard Rolle
sur les premiers versets du *Cantique des Cantiques*', *Mélanges de Sciences
Religieuses* 7 (1950) pp. 311–25; for a Modern English translation, see Richard
Rolle, *Biblical Commentaries: Short Exposition of Psalm XX, Treatise on the
Twentieth Psalm, Comment on the First Verses of the Canticle of Canticles,
Commentary on the Apocalypse* trans. Robert Boenig, Salzburg Studies in
English Literature: Elizabethan & Renaissance Studies 92:13 (Salzburg:
Institut für Anglistik und Amerikanistik, 1984) pp. 56–141.

11. For a description of the manuscripts, see Allen, *Writings*, pp. 64–8.

12. For a study of the Latin vocabulary of the spiritual experience, see Pierre
Miquel, *Le Vocabulaire latin de l'expérience spirituelle dans la tradition monas-
tique et canoniale de 1050 à 1250* Théologie Historique 79 (Paris: Aubier,
1989), esp. pp. 97–213.

13. See Clark, 'Richard Rolle', *Downside Review* 104 (1986) pp. 168–73; see also
his 'Richard Rolle: a Theological Re-Assessment', *Downside Review* 100
(1983) pp. 108–39.

14. The copyist of MS Bodley 953, an early fifteenth-century manuscript, high-
lights the first letter of each Latin verse in blue. There is a paragraph marking
in red ink at the beginning of both translation and exposition. The translation
is underlined in red ink.

15. H.R. Bramley (ed.) Richard Rolle, *The English Psalter* (Oxford: The
Clarendon Press, 1884) pp. 4–5.

16. See Paul Theiner (ed.) Richard Rolle, *The Contra Amatores Mundi* (Berkeley
and Los Angeles: University of California Press, 1968); see also E.J.F.
Arnould (ed.) Richard Rolle, *The Melos Amoris* (Oxford: Basil Blackwell,
1957); see also F. Vandenbroucke (ed.) *Richard Rolle, Le Chant d'Amour
(Melos Amoris)*, 2 vols., Sources Chrétiennes 168–9 (Paris: Editions du
Cerf, 1971).

17. Rolle, *The English Psalter* p. 5.

18. *Super Threnos, Super Apocalypsim, Six Old Testament Canticles* and the
English Magnificat belong also to this category of commentaries built around
the standard Gloss; see Clark, 'Richard Rolle', *Downside Review* 104 (1986)
p. 165.

19. See Watson, *Richard Rolle*, pp. 113–41; Watson describes *Incendium Amoris*
as a new starting point in Rolle's writing career, marked by the firm proclama-
tion of his status as Christian, a hermit and as a spiritual authority.

20. See Bernard of Clairvaux, *On the Song of Songs* I, trans. Kilian Walsh Cistercian Fathers Series 4 (Spencer, Mass.: Cistercian Publications, 1971) p. 6.
21. See William of St Thierry, *The Works of William of St Thierry ii: Exposition on the Song of Songs* trans. Mother Columba Hart Cistercian Fathers Series 6 (Spencer, Mass.: Cistercian Publications, 1970) p. 6.
22. For a fine study of Biblical imitatio in the writings of Rolle, see John A. Alford, 'Biblical Imitatio in the Writings of Richard Rolle' *English Literary History* 40 (1973) pp. 1–23, esp. p. 6. For a general study of the Bible as literature, see Robert Alter, *The Art of Biblical Narrative* (London: George Allen & Unwin, 1981) and John B. Gabel and Charles B. Wheeler, *The Bible as Literature: An Introduction* (Oxford, New York: Oxford University Press, 1986); see esp. pp. 16–41.
23. See Matter, *The Voice of My Beloved*, pp. 151–200.
24. See Richard of St Victor, *The Twelve Patriarchs: The Mystical Ark: Book Three of the Trinity* trans. Grover A. Zinn, The Classics of Western Spirituality (New York: Paulist Press, 1979). The use of the Song of Songs' language and imagery pervades books four and five of *The Mystical Ark*; see also Robert Javelet, 'Thomas Gallus et Richard de St Victor Mystiques' *Recherches de Théologie Ancienne et Médiévale* 29 (1962) pp. 206–33, 30 (1963) pp. 88–121, and Astell, *The Song of Songs*, pp. 33–5, 77–89.
25. See Copeland, *Rhetoric*, p. 65.
26. R. Freyhan, 'The Evolution of the Caritas Figure in the Thirteenth and Fourteenth Centuries' *Journal of the Warburg and Courtauld Institute* vol. 11 (1948–9) pp. 68–86; for a definition of caritas as mother of all the virtues, see p. 68 n. 2; for a survey of the notion of *caritas*, see *Dictionnaire de Spiritualité* ii, cols. 507–691.
27. See Clark, 'Richard Rolle', *Downside Review* 104 (1986) p. 187.
28. G. Dumeige (ed. and trans.) *Epitre à Séverin sur la Charité: Richard de Saint-Victor, Les Quatres Degrés de la Violente Charité* (Paris: J. Vrin, 1955) p. 110 (used for all citations from the work in this paper).
29. Richard of St Victor *De IV Grad.* p. 143.
30. Richard of St Victor *De IV Grad.* p. 151.
31. Richard of St Victor *De IV Grad.* p. 153.
32. Richard of St Victor *De IV Grad.* p. 153.
33. Richard of St Victor *De IV Grad.* p. 157; see also Margaret Jennings, 'Richard Rolle and the Three Degrees of Love' *Downside Review* 93 (1975) pp. 193–200, esp. p. 195.
34. Richard of St Victor *De IV Grad.* p. 167; Allen, *Writings* pp. 66–8; see also Clark, 'Richard Rolle', *Downside Review* 104 (1986) pp. 185–6.
35. See Clark, 'Richard Rolle', *Downside Review* 104 (1986) pp. 124–6, who suggests that Rolle's degrees of love derive directly from the *De IV Grad.*; see also Jennings, 'Three Degrees', pp. 197–200.
36. Astell, *The Song of Songs* p. 108.
37. See Rolle, *Super Cant.*, p. 2. Unless indicated otherwise, translations are my own. For an alternative modern English translation, see Richard Rolle, *Biblical Commentaries*, trans. Boenig p. 57.
38. See also Watson, 'Translation and Self-Canonization', *The Medieval Translator* (1989) pp. 174–9.
39. See Wolfgang Riehle, *The Middle English Mystics* trans. Bernard Standring (London: Routledge and Kegan Paul, 1981) pp. 34–5.

40. For a case study of the conceptualization of feeling, see George Lakoff, *Women, Fire and Dangerous Things: What Categories Reveal about the Mind* (Chicago and London: University of Chicago Press, 1987) pp. 377–415.

41. See Rolle, *Super Cant.* p. 10; Boenig, p. 66, translates: 'They have venerated the filling of their stomach rather than embraced Christ.' This translation is inaccurate, as the word venerem cannot stand for a third person plural in any of the tenses of the verb venerare. Madon, 'Le Commentaire de Richard Rolle', pp. 324–5, gives a correct French translation: 'Un ventre rassasié embrasse Venus beaucoup plus que le Christ.'

42. For autobiographical accounts showing Rolle dealing with secular ladies, see Rolle, *Super Cant.* pp. 47–8; see also Margaret Deanesly (ed.) *Richard Rolle, The Incendium Amoris* (Manchester: Manchester University Press, 1915) pp. 178–9; for a modern English translation, see *Richard Rolle, The Fire of Love* trans. Clifton Wolters, 3rd edn. (Harmondsworth: Penguin Books, 1988) pp. 81–2; see also Watson, *Richard Rolle* pp. 129–30. For studies on the importance of the role of women in Rolle's writings, see Arnould (ed.) *Melos Amoris* pp. xl–lvii; see also Ann W. Astell, 'Feminine Figurae in the Writings of Richard Rolle: a Register of Growth' *Mystics Quarterly* 15 (1989) pp. 117–24.

43. See Rolle, Super Cant. p. 22; see also Rolle, *Biblical Commentaries* p. 78.

44. See Alford, 'Biblical Imitatio' pp. 8–9; Alford notices that Rolle is indebted to Apoc. 2:17 for his description of *canor*.

45. See Riehle, *The Middle English Mystics* pp. 110–113.

46. See Sara de Ford, 'Mystical Union in the Melos Amoris of Richard Rolle' in Marion Glasscoe (ed.) *The Medieval Mystical Tradition in England* (Exeter: University of Exeter Press, 1980) pp. 173–201.

47. Eva Kittay, *Metaphor: Its Cognitive Force and Linguistic Structure* (Oxford: Oxford University Press, 1987) p. 32. My debt to Eva Kittay concerning my own adaptation of a metaphorical cognitive theory for mystical and devotional texts will be apparent throughout the second part of this paper; see also Stephen H. Phillips, 'Mysticism and Metaphor' *International Journal for the Philosophy of Religion* 23 (1988) pp. 17–41; see also Cyril Barrett, 'The Language of Ecstasy and the Ecstasy of Language' in Martin Warner (ed.) *The Bible as Rhetoric: Studies in Biblical Persuasion and Credibility* (London: Routledge, 1990) pp. 205–21.

48. See Copeland, *Rhetoric* p. 83.

49. For a survey of the meaning of the kiss in secular and religious literature, see Nicolas James Perella, *The Kiss Sacred and Profane: An Interpretative History of Kiss Symbolism and Related Religio-Erotic Themes* (Berkeley: University of California Press, 1969) p. 39. Perella considers Origen of Alexandria as the father of the doctrine of the spiritual senses. For a study of the kiss as a means of unitive expression for the mystic, see Riehle, *The Middle English Mystics* pp. 104–27.

50. See Rolle, *Super Cant.* p. 1; see also Rolle, *Biblical Commentaries* p. 56.

51. Rita Copeland, 'Richard Rolle and the Rhetorical Theory of the Levels of Style' in Marion Glasscoe (ed.) *The Medieval Mystical Tradition in England* (Cambridge: D.S. Brewer, 1984) pp. 55–80; see esp. p. 76.

52. See Rolle, *Super Cant.* pp. 20–1; see also Rolle, *Biblical Commentaries* pp. 76–7. *Laicus*, with *illiteratus*, *rusticus* and *idiota* were used to name the illiterate; see Stock, *The Implications of Literacy* p. 27.

53. Of related interest on this point, see Margaret Aston, *Lollards and Reformers:*

Images and Literacy in Late Medieval Religion (London: Hambledon Press, 1984) pp. 101–33.

54. See Rolle, *Super Cant.* p. 31; see also Rolle, *Biblical Commentaries* p. 88.
55. See Beryl Smalley, *The Study of the Bible in the Middle Ages* (Oxford: Basil Blackwell, 1952, repr.. 1983) esp. pp. 214–263.
56. Copeland 'Rolle' p. 56.
57. Gilbert of Hoyland gives an excellent description of ruminatio in his fifth sermon on the Song of Songs; see *The Works of Gilbert of Hoyland: Sermons on the Song of Songs* i, trans. L.C. Braceland, Cistercian Fathers Series 14 (Kalamazoo: Cistercian Publications, 1978) pp. 85–86.
58. See Copeland, *Rhetoric* p. 43.
59. See Minnis, *Medieval Theory* pp. 57–58.
60. See Vincent Gillespie, 'Mystic's Foot: Rolle and Affectivity' in Marion Glasscoe (ed.) *The Medieval Mystical Tradition in England* (Exeter: University of Exeter Press, 1982) pp. 199–230.
61. See Rolle, *Super Cant.* p. 1; see also Rolle, *Biblical Commentaries* p. 56.
62. See Rolle, *Super Cant.* p. 49; Boenig's translation (Rolle, *Biblical Commentaries* p. 107) wants a translation of the words 'flagrans . . . omnem modum excedens' and misreads 'ascendens' as 'ardens'.
63. See Rolle, *Super Cant.* p. 67; see also Rolle, *Biblical Commentaries* p. 126.
64. It is beyond the scope of this work to study the relations between metaphors and images. However, the reproduction and interpretation through images of the whole of the Song of Songs in *La Bible Moralisée* is revealing of the ways the vocabulary of love could be set into pictures; see *La Bible Moralisée Conservée à Oxford, Paris et Londres ii. Reproduction Intégrale du Manuscrit du XIIIè Siècle* (Paris, 1912), plates 290–317 (fols. 66–93^v in Paris, Bibl. Nat. lat. 11560).
65. Admittedly, some authors fail to make or sustain the distinction between the semantic field of love and courtship and the content domain of Christ in his humanity. The writing of an author like Margery Kempe evidences this fact forcefully; see H.E. Allen and S.B. Meech (eds) *The Book of Margery Kempe* Early English Text Society O.S. 213 (London: Oxford University Press, 1941, repr. 1961) esp. pp. 70–1, 86–8; Margery's intense devotion to the humanity of Jesus prevents her from marrying God mystically; also, as a result of that, she is spiritually moved before the sight of children and young men.

Chapter 10

Le Théologien et le Poète: Deux Traductions en Français Moderne de *The Cloud of Unknowing*

RENÉ TIXIER

Nous ne connaissons pas de traductions françaises de *The Cloud of Unknowing* antérieures au vingtième siècle. La première traduction parut en 1925, dans la collection «Mystiques anglais». C'est Dom Maurice Noetinger (1867–1930), moine bénédictin de Solesmes, qui, mettant à profit l'exil de la communauté à Quarr Abbey,[1] présenta au public français *Le nuage de l'inconnaissance*, traduction rééditée sans changement en 1977 par les Éditions de Solesmes. En 1977 paraissait également, aux Éditions du Seuil, *Le nuage de l'inconnaissance*, réédition de la traduction d'Armel Guerne (1911–1981) parue en 1953 aux Cahiers du Sud.[2] À côté de l'anthologie publiée en 1957 par Paul Renaudin, dans laquelle l'auteur indique qu'il a utilisé les traductions des bénédictins de Solesmes «à très peu de chose près» (p. 9), la diffusion de *The Cloud of Unknowing* et de son corpus auprès des milieux français non anglicistes reste donc essentiellement liée au nom d'un théologien de la vie spirituelle, Dom Maurice Noetinger, et à celui d'un poète, Armel Guerne.

Profondément unis dans leur foi commune, les deux hommes n'en diffèrent pas moins considérablement dans leur manière d'aborder le texte et de le rendre en français. La différence de méthode se reflète de prime abord dans la différence physique des deux livres: aux deux pages d'introduction et aux quatre notes qui accompagnent la traduction d'A. Guerne s'opposent une cinquantaine de pages d'introduction et plus de quatre-vingts notes dans le texte de M. Noetinger. Si l'on ajoute à la traduction

218

de *The Cloud* celles que M. Noetinger propose de *The Book of Privy Counselling, The Epistle of Prayer, The Epistle of Discretion of Stirrings* et *A Treatise of Discernment of Spirits*, ce sont au total plus de cent cinquante notes qui accompagnent l'édition «Mystiques anglais», dont un tiers environ apportent au lecteur des explications historiques et doctrinales, un autre tiers des illustrations tirées des grands textes spirituels parallèles, des Pères du désert jusqu'au grand siècle mystique français, le dernier tiers des notes étant constitué de références internes soulignant la continuité des thèmes. Il ressort de cette première comparaison, même rapide, que la traduction bénédictine, accompagnée de ses notes riches et abondantes, est beaucoup plus qu'une simple traduction: c'est en réalité un travail d'explication, d'expansion, de description et d'interprétation du texte original, ce que confirme l'avant-propos de la réédition de Solesmes: «Comme la Bible elle-même, ce livre demande en effet à être interprété en fonction de la vie, de la théologie spéculative et de la tradition» (pp. iii–iv). M. Noetinger se présente ici d'emblée comme historien de la spiritualité, théologien de la vie spirituelle, et pour tout dire père spirituel soucieux avant tout de la formation et du progrès de son lecteur. Il est en ceci entièrement fidèle à l'esprit qui anime ces textes, puisqu'il s'agit avant tout de lettres de direction spirituelle écrites à l'intérieur d'une tradition toujours vivante. Par contraste, A. Guerne, en artisan du verbe et en puriste, s'attache essentiellement au texte, et cherche systématiquement à en extraire toute la saveur originelle. Il en préserve ainsi la densité, la vigueur, voire la nature chaotique; il en résulte une traduction souvent plus littérale, plus concrète, aux images plus heurtées et aux constructions plus elliptiques. Le lecteur moderne risque cependant d'être fréquemment dérouté, dans la mesure où le traducteur a choisi de présenter le texte en un français ancien reconstitué, dont le pseudo-archaïsme pourrait finir par constituer un obstacle.

Le but de la présente étude n'est pas toutefois d'opposer ces deux méthodes, mais bien plutôt d'essayer de faire justice à deux entreprises courageuses en montrant qu'elles sont complémentaires, que chacune porte ses fruits, au service l'une comme l'autre d'un texte réputé difficile qu'il s'agit de transmettre dans la fidélité. Chacun des deux traducteurs a fait ses choix; chacun de ces choix, en retour, implique un certain nombre de risques qu'il faut savoir affronter. Au risque affronté par M. Noetinger, dans un souci pédagogique évident, d'améliorer l'original et de produire un texte plus limpide et parfois plus simple que l'original, correspond le risque, couru par A. Guerne, de décourager le lecteur moderne en proposant une version rendue artificiellement obscure d'un texte parfois déjà lui-même obscur. Par ailleurs, il ressort clairement que les deux traducteurs ont voulu faire oeuvre d'amour, chacun à sa manière (*G.*, p. 10). Il s'agit donc ici de comparer quelques unes des solutions qui ont été retenues, tout en examinant respectivement leurs mérites comme leurs limites.

L'une des grandes difficultés que doit affronter tout auteur spirituel tient à la nécessité de conceptualiser les réalités intérieures qu'il cherche à décrire et à communiquer. La solution la moins maladroite se trouve souvent dans l'emploi d'un langage métaphorique où les images parlent autant au coeur qu'à l'intellect. La contemplation dite obscure, de type dionysien, que recommande l'auteur de *The Cloud of Unknowing*, est un dur travail d'arrachement aux images qui pourtant se formule en partie en images. Dix concepts-clés de cette contemplation, accompagnés de leurs images et formulations, ont été retenus ici comme points de rencontre et de comparaison entre les deux traductions.

1. *L'union dans l'amour.* L'union de l'homme et de Dieu dans l'amour trouve sa formulation, traditionnelle, dans l'image du noeud (*knot*). L'un des enseignements essentiels de l'auteur de *The Cloud* se trouve concentré au ch. 4: *Loue is soche a might that it makith alle thing comoun. Loue therfore Iesu, & alle thing that he hath it is thin (. . .) Knyt thee therfore to him by loue & by beleue: & than by vertewe of that knot thou schalt be comoun parcener with him & with alle that by loue so ben knittyd vnto him* (*Cloud* 12/2–9). «Unis-toi à Lui, par amour et par foi, et ainsi, par l'effet et vertu de ce lien, tu percevras en commun avec Lui, et avec tous qui par l'amour sont aussi liés à lui,» écrit A. Guerne (p. 28), M. Noetinger préférant «Attache-toi donc à lui par l'amour et par la foi, et tu auras part à ses biens, en commun avec tous ceux qui lui sont ainsi unis par l'amour» (p. 79). La force ou solidité de ce noeud (*vertewe*) n'est plus qu'implicite dans la traduction de M. Noetinger, alors qu'A. Guerne renforce le concept par l'utilisation d'un doublet, «l'effet et vertu», procédé qu'il semble affectionner et qu'il reprendra peu après dans sa traduction de cette autre affirmation-clé, *to be knit to God in spirite* (ch. 8), «attaché et uni à Dieu en esprit» (p. 45).

2. *Le travail d'amour.* Le travail d'amour qu'est la contemplation unitive s'exprime essentiellement par trois mots, *worching*, *werk*, et *trauayle*. Ces trois mots correspondent à au moins cinq mots français, la distinction entre l'activité décrite et le produit de cette même activité n'étant pas plus possible dans les traductions que dans le texte original. Le mot «oeuvre», traduction favorite de M. Noetinger, peut indiquer que ce travail d'amour est une forme de l'*opus Dei*, ce que confirme la préférence de l'auteur anglais pour la prière liturgique comme activité majeure du contemplatif (ch. 37). A. Guerne utilise le plus souvent les mots «travail», «ouvrage» ou «opération», le mot *exercise* étant conservé en français chez les deux traducteurs. Quant à *trauayle*, il conserve dans le français

«travail», sous la plume d'A. Guerne, ses connotations de travail d'ac-
couchement pour un enfantement à la vie dans l'Esprit, M. Noetinger
faisant plutôt ressortir la dimension ascétique de l'effort contemplatif en
utilisant le mot «peine», fidèle également à l'auteur qui souvent emploie
le mot *pyne* pour insister sur l'aspect douloureux de ce dur travail de
purification, au point d'y voir parfois un purgatoire, pour ne pas dire un
enfer (chs. 33, 69).

3. *Dieu et l'homme au travail.* Dans *The Cloud of Unknowing*,
l'amour travaille et fait travailler, le travail d'amour auquel se livre
l'homme n'étant en réalité que la réponse au travail auquel se livre sur lui
le Dieu-Amour. L'un des mots les plus utilisés pour exprimer cette action
d'agitation de Dieu-Créateur sur sa créature est le mot *stiring*, en relation
fréquente avec *loue, meek, blynde, nakid, synne* et *kynde*. Les deux
traducteurs utilisent tour à tour les mots français «mouvement», «élan»,
«impulsion», «motion», M. Noetinger ayant recours également au mot
«aspiration», sous l'influence, entre autres, d'Augustine Baker.[3] Cette
dynamique du désir qui met l'homme en marche vers la Source de
l'amour, *a sodeyn steryng, & as it were vnauisid, speedly springing unto
God as sparcle fro the cole* (*Cloud* 12/22–4), est «un élan soudain et
comme spontané qui jaillit avec force vers Dieu» (*Noet.* p. 80), ou «un
brusque mouvement, et comme inattendu, qui s'élance vivement vers
Dieu» (*G.* p. 29). Le lieu privilégié de cette «agitation» est le coeur,
organe central de l'activité de perception et de décision de la piété affective. Toutefois, cette motion intérieure affecte aussi l'intellect (*the scharp
steryng of thin vnderstondyng, Cloud* 18/25); A. Guerne traduit littéralement «ce mouvement aigu de ton intelligence» (p. 47), alors que M.
Noetinger décrit et explicite plus qu'il ne traduit: «toutes ces pensées qui
feront irruption dans ton intelligence» (p. 97). De plus, ces motions
intérieures sont d'une extrême importance pour la vie spirituelle, et
doivent être l'objet d'un discernement attentif et constant, car de leur
interprétation dépend la qualité du «travail» du contemplatif; en ce
domaine les risques d'erreur sont considérables (ch. 34) et l'ennemi
travaille à établir la confusion (chs. 51–2). Beaucoup se sont perdus pour
n'avoir pas su interpréter ces mouvements intérieurs, *with many other that
knowen not theire sterynges* (*Cloud* 27/13–4). M. Noetinger, élargissant la
question, parle des «dispositions intérieures» du contemplatif (p. 123),
tandis qu'A. Guerne perd ici toute précision en évoquant simplement la
«vie intérieure» (p. 76). Pourtant, s'il est parfois délicat à traduire, le mot
steryng n'en est pas moins précis; il indique essentiellement une agitation,
une stimulation, une mise en mouvement. C'est ainsi qu'au début du texte
l'auteur de *The Cloud*, en bon père spirituel, ne cache pas son intention
à son dirigé: *therfore haue no wonder thof I stere thee to this werk* (*Cloud*

11/9); A. Guerne l'a bien compris, qui traduit doublement «ne t'étonne donc pas si je te pousse et t'incite à cette oeuvre» (p. 26), mais M. Noetinger, qui manifestement pèse chaque mot, n'a pas craint d'affirmer: «Ne t'étonne donc pas si je t'excite à cette oeuvre» (p. 77).

4. *L'Intention et la volonté.* L'amour est avant tout un acte de la volonté, le mot des scolastiques *affectus* signifiant les deux. L'un des mots les plus importants du texte est le mot *entent*. Au moment de prendre congé de son lecteur, le maître spirituel dira que Dieu, dans sa tendresse, regarde bien plus en avant qu'en arrière, vers le bien que l'homme désire plutôt que vers ses misères passées (ch. 75). C'est l'intention d'aimer qui est première, au point que l'auteur définit ainsi la prière: *Preyer in itself propirly is not elles bot a deuoute entent directe vnto God* (*Cloud* 42/32–3). C'est «une aspiration de l'âme qui tend directement et avec ferveur vers Dieu,» écrit M. Noetinger (p. 170) qui en profite pour rappeler en note que cette définition se retrouve chez plusieurs autres auteurs, dont Guigues II le Chartreux, source probable de la formule moyen-anglaise qui lui correspond exactement, *Oratio est devota cordis in Deum intentio.*[4] La prière initiale du maître, sur laquelle s'ouvre le texte de *The Cloud,*[5] comporte elle aussi le mot *entent*: *God, unto whom alle hertes ben open, & unto whom alle wille spekith (. . .) I beseche thee so for to clense the entent of myn hert with the unspekable gift of thi grace* (*Cloud* 1/2–4). Il est regrettable que cette dynamique de l'amour qu'exprime le mot *entent* n'ait pas été réellement rendue dans les deux traductions; la tension, même paisible, de l'amour n'apparaît guère dans la formule «dispositions de mon coeur» (*Noet.* p. 61), et reste peu perceptible dans «les desseins de mon coeur» (*G.* p. 13). De même, l'adverbe *ententively*, si important dans l'envoi (*the fourme of leuyng that thou hast ententively purposed, Cloud* 7/24–5) reste intraduit dans les deux éditions françaises («la forme de vie que tu as embrassée», *Noet.* p. 65; «forme de vie dont tu as pleinement fait choix», *G.* p. 17), alors qu'au ch. 39 la traduction du même adverbe rend bien mieux compte de l'activité de la volonté au service de l'amour («nous voulons diriger notre prière», «notre prière tend à obtenir tout bien», *Noet.* p. 170; «nous voulons intensément prier», *G.* p. 128). Toutefois, c'est James Walsh S.J. qui, dans son édition en anglais moderne, traduit avec le plus de force et de clarté, en liant l'*intentio* au *propositum*, cet engagement du contemplatif dans la vie religieuse: 'the manner of life that you have undertaken with full deliberation'.[6]

5. *Pureté et perfection du travail d'amour.* L'image la plus insistante pour parler de la pureté du travail de contemplation et de la nécessité d'un dépouillement intérieur est celle de la nudité. L'adjectif *nakid* et son adverbe *nakidly* accompagnent régulièrement, dans *The Cloud*, les mots

entente, *thought*, *being*, de même que le mot essentiel *offring*, dans *The Book of Privy Counselling*. C'est sur ce point tout particulièrement que M. Noetinger, plus fidèle à l'esprit qu'à la lettre, fait oeuvre de théologien de la vie spirituelle, explicitant tout autant que traduisant ce concept fondamental de la mystique dionysienne, à la fois fort simple et fort trompeur pour qui n'est pas averti. Ses traductions se révèlent beaucoup plus riches que celles, plus littérales, d'A. Guerne. La première interprétation de la nudité mystique en fait un synonyme de la pureté, de la simplicité et du détachement, équivalence clairement exprimée dans *The Pistle of Preier*. C'est également, pour reprendre une formule du Nécrologe solesmien, une image de ce «vide du créé» qu'avait établi pour lui-même M. Noetinger (*Noet.* avant-propos p. v); c'est un chemin d'anéantissement devant préparer la rencontre d'amour avec le Néant qui est aussi le Tout (*Cloud* ch. 68), une image pour *imaginum absentia et privatio* telles que les définira au dix-septième siècle le jésuite hollandais Sandaeus.[7]

A cet égard, le premier chapitre de *The Book of Privy Counselling*, correspondance ultérieure entre le maître de *The Cloud* et son dirigé, est essentiel. Explicitant son enseignement sur les deux nuages, celui de l'oubli et celui de l'inconnaissance, l'auteur affirme: *Loke that nothing leue in thi worching mynde bot a nakid entent streching into God* (*PC* 75/18–9), ce que M. Noetinger traduit «un simple regard fixé sur Dieu» (p. 333); par contre le conseil *thenk nakidly* (*PC* 76/14–6), invitation à renoncer à toute curiosité humaine au sujet de Dieu, est rendu littéralement par «pense purement» (p. 337). Le maître invite d'ailleurs son disciple à voir dans son effort de mise à nu un travail de purification spirituelle: *that thi thought be nakid & thi felyng nothing defoulid, & thou, nakidly as thou arte, with the touching of grace be priuely fed in thi felyng oñly with hym as he is* (*PC* 76/8–10). Le traducteur de Solesmes donne ici toute sa force à l'adverbe dans cette belle traduction: «que ta pensée soit nue et tes impressions purifiées. Alors, dans cette nudité, par la touche de la grâce, tu seras secrètement nourri de lui seul tel qu'il est» (p. 337). Face à la même formule dans *The Cloud*, *thou felist in thi wille a nakid entente vnto God* (*Cloud* 9/30–1), A. Guerne traduit littéralement «tu sens dans ta volonté un élan nu vers Dieu» (p. 23), mais le théologien choisit d'expliciter: «tu constateras dans ta volonté une aspiration nue et pure vers Dieu» (p. 72). C'est encore ce souci pédagogique de pasteur qui conduit M. Noetinger, traduisant plus loin la même formule à l'intérieur d'un paragraphe-clé, à bien préciser: «il n'est besoin que de tendre directement vers Dieu dans une nudité complète d'esprit et sans autre motif que lui-même» (*Cloud* 15/24–9; *Noet.* pp. 89–90). De même encore, au ch. 43 qui fait écho au ch. 16 exposant le renoncement de Marie de Béthanie, grand modèle des contemplatifs, le théologien a jugé insuffisante la traduction littérale, pourtant retenue par le poète, «une connaissance nue et un sentiment de ton être propre» (*G.* p. 138), puisqu'il n'a pas craint d'expliciter: «il te restera encore, interposées entre toi et ton Dieu et dépouillées de toute considération, la connaissance et la conscience de ton être propre» (*Noet.* p. 181) (*a nakid weting & a felyng of thin owne beyng* (*Cloud* 46/2–8).

La deuxième interprétation de la nudité mystique en fait un moyen de perfection. Cet exigeant travail de mise à nu et de purification de tout l'être est en effet un chemin qui doit conduire de l'imperfection vers la perfection, à la rencontre du Seul Parfait, Dieu. L'auteur de *The Cloud* l'expose clairement: *the substaunce of this werke is not elles bot a nakid entente directe vnto God for himself (. . .) in this werke God is parfitely loued for hymself* (*Cloud* 32/22–31). Celui qui s'engage résolument dans ce travail est appelé *parfite prentis, parfite worcher* («bon ouvrier», *Noet.* p. 139; «parfait ouvrier», *G.* p. 93); dans son imperfection, il travaille à acquérir la perfection, car il s'est mis à la suite et à l'école du Christ-Perfection (*a parfite folower of Criste, Cloud* Prolog. 1/15–6), lui l'Ouvrier Parfait qui ne regarde pas à sa peine (ch. 24), l'Amant Parfait (ch. 43) qui, nu sur la Croix, étend les bras et aime tout homme sans distinction aucune (ch. 25). C'est avec ce modèle au coeur que travaille l'apprenti contemplatif. *Schere awey couetyse of knowyng, for it wil more let thee than help thee. It suffisith inowgh vnto thee that thou fele thee steryd likyngly with a thing thou wost neuer what, ellys that in thi steryng thou haue no specyal thought of any thing vnder God, & that thin entent be nakidly directe vnto God* (*Cloud* 39/6–10). «Retranche tout désir de comprendre» (*Noet.* p. 158): ce renoncement amoureux et parfois douloureux à toute satisfaction intellectuelle s'accompagne d'un grand désir de malléabilité entre les mains de Dieu-Artisan (*Cloud* 39/1–6), et cette docilité, fruit de l'amour et de l'humilité (*meek*), fait du contemplatif un imitateur du Christ nu, humble et humilié (ch. 2). La recherche de la nudité de l'âme dans le dépouillement des sens comme de l'intellect, chemin de purification passive, est une condition de la perfection; A. Guerne restitue au texte toute sa force et parle d'un «élan nu directement dirigé vers Dieu» (p. 115); M. Noetinger quant à lui préfère expliciter, écartant sur ce point capital tout risque d'ambiguïté et rappelant le but de toute ascèse chrétienne: «ton âme tend vers Dieu dans une nudité parfaite» (p. 158).

6. *L'obscurité du travail mystique.* Le caractère intérieur et caché de la vie spirituelle, toute tournée vers «Celui qui voit dans le secret», en fait une activité obscure aux yeux des hommes. Elle l'est tout autant au regard de celui qui s'y donne. Le lecteur averti de *The Cloud of Unknowing*, qu'il aborde le texte dans l'original comme dans n'importe quelle traduction, saura que l'adjectif «mystique», si dévoyé dans le monde moderne, a une

histoire précise, qu'il renvoie étymologiquement et irréductiblement à des réalités cachées le rattachant au Mystère, celui des origines, celui du Verbe Incarné. Le *De Mystica Theologia* du Pseudo-Denys, texte essentiel pour la compréhension du corpus de *The Cloud*, a été traduit et paraphrasé par notre auteur sous le titre *Denis Hid Diuinite*, que J. Walsh a choisi de rendre en anglais moderne par *Denis's Hidden Theology*. Cette obscurité, lieu de l'union d'amour entre Dieu et chaque âme humaine tant qu'elle «réside en cette chair mortelle» (fin ch. 8 & chs. 13, 14), est constitutive de la théologie négative qui, à sa façon tâtonnante, tente de balbutier quelque chose du Mystère de Dieu.[8] Rien d'étonnant, donc, si le corpus de *The Cloud* est rempli de substantifs et d'adjectifs se rapportant au caché, à l'enfoui, au profond, ainsi que de formules obscures.[9] Parmi ces mots, l'adjectif *blynde* occupe une place privilégiée, d'une part en raison de la réalité qu'il décrit, mais aussi du fait de sa conjonction fréquente avec des mots aussi essentiels que *steryng*, *felyng* ou *beholdyng*. Il importe ici de comprendre que le concept d'obscurité peut renvoyer, selon le cas, à la cécité de l'âme et de l'esprit, condition de leur avancée vers le Dieu caché (*Cloud* ch. 9), comme à leur incapacité à le regarder en face, c'est-à-dire, à proprement parler, leur aveuglement. L'âme progresse à tâton, en aveugle, vers sa rencontre obscure, dans «un pieux et humble aveugle élan d'amour» (*G.* p. 30) (*a deuoute & a meek blynde stering of loue*, *Cloud* 12/33–4). M. Noetinger parle ici de «l'humble et pieux mouvement d'un amour aveugle» (p. 81). Les deux traducteurs parlent des «sentiments aveugles» que l'homme a de sa propre misère ou de la bonté de Dieu (*blynde felynges of theire owne wrechidnes, or of the goodnes of God*, *Cloud* 40/16–8), mais à la «considération et aveugle contemplation de la faute ou péché» (*G.* p. 120), M. Noetinger préfère la «considération obscure du péché» (p. 164) (*this blynde beholdyng of synne*, *Cloud* 40/31–2).

Force est de reconnaître ici l'extrême difficulté de tels passages, non tant à cause des hardiesses de formulation—déjà remarquables—qu'en raison de la nature surhumaine des réalités qu'il s'agit d'essayer de décrire. Ces réalités sont, en vérité, beaucoup trop fortes pour une langue d'homme, et tout se passe comme si, à leur contact, le langage se brisait pour éclater en morceaux, chaque morceau reflétant à sa manière quelque chose de la vision entrevue. C'est ainsi, en particulier, que peut s'expliquer pour une bonne part l'usage si fréquent du paradoxe dans les écrits mystiques; c'est ainsi également que s'explique la présence de formules si extraordinaires dans le grec du Pseudo-Denys qui est sous-jacent à notre texte moyen-anglais, à travers le latin de Jean Sarracène et ses commentaires médiévaux.[10] L'un des passages les plus difficiles à rendre en français se trouve dans le ch. 68, qui est justement l'un des chapitres les plus dionysiens de tout le corpus de *The Cloud*. Tout se concentre ici en un combat de formules ramassées, où l'accumulation des tensions ne peut que produire un «discours blessé».[11] Au combat obscur de Jacob avec l'Ange correspond ici non seulement la lutte de l'âme aimante avec le tout et le rien de son amour, mais aussi l'affrontement du traducteur avec un texte en vérité insurmontable. Quoi qu'il advienne de ce texte dans son difficile passage d'une langue à l'autre, son lecteur comme son traducteur est appelé à souffrir.

> Loke than besily that thi goostly werk be noghwhere bodely (. . .) & lete nought, therfore, bot trauayle besily in that nought with a wakyng desire to wilne to haue God, that no man may knowe. For I telle thee trewly that I had leuer be so nowhere bodely, wrastlyng with that blynde nought, than to be so grete a lorde that I might when I wolde be euerywhere bodely, merily pleiing with al this ought as a lorde with his owne (. . .) This nought may betir be felt then seen; for it is ful blynde & ful derk to hem that han bot lityl while lokid therapon. Neuertheles, if I schal sothlier sey, a soule is more bleendid in felyng of it for habundaunce of goostly light, then for any derknes or wantyng of bodely lightte. (*Cloud* 67/37–68/18)

M. Noetinger lutte avec «ce néant obscur» (pp. 244–6), tandis qu'A. Guerne lutte et combat «avec cet aveugle rien» (pp. 205–7); pour le théologien soucieux de réduire les risques d'erreurs en un passage aussi délicat, ce «rien» est «invisible et obscur» (p. 245), et pour le poète il est «tout aveugle et tout obscurité» (p. 206). Il faut ajouter que cette souffrance du texte, qui reflète la souffrance de l'âme en sa progression obscure, accompagne aussi la mise à nu de celle-ci, son dépouillement de toute image: la relation entre *blynde* et *nakid* est en effet très forte, au point que dans *Privy Counselling* les deux adjectifs sont interchangeables (*blynde beholdyng, nakid beholdyng, nakid blynde beyng, nakid blynde felyng of thin owne beyng*), preuve s'il en fallait encore du lien profond entre l'impérieux besoin de reculer les limites conceptuelles du langage, et le désarroi croissant des mots à l'approche du Mystère. En dernière analyse, si *The Cloud* est un texte qui fait souffrir lecteurs et traducteurs, il est clair qu'une telle souffrance est encore celle de l'amour au travail (*trauayle*).

7. *L'intimité de l'amour.* «Or, quel est-il, celui qui l'appelle un rien? Assurément, c'est l'homme extérieur, et non pas l'homme intérieur. Notre homme intérieur l'appelle un Tout» (*G.* p. 207) (*Noet.* pp. 245–6). Cette fin du ch. 68, opposant le «Tout» de l'homme intérieur, spirituel, au «rien» de l'homme extérieur, charnel, confirme ce qui était indiqué dès les premières lignes de *The Cloud* et que tout amant, du ciel comme de la terre, aura découvert pour lui-même au long de son apprentissage:

l'amour est une nourriture qui se partage et se goûte dans l'intimité (*Cloud* ch. 26 & *PC* 76/10, *priuely fed*). Le Christ, Amant-Parfait, est un amant jaloux qui ne souffre aucun rival (ch. 2). En revanche, il se donne entièrement à qui le choisit pour son Tout (ch. 4). Ce don mutuel total, loin des regards indiscrets comme des distractions des sens corporels, ce don qui échappe à tous sauf à Celui qui voit dans le secret, s'exprime au long du texte tout particulièrement par l'adjectif priue, dans des conjonctions sémantiques toujours très importantes. Le travail de contemplation unitive que recommande le maître est défini comme *a priuy loue put apon the clowde of unknowing* (ch. 9). C'est un «secret empressement en ce nuage d'inconnaissance», écrit A. Guerne (p. 48). Plus loin, *priue loue* sera traduit par «amour intime» (*G.* p. 63), ou «amour secret» (*Noet.* p. 113). Mais c'est au début du ch. 21, où l'auteur explique comment Marthe et Marie représentent les deux vies, active et contemplative, que les deux traducteurs diffèrent le plus dans leur présentation: A. Guerne dit de ces deux vies, *priuely vnderstonden*, qu'elles sont «secrètement entendues» (p. 83); M. Noetinger, en théologien, préfère le terme technique et écrit que «ces deux vies sont mystiquement figurées dans le récit de l'Evangile par les deux soeurs» (pp. 129–30).

8. *Les sens spirituels.* La nécessité d'un langage analogique pour rendre compte des réalités de l'expérience spirituelle a conduit très tôt les auteurs à recourir, spontanément ou consciemment, au langage des sens corporels en donnant à ce dernier un contenu spirituel.[12] Des cinq verbes désignant les activités des sens, *taast, fele, see, smel, here*, trois sont principalement utilisés dans ces textes pour décrire la possession fruitive, ou jouissance de Dieu (*fruitio Dei*): *taast, fele*, et *see*. La preuve que l'activité des sens spirituels est à mettre en relation étroite avec la possession de Dieu par l'homme est fournie dans la remarquable conjonction de ces trois verbes, *see, fele, haue* (*Cloud* 48/32–3 & *PC* 80/34). Les deux traductions françaises font apparaître des différences d'appréciation, A. Guerne préférant s'en tenir généralement au sens littéral, alors que M. Noetinger fait ressortir, par ses fréquentes transpositions d'un sens spirituel à l'autre, la nature unique de l'expérience spirituelle pourtant décrite de manières multiples. La traduction du théologien fait sans doute parfois perdre à l'original un peu de sa force sensuelle; par contre elle a l'avantage de manifester, face à la traduction du poète, quelque chose de l'indivisible unité de cette expérience d'amour par ailleurs si difficile à cerner comme à décrire. Il importe en effet de prendre conscience de cette profonde unité de l'expérience fruitive de Dieu attestée, de façon certes encore bien obscure, par les différents sens spirituels. C'est ainsi que *taast*, traduit habituellement par «goûter» chez A. Guerne, est parfois rendu dans le texte de M. Noetinger par «éprouver», ce qui l'apparente à *fele*. Le verbe

fele, en retour, pose au traducteur le délicat problème du choix entre une perception purement physique (sensation) et une réaction mentale, psychologique, voire affective (sentiment). *For alle vertewes thei fynden & felyn in God* (*Cloud* 44/3–4): «en toute vertu il trouve et voit, reconnaît et a le sentiment de Dieu» (*G.* p. 131), «ne trouvent-ils pas et ne goûtent-ils pas toutes les vertus en Dieu?» (*Noet.* p. 174). Il est intéressant de remarquer qu'ici le poète a dédoublé sa traduction, quand le théologien a serré le texte tout en transposant *fele* en *taast*. De même, pour la difficile traduction de *fele God* dans la formule *thou woldest see hym & haue hym or fele hym* (*Cloud* 48/32–3), Noetinger préfère «goûter Dieu» (p. 189) à «avoir le sentiment de Dieu» (*G.* p. 146), mais dans le conseil donné à la fin de *Privy Counselling*, *seche more after felyng then after kunning; for kunnyng oft-tymes disceyuith with pride, bot meek louely felyng may not begile (. . .) In knowyng is trauaile, in feling is rest* (*PC* 98/36–9), il couple les deux traductions: «Cherche plus à goûter qu'à connaître. La science fait souvent tomber dans l'erreur à cause de l'orgueil; mais il ne peut y avoir d'illusion à goûter dans l'humilité ce sentiment d'amour (. . .) La science exige le travail, l'expérience du sentiment spirituel donne le repos» (p. 406). L'étroite parenté entre *fele* et *taast* quand il s'agit de tenter une description de l'expérience directe de Dieu est d'ailleurs soulignée par l'auteur lui-même, dans la mesure où il les emploie conjointement (*taast of goostly felyng in God*, *PC* 98/34–5; «c'est par la grâce seule qu'il peut goûter un sentiment spirituel de Dieu» *Noet.* p. 406). Ici les traducteurs anglais bénéficient de l'existence du mot «experience» qui permet de faire immédiatement l'unité entre les diverses activités des sens spirituels ('He cannot experience God by spiritual taste except through grace. . . . Seek rather experience than knowledge. For knowledge often leads us astray through pride, but humble loving aware-ness cannot beguile us' *J.W.* 2, p. 247).

Cette rencontre de Dieu, au plus profond de l'être, conservera néces-sairement un caractère obscur, ce qui explique en partie l'inévitable maladresse avec laquelle s'expriment les auteurs spirituels. Par ses sens spirituels, il peut être donné à l'homme intérieur, uni à Dieu dans l'amour, d'avoir une perception directe, à la fois réelle et obscure, de Celui qui l'attire ainsi à Lui (*Cloud* ch. 9); mais au moment d'en rendre compte à l'aide des mots de la perception sensorielle commune, le caractère immédiat d'une telle expérience lui échappe. En réalité, tout discours de l'homme sur Dieu ne peut que demeurer un discours indirect (*PC* 87/20–1). Ce tâtonnement conceptuel, très perceptible dans le texte original de *The Cloud* et de *Privy Counselling*, comme dans de si nombreux autres textes ascétiques et mystiques, ne peut qu'affecter toute tentative de traduction. D'un certain point de vue, l'exigence de fidélité qui anime le traducteur le conduit à reproduire ce tâtonnement en une maladresse lexicale et syntaxique de la plus haute signification. La traduction fidèle d'un discours blessé peut-elle produire en vérité autre chose qu'une nouvelle forme du même discours blessé? Le mot *felyng* s'oppose à *cleer sight* pour désigner cette avancée à tâton, comme à l'aveuglette, de l'âme vers son Amant. Mais une variante extrêmement significative laisse planer la confusion entre cette approche maladroite de l'âme aveuglée (*grope*, *Cloud* 19/7) et la jouissance de la saisie directe, à la fois ferme et douce (*grappe*).[13] Toute traduction se doit ici de faire ressortir, sans aucune équivoque possible, mais en intégrant toute la richesse des harmoniques du langage de l'amour humain, le caractère fortement amoureux de tels passages où la mystique dionysienne rejoint la mystique nuptiale pour célébrer, dans une «érotique théologique»,[14] les Noces de l'âme et de son Créateur. A la «claire vision» A. Guerne oppose le «sentiment» (p. 48); à la «vision» Noetinger oppose ici l'«expérience», et établit une équation entre cette expérience fruitive et la saisie immédiate et obscure de Dieu dans l'amour: «tu peux du moins le saisir et en avoir l'expérience dès cette vie par la grâce. La vision est impossible ici-bas, mais l'expérience est possible à l'aide de la grâce, quand Dieu daigne la donner» (*Noet.* pp. 98–9) (& *loke thou haue no wonder of this; for mightest thou ones se it as cleerly as thou maist bi grace com to for to grope it & feele it in this liif, thou woldest think as I say. Bot seker be thou that cleer sight schal neuer man haue here in this liif; bot the felyng mowe men haue thorow grace when God vouchethsaaf, Cloud* 19/6–10).

9. *La concentration dans le travail*. L'effort du contemplatif, qui dans la veine dionysienne à l'origine de ces textes est un essort dans et par la contemplation,[15] est un dur labeur à base d'oubli et de concentration. Il s'agit de tout oublier, de tout recouvrir d'un épais «nuage d'oubli» pour mieux se concentrer sur l'Unique Nécessaire, Dieu lui-même, non en ce qu'il est, mais dans le fait même qu'Il est (*PC* 75/18–21), et ainsi entrer dans le second nuage, celui de l'inconnaissance, demeure du Tout-Autre. Ce travail d'attention à Dieu et aux différentes motions intérieures qu'il suscite, ce nécessaire «discernement des esprits» sans lequel tout est péril est fréquemment présenté dans le texte par le mot *beholdyng*. Ce mot désigne tantôt la contemplation en tant qu'activité de concentration sur Dieu, tantôt l'attention psychologique portée sur tel ou tel aspect du travail du contemplatif. Les traductions varieront donc entre «contemplation» et «considération», ou «observation», selon que le mot sera accompagné d'adjectifs comme *besi, clere, blynde*, ou encore selon que cette attention se portera sur Dieu, sur le but à atteindre, ou sur la masse de péché qu'est l'homme en soi (ch. 36). C'est la notion de considération attentive, ou soutenue, qui dans les deux textes français traduit le conseil du maître concernant la vocation de son jeune disciple (*besi beholding*,

Cloud 7/22). L'attention que Marie de Béthanie, perdue dans sa contemplation amoureuse, avait cessé de porter à la précieuse humanité de son Seigneur (*lityl specyal beholdyng unto the beute of his precious & his blessid body*, *Cloud* 26/2–3) est traduite par A. Guerne en termes de regard (p. 71) et par M. Noetinger en termes d'occupation (p. 119). C'est encore un «regard» que, selon A. Guerne, Marie jette sur sa misère passée (p. 69), alors que M. Noetinger parle ici de «considération» (p. 117) (*the beholdyng of hir wrechidnes*, *Cloud* 25/3). Dieu mesure la «contemplation» de chacun selon ses capacités, en fonction de la nature et de la grâce (*G.* p. 60 & *Noet.* p. 110) (*he mesurid theire beholdyng after theire abilnes in kynde & in grace*, *Cloud* 22/28–9). Par ailleurs, ce n'est pas le moindre des paradoxes de *The Cloud*, du moins en apparence, que de présenter l'adjectif *blynde* en compagnie de *beholdyng*; *blynde* s'oppose en réalité à *clere* pour désigner la concentration sur Dieu, tâtonnante et maladroite, aveuglée par l'abondance de lumière divine (ch. 68), par contraste avec les constructions intellectuelles logiques et satisfaisantes pour l'esprit, mais qui ne sont qu'autant de projections trop humaines sur Dieu, et que la théologie négative récuse comme trompeuses: *Put doun soche clere beholdinges* (*Cloud* 18/33), dit le maître, conseil que M. Noetinger traduit: «dépose toute considération précise» (pp. 97–8). De même pour le péché qui doit rester l'objet d'une «considération obscure» (*Noet.* p. 164), qu'A. Guerne appelle ici une «considération et aveugle contemplation de la faute ou péché» (p. 120). Cette appréhension obscure du péché (*blynde beholdyng of synne*, ch. 36) imite, dans sa méthode, cette autre considération obscure de Dieu, pur fruit d'un amour dépouillé de toute image, qu'est la contemplation unitive de Marie de Béthanie (*a louyng steryng & a blinde beholdyng vnto the nakid beyng of God him-self only*, *Cloud* 17/32–3). Pour A. Guerne il s'agit ici d'un «élan d'amour» et d'une «aveugle considération de l'Etre pur de Dieu» (p. 44), et M. Noetinger n'hésite pas à parler d'un «élan d'amour» et d'un «regard aveugle qui se portent sur l'être nu de Dieu» (p. 95). Plus loin dans le corpus, présentant un passage de *Privy Counselling* où l'auteur explicite son enseignement sur le même sujet, le traducteur de Solesmes écrira: «L'âme simple peut dormir doucement et se reposer dans l'amoureuse contemplation de Dieu tel qu'il est» (p. 368) (*the sely soule may softely sleep & rest in the louely beholdyng of God as he is*, *PC* 86/21–2).

10. *Les jeux de l'amour.* Une telle exigence de concentration et de vigilance constante pourrait vite devenir très lourde à porter, surtout si elle se trompe d'objet. En réalité, à lire attentivement les textes, il apparaît que cet effort de concentration et d'oubli est tout simplement un jeu d'enfant. C'est là l'un des profonds paradoxes de la vie spirituelle

chrétienne, vérifié quotidiennement auprès des grands spirituels qui se sont enfoncés dans l'abandon. Ce jeu d'enfant est celui qui occupe et ravit Benjamin, figure de la contemplation abandonnée dans le texte de Richard de Saint-Victor à la base de *The Study of Wisdom*. *Ibi Beniamyn adolescentulus in mentis excessu* (*BM* 145/7): l'auteur de *The Cloud* reprend ce texte dans *Privy Counselling* et prend soin de rappeler que pour que Benjamin vive, il a d'abord fallu que Rachel, sa mère, meure en lui donnant le jour (*PC* 85/11–29). La contemplation infuse, de nature extatique, ne peut se développer et jouir de son «excès» en Dieu qu'une fois morte la raison. *The Cloud of Unknowing* contient, de façon éparse il est vrai, un certain nombre de références au *ludus amoris*, que ce soit l'amour conjugal ou l'amour parental, ce qui place ce texte, avec son corpus, à la croisée de la mystique nuptiale et de la mystique de l'essence.[16] Le ch. 46 est particulièrement important en ce domaine: *gamenly, gamesumli, childly, pleyingly* accompagnent le mot *pley*, lui-même lié à l'image du père jouant affectueusement avec son enfant (*Cloud* 48/16–20 & 26–37). A. Guerne (p. 146) comme M. Noetinger (p. 189) parlent ici de «jeu» et d'«enfantillage». Le mot *sleight* (*Cloud* 37/9–22), si important au ch. 32 où le père vient consoler son enfant, désigne une astuce qui elle aussi s'apparente au jeu. M. Noetinger opte ici pour «stratagème» (pp. 152–3), mais A. Guerne ne parle que d'un «moyen» (p. 109). Sa traduction de *cauteel* (*Cloud* 74/7) par «dessein fort habile» (p. 225), au ch. 75 décrivant le salutaire jeu de cache-cache auquel Dieu se livre avec l'âme aimante, ne rend que partiellement compte du caractère bienveillant de ce comportement, de même que celle de M. Noetinger («un détour plein d'habileté», p. 261). Il est vrai qu'ici tous deux ont peut-être été influencés par la traduction en anglais moderne d'Evelyn Underhill,[17] parlant de 'artful device' (p. 313), ou par J. McCann O.S.B. qui utilise la formule 'on purpose' (p. 99). Il est vrai également qu'en anglais médiéval, comme en anglais moderne, le mot *pley* peut renvoyer à une simple «activité», à la manière du français «jeu» (par ex. le jeu d'un piston). Est-ce la raison pour laquelle l'exclamation du maître, prenant vivement la défense des contemplatifs à la fin du ch. 21, *Lat hem sit in here rest & in here pley, with the thrid & the best partye of Marye* (*Cloud* 30/24–9), a été rendue par les deux traducteurs en termes d'«occupation» (*Noet.* p. 133; *G.* p. 86)? Dans *Caligo ignorancie*, sa traduction latine de *The Cloud* au quinzième siècle, le chartreux Richard Methley a pourtant choisi un mot qui, à côté du repos, donne toute sa part à la récréation: «in sua quiete et suo solacio.»[18]

«Quelle chose admirable et sublime que l'amour de Dieu! Il n'est pas de langue assez parfaite pour en faire comprendre la moindre parcelle, sinon par des suppositions impossibles. Comme il dépasse l'intelligence humaine!» (*Noet.* pp. 275–6). Cette exclamation du maître, dans *The*

Epistle of Prayer, résume en quelque sorte l'ambition et les difficultés de la contemplation dite obscure, relevant de ce qu'on a appelé la «mystique des ténèbres» par opposition à la «mystique de la lumière». Ces «exemples impossibles qui passent l'entendement» (*inpossible ensaumples & passing the vnderstonding of man*, Pr. 104/19–23) constituent sans doute la moins maladroite des solutions pour l'auteur. Pour le traducteur, ce sont autant de pierres d'achoppement. La plupart de ces passages «impossibles», formés de locutions paradoxales ou de constructions elliptiques concentrées, se trouvent dans *The Book of Privy Counselling*, ce qui n'est guère surprenant puisqu'il s'agit en fait d'une mise au point technique, d'un mode d'emploi raisonné de *The Cloud* où le maître justifie avec hardiesse les hardiesses de son propre enseignement. Le lecteur français ne dispose actuellement que d'une seule traduction moderne de *Privy Counselling*, celle de M. Noetinger,[19] A. Guerne n'ayant pu, malgré son désir, mener à bien le reste de sa traduction (*G*. p. 10). La comparaison sera établie ici avec les solutions proposées par cet autre grand explicateur et traducteur moderne du corpus de *The Cloud* que fut le jésuite James Walsh.

Thus schalt thou knittingly, & in a maner that is meruelous, worschip God with himself (*PC* 81/7–8): «Cette offrande de toi-même rendra à Dieu un hommage très élevé et t'unira à lui», écrit M. Noetinger (pp. 351–2), dans une traduction où apparemment l'image du noeud contenue dans l'adverbe *knittingly* et l'affirmation selon laquelle, dans la contemplation, l'homme et Dieu ne font plus qu'un, sont regroupées dans le concept d'union exprimé par le verbe français. J. Walsh traduit en serrant le texte de plus près: 'And so through this union, in a way that is wonderful, you shall worship God with God himself' (*J.W.* 2, p. 226), mais en fournissant comme en justification un rappel de l'affirmation du Pseudo-Denys sur l'immanence de Dieu dans ses créatures (*Noms Divins*, ch. 5, par. 10). M. Noetinger avait estimé nécessaire, il est vrai, d'accompagner sa traduction d'une note de rappel sur l'exemplarisme divin. Plus loin, la formule paradoxale *fully mekyd in booldnes & strengtheed of loue* (*PC* 86/6–7), dont le parallélisme avec *fully mekid in noughtnyng of it-self* (*PC* 84/21) offre des perspectives sur le travail d'amour des contemplatifs, fait l'objet d'une fort belle traduction: «ils sont devenus pleinement humbles dans la hardiesse et la vigueur de leur amour» (*Noet.* p. 367). La traduction de J. Walsh s'accompagne ici d'une référence à St Paul (2 Cor.12:1–9). Par ailleurs, le couplage paradoxal de *nakidly* et de *clothed* dans la formule très concentrée *vtterly spoylid of thiself & nakidly clothed in hymself as he is, vnclothed & not lappid in any of thees sensible felynges* (*PC* 97/17–9), donne lieu à deux interprétations différentes: M. Noetinger associe nudité et recherche de «simplicité», au sens où le mot apparaît par exemple dans le *Miroir des simples âmes* de Marguerite Porete («dépouillé de soi-même et revêtu de lui seul», p. 402), alors que J. Walsh explicite et en quelque sorte déconcentre la formule en la décomposant en une séquence chronologique: pour pouvoir revêtir le Christ, il faut commencer par se présenter nu à lui ('you are utterly despoiled of yourself and your naked-ness is clothed in him, as he is. You are unclothed: that is, you are not wrapped in any of the sensible consolations which may be experienced in this life . . .', p. 245). Il est hautement significatif qu'ici J. Walsh, en théologien, ait jugé utile d'accompagner sa traduction d'une note (p. 281). Cette note présente un extrait du traité *Mystica Theologia* (ou *Viae Syon Lugent*) du chartreux Hugues de Balma: 'The spirit must first leave all consideration and love of sensible things, and the contemplation of all intelligible things. For the loving power must ascend in all purity without defilement from the intellect, to him whom it recognizes in its striving as the fulfilment of its desires, so that it may be more intimately united with him' (*Mystica Theologia*, III, 4). Ce texte d'Hugues de Balma, qui a peut-être influencé l'auteur de *The Cloud* (*J.W.* 1, p. 20), est fréquemment cité en note par le traducteur qui semble l'utiliser, en compagnie d'autres textes d'origine cartusienne, comme une glose devant aider le lecteur à mieux comprendre un texte souvent très dense. Cette nécessité d'une glose quasi permanente, en présence de textes difficiles, a été fortement ressentie par de nombreux traducteurs au cours du temps.

L'un des exemples les plus frappants du recours à la glose est fourni au début du ch. 69 de *The Cloud* avec l'affirmation *Wonderfuly is a mans affeccion varied in goostly felyng of this nought when it is nowhere wrought* (*Cloud* 68/23–4). Curieusement, les deux traducteurs français s'en tiennent strictement au texte, certes limpide pour qui a commencé d'entrer dans l'expérience vécue d'un tel dépouillement, mais d'aspect résolument énigmatique pour qui l'aborde sans préparation. Au «senti-ment spirituel de ce rien» exercé dans ce «nulle part» de M. Noetinger (p. 246) correspond «ce rien conçu nulle part» sous la plume d'A. Guerne (p. 208). Pourtant, dès le quinzième siècle, Richard Methley estime qu'il doit quelque éclaircissement au lecteur de sa traduction latine. J. Walsh reprend en note cette glose dans le même souci pédagogique.[20] En ce sens il se montre fidèle à l'esprit dans lequel a circulé ce texte, et prolonge la tradition de la version glosée à laquelle avait également contribué, au dix-septième siècle, le grand bénédictin Augustine Baker, dont le texte accompagne justement la version en anglais moderne de Dom Justin McCann.[21]

Face à tant de difficultés de conceptualisation et de formulation, le traducteur en vient à se demander s'il n'aurait pas plutôt intérêt à appliquer pour lui-même, et pour la pratique de son art somme toute ambigu, le bien sage conseil que le maître donnait déjà à son disciple en présence de choix «impossibles»:

Do thou thus: sette the tone on the to honde and the tother on the tother, and chese thee a thing the whiche is hid bitwix hem, the whiche thing when it is had, geueth thee leue, in fredom of spirite, to beginne and to seese in holding any of the other (. . .) Bot now thou askest me what is that thing. I schal telle thee what I mene that it is. It is God for whom thou schuldest be stille, if thou schuldest be stylle; and for whom thou schuldest speke, if thou schuldest speke (. . .) For silence is not God, ne speking is not God; fastyng is not God, ne etyng is not God; onlines is not God ne companye is not God; ne yet any of alle the othir soche two contraries. He is hid betwix hem, and may not be founden by any werk of thi soule, bot al only bi loue of thin herte. He may not be knowen by reson. He may not be thought, getyn, ne trasid, by vnderstonding. Bot he may be loued and chosen with the trewe, louely wille of thin herte. Chese thee him; and thou arte silently spekyng & spekingly silent, fastyngly etyng and etyngly fasting; and so forth of alle the remenant. Soche a louely chesing of God, thus wisely lesing and seking him oute with the clene wille of a trewe herte bitwix alle soche to, leuyng hem bothe whan thei come and profren hem to be the poynt and the pricke of oure goostly beholding, is the worthiest trasing and sekyng of God that may be getyn or lerned in this liif . . . (*St.* 14/33–115/18)

«Voici comment tu agiras: de ces deux procédés opposés, prends l'un dans une main, l'autre dans l'autre, et choisis pour toi ce qui est caché ente les deux (. . .) Tu me demanderas alors qu'est-ce qui est ainsi caché; et je te répondrai: c'est Dieu, Dieu pour qui tu dois te taire, si tu dois rester silencieux, et pour qui tu dois parler, s'il te faut parler (. . .) il en est de même de toutes ces pratiques opposées. Dieu se trouve caché entre elles, et ne peut être trouvé par aucune opération de l'âme, si ce n'est par l'amour de ton coeur. (. . .) Choisis-le donc (. . .) Ce choix de Dieu par amour, réalisé en écartant toute autre chose, cette recherche de lui dans la volonté sincère d'un coeur pur, en passant entre ces exercices qui s'offrent à nous comme but et fin de notre considération spirituelle, voilà sans contredit la manière la plus noble de poursuivre et de chercher Dieu que l'on puisse pratiquer ou apprendre en cette vie» (*Noet.* pp. 299–301 *passim*). Un tel choix est donc bien, dans la pensée du maître, un choix d'amour (*a louely chesing of God*) qui va procurer la liberté dans l'Esprit (*St.* 114/16–29). C'est justement à la suite de ce passage essentiel qu'apparaît cet autre conseil, tout aussi essentiel, *Bot euer when reson defaileth, than list loue liue and lerne for to plei* (*St.* 115/31–2). «Quand la raison défaille, apprends à jouer.» Convaincu de la vraie nature de ce jeu, M. Noetinger a traduit: «apprends à exercer ton amour" (p. 302).

«Passer entre.» En choisissant de mettre ainsi en valeur la préposition *bitwix*, M. Noetinger invite semble-t-il son lecteur à une expérience pascale. Ce passage, ce chemin de liberté entre les paradoxes de la vie spirituelle, eux-mêmes transposés en paradoxes textuels, est lui aussi une forme de l'amour au travail. *Ubi spiritus Domini, ibi libertas* (*St.* 114/28). Mais, par le détachement que procure l'indifférence, ce travail va peu à peu devenir un jeu d'enfant. En christianisme, en effet, le paradoxe n'affecte que l'apparence, la surface des choses. Ici, il n'affecte que la surface du texte; c'est pourquoi le traducteur, à l'image du disciple, doit apprendre à se glisser entre des exigences d'aspect contradictoire pour gagner la profondeur. En choisissant de pratiquer cette forme très particulière de détachement, lui aussi choisira Dieu, caché entre les mots. L'exercice intellectuel qu'est la traduction d'un texte spirituel tend alors à se transformer, par l'approfondissement du sens et le renoncement amoureux à d'autres formes possibles, en un authentique exercice spirituel.

Il paraît bon ici d'évoquer, pour finir et comme champs d'application de cet «enfantillage», fruit de l'amour au travail qui doit apprendre à «passer entre», deux domaines qui, dans l'histoire collective de la spiritualité comme dans l'histoire singulière des âmes, ont été souvent l'occasion de souffrance autant que d'abandon confiant. Cette souffrance résulte d'une tension et tient, encore une fois, aux limites du langage humain face aux réalités pourtant si simples de l'amour. Les difficultés qui entraînent cette souffrance n'apparaissent d'ailleurs vraiment que dans la mesure où, pour une raison précise, il est jugé nécessaire ou souhaitable que telle ou telle expérience intime de l'amour de Dieu soit communiquée à la communauté ecclésiale, large ou restreinte, pour le bien spirituel de ses membres. C'est ici un problème bien connu des directeurs spirituels. Il n'est donc pas surprenant que ces difficultés de formulation qu'affronte l'auteur se transforment sous la plume du traducteur en autant de difficultés de traduction. Toutefois, seule une comparaison minutieuse avec l'original permettra au lecteur des deux éditions françaises de *The Cloud* de déceler un désir de précaution face à certaines hardiesses du texte.

Le premier de ces deux domaines est celui de la sexualité. Il ne s'agit pas ici de la sexualité en soi, mais dans ses rapports avec l'amour spirituel et ses manifestations, en particulier sous son aspect ascétique. Les grands spirituels font souvent preuve, dans la représentation de telles expériences intimes, d'une liberté qui témoigne de leur remarquable équilibre. Le langage remplit alors sa fonction analogique, et les images de l'amour humain, *mutatis mutandis*, apportent toute leur vérité et toute leur force dans l'évocation de l'union amoureuse de Dieu avec l'homme. Cependant les risques de confusion demeurent, ce qui justifie les mises au point rencontrées dans les textes. C'est ainsi que, par deux fois, l'auteur de *The Cloud* fait directement référence à la vie sexuelle. Il ne fait pas de doute, en effet, que les preue membres dont il est question aux chapitres 12 et 52 sont ceux dont parle Chaucer dans *The Parson's Tale*, c'est-à-dire les organes génitaux. Or rien dans les deux traductions françaises ne permet de le comprendre.

«Jeûne autant que tu voudras, veille aussi tard et lève-toi aussi matin qu'il est possible, couche sur la dure, porte la haire la plus rude, oui, et s'il était permis de le faire, ce qui n'est pas, coupe-toi la langue, arrache-toi les yeux, bouche-toi hermétiquement les oreilles et le nez, découpe-toi les membres, inflige à ton corps toutes les souffrances que tu peux imaginer, tout cela ne te servira de rien: les mouvements et les soulèvements du péché ne seront pas détruits en toi» (*Noet.* p. 105). («Tranche-toi les membres», *G.* p. 57). Il est vrai que le traducteur théologien assortit son texte d'une très abondante note sur «la pratique de la mortification» (pp. 105–6). Constatant la fréquence de telles recommandations dans la littérature ascétique contemporaine et antérieure, M. Noetinger ajoute: «Une préoccupation aussi constante suppose des abus qu'il fallait combattre. Peut-être les excès des moines irlandais avaient-ils créé une sorte de légende autour de leurs pratiques?» L'allusion à l'activité des quatre premiers organes des cinq sens corporels (yeux, langue, nez, oreilles) pourrait faire penser qu'après la vue, le goût, l'odorat et l'ouïe, c'est le toucher, au sens large, qui est l'objet de l'avertissement concernant les membres. L'ascèse des moines irlandais, héritiers des grands ascètes du Désert, les conduisait-elle à appliquer à la lettre le conseil de Jésus «Si ta main est pour toi une occasion de péché, coupe-la» (*Mc.* 9:43–8)? Un homme en tout cas, d'après la tradition, crut devoir le faire, et fut blâmé dans l'Eglise pour un tel acte. La castration volontaire d'Origène, en application littérale de la remarque de Jésus (Mat.19:12), apparaît comme une référence possible, voire comme l'exemple de ce qu'il ne faut pas faire, dès lors qu'est rétabli le sens complet des *preue membres* que dans son zèle un disciple encore peu formé pourrait être tenté de se retrancher (*schere awei thi preue membres, Cloud* 21/23). L'argumentation du maître s'en trouverait renforcée. De même, au ch. 52, l'auteur s'en prend aux «contemplatifs du diable» qui, dans leur fausse contemplation, inversent le cours de la nature et travaillent à leur propre perte. Eux aussi ont entendu parler des sens spirituels, mais dans leur ignorance ils appliquent leurs sens corporels à des fins spirituelles et accordent à leurs sensations physiques une valeur indue: «De même pour leur imagination: ils la fatiguent avec tant d'indiscrétion qu'ils finissent par se mettre la cervelle à l'envers. Il n'en faut pas plus pour permettre au diable de leur faire voir de fausses lumières ou entendre de fausses mélodies, de présenter à leur odorat ou à leur palais de douces sensations, et de répandre un feu ou une chaleur extraordinaire, dans leur poitrine, leur dos, leurs reins ou leurs membres» (*Noet.* p. 204) («maintes flammes et chaleurs bizarres dans leur dos ou dans leurs reins, et dans leurs membres», *G.* p. 163).

Ainsi, par la disparition de l'adjectif *preue*, l'argument ascétique à la lumière de l'histoire de l'Eglise se trouve affaibli (ch. 12), de même que la critique de certains hérétiques aux moeurs sexuelles suspectes (ch. 52).[22] Il serait pourtant injuste de reprocher une telle omission aux deux traducteurs français. Leur travail est antérieur à la parution de l'édition critique de Phyllis Hodgson (1944). M. Noetinger, pour sa part, semble avoir basé sa traduction essentiellement sur le texte, en anglais moderne, de Justin McCann (1924) qui disposait lui-même de plusieurs manuscrits,[23] dont la version dite «de Baker» (1677), et de la traduction moderne d'Evelyn Underhill (1912). Cette dernière traduction, l'une des plus fidèles, ne précise pas la nature des membres cités aux chapitres 12 et 52, alors que le manuscrit MS. Harley 674 qui lui sert de base comporte la précision *preue*.[24] Il est vrai que, si dans l'édition de 1947, J. McCann n'a pas encore ajouté l'adjectif *preue* à la lumière de l'édition critique alors toute récente, il l'a fait dans sa 6ème édition, révisée, de 1952. Pourtant en 1947 sa cinquième édition comportait déjà en note des extraits de la traduction latine *Nubes Ignorandi* (MS. Bodley 856); les *carnalibus titillationibus* indiquées en note au ch. 12 laissent peu de doutes sur la nature du combat à mener, et d'ailleurs le texte complet de cette traduction latine, pour les deux passages cités, est explicite: *verenda tua* (ch. 12) et *priuatis membris* (ch. 52), bien qu'ici le traducteur ait ajouté *ceteris*.[25] De sorte que la question est reportée plus haut dans la chaîne des dépendances textuelles, elle reste cependant posée: qui a jugé opportun, ou préférable, de faire disparaître de l'argumentation l'adjectif *preue*, supprimant ainsi pour le lecteur à venir une donnée ascétique et historique d'un intérêt non négligeable?

Un deuxième domaine, bien plus fondamental et délicat, concerne les hardiesses qui accompagnent inévitablement tout effort de formulation théologique des étapes de l'union spirituelle. La théologie mystique abonde en degrés, modes, itinéraires et demeures dont les gradations aboutissent souvent à une architecture complexe. Pour rassurantes qu'elles puissent paraître, et mis à part leur très réel intérêt pédagogique, ces mises en systèmes conservent quelque chose de bien artificiel dans la mesure où, encore une fois, elles ne font que reproduire des projections mentales très humaines. Ici la mathématique mystique, tout comme le langage de l'érotique humaine dans ce qu'elle a de meilleur pour exprimer un pur désir d'abandon total, n'en demeure pas moins une construction bien insatisfaisante, car toujours incapable de rendre compte, en vérité, de la réalité qu'elle cherche à appréhender. C'est bien sûr le coeur de l'expérience d'amour intime qui est visé, mais c'est encore sa périphérie qui est décrite, car l'extrême pureté de cet échange mystérieux en fait quelque chose d'une simplicité telle qu'elle échappe normalement à l'appréhension de l'homme dans son état terrestre. Les spirituels en sont très conscients, et l'auteur de *The Cloud* le rappelle à sa manière: *For al that is spokyn of it is not it, bot of it* (*PC* 87/20–1). De telles mises en systèmes reflètent à l'évidence un très grand souci de prudence dans la formulation humaine des mystères divins, mais l'histoire trop humaine de la mystique confirme qu'entre cette pulsion de l'amour qui tend à produire des «mises en fable»,[26] et les réflexes compréhensibles de prudence et de crainte face aux risques de glissements vers l'erreur, le chemin reste bien étroit.[27] Par sa façon volontairement nébuleuse de procéder, par ses invitations répétées à tout oublier, à entrer dans l'inconnaissance et à demeurer quelque part en un mi-lieu de l'amour à la fois très précis et indéterminé,[28] le maître de *The Cloud* fait preuve lui-aussi d'une grande prudence, tout en échappant avec réalisme à ces constructions mentales qui mettent Dieu «au péril du nombre».[29]

Mais que dire alors d'une affirmation aussi entière et périlleuse que celle du chapitre 4: *For he is euen mete to oure soule by mesuring of his Godheed; & oure soule euen mete unto him bi worthines of oure creacion to his ymage & to his licnes* (*Cloud* 10/22–4)? («Il [Dieu] descend au niveau de notre âme, et lui proportionne sa Divinité, et notre âme peut s'élever jusqu'à lui à cause de la dignité dans laquelle nous avons été créés à son image et à sa ressemblance», *Noet.* p. 75; «Il vient même à la convenance de notre âme par la mesure qu'Il donne à sa Divinité; et notre âme également est à sa convenance par l'excellence originale de notre création 'à Son image et à Sa ressemblance'», *G.* p. 25). Dans ce passage, qui précède cette autre affirmation audacieuse *Loue is soche a might that it makith alle thing comoun. Loue therfore Iesu, & alle thing that he hath it is thin* (*Cloud* 12/2–3), l'auteur n'énonce rien de moins que l'égalité (*euen mete*) entre le Créateur et sa créature, égalité qu'il présente en termes de quantité (*mesuring*) et de qualité (*worthines*). Commentant «ce motif de la grandeur infinie de l'homme et donc d'un amour de réciprocité entre égaux» dans son étude sur la littérature mystique au Moyen Age, Albert Deblaere S.J. a retenu ce passage et écrit: «Aucune des deux traductions françaises modernes ne rend l'original: dans ces traductions, Dieu daigne descendre à la mesure de notre petitesse. Il 'descend au niveau de notre âme, et lui proportionne sa Divinité' (*Noet.*); ou bien 'Il vient même à la convenance de notre âme par la mesure qu'Il donne à sa Divinité.' (*G.*) Ces traductions insistent sur l'inégalité, alors que l'auteur répétait expressément la *euen mete* de la réciprocité d'égal à égal.» Et le collaborateur du *Dictionnaire de Spiritualité* ajoute:

> Ceci n'est qu'un exemple entre mille; et c'est le moment opportun de le dire une bonne fois (dans un ouvrage de consultation comme le *DS*, qui a gardé quelque prétention scientifique): pour un lecteur francophone qui ignore l'anglo-saxon, le moyen-anglais, le moyen-haut-

allemand ou le moyen-néerlandais (on pourrait ajouter le castillan de Jean de la Croix), la lecture de ces mystiques est rendue inaccessible par les traducteurs. A quelques rares exceptions près . . . les traducteurs français semblent surtout soucieux d'aménager les écrits de ces génies aux dimensions de leur théologie un peu courte, et, dans ce lit de Procuste, ils leur coupent allègrement tête et pieds. Etant ainsi assurés que ces textes manipulés ne feront plus tort aux âmes dévotes, ils s'étonnent de voir ces mêmes âmes se demander pourquoi ces auteurs sont tellement exceptionnels et remarquables.[30]

De fait, devant ce texte très difficile, la plupart des traducteurs anglais[31] semblent eux aussi embarrassés, et font ressortir d'une manière ou d'une autre la supériorité de Dieu sur sa créature, comme l'énoncera clairement le maître au ch. 67: *onli bi his mercy withouten thi desert [thou] arte maad a God in grace (. . .) So that, though thou be al one with hym in grace, yet thou arte ful fer binethe hym in kynde* (*Cloud* 67/8–21). Ainsi, l'auteur de *The Cloud* apporte les précisions nécessaires en fournissant son propre commentaire. De même, le recours à la glose est pour beaucoup de traducteurs la solution retenue. J. McCann, par exemple, accompagne sa traduction littérale du commentaire suivant: 'He condescends to the soul, adapting his Godhead to its reach. The reference may be to the Incarnation, or generally to God's dealings with the individual soul', ajoutant, comme pour justifier à la fois sa traduction littérale et la glose qu'il en donne, ce passage de la traduction latine *Nubes Ignorandi* «*Ipse aeque animabus nostris aptus est per suae deitatis mensurationem*» accompagné de la remarque 'a very literal translation' (p. 9). 'For God created us in his image and likeness, making us like himself, and in the Incarnation he emptied himself of his divinity becoming a man like us', écrit William Johnston S.J. (p. 50), peut-être sous l'influence de ce même commentaire. Clifton Wolters traduit «For he comes down to our level, adapting his Godhead to our power to comprehend. Our soul has some affinity with him, of course, because we have been created in his image and likeness» (p. 62). Quant au choix de l'adjectif 'apt' par Robert Way ('*He is apt to our souls by the measuring of his Godhead, and our souls are apt to Him by the worthiness of our creation in His image and likeness*' (p. 13)), il se peut qu'il ait été lui aussi influencé par le *aptus* de la citation latine donnée en note par McCann. J. Walsh, pour sa part, lit et traduit *The Cloud* à la lumière d'une autre version latine, glosée elle aussi, celle de Richard Methley, *Caligo Ignorancie*, qu'il cite abondamment en notes; toutefois, sur ce passage délicat, il ne cite pas le travail de Methley; il traduit 'He fits himself exactly to our souls by adapting his Godhead to them; and our souls are fitted exactly to him by the worthiness of our creation after his image and his likeness', mais accompagne sa traduction d'une glose, cette fois tirée d'un commentaire de Thomas Gallus sur les *Noms divins* du

Pseudo-Denys.[32] Il est vrai que, dans sa volumineuse introduction, il avait préparé son lecteur en commentant ainsi ce passage du ch. 4: 'God both adapts himself to our condition and lifts us up by grace to his own' (p. 56). À ce point de notre réflexion, il est encore intéressant de constater le scrupule qui a peut-être saisi le scribe du manuscrit Harley 674 dans son désir de produire une formulation «au plus juste»: *he is euen mete* reçoit la précision *he is maad euen mete.*[33] Constatons, pour finir, que Phyllis Hodgson, elle aussi, a subi l'influence des traducteurs qu'elle a influencés, car la comparaison de ses deux éditions critiques fait apparaître une évolution dans le choix de sa glose.[34] Quoi qu'il en soit, au 16ème siècle, cette affirmation *euen mete* a également retenu l'attention d'un lecteur du manuscrit University College 14, car elle fait partie des phrases qui ont été soulignées en rouge dans le texte. De plus, un index a été dessiné dans la marge en face de ce même passage, ce qui confirme son importance dans la démonstration (voir la reproduction en face).[35]

Il serait possible de proposer d'autres exemples de telles difficultés, et de comparer les solutions retenues par ces mêmes traducteurs, en particulier devant cette autre affirmation audacieuse: *mene God al, & al God* (*Cloud* 44/7–8).[36] Face à de tels passages où la raison vacille, les possibilités de choix du traducteur sont limitées, et se résument à celles qui viennent d'être analysées. Les deux attitudes fondamentales, celle du traducteur poète qui affronte le texte pour ainsi dire à main nue, sans outils théologiques, et celle du traducteur théologien qui dispose sur le sujet d'autres textes apparentés lui permettant des mises en perspective, se retrouvent d'une langue à l'autre, comme l'a montré la présente étude. Le contraste observé initialement entre les choix d'A. Guerne et ceux de M. Noetinger s'observe également chez les traducteurs en anglais moderne. Aux cent-cinquante pages de *The Cloud* et *Privy Counselling* et à la quarantaine de notes qui les accompagnent dans la traduction du poète Robert Way correspondent plus de six cents pages de texte et onze cents notes d'explication et commentaires dans les deux volumes du théologien J. Walsh. J. McCann avait lui aussi jugé bon d'accompagner sa traduction de notes et d'un commentaire emprunté à un autre théologien et directeur spirituel hors pair, le bénédictin Augustine Baker (1575–1641). La question est donc toujours posée, et resurgit à chaque entreprise nouvelle: faut-il suivre et rendre le texte dans sa nudité, ou s'inspirer du choix fait par l'auteur de *The Cloud* face au texte du Pseudo-Denys: *Therfore, in translacioun of it, I haue not onliche folowed the nakid lettre of the text, bot for to declare the hardnes of it, I haue moche folowed the sentence of the Abbot of Seinte Victore, a noble & a worthi expositour of this same book* (*DHD* 119/7–10)? Autrement dit, faut-il livrer un texte dans son état brut, alors qu'il est déjà probablement le produit de plusieurs remodelages, ou bien vaut-il mieux l'accompagner, l'expliciter,

IHC

MS University College Oxford 14, fol. 4ᵛ, reproduced by kind permission of the Master and Fellows of the College.

l'éclairer à l'aide de textes apparentés, et ainsi, de glose en glose, remonter le courant vers sa source? Mais jusqu'où? Augustine Baker, qui présentait à ses dirigées *The Cloud of Unknowing* accompagné d'un commentaire chapitre par chapitre, était très conscient du problème, au point d'écrire:

> I must take heed that I, becoming a commentator upon an obscure work, become not more obscure in my exposition than the text itself which I would expound. It is said of the commentators on St Denis— and our *Cloud* is one comment upon it—that they are as obscure as is the writing itself. And if one cannot write more clearly than the text itself, he may better forbear to write at all upon it. And therefore I shall pass over without any expressment what I cannot express better to the understandings of others—howsoever I think myself to understand the same—lest I should seem to expound that which is obscure by that which is more obscure. (McCann, p. 183)

NOTES

Abréviations des principaux documents discutés dans la présente étude:

Noet.: *Le nuage de l'inconnaissance et les épîtres qui s'y rattachent, par un anonyme anglais du quatorzième siècle*, traduits par D.M. Noetinger, moine de Solesmes, collection «Mystiques anglais» (Tours: Mame, 1925; réédition Solesmes, 1977);

G.: *Le nuage d'inconnaissance*, trad. A. Guerne (Les Cahiers du Sud, 1953; réédition, collection «Points Sagesse», Paris: Seuil, 1977);

Cloud1: *The Cloud of Unknowing and The Book of Privy Counselling*, ed. Phyllis Hodgson Early English Text Society OS 218 (London: Oxford University Press, 1944 (for 1943); *Cloud2*: *The Cloud of Unknowing and Related Treatises*, ed. Phyllis Hodgson, Analecta Cartusiana 3 (Salzburg, 1982) (sauf indications contraires, les références aux pages et lignes des textes originaux renvoient à cette seconde édition critique dont les citations sont légèrement modernisées);

McCann: *The Cloud of Unknowing and other Treatises by a 14th-century English Mystic*, trad. J. McCann O.S.B., Orchard Series (London Burns Oates, 6ème édition révisée 1952 (1ère ed. 1924));

J.W.1: *The Cloud of Unknowing*, edited with an introduction by J. Walsh S.J., Preface by S. Tugwell O.P. The Classics of Western Spirituality (London: Paulist Press, SPCK, 1981);

J.W.2: *The Pursuit of Wisdom and Other Works by the Author of The Cloud of Unknowing*, translated, edited and annotated by J. Walsh S.J. The Classics of Western Spirituality (New York and Mahwah: Paulist Press, 1988);

J. Walsh S.J. et E. Colledge O.S.A. avaient préparé pour une collection italienne une édition critique de *Caligo ignorancie* (Pembroke College, Cambridge, MS. 221), version latine glosée de *The Cloud* due au chartreux Richard Methley. Le projet a été repris récemment sous une forme différente par le Rev Dr J.P.H. Clark et le Dr J. Hogg; *The Latin Versions of The Cloud of Unknowing* formera quatre volumes dans la collection Analecta Cartusiana, N° 119: J. Clark a publié *Nubes Ignorandi* (119/1), MS. Harley 959 (119/2) et prépare un volume d'introduction générale, J. Hogg préparant une nouvelle édition critique de *Caligo ignorancie*;

AC: Dr J. Hogg (ed.) Analecta Cartusiana (Universität Salzburg, Salzburg, Austria, Institut für Anglistik und Amerikanistik);

SC: Collection «Sources Chrétiennes» (Paris: Le Cerf);

DS: *Dictionnaire de Spiritualité, ascétique et mystique, doctrine et histoire* (Paris: Beauchesne, 1932–);

'Mystique et pédagogie': René Tixier, 'Mystique et pédagogie dans The Cloud of Unknowing' (Thèse de Doctorat Nouveau Régime, Université de Nancy II, 1988) 4 vols., (Microfiches disponibles auprès de l'Atelier National de Reproduction des Thèses, Université de Lille III, 9, rue A. Angellier, 59046 Lille Cedex, ref. 88.15.07714/89).

1. Au tout début du siècle, les lois anticléricales d'E. Combes forcèrent les communautés religieuses françaises à s'exiler dans les pays voisins.

2. *Mystiques anglais* (Oeuvres de Richard Rolle, Juliane de Norwich, Walter Hilton, *Le nuage de l'inconnaissance*), introduction et choix de textes par P. Renaudin, collection «Les maîtres de la spiritualité chrétienne» (Paris: Aubier, 1957).

3. Augustine Baker O.S.B., 'Of the Prayer of Aspirations' dans *Holy Wisdom* (Wheathampstead: Anthony Clarke Books, 1972) pp. 456–65.

4. Guigues II le Chartreux, *Lettre sur la vie contemplative* (*L'échelle des moines*) introd. et texte critique par E. Colledge O.S.A et J. Walsh S.J., SC N° 163 (Paris: Cerf, 1970) p. 84/35–6; édition anglaise, *The Ladder of Monks* Cistercian Studies N° 48 (Oxford: Mowbray, 1978).

5. Le texte de cette prière est en réalité celui de la collecte de la messe votive *Ad postulandam gratiam Spiritus Sancti* (*Noet.* p. 61n).

6. *J.W.1* p. 115. Voir la note 3 p. 101, où *hole entent* (*Prol.* 1/15) est traduit par 'steadfast determination'.

7. M. Sandaeus, *Pro theologia mystica clavis* (Cologne, 1640) reproduction anastatique, Editions de la Bibliothèque S.J. (Heverlee-Louvain, 1963).

8. Ce balbutiement au sujet du travail de Dieu en l'homme est très précisément inscrit dans le texte: *For of that werke that fallith to only God dar I not take apon me to speke with my blabryng fleschely tonge* (*Cloud* 34/36–8).

9. 'Mystique et pédagogie' pp. 707–80.

10. Parmi les commentaires médiévaux du corpus dionysien, l'*Explanatio* et l'*Extractio* du victorin Thomas Gallus ont exercé une forte influence sur l'auteur de *The Cloud* qui reconnaît en lui 'a noble & a worthi expositour' (*Cloud2* p. 119/10).

11. A. Lion O.P., «Le discours blessé: sur le langage mystique selon Michel de Certeau» *Revue des Sciences philosophiques et théologiques* N° 71 (1987) pp. 405–20.

12. Gerson définit la contemplation unitive comme *experimentalis cognitio habita de Deo per amoris unitivi complexum* (*Theologia mystica*, Consid. 28, *Opera*, t. 3); ailleurs il précise que cette connaissance intime, à base d'expérience, est une *praegustatio quaedam gloriae* (*Tractatus septimus super Magnificat*) (*DS*). Cette image sensorielle d'une pré-libation se retrouve dans *The Cloud*: l'âme est nourrie par ses sens spirituels (*som taast*), en attendant la totalité de la nourriture céleste (*the fulle food*) (*Cloud* 11/5–8).

13. *Cloud1* 34/16 et Note 16 sur MS. Har. 2. (= MS BL Harley 2373) (Voir l'OED *s.v. grappe.*)

14. Jean Bastaire, *Eros sauvé, ou le jeu de l'ascèse et de l'amour* (Paris: Desclée, 1990) p. 19.

15. *Ignote consurge ad ejus unitionem qui est super omnem substantiam et cognitionem*, Pseudo-Denys, *De Mystica Theologia*, cap. 1.

16. R. Tixier, «*Good gamesumli pley*: les jeux de l'amour dans *The Cloud of Unknowing*» *Caliban* N° 24, «Ecrivains catholiques anglo-saxons» (Université de Toulouse-Le Mirail, 1987) pp. 12–3; traduction anglaise dans *The Downside Review* 108, N° 373 (1990) pp. 239–40.

17. Evelyn Underhill, *The Cloud of Unknowing* (London: John Watkins, 1912).

18. *J.W.1* p. 165, n. 160.

19. Mis à part les six courts extraits que P. Renaudin a joints à la sélection de chapitres du *Nuage* qu'il propose dans *Mystiques anglais* (voir supra Note 2). Comme il l'indique en l'introduction, sa traduction des extraits de *L'Epître de la direction intime* est une reprise, «à très peu de chose près», de celle de M. Noetinger.

20. 'He does not say that nothing is something, since nothing is nothing, that is, no thing. But because next to nothing (*quasi nihil*) is something, a man labours to cut away everything that exists that he might be purified and naked, according to that knowledge which is unknowing (*cognitionem incognitam*)': *J.W.1* p. 253 n. 437.

21. '*Secretum sive Mysticum*, being an Exposition of *The Cloud of Unknowing*, by Father Augustine Baker, Monk of the English Benedictine Congregation.' Ce commentaire, qui accompagne la traduction de J. McCann dans la collection «Orchard Series» (1947, 1952), n'a pas été réédité dans la collection «Golden Library» (Wheathampstead: Anthony Clarke, 1964).

22. Plusieurs documents médiévaux attestent l'existence d'un lien fréquent entre hérésie et dérèglement sexuel (voir R. Lerner, *The Heresy of the Free Spirit in the Later Middle Ages* (University of California Press, 1972)); les hérétiques sont trompés par le diable (*Cloud* chs. 51–7), et la sexualité offre un terrain particulièrement vulnérable (sur l'utilisation possible de modèles continentaux dans les condamnations et avertissements de l'auteur de *The Cloud* voir J. Bazire & E. Colledge (eds) *The Chastising of God's Children and The Treatise of Perfection of the Sons of God* (Oxford: Blackwell, 1957) pp. 49–56).

23. McCann (1947) pp. x–xi.

24. Phyllis Hodgson ne signale aucune variante faisant apparaître l'absence de cet adjectif (*Cloud1* 39/1 et notes). Je remercie le Dr Roger Ellis, University of Wales College of Cardiff, d'avoir très aimablement vérifié pour moi la présence de *preue* aux chs. 12 et 52 dans MS. Harley 674 (Har. 1).

25. J.P.H. Clark (ed.) *Nubes ignorandi* AC 119/1, pp. 48/21–5, 118/11–2.

26. *Per figuras amatorias*, Guillaume de St Thierry, *Super Cantica Canticorum*, Chant 1, final 144; trad. J-M.Déchanet, SC 82, pp. 304–5. Voir aussi M. de Certeau S.J., *La fable mystique* (Paris: Gallimard, 1982).

27. Marguerite Porete et son *Miroir des simples âmes* ne représente qu'un cas parmi d'autres. 'It is obvious, of course, that the situation in England at the time when *The Chastising* was written was very different from the state of affairs in the Low Countries during Ruysbroek's lifetime (. . .) But though it is true that such sects as hers [Bloemardinne's] never became organized in pre-Reformation England, there is evidence enough to show that their spread

to England was constantly feared by the Church and the civil authorities, who took every precaution to guard against such an event' (Bazire & Colledge, *The Chastising* pp. 50–1); voir aussi Y. Congar O.P., «Langage des spirituels et langage des théologiens» dans *La mystique rhénane*, Actes du Colloque de Strasbourg (16–19 mai 1961), Bibliothèque des Centres d'Etudes Supérieures Spécialisés Paris P.U.F., 1963) pp. 15–34.

28. 'Mystique et pédagogie', pp. 738–80.
29. André Manaranche S.J., *Des Noms pour Dieu* (Paris: Fayard, 1980) p. 65.
30. Albert Deblaere S.J., *DS*, article «Mystique», col. 1907–8.
31. À côté des traductions déjà citées, comparer W. Johnston S.J., *The Cloud of Unknowing and The Book of Privy Counselling* Image Books (New York: Doubleday 1973); Clifton Wolters, *The Cloud of Unknowing and Other Works* Penguin Classics (Harmondsworth: Penguin Books, 1978); Robert Way, *The Cloud of Unknowing and the Letter of Private Direction* (Wheathampstead: Anthony Clarke, 1986).
32. 'So great is the power of the true love of the good and the beautiful that not only does it lead men and angels to outstrip their natural powers so that they can ascend to God, but it causes God to leave behind as it were his own nature, and to descend below it to the creature', Th. Gallus, *Explanation on the Divine Names*, ch. 7 (*J.W.1* p. 122 n. 41).
33. *Cloud1* p. 18 n. 13, mais il apparaît que cette addition a été barrée.
34. La note 18/13 de la première édition critique (*Cloud1*, 1943) était tout simplement la reprise, reconnue comme telle, de la glose de *Nubes Ignorandi* citée en note par McCann (1924, p. 14n), et qui a probablement guidé Noet. dans sa traduction (p. 75), mettant en valeur la «descente» de Dieu vers l'homme. Mais la note 10/22 de la seconde édition critique (*Cloud2* 1982) est un passage des *Noms divins* du Pseudo-Denys: 'Divine things are revealed unto each created spirit in proportion to its powers, and in this measure is perception granted through the workings of the Divine Goodness, the which in just care for our preservation divinely tempereth unto finite measure the infinitude of things which pass man's understanding' (ch. 1, trad. C.E. Rolt (London: SPCK, 1920) p. 52). Le passage de l'*Explanatio* de Gallus choisi comme glose par J. Walsh portait également sur les *Noms divins* (voir supra Note 32). Bien difficile de ne pas voir ici l'effet d'une série d'influences.
35. Ce manuscrit a appartenu au 16ème siècle à John Jewel, évêque de Salisbury. Il se trouve que l'index dessiné en marge du passage cité est unique dans le texte. Le Dr Vincent Gillespie, St Anne's College, Oxford, a très aimablement examiné les marginalia et les passages soulignés, et je suis heureux de l'en remercier ici. Une description de University College MS. 14 est fournie par Phyllis Hodgson (*Cloud1* p. xvii).
36. L'audace fait place à la prudence dans la variante qu'apporte le MS. Pa (i.e. Parkminster): *mene nothing els but God* (*Cloud1*, p. 79 n. 11). E. Underhill a traduit mot-à-mot la leçon de Harley 674 (p. 201); J. McCann a semble-t-il fait preuve d'une prudence comparable à celle du MS. Pa et traduit 'mean God wholly, and wholly God' (p. 57), suivi exactement en cela par R. Way (p. 64); J. Walsh (p. 198) et C. Wolters (p. 108) proposent une interprétation très proche; W. Johnston reste lui aussi très proche de McCann (p. 100), de même que Noet. («propose-toi Dieu comme tout bien, et Dieu tout entier», p. 174); *G.* est beaucoup plus proche de l'original quand il traduit «entends Dieu en tout, et en tout Dieu» (pp. 131–2).

SELECT BIBLIOGRAPHY

Barratt, A. (ed.) *Women's Writing in Middle English* (London and New York: Longman, 1992)

Barratt, A., 'Dame Eleanor Hull: a Fifteenth Century Translator', in Ellis (ed.) *Medieval Translator* (1989) pp. 87–101

Bassnett-Maguire, S., *Translation Studies* rev. ed., New Accents (London and New York: Routledge, 1991)

Batt, C., 'Clemence of Barking's Transformations of *Courtoisie* in *La Vie de Sainte Catherine d'Alexandrie*' *New Comparison* 12 (1991) pp. 102–23

Beer, J., *Li Fet des Romains (A Medieval Caesar)*, Etudes de Philologie et d'Histoire 30 (Geneva: Droz, 1976)

Beer, J., *Narrative Conventions of Truth in the Middle Ages* Etudes de Philologie et d'Histoire 38 (Geneva: Droz, 1981)

Beer, J., (ed.) *Medieval Translators and their Craft* Studies in Medieval Culture XXV (Kalamazoo: Western Michigan University, 1989)

Belloc, H., *On Translation*, The Taylorian Lecture 1931 (Oxford: Clarendon Press, 1931)

Benjamin, W., 'The Task of the Translator: an Introduction to the Translation of Baudelaire's *Tableaux Parisiens*', in *Illuminations*, ed. H. Arendt, trans. H. Zohn (New York: Schocken Books, 1968), pp. 69–82

Brislin, R.W. (ed.) *Translation Applications and Research* (New York: Gardner Press, 1976)

Burnley, D., 'Late Medieval English Translation: Types and Reflections', in Ellis (ed.) *Medieval Translator* (1989) pp. 37–53

Chamberlain, L.,'Gender and the Metaphorics of Translation' *Signs* 13:3 (1988) pp. 454–71

Clanchy, M.T., *From Memory to Written Record* (London: Arnold, 1979)

Copeland, R., 'Rhetoric and Vernacular Translation in the Middle Ages' in T.J. Heffernan (ed.) *Studies in the Age of Chaucer* 9 (Knoxville, Tennessee: New Chaucer Society, 1987) pp. 41–75

Copeland, R., 'The Fortunes of "non verbum pro verbo": or, why Jerome is not a Ciceronian', in Ellis (ed.) *Medieval Translator* (1989) pp. 15–35

Copeland, R., *Rhetoric, Hermeneutics, and Translation in the Middle Ages: Academic Traditions and Vernacular Texts* (Cambridge, New York and Melbourne: Cambridge University Press, 1991)

de Man, P., '"Conclusions": Walter Benjamin's "The Task of the Translator"' in *The Resistance to Theory* (Minneapolis: University of Minnesota Press, 1986) pp. 73–105

Ellis, R., 'The Choices of the Translator in the Late Middle English Period' in M. Glasscoe (ed.) *The Medieval Mystical Tradition in England* (Exeter: University of Exeter Press, 1982) pp. 18–48

Ellis, R. (ed.) assisted by Jocelyn Price, Stephen Medcalf and Peter Meredith *The Medieval Translator: The Theory and Practice of Translation in the Middle Ages: Papers Read at a Conference Held 20–23 August 1987 at the University of Wales Conference Centre, Gregynog Hall* (Woodbridge, Suffolk: D.S. Brewer, 1989)

Ellis, R. (ed.) *The Medieval Translator II* Westfield Publications in Medieval Studies 5 (London: Centre for Medieval Studies, Queen Mary and Westfield College, 1991)

Ellis, R. (ed.) *New Comparison* 12: *Translation in the Middle Ages* (1991)

Evans, R., 'Women Inside and outside the Text: Translation and Position', *New Comparison* 12 (1991), pp. 89–101

Genette, G., 'Introduction to the Paratext' *New Literary History* 22 (1991) pp. 261–72

Gentzler, E., *Contemporary Translation Theories* Translation Studies (London and New York: Routledge, 1993)

Graham, J. (ed.) *Difference in Translation* (Ithaca: Cornell University Press, 1985)

Halkin, A.S., 'Translation and Translators (Medieval)' *Encyclopaedia Judaica* (Jerusalem: Keter Publishing House, 1971) Vol. 15 pp. 1318–1329

Hermans, T., *The Manipulation of Literature: Studies in Literary Translation* (London and Sydney: Croom Helm, 1985)

Holmes, J. S. (ed.) *The Nature of Translation: Essays on the Theory and Practice of Literary Translation* (The Hague: Mouton; Bratislava: Publishing House of the Slovak Academy of Sciences, 1970)

Jakobson, R., 'Linguistics and Poetics' in *Selected Writings*, Vol. 3 (The Hague: Mouton, 1981) pp. 18–51

Johnson, I., 'Prologue and practice: Middle English lives of Christ' in Ellis (ed.) *Medieval Translator* (1989) pp. 69–85

Kelly, L. G., *The True Interpreter: A History of Translation Theory and Practice in the West* (Oxford: Basil Blackwell, 1979)

Lefevere, A. (ed.) *Translation/History/Culture: a Sourcebook* (London and New York: Routledge, 1992)

Lefevere, A., *Translation, Rewriting, and the Manipulation of Literary Fame* (London and New York: Routledge, 1992)

Legge, M. Dominica, *Anglo-Norman Literature and its Background* (Oxford: Oxford University Press, 1963; repr. Greenwood Press, 1978)

Meale, C. (ed.) *Women and Literature in Britain 1150–1500* (Cambridge: Cambridge University Press, 1993)

Mills, M., 'Techniques of Translation in the Middle English Versions of *Guy of Warwick*', in Ellis (ed.) *Medieval Translator II* (1991) pp. 209–29

Minnis, A. J., *Medieval Theory of Authorship: Scholastic Literary Attitudes in the Later Middle Ages* (London: Scolar Press 1984: rev. ed. Aldershot: Wildwood House, 1988)

Minnis, A.J., and Scott, A.B. (eds) with the assistance of David Wallace *Medieval Literary Theory and Criticism c.1100–c.1375: The Commentary Tradition* (Oxford: Clarendon Press, 1988; repr. 1991)

Nida, E., *Toward a Science of Translating* (Leiden: Brill, 1964)

Niranjana, T., *Siting Translation: History, Post-Structuralism, and the Colonial Context* (Berkeley, Los Angeles and Oxford: University of California Press, 1992)

Steiner, G., *After Babel: Aspects of Language and Translation*, 2nd ed. (Oxford: Oxford University Press, 1992)

Steinschneider, M., *Die hebräischen Übersetzungen des Mittelalter und die Juden als Dolmetscher* (Berlin: H. Itzkowski, 1893; repr. Gräz: Akademische Druck und Verlagsamstalt, 1956)

Stock, B., *The Implications of Literacy: Written Language and Models of Interpretation in the Eleventh and Twelfth Centuries* (Princeton, New Jersey: Princeton University Press, 1983)

Toury, G., *In Search of a Theory of Translation* (Tel Aviv: Porter Institute, 1980)

Tymoczko, M., 'Translation as a Force for Literary Revolution in the 12th Century Shift from Epic to Romance', *New Comparison* 1 (1986), pp. 7–27

Venuti, L. (ed.) *Rethinking Translation: Discourse, Subjectivity, Ideology* (London and New York: Routledge, 1992)

Warner, M. (ed.) *The Bible as Rhetoric: Studies in Biblical Persuasion and Credibility* (London: Routledge, 1990)

Watson, N., 'Translation and Self-Canonization in Richard Rolle's *Melos Amoris*' in Ellis (ed.) *Medieval Translator* (1989) pp. 167–80

Watson, N., 'Misrepresenting the Untranslatable: Marguerite Porete and the *Mirouer des Simples Ames*', *New Comparison* 12 (1991), pp. 124–37

Worth, V., *Practising Translation in Renaissance France: The Example of Etienne Dolet* (Oxford: Clarendon Press, 1988)

Index

INDEX